The Almost Impossible Ally

The Almost Impossible Ally

Harold Macmillan and Charles de Gaulle

PETER MANGOLD

I.B. TAURIS

LONDON · NEW YORK

Published in 2006 by I.B.Tauris & Co Ltd
6 Salem Road, London W2 4BU
175 Fifth Avenue, New York, NY 10010
www.ibtauris.com

In the United States of America and in Canada distributed by
Palgrave Macmillan a division of St. Martin's Press,
175 Fifth Avenue, New York NY 10010

ISBN 1 85043 800 5
EAN 978 1 85043 800 7

A full CIP record for this book is available from the British Library
A full CIP record for this book is available from the Library of Congress

Library of Congress Catalog Card Number: available

Printed and bound in Great Britain by TJ International Ltd, Padstow, Cornwall
camera-ready copy edited and supplied by the author

Contents

CONTENTS

Acknowledgements

I would like to thank Clare Brown, Piers Dixon and John Pearce for help at various stages with this book. Christiane and John Tod generously provided me with hospitality during parts of the research. I owe a particular debt of gratitude to John Eidinow for providing the original inspiration and encouragement. The responsibility for the final text is, needless to say, my own.

I am also grateful to Jane Reilly for permission to quote from Sir Patrick Reilly's Unpublished Memoirs. Extracts from the diary of Harold Macmillan are reproduced by kind permission of the Trustees of the Harold Macmillan Book Trust.

Peter Mangold
Stonor, June 2005.

Introduction

Bathing at Tipasa

Tipasa lies some forty miles west of Algiers along the North African coast. In the Second World War it was little more than a fishing village, with a few houses, a sleepy post office, and an inn. Behind this was a cliff, from which, half hidden by shrubs and wild lavender could be seen the ruins of a partially excavated Roman town set on a promontory. It was here that on 13 June 1943, Whit Sunday, two men came out from the Algerian capital to bathe and relax. Both had just been involved in a fierce power struggle for control of what was to become France's post-war government. It was a curious scene. One, the British Resident Minister at Allied Forces Headquarters, (AFHQ), bathed naked, as was the fashion among British troops in North Africa. The other, a French general, sat in a dignified manner on a rock with his military cap, uniform and belt. Afterwards Harold Macmillan and Charles de Gaulle walked among the Roman ruins and dined at the inn. Like the walrus and the carpenter they talked of many things - politics, philosophy, religion, ancient and modern history. 'It is very difficult to know how to handle him,' Macmillan wrote the next day in his diary. 'I do my best, and I know that he likes me and appreciated having somebody whom he trusts and with whom he can talk freely.'[1]

Nearly twenty years later a very different scene unfolded in the ornate Salon de Fêtes in the Elysée Palace in Paris. On 14 January 1963 President de Gaulle gave one of his semi-annual press conferences to an audience of some eight hundred people. They included not only journalists, the majority foreign, but members of the French cabinet, senior civil servants, and foreign diplomats. De Gaulle prepared himself meticulously for these occasions, memorising in advance answers to what were for the most part planted questions. This conference had already been billed by the Elysée as a 'conference de choc'. One of the questions concerned the British application to join the Common Market. Without any previous consultation of his five EEC partners, de Gaulle proceeded to announce what was in effect, though the word was never actually used, a French veto. Having outlined some of his reasons, paid tribute to Churchill and the British role in the two world wars, de Gaulle concluded in lofty tones that it was:

> 'very possible that Britain's own evolution, and the evolution of the universe, might bring the English towards the Continent, whatever delays this achievement might demand. For my part, that is what I readily believe, and this is why, in my opinion, it will in any case have been a great honour for the British Prime Minister, my friend Harold Macmillan, and for his Government, to have discerned that goal in good time, to have had enough political courage to have proclaimed it, and to have led their country the first steps along the path which one day, perhaps, will lead it to moor alongside the Continent.'[2]

It was a political blow from which Macmillan never recovered.

Friendships at the highest level between British and American leaders have been a feature of the Anglo-American 'special relationship'. They began with Churchill and Roosevelt and continued with Macmillan and both Eisenhower and Kennedy, and later Thatcher and Reagan. More recently Tony Blair has succeeded in forming close personal links with both Clinton and George W. Bush. They have been much less prominent in the older Anglo-French *Entente Cordiale*. Lloyd George and Clemenceau enjoyed each other's company, but differing perceptions of national interest obstructed understanding between them. De Gaulle and Churchill admired one another greatly, but quarrelled, at times violently. The only two leaders whose friendship had any discernible political impact, in the form of the eventual British entry into the EEC in 1973, were Ted Heath and Georges Pompidou.[3]

The political friendship between Macmillan and de Gaulle was a peculiarly feline and manipulative affair. No other Anglo-French friendship began under quite such unconventional circumstances, or proved so dramatic in its denouement. No other modern British and French leaders have had so much influence on one another's political fortunes. No other French peacetime leader, with the recent exception of President Chirac during the 2003 Iraq war, has appeared to rebuff a British prime minister so publicly; certainly none has done his British counterpart so much harm. And no other Anglo-French political friendship has spanned such a lengthy and dramatic period.

Macmillan and de Gaulle were contemporaries, born in the last decade of the nineteenth century. Each had fought with distinction in the First World War, and been deeply frustrated by his respective government's diplomatic and military policy in the face of the growing German threat in the 1930s. The turning point in both men's careers had come with the ending of the so-called

'Phoney War' in the spring of 1940. Following the failed Anglo-French Norwegian campaign, Chamberlain had been forced to resign as Prime Minister, and it was the leader of the new British government, Winston Churchill, who in mid-May gave Macmillan his first government post. Three weeks later, as the German army advanced relentlessly into France, de Gaulle was appointed Under-Secretary of War. But while Macmillan and de Gaulle were personal beneficiaries of these events - Macmillan liked to say that it had taken Hitler to make Churchill Prime Minister and himself a parliamentary under-secretary - the ramifications for their two countries, as for the old *Entente Cordiale*, were to profoundly unsettling. [4]

Macmillan and de Gaulle first met in London, where de Gaulle had established his wartime headquarters. But they first got to know each other in North Africa in 1943. By this stage in the war power was beginning to pass from Britain to the US. Indeed the immediate reason for Macmillan's appointment as Minister Resident at AFHQ, was to increase British influence with the Americans, who sometimes appeared to be riding roughshod over British interests. At the same time Britain remained one of the wartime Big Three and a Great Power. France by contrast remained occupied by the Germans, and *hors de combat* as far as the strategic direction of the war was concerned. Politically it was badly divided and much of Macmillan's time in Algiers was spent promoting the cause of unity between rival French factions. Few, if any British ministers have exercised so much influence in the political affairs of modern France: one French historian describes his role as that of 'confidant, adviser, temporiser, arbiter and spur'.[5] De Gaulle was the major beneficiary of Macmillan's efforts, and his success in handling a man who had already gained such a reputation for being cantankerous and difficult helped turn Macmillan from an obscure junior minister into the leading Conservative figure, who was to become Prime Minister in 1957.

The second act of the de Gaulle-Macmillan drama opened with de Gaulle's return to power a year later. (His brief wartime spell as French Prime Minister had ended with his resignation in 1946.) The canvas had now broadened from domestic French intrigues to the heady world of international power politics. Macmillan and de Gaulle both represented states which were used to playing a global role. Despite Europe's loss of international primacy, and their own countries' supercession by the two superpowers, the United States and the Soviet Union, neither man had the slightest intention of abjuring the world stage. A contemporary cartoon, quoting the opening words of de Gaulle's *War Memoirs*, 'All my life I have always had a certain idea of France,' depicted a map of the world with the western coast of the American continent, and the eastern coast of Russia and China, modelled as the General's face. Macmillan's penchant for global personal diplomacy was nicely satirised in the 1960s *Beyond the Fringe* review. The actor Peter Cook stood beside a table with a globe. He used this to point out where he had been travelling, at his audience's expense, and incidentally also on their behalf, to exchange some frank words with the powerful chaps with whom he was hoping to shape the future.[6]

It was now that the Macmillan-de Gaulle friendship began to turn sour. In contrast to North Africa, this was a much more prolonged encounter, lasting until Macmillan's resignation in the autumn of 1963. And from the outset there was trouble. Britain and France faced remarkably similar problems - decolonisation, the creation of their own nuclear deterrents, the need to find a post-colonial role. But de Gaulle and Macmillan had very different styles and priorities. These were not to be glossed over by the exquisite courtesies of their country-house weekend *tête-à-têtes*, when they claimed to preserve something of the informality of the old Algiers day. As leaders of their respective countries, the two men were now rivals as well as allies, and where they did discuss alliance business, such as the handling of the Berlin crisis which the Soviet leader Nikita Khrushchev first precipitated at the end of 1958 and the reform of NATO, they were often at odds. What brought matters to a head was the British bid to join the Common Market, which de Gaulle saw as a threat to his own vision of a French-led Europe, allied to yet independent of the United States.

Running through this Macmillan-de Gaulle dialogue of the late 1950s and the early 1960s was a debate about the future of Europe and Trans-Atlantic relations, which forty years on often has a remarkably contemporary resonance. The General foresaw the end of the Cold War - then still some thirty years hence - and a Europe united from the Atlantic to the Urals. His intense suspicion of American power, if premature in the late 1950s and early 1960s, remains a dominant theme of French foreign policy today, as does his notion of Europe as a counterweight to US hegemony. Europe, Dominique de Villepin argued in 2005, developing ideas de Gaulle had put more than four decades earlier, must move rapidly to become a Power. With the great international poles now being constituted around the American continent and Asia, the European continent can play a pivotal role.[7]

Macmillan on the other hand talked of the need for a partnership of equals between Europe and the United States, and of Britain as a 'bridge' between the two sides of the Atlantic, the image later much used by Tony Blair. One of the wartime pioneers of the 'special relationship' with the Americans, it had fallen to Macmillan to reverse the long tradition of British aloofness from Continental Europe. He thus became the first British Prime Minister to try to grapple with one of the thorniest problems of post-war British foreign policy: how to balance Britain's relationship between a Europe in which it has never felt really at home, with its intimate links towards Washington, to which it seems instinctively to gravitate. Macmillan's failure raises questions which have still to be satisfactorily answered.

The Macmillan-de Gaulle story has an additional relevance to the contemporary diplomatic scene in which 'summit' diplomacy has become a way of life and relationships between heads of government are heavily emphasised. It offers an object lesson in the possibilities and pitfalls of political friendship. To some this is an essentially artificial, if not downright misleading, concept. 'In what sense,' asks Timothy Garton Ash, 'were Churchill and Roosevelt ever really friends?' [8] Friendship between foreign statesmen can, of course, be genuine.

But it is more often a tool, if not actually a weapon of international diplomacy, especially for those lacking more tangible assets.

The way in which national leaders go about wooing, flattering and then trying to influence and manipulate one another, is among the most fascinating aspects of international diplomacy. But in revealing the more human face of a subject usually discussed primarily in terms of calculation and manoeuvre, personal diplomacy also raises questions about the conflict between national interest and the obligations of friendship. At what point can friendship be said to have been abused? Under what circumstances can it be said to have been betrayed? Was de Gaulle's *Realpolitik* an anachronism, or an uncomfortable reminder of how little the international diplomacy of post-war Europe had in fact changed? The answers, as the following chapters underscore, would prove anything but straightforward.

PART ONE:

REBELS AND RIVALS, 1320-1941

Chapter 1

Anglo-French Contemporaries

In the late November of 1890, Jeanne de Gaulle returned to her mother's home in the northern French industrial city of Lille for the birth of the third of her five children, Charles-André-Joseph-Marie. A serious girl whose passion for her country was equalled only by her religious piety, Jeanne had married into the minor aristocracy.[1] Her husband (and first cousin) Henri de Gaulle had fought in the Franco-Prussian war of 1870, but had been too poor to pursue a military career. He had gone instead into teaching, becoming headmaster of two distinguished Jesuit high schools in Paris, where the family lived. Charles described his father as a thoughtful, cultivated, traditional man, imbued with a feeling for the dignity of France'. [2]

The de Gaulles were a somewhat eccentric family. Grace at meals was followed by short extempore speeches in Latin, and in the evening there were constant readings from such improving authors as Rostand and Seneca. Discussion of contemporary political events was intense.[3] Henri de Gaulle's lectures on these subjects reflected the political values of the Right - a deep attachment to monarchy, fierce patriotism and fear and distress over the decline of France. A certain anxious pride in their country came as second nature to the young de Gaulles. 'As a young native of Lille living in Paris', Charles wrote,

'nothing struck me more than the symbols of our glories: night falling over Notre Dame, the majesty of evening at Versailles, the Arc de Triomphe in the sun, conquered colours shuddering in the vault of the Invalides. Nothing affected me more than the evidence of our national successes: popular enthusiasm when the Tsar of Russia passed through, a review at Longchamp, the marvels of the

Exhibition, the first flight of our aviators. Nothing saddened me more profoundly than our weaknesses and our mistakes, as revealed to my childhood gaze by the way people looked and by things they said: the surrender of Fashoda, the Dreyfus case, social conflicts, religious strife.' [4]

And nothing, as he goes on to narrate at the outset of his *War Memoirs*, moved him more than the story of France's past misfortunes, in which the French defeat in the Franco-Prussian War, which his parents remembered all too clearly, featured prominently.[5]

The young Charles was not an easy child, and already at secondary school, he had begun to stand apart. It was only towards the end of his school days that he began to apply his formidable intelligence. His career options were limited by the family's genteel poverty. He gave some consideration to the Church. But the army was a more natural choice for a boy who in 1905, when he was fifteen and a crisis over the Moroccan port of Agadir was giving rise to talk about a possible Franco-German war, was already fantasising about how as a General with an army of 200,000 men and 518 guns, he would save France from German attack.[6] The choice may also have been influenced by the prevailing atmosphere of uncertainty and national division, in which the army was the one institution offering order and structure.[7]

'The huge asparagus', as the strikingly tall officer cadet was soon nick-named, only came 119th out of 221 in the entrance exams to St. Cyr, the École Speciale Militaire at Versailles, which trained aspiring French officers.[8] By the time he graduated as a second-lieutenant two years later in 1912, he was described as a 'very highly gifted cadet', with energy, zeal, and enthusiasm, as well as power of command and decision.[9] His first posting was with the 33rd Infantry Regiment, commanded by another soldier who was to play a prominent, although in the event very different, role in French political life, Colonel, later Marshal, Philip Pétain. The regiment saw action immediately after the outbreak of the First World War in August 1914, and de Gaulle was wounded. By September 1915 he had been promoted captain, awarded the Croix de Guerre and suffered a second wound. Then in March 1916, de Gaulle was taken prisoner during the great German onslaught on Verdun. Despite repeated escape attempts, the rest of his war was spent in German prisoner of war camps. Typically the time was not wasted. He improved his German, lectured to his fellow prisoners, who regarded him with awe and listened with fascination, and used the opportunity to think hard about leadership and war.

The two decades which followed the end of the war in 1918 were, by later standards at least, uneventful. In 1921, following a secondment to the Polish army, he married Yvonne Vendroux. The daughter of a Calais family, which claimed the illegitimate daughter of a pope as an ancestress, she was a pretty if not beautiful girl with large black eyes, oval face, high forehead and a mass of swept back hair. Personality and charm were tempered by a certain puritanism and shyness, and she had little taste in later life for the public side of her husband's career. Writing to the Queen shortly before the General's State Visit to Britain in April 1960, about the lady irreverently known within the de Gaulle entourage as 'Tante Yvonne', Macmillan described her as 'very shy' and speaking practically no English. 'She is a woman of considerable character: I have even heard it said that she is the only human being of whom the General stands mildly in awe - but I can scarcely believe this.'[10] The couple had three children, the youngest of whom Anne, born in 1928, suffered from Downs syndrome. De Gaulle was devoted to her, and after her death in 1948 is reputed to have said, 'Without Anne, perhaps I should not have done all that I have done. She made me understand so many things. She gave me so much heart and spirit.' [11]

The year after his marriage, de Gaulle joined the staff at St Cyr, where he taught history. There followed staff college, the École Supérieur de Guerre, a period on Pétain's personal staff, command of a rifle battalion and a posting to Lebanon. Between 1932 and 1937 he served in the Secretariat of the Conseil Supérieur de la Défense Nationale, a posting which brought him to the nerve centre of French strategic power.[12] Promoted colonel in 1937, the forty-seven-year old de Gaulle was given command of a regiment of tanks at Metz, a post he was to hold until just before the outbreak of war in September 1939.

While scarcely a meteoric rise up the staid French military hierarchy of the interwar years, it was nevertheless very quickly evident that here was no ordinary soldier. Pétain, whose protégé for a time he became, once described him as 'the most intelligent officer in the French army'.[13] When in 1927 de Gaulle was promoted major and given his first command, the director of infantry on the general staff and responsible for senior postings was aware from gossip that he was placing a future Commander in Chief.[14]

At the same time de Gaulle was also proving himself an independent, if not necessarily original, military thinker. His books, articles and lectures dealt both with immediate issues - he was a keen advocate of the tank - as well as with larger questions, such as the nature of leadership and war, and the relationship between government and High Command. And he had a presence which impressed. Philippe Serre, a French deputy and later minister wrote of de Gaulle's 'Olympian side...an authority, a command and an eloquence that compelled recognition straight away. He spoke with a kind of majesty, like someone who feels he is invested with a lofty mission.'[15] In October 1936, the then Prime Minister, Leon Blum, invited de Gaulle to meet him. Blum describes seeing 'a man whose height, breadth and bulk had something gigantic about them: he walked in with an easy, even placid calmness. Straight away one felt that he was "all of a piece". He was so in his physical being, and all his gestures seemed to move his body as a whole, without friction. He was so in his psychological behaviour.'[16]

What struck many of his military superiors, however, was just what a difficult subordinate he could be. De Gaulle was a natural rebel with what one of his French biographers describes as an 'itch to challenge', a 'temptation to clash with his superiors (whether they were internal hierarchies or states) which perpetually goaded him'. And he was arrogant. A report written of his period at the École de Guerre Supérieur remarked on his excessive self-confidence, severity towards the opinions of others, and an attitude of a 'king in exile'. (Nearly four decades later a despatch from the British embassy in Paris noted that de Gaulle 'knows with a disconcerting and unshakeable certainty that he is right.') [17]

To complicate matters further, de Gaulle was fundamentally out of sympathy with the conservative doctrine of the French army, which, far from accepting his ideas about mobile warfare, had decided to dig in behind the Maginot line. As the international situation deteriorated following Hitler's accession to power in 1933, the restless French staff officer felt he had no alternative but to crusade publicly for his ideas. As he himself later put it, 'I could not bear to see the enemy of tomorrow endowing himself with the means of victory while France was still without them. And yet, in the incredible apathy in which the nation was plunged, no voice in authority was lifted to demand the required action. The stake was so great that it did not seem to me permissible to maintain my reserve, slight as were my importance and my fame.'[18]

To this end he solicited not only editorial but also political support. The Left was broadly unreceptive. On the Right, Paul Reynaud, a former Finance Minister to whom de Gaulle was introduced in 1934, came to treat him as his military adviser, quickly becoming known on the General Staff as 'de Gaulle's gramophone'. In late 1937 when de Gaulle was perhaps not very surprisingly left off the promotion list to the rank of colonel, he got Reynaud to intervene, and his promotion was duly gazetted. When he left for his new command, the Defence Minister General Maurin remarked, 'You have given us enough trouble with your paper tanks. Let us see what you make of the metal sort.' [19] But his battle was still far from won. His new commanding officer, General Henri Giraud, remarked that while Colonel de Gaulle's ideas might be brilliant, they were of a kind that might lose France the next war.[20]

* * *

At first sight Harold Macmillan's early life reads very differently from that of his French contemporary. Four years younger than de Gaulle, Macmillan was born on 10 February 1894 at 54 Cadogan Place, London SW1. His childhood was spent in what he later described as 'the last decade of that one hundred years of almost unchallenged authority which the British people exerted from the battle of Waterloo to the outbreak of the First World War.'[21] British power, in marked contrast to that of France, was at its apogee, and one of Harold's first recollections was of Queen Victoria's Diamond Jubilee in 1897. Other childhood memories of this Imperial high noon included the crowds which gathered three years later to celebrate the relief of Mafeking during the Boer war, and the death of Victoria in 1901.[22]

The Macmillan family nevertheless lived a much more placid and apolitical existence than the de Gaulles. Harold's great-grandfather had been a Scottish crofter. His grandfather, Daniel, one of twelve children born into great poverty, was a self-made businessman who in 1843 had founded the Macmillan publishing company.[23] His second son, Maurice, shared both his father's scholarly bent and his business sense. A shy, taciturn and very controlled man, in 1883 he met in Paris and fell in love with a woman of a very different stamp. Her name was Helen Belles and she came from a small American prairie town in Indiana. She loved her country by adoption, Harold Macmillan later wrote, but never forgot her own.[24] His mother's origins were a subject on which Harold was always later keen to remind his American audiences.

Helen Macmillan was a small, dark-haired woman with strong religious views and her determined features reflected a powerful personality. Her impact on the Macmillan family extended to the business - at one point she insisted that her sons bought the rights to *Gone with the Wind*.[25] At home, however, her dominating influence may have been less beneficial, helping to make all her children, for whom she was immensely ambitious, repressed and withdrawn.[26] In his memoirs, Macmillan acknowledged his great debt to her devotion and support.

> 'In everything I tried to do I was apt to fail or lose heart at the first set-back. Without my mother's encouragement and the high standard of work she insisted upon in my youth, I should never have attained even the slightest academic distinction. If I failed in the first attempt, she felt certain I would succeed in the next; and so it often proved. In my disagreements with my political leaders and the indiscipline which I showed, my mother was sympathetic. She always said, 'You will win in the end.'"[27]

His private feelings, as even the public account hints, were more ambivalent. 'I admired her,' he told a friend after he had become Prime Minister, 'but never really liked her.......she dominated me and she still dominates me.'[28]

The young Harold's upbringing was austere and solitary. His brothers were four and eight years older. He saw little of his father, who was always at work, and gained most affection from his Nanny.[29] A series of French nursery maids and a French governess taught the young boy to speak the language. The initial part of his formal education, however, was more conventional - preparatory school: Summerfields on the outskirts of Oxford, followed in 1906 by Eton. Photos of the young Harold at this time show what his official biographer, Alistair Horne, describes as a good-looking boy with sensitive, full mouth, a wistful face and 'a hint of steel in his eyes.'[30] But he was withdrawn from Eton after three years on health grounds. Preparation for the Oxford scholarship exam was thus undertaken by private tutors, one of whom, Ronald Knox, came close to converting him to Catholicism. He went up to read classics at Balliol, a subject for which he was to retain a life-long affection. Oxford was something of a liberation after the disciplines and emotional constrictions of home life, but in the summer of 1914, having gained a First in 'Mods', he found himself 'sent down by the Kaiser'.[31]

Macmillan enlisted in the autumn of 1914, although it was only in the following August, after a transfer to the Grenadier Guards, engineered by his mother, that he left for France. A wound at the battle of Loos five months later left him with a permanently weakened hand. He was back in France in April 1916. In July he was again wounded. He refused to be sent back to England and at the end of the month his battalion was moved to the Somme front where on 15 September, Captain Macmillan was once more wounded, this time much more seriously. When the war ended two years later, he was still on crutches; he was in pain for the rest of his life. Although he was never decorated, he had been recommended for both the MC and DSO.[32] Unlike de Gaulle, Macmillan was to remain haunted by the magnitude of the suffering he had witnessed, and by a sense of guilt at having survived.[33]

After the war Macmillan went to Canada, as ADC to the Governor-General, the Duke of Devonshire. Here he met his future wife, the twenty-year-old Lady Dorothy Cavendish. A striking girl, Lady Dorothy had warmth, charm and a sense of humour, along, according to Harold, with a better judgement of character than his own.[34] Unlike Madame de Gaulle, Lady Dorothy took readily to public life, but the marriage was to bring Macmillan much personal unhappiness. A life-long affair with a friend of his, Robert Boothby, which Lady Dorothy began in 1929, hurt Harold deeply. How much it contributed to a serious breakdown he suffered in 1931, during which there is at least a hint of a suicide attempt, is unclear. But by his own admission, the affair strengthened Macmillan's character; it also sharpened his political ambition.[35]

He had entered parliament in 1924 at the age of thirty as the Conservative MP for the northern industrial constituency of Stockton-on-Tees. Stockton had been one of the first boom towns of the industrial revolution, but trade had collapsed in the post-war slump, and the shipyards closed down. Unemployment was cruelly high; the despairing faces of the men as they tramped up and down the High Street left a lasting impression on Macmillan. The new MP naturally focused his attention on economic, social and industrial issues, and soon became an advocate of the then unfashionable idea of state planning, on which he wrote a series of books and pamphlets.[36]

Macmillan had made a favourable early impression in the House of Commons. He attracted the attention of Lloyd George, and formed an early connection with Winston Churchill, under whose spell he quickly fell, although it is unclear how far Churchill returned his admiration.[37] Yet while contemporaries such as Anthony Eden quickly gained promotion, Macmillan remained on the backbenches for sixteen years. He was not yet the skilful, self-confident political operator who was to emerge during the Second World War, but rather an impractical, somewhat academic figure who seemed more at home with ideas than the real world. And, particularly in the 1930s, Macmillan was very much out of sympathy with the government, which he considered had totally failed to come to grips with the gravity of the social and economic problems facing the country. If not perhaps a born rebel like de Gaulle - the element of the frustrated careerist must also be taken into account - Macmillan was no conventional Tory.[38] According to Attlee, who described him as a 'real left-wing radical in his social, human and economic thinking', Macmillan subsequently came close to joining the Labour Party.[39] He certainly toyed with the idea of forming a Centre Party including the left of the Conservatives and the right of the Labour Party.

The division between the Conservative Party and its radical member for Stockton was widened by the foreign policy crises of the mid and late 1930s. Macmillan was a strong supporter of collective security and the League of Nations, and in the summer of 1936 he was one of only two Conservatives to vote against the government over the Anglo-French Hoare-Laval Pact which would effectively have carved up Abyssinia to the benefit of Mussolini. For a time he resigned the Party Whip. He regarded the Munich agreement with Hitler of September 1938 as 'a complete capitulation to the racial principles of Nazi philosophy',[40] campaigning in protest that autumn in the Oxford by-election for his former tutor, A.D.Lindsay, against the official Conservative candidate, Quentin Hogg, (the future Conservative minister, Lord Hailsham.) A less dramatic protest came at the Macmillan family bonfire party on 5 November, when the guy was dressed up as Neville Chamberlain, in black Homburg hat and with a rolled umbrella. [41] 'You may hear,' he told constituency critics in early 1939 'that I am a bit of a "Bolshie" and sometimes make myself a bit of a nuisance in the House. Frankly, I feel it is a role that must be played by *someone* in the party.'[42] At the end of the decade, Macmillan could take satisfaction for having been more far-sighted than the government over some of the major foreign and domestic issues of the day. But he was also ambitious, and on the eve of the Second World War he seemed to be a politician without a future.

* * *

Certain parallels between the lives and characters of these two products of what de Gaulle once described as the generation of catastrophes are immediately apparent, notably ability, bravery, and the courage of their convictions. Both also had a sense of style, and an extensive knowledge of history and the classics. Each was moved by the drama of great events, and thought, and sought to act, on the grand scale. Each looked ahead - de Gaulle far into the future. As politicians they would prove themselves to be highly skilled communicators, who knew how to put a sense of theatre to effective use, although de Gaulle's penchant for the dramatic gesture contrasted with the more subtle, lower-key skills of the actor-manager which Macmillan presented himself as. Each played his cards close to his chest. Each knew how to hide behind a mask.

To those who did not know Macmillan, this could be disconcerting. At his first meeting with him, in 1960, Sir Gawain Bell, a colonial governor in Nigeria, was struck by a lackadaisical manner, a marked drawl of speech and an air of languid nonchalance which seemed to amount almost to a measure of irresponsibility and levity. It was unnerving to be addressed as 'My dear old boy' and complimented on a 'splendid figure', and as Bell remarks, 'a little rum.' Like others, however, Bell soon realised that this was an extremely deft act, and that the image of easy-going non-professionalism was no more than a facade. Behind it was a highly professional politician.[43] The mask served an additional purpose. Like de Gaulle, Macmillan was a shy and very private person, who rarely gave much of himself away and felt something of an outsider. A public style was necessary for a man so acutely self-conscious and sensitive, one who, like his hero Disraeli, needed to create an elaborate role in order to be publicly effective.[44]

Macmillan and de Gaulle also shared something more debilitating: both were prone to depression. From childhood onwards Macmillan suffered from bouts of despondency, known as 'Black Dog', from which he sought relief by retreating into himself, and reading Jane Austen. On occasion, after he became Prime Minister, his deputy, R.A.Butler, stepped in and took over the Cabinet, saying that he had 'told the PM to go away for a few days'.[45] In de Gaulle's case depression tended to be associated with tension or failure; indeed in the aftermath of his unsuccesful attempt to regain the West African port of Dakar from Vichy control in September 1940, he appears to have briefly contemplated suicide.[46]

Above all, both men were highly complex characters. Sir Pierson Dixon, Macmillan's ambassador in Paris in the early 1960s, once commented that nothing one wrote about the General could quite attain to the inner truth.[47] Classicist and romantic, de Gaulle combined passion and control, discipline and rebellion, a heroic notion of leadership with a pragmatic respect for circumstance. But these polarities were, at least for much of the time, in a creative tension.[48] In Macmillan's case the contrasts and contradictions seem more dissonant. There often seemed to be several different Mr Macmillans.[49] There was on the one hand the fatalist and on the other the man of persistent determination, unwilling to let go even when the odds were heavily against success. There was the pragmatic realist who adapted to facts and accepted change at which others bridled. This Mr Macmillan was dispassionate, hard-headed and clear-sighted. But there was also a much more emotional man, given to wishful and sometimes woolly thinking. Macmillan carefully and successfully cultivated the image of the unflappable 'Supermac'. The diplomat Sir Patrick Reilly recalled once hearing a French simultaneous translator, in a context completely unconcerned with the Prime Minister, translate the word 'unflappability' as 'Macmillanisme'.[50] Yet the reality was of a highly-strung, nervous man, given to hypochondria, who could often exaggerate danger, and could on occasion panic. When in the autumn of 1942 Macmillan's name briefly came up during the search for a new Viceroy of India, Churchill thought he would be too unstable.[51]

Yet for all the parallels and similarities, some of which helped make for a sympathy and rapport at the personal level, it is the differences which are the more striking. Ultimately the two were not in the same league. De Gaulle, the man who twice saved France, following Pétain's capitulation in 1940 and again in the face of incipient civil war over Algeria in 1958, was in Churchill's words a 'figure of magnitude'. 'No statesman of our time,' a *Sunday Times* writer noted in April 1960, on the eve of the General's State Visit to Britain, 'excites more admiration and curiosity, more of the feelings men have for someone whose roots seem to be in no ordinary soil.' Today de Gaulle is a French national hero ranking with Napoleon and Charlemagne, commemorated in the names of France's nuclear aircraft carrier and Paris's main international airport.[52] Macmillan was a man of great ability, who never, however, entered the pantheon of the Greats.

They were also in key respects very different people, with different concepts of their respective roles. The English parliamentarian who frequented the great London clubs and the House of Common's smoking room, stands in marked contrast with the French General, and later President, who consciously cultivated a sense of mystery and aloofness. More subtle, but no less telling, are the respective titles and subject matters of de Gaulle and Macmillan's main books from the interwar years. De Gaulle's *The Edge of the Sword* is very much a soldier's book. It is a study in leadership, clearly influenced by the ideas of the German philosopher, Friedrich Nietzsche, which has been described as a self-portrait in anticipation.[53] Macmillan's *The Middle Way*, published in the late 1930s, drew its influence from the economist John Maynard Keynes. This was an attempt to chart a path between the then apparently irreconcilable extremes of Socialism and *laissez-faire* Capitalism, by a politician who gravitated naturally to the centre ground.

Whereas de Gaulle sought instinctively to impose his will on events, Macmillan was essentially a man of manoeuvre who operated indirectly, often by stealth. The secret of his success, wrote his private secretary and confidant, John Wyndham, 'was that he had the remarkable gift of inserting his guiding thoughts into other men's minds and making them think that the thoughts had all along been their own.'[54] A diplomat, George Mallaby, describes Macmillan's liking for the oblique method:

'He sent for you because he wanted to see you, he liked your company, he wanted to talk about his ancestry and yours, his Oxford days and so on; and, as a sort of incidental offhand suggestion muttered out not very clearly as he shuffled out of the room, perhaps you would be so good as to think up some way of overcoming the obstruction being erected against him by some Ministry or Department.'[55]

This might be good political tactics, but it was as much a reflection of a dislike of the kind of open conflict which de Gaulle relished. De Gaulle was a much more angular and awkward character than Macmillan, a man of heavy weather happy only in squalls, with the harder, more 'driven' personality.[56] Macmillan could be manipulative and ruthless, as the victims of the 'Night of the Long Knives', when in 1962 he sacked a third of his cabinet, were to discover. Macmillan himself confided to a friend at his son's funeral; 'Maurice was much nicer than me. I was always a shit. Maurice wouldn't be one so that's why he didn't get on in politics like me.'[57] But, as his concern for the men in his company during the First World War and his reaction to the miseries of the unemployment of the interwar years demonstrate, Macmillan had a warmth and compassion which de Gaulle lacked. One cannot imagine the General taking Macmillan's satisfaction from the 'surgeries' in Stockton, where the young MP tried to help with his constituents' practical day-to-day problems.[58]

De Gaulle operated at an altogether remoter, and less human level. He had little difficulty in acting as the agent of the state, an entity which like Nietzsche, he regarded as 'the coldest of all the cold monsters'. Unlike Macmillan he had a bleakly Hobbesian view of the world, regarding life as a matter of combat and struggle. British wits in North Africa during the war had nicknamed him 'Charlie Wormwood' and 'Ramrod', on the grounds that he had all the rigidity of a poker with none of its warmth. To many, however, this was no laughing matter. So disillusioned were the officers of the division de Gaulle briefly commanded in May 1940 with the General's intolerance for the opinions of others, his impatience of human failing, and occasional outbursts of rage when crossed, that none of them subsequently joined him in London.[59] Ruthless and brutal were terms often applied.

There were also pettier elements to his character. Acutely suspicious, he easily took offence and as one British diplomat who got to know him well during his wartime stay in London put it, was 'always ready to be insulted'.[60] He did not readily forgive and forget and, again very much unlike Macmillan, bore rancour. He could be sarcastic, contemptuous and malicious. Although personally devoid of arrogance and vanity - his grave in Colombey-les-Deux-Eglises is quite simple - his behaviour often gave a very different impression. 'Whatever good qualities he may have had,' wrote Field Marshal Lord Alanbrooke, 'were marred by his overbearing manner, his "megalomania" and his lack of cooperative spirit.' Macmillan wrote of the General's approach as that of an egocentric who had no notion of 'working as a member of a collective body unless he can dominate it'.[61]

One final characteristic is important. De Gaulle had a passionate commitment to, and almost mystical self-identification with the idea of France, which finds its most famous expression in the opening pages of his *War Memoirs*:

> All my life I have thought of France in a certain way. This is inspired by sentiment as much as reason. The emotional side of me tends to imagine France, like the princess in the fairy stories or the Madonna in the frescoes, as dedicated to an exalted and exceptional destiny. Instinctively I have the feeling that Providence has created her either for complete successes or for exemplary misfortunes.'[62]

There is no comparable passage in any of Macmillan's writings. But discussing de Gaulle's veto of British EEC membership, Macmillan quotes a section from Lloyd George's *War Memoirs* about two French diplomats of an earlier generation, Jules and Paul Cambon:

'They were intensely patriotic. France was their faith - their shrine - their worship - their deity. The first commandment of the true French patriot is: "Thou shalt have no other gods but France." It is a type of quality of patriotism which springs more naturally from the soil of France than from any other land. Are Englishmen also not patriots? Yes, they are, but with them patriotism is a duty, with Frenchmen it is a fanaticism.'[63]

Chapter 2

Mesentente Cordiale

In the aftermath of the January 1963 press conference, the former French Prime Minister Paul Reynaud sent his old protégé a letter of remonstrance, pointing out Britain's role in saving France in the two world wars. The reply came in the form of an empty envelope addressed in the General's hand, on the back of which was written, 'In the case of absence please forward to Agincourt (Somme) or to Waterloo (Belgium.)'[1] Like Macmillan, de Gaulle was a man immersed in history, and he was particularly well aware of the long tradition of Anglo-French rivalry. Speaking to French officers in Britain in 1943, he described 'les Anglais' as our hereditary enemies 'just like the Germans.'[2] Nineteen years later when discussing the impending State Visit to France of the West German Chancellor, Konrad Adenauer, he again spoke of Britain rather than Germany as France's greatest hereditary enemy. From the Hundred Years War to Fashoda she had barely ceased to struggle against France. The General might admire Britain, but as a brief for the Queen written at the time of his 1960 State Visit to London noted, dislike, envy and mistrust predominated.[3]

There were in fact few foreign countries the General obviously liked, and his attitude towards both the Americans and the Germans was no less ambivalent. Anglo-French relations, as the British embassy in Paris reflected in the 1960s, have however, always been a particularly complex affair.

'As nearest neighbour, oldest friends and worst enemies, sharing common blood and traditions but profoundly unlike each other, Britain and France have evolved a relationship so deep, various and inconsistent that neither are or can be fully conscious of it. At one moment the two countries seem by their circumstances and common heritage to be natural partners in an uncertain world; at another they are like scorpions in a bottle seeking to escape or ignore each other, or, with a certain relish, to do each other harm.'[4]

Historically it was the hostile side of the relationship which predominated. Negative stereotypes took deep root on both sides of the Channel. The British were seen in France as 'perfidious Albion', a term certainly used among the de Gaulle family. 'Perfidious?' Henri de Gaulle is once reported to have said. 'The adjective hardly seems strong enough.'[5] For their part the British readily reciprocated, attributing a variety of disobliging qualities to the French.[6]

The origins of this antagonism can be dated back to the Battle of Sluys in 1340. The Hundred Years War produced what one historian has described as 'a particularly luxuriant seedbed of nationalist prejudices'. The English came to regard the French as their natural prey, and to develop feelings of hatred and contempt for them. The French, on whose territory the war was largely fought, and whose towns and villages had been despoiled, brooded long over the consequences of defeat and the iniquities of the British invaders.[7] A de Gaulle ancestor had fought at Agincourt. 'The fact that Sieur Charles de Gaulle was one of the Knights attendant upon St. Jeanne d'Arc', Macmillan wrote in early 1944 at the end of his first prolonged encounter with the General,

> 'may or may not be a historic fact. Whatever its importance in the middle ages, it has had a most unfortunate influence upon modern times. For undoubtedly General de Gaulle regards himself not merely as the lineal but also the spiritual descendant of this Knight. Nor can he ever get out of his mind the French version of the death of the unfortunate Maid, conveniently forgetting that it was the Burgundians who condemned her to death, the English being guilty of nothing more than acquiescence in the outcome of one of those internal disputes which appear to be endemic in France. But de Gaulle in moments of antipathy against the English seems almost to feel physically the hot, singeing fire of those burning flames.'[8]

He was no means alone. The Anglophile, Andre Maurois, noted how in more than one French province between 1919 and 1939, he had encountered memories of the Hundred Years War.[9]

Although the British lost their last French foothold with the fall of Calais in 1540, the conflict between the two countries was very far from over. Over the next three centuries it variously took dynastic, religious, commercial, imperial and following the French Revolution of 1789, ideological form. Between 1689 and 1815 Britain and France fought no fewer than eight wars, the battles extending beyond Europe to North America and India. Waterloo was the last occasion on which French and British armies faced each other on the

European battlefield. But while the next decades witnessed an improvement in Anglo-French relations - by the 1840s there was already talk of an *entente cordiale* - cooperation and expressions of goodwill alternated with more traditional expressions of hostility and suspicion.

Much of the latter was Imperial. There had been a strong reaction in France when in 1840 the English seized Beirut and the Royal Navy blockaded the Syrian and Egyptian coasts. 'I do not blame the French for disliking us,' wrote Palmerston the same year. 'Their vanity prompts them to be the first nation in the world; and yet at every turn they find we outstrip them in everything.' Seven years later Palmerston was complaining that 'you can't trust them from one week to another, or even from one day to the next.'[10]

The intensification of the scramble for Africa in the last decades of the nineteenth century, when the two countries found themselves jostling for possession of often unpronounceable places and territories which politicians in London and Paris sometimes had difficulty finding on the map, became a major source of tension. The most damaging incident took place in 1898 at Fashoda, an abandoned mud-built fort in the Sudan, some seven hundred miles south of Khartoum. The French had sent an expedition to cross Africa from the Congo, in an attempt to prevent the construction of a British rail link between north and southern Africa. The French commander Jean-Baptiste Marchand was quickly challenged by a superior British force under General Kitchener. Unable to reach agreement the two men referred to their respective capitals for instructions. The British Prime Minister, Lord Salisbury, held firm. The Mediterranean fleet was mobilised, and parts of the Channel fleet were sent to Gibraltar. Having no prospect of reinforcing the Fashoda garrison, Paris reluctantly ordered a French withdrawal.[11]

In deference to French sensitivities, the name Fashoda was subsequently erased from the map.[12] But the damage had been done. The humiliation of the withdrawal was deeply felt in France. A cartoon in a leading humorous political journal depicted Albion as a bird of prey. Another showed France as Little Red Riding Hood, carrying fruit labelled Fashoda, and Britannia as the wolf. This was no passing affair. In part perhaps because Britain was then at the very height of its wealth and power while France was in relative decline, the resentment created by Fashoda bit deep into parts of French society, including the officer corps.[13] The incident was discussed with indignation in the de Gaulle household, and was long remembered by Charles as a supreme example of French impotence and British treachery.[14]

Yet only six years after Fashoda, in 1904, Britain and France signed the *Entente Cordiale*. Speaking in Oxford in 1941 de Gaulle attributed this dramatic reversal in Anglo-French relations to the rise of Germany and the threat it posed to the European balance of power.[15] In fact the original *Entente*, negotiated on the British side by the Foreign Secretary, Lord Lansdowne, (godfather to Macmillan's future wife, Lady Dorothy Cavendish), was essentially a colonial settlement. Britain gained the free hand it wanted in Egypt and the Nile valley in return for the safeguarding of France's special interests in Morocco. It was certainly not an alliance, and despite its name did not involve a radical revision of the traditionally suspicious and hostile view the two countries held of each other. No towns were twinned or youth exchanges inaugurated, as they were after the Franco-German treaty of 1963. Dislike, irritation and rivalry were to remain mutual. But the rapid assertion of German power led the two countries to enter into unprecedented, and highly secret Staff talks. Although British ministers insisted that no commitment was implied, their protestations were never convincing, if only because ever mindful of the need to maintain a European balance of power, Britain could not afford to risk France's defeat in a major European war. After the briefest of hesitations, a British Expeditionary Force (BEF) was despatched to France on the outbreak of war in August 1914.

Northern France was an area which British soldiers were to come to know all too well. By mid 1918 the BEF, which had originally numbered 160,000, had been expanded into a force of some one and a half million men. Their contribution to the war effort was critical. In May 1916, against the background of the German onslaught at Verdun, where de Gaulle had been captured two months earlier, the French told Haig that without a major British diversionary move, their army would cease to exist. Although aware that his forces were not fully trained, the British commander agreed to advance the date of his planned offensive on the Somme, the scene of Macmillan's near-fatal wound. The following year the BEF stood firm at the time of the mutinies in the French army. In March 1918 it was the British who bore the brunt of Germany's last great offensive. The great cemeteries in France - along with the countless war memorials in churches, schools, colleges and town squares across Britain - are testimony to the scale of the British commitment.

None of this of course prevented Anglo-French friction and recrimination, both at the time and later. De Gaulle for one was critical of British military conduct, notably the absence of British forces from the battle of the Marne in August 1914 and the initial speed with which they had pulled back in the face of the German attack of March 1918.[16] Nor did things improve during the interwar years, when the two countries seemed constantly to be annoying or frustrating each other. 'Nothing,' a Foreign Office memorandum opposing the construction of a Channel tunnel declared in 1920, 'can alter the fundamental fact that we are not liked in France, and never will be, except for the advantages which the French people may be able to extract from us.'[17] Three years later, the French Prime Minister, Raymond Poincaré, while describing the *entente* as an absolute necessity, went on to say that he had 'no illusion as to the real feelings of Great Britain towards France. She is as she has always been: a great rival who will remain with us because she needs us as we need her.'[18]

Rivalry was particularly acute in the Levant, and when in 1929 de Gaulle was posted to Beirut, he quickly came to share the suspicion rife among French officers of British machinations in the region.[19] But the central point of dissension was inevitably Germany. The French wanted a British security guarantee against the revanchism which was desperately feared in Paris. The British, all too mindful of the losses they had just sustained on the Western Front, and anxious to retain their traditional free hand in Europe, would not give it. They preferred to see themselves as a mediator between France and Germany. In his *War Memoirs*, de Gaulle writes of England treating Berlin gently 'in order that Paris might have need of her'.[20] But de Gaulle also had more specific charges against Britain's thoroughly undistinguished interwar policy towards Germany. These included the pressure on France over the Versailles settlement, preventing the French from opposing German rearmament, and, rather more dubiously, forbidding France to react to the German reoccupation of the Rhineland in 1936.[21]

By the late 1930s, however, as the threat posed by Hitler became increasingly difficult to ignore, and with the United States firmly isolationist, France came to be recognised as Britain's only major ally against Germany. Indeed British military planning was now premised on the strength of the French army. When in September 1939 war again broke out, another British Expeditionary Force was despatched across the Channel. But it was poorly trained and less well equipped than its predecessor. Even more ominously, it was sent to a country which had been morally and politically weakened by ideological conflict and where the scars of the bloodletting of the Western Front had not healed. Unlike Britain, France entered the Second World War in a mood of acute pessimism.[22]

* * *

While the Second World War heralded disaster for France and the *Entente*, it was to be the making of de Gaulle's and Macmillan's careers. This was not immediately evident, least of all to Macmillan who, having tried unsuccessfully to join his old regiment, briefly, or so at least he subsequently claimed, envisaged his war service as being confined to the unexalted role of lorry driver for the Cuckfield Rural District Council.[23] But in May 1940 the failure of the Norwegian campaign forced a parliamentary debate in which Chamberlain's majority was reduced to 81. Lady Violet Bonham-Carter, daughter of the Liberal Prime Minister, Herbert Asquith, recorded the scene. 'Cheers - shouts of "resign" - "Go" - Prim respectable Conservatives like Harold Macmillan - with his high white collar and tightly fixed pince-nez yelling "Go! Go! Go!" like inspired baboons.' When Churchill formed his government, he included the forty-six-year old Macmillan as Parliamentary Secretary to the Ministry of Supply. It was in this decidedly junior post that Macmillan's talent, and also ambition, first became evident.[24]

The change in premiership had come none too soon. The very day of Churchill's appointment, Hitler had attacked the Low Countries. Three days later, on 13 May, the German army launched Operation *Sichelschnitt*, the daring assault which outflanked the Maginot line by attacking France through the thick woods of the Ardennes, which the French high command had believed impassable. By 21 May German tanks had reached the coast. De Gaulle, who had been given command of a tank division shortly before the German assault, had seen action. Although he had acquitted himself honourably, he had not displayed what one biographer describes as that 'feeling for places, men and moments, that hunter's instinct, that almost animal flair' which puts a commander in the first class.[25] The point, however, quickly became academic. Although he always remained known as 'the General' - he had been promoted brigadier-general, the youngest in the French army - it is as a political rather than a military leader on which his fame and reputation rests. On 5 June the French Prime Minister, Paul Reynaud, appointed de Gaulle Under-Secretary of State for War.

By now the Allies were in deep crisis. The French army was in full retreat, and the last British troops had been evacuated from the beaches at Dunkirk. In London the cabinet had already considered and rejected the idea of a peace overture. Capitulation was not in Churchill's style, and like de Gaulle Churchill believed that only nations which went down fighting rose again.[26] But unlike France, Britain enjoyed the protection of the Channel, and assuming full American economic and financial support, the Chiefs of Staff believed that Britain could fight on alone.[27] One of de Gaulle's first ministerial tasks was to go to London to correct the impression that France was wavering. As Reynaud put it in his Memoirs, 'I was happy to show the English a general with an aggressive spirit.'[28]

From the conventional diplomatic point of view the General was not an obvious choice. In Jean Lacouture's words, in June 1940 de Gaulle might be considered an anglophobe, although this is disputed, not least by his son, Philippe. Family tradition, his St.Cyr education, the influence of the right-wing *Action Française,* as well as of his Levant posting, all inclined him to a highly suspicious of British foreign and colonial policy. In a paper written in 1932 he had shown a clear preference for alliance with the Soviet Union rather than Britain. He spoke only halting English, although he understood the language quite well, and had few if any contacts in a country which he had never previously visited.[29]

His first impressions were by no means favourable. In sharp contrast to Paris, which the French government was on the point of evacuating, London, as he later wrote,

'had a look of tranquility, almost indifference. The streets and parks full of people peacefully out for a walk, the long queues at the entrances to the cinemas, the many cars, the impressive porters outside the clubs and hotels, belonged to another world than the one at war.'

To English feelings, he concluded 'the channel was still wide'.[30] It was a theme to which he would return.

Nor were his initial dealings with the British government satisfactory. Churchill refused the General's request on 9 June to give a date when British forces could return to the battle, or to send additional British fighters.[31] At a meeting in France a few days later, de Gaulle's deeply-ingrained suspicions of British policy contributed to his wrongly attributing to the British Prime Minister a willingness to barter the release of France from her commitment not to negotiate a separate armistice or peace treaty, for guarantees over the future of the French fleet. [32] On the other hand he had been impressed by Churchill.[33]

De Gaulle returned to Britain by destroyer on 15 June, together with the stock of heavy water acquired as part of the early French nuclear research programme. By a strange coincidence in view of their later dealings on nuclear matters, it was Macmillan at the Ministry of Supply who was initially called upon to deal with this unexpected arrival. At the time Macmillan did not know what heavy water was, and was too confused to ask.[34] The real drama of this second visit, however, played out in Whitehall, where de Gaulle became involved in one of the strangest and most dramatic incidents in the history of the *Entente*. With the prospect of French surrender now imminent, a small group of British and French officials had drawn up a proposal for an Anglo-French union, with joint organs for defence, finance and economic policies, a single War Cabinet and common citizenship.[35] Many of the details, including the question of whether the union would continue after the war, were obscure. It did not matter. The main point, as de Gaulle immediately realised, was that it offered Reynaud an argument for tenacity vis-a-vis his wavering ministers.[36]

On June 16 the man normally viewed as the supreme champion of French national sovereignty persuaded an initially reluctant Churchill to get the British Cabinet to accept the proposal. Reynaud's response was enthusiastic; that of his government, which by now had retreated to Bordeaux, was not. The octogenarian Marshal Pétain spoke of 'a marriage with a corpse'. Other members declared that they did 'not want to be a British dominion.'[37] It was the last straw. Reynaud resigned later the same day and his successor, Pétain, immediately asked for an armistice which was signed on 22 June. The Germans occupied the north, along with a zone along the Atlantic coast, leaving an Unoccupied southern zone covering some 45 per cent of the country. It was here that Pétain set up his government, with its capital in the sleepy spa town of Vichy. France's future, the German Propaganda Ministry declared on 9 July, was to become 'a greater Switzerland....a country of tourism and fashion.'[38]

* * *

June 1940 is one of the great turning points in modern history. Never before had the European balance of power shifted so completely in so short a time. Germany now occupied much of the Continent. Britain was on its own, about to face at once its darkest, but also its finest, hour. France was entering the lowest ebb in its fortunes since at least the wars of religion of the sixteenth century. It had suffered much more than a defeat. Unlike other countries overrun by the Germans, the Vichy government had, in de Gaulle's words, 'sold its soul' and collaborated. For the General it was a shameful act.[39] Alone among senior French political or military figures, de Gaulle decided on exile in Britain.

On 18 June, the day after his arrival, and coincidentally the one hundred and twenty-fifth anniversary of the battle of Waterloo, he made his now famous BBC broadcast, calling for the continuation of French resistance in defiance of Pétain and Vichy. In the words of the despatch written by the British embassy in Paris after the General's death in 1970, de Gaulle had snatched the tricolore from the hands of the dying Republic, and held it aloft as a rallying call for those who refused to accept French capitulation.[40]

The road ahead was to prove long and lonely. To many, particularly in the French army, de Gaulle was not a hero but a deserter who had defied orders.[41] His official British hosts had mixed feelings about this largely unknown, although already controversial officer, and it was in large measure due to Churchill that within ten days the General was recognised as the 'leader of all Free Frenchmen who rally to him in support of the Allied cause.' By the late summer the two men were sufficiently close for de Gaulle to be a regular visitor to Chequers.[42]

The mutual respect and admiration would last a lifetime. On the eve of Churchill's death in 1965, de Gaulle talked about the former Prime Minister to the retiring British ambassador, Sir Pierson Dixon. 'The impression he gave me,' Dixon noted in his diary, 'was a strange one. It was that in Winston he recognised perhaps one human being whose claim to greatness was stronger than his own. His attitude was if anything humble, and I have never noticed a trace of humility in the General before.'[43] Yet the honeymoon which had begun in the grim summer of 1940 had been over within a year, and de Gaulle and his British hosts found themselves locked into a vicious circle of mutual frustration and exasperation.[44] In a note for the cabinet in 1943, Churchill described his former protégé as:

'animated by dictatorial instincts and consumed by personal ambition. All those who have worked with him know that he shows many of the symptoms of a budding Führer...He seeks to appropriate for himself and his followers the title-deeds of France. There is no doubt in my mind that he would bring civil war to that country...He would I have no doubt make anti-British alliances and combinations at any time when he thought it in his interests to do so, and he would do this with gusto.'[45]

One senior Foreign Office official complained that all those who had dealt with de Gaulle were 'unanimous in finding his methods almost intolerable'. The Foreign Secretary, Anthony Eden, who was usually sympathetic to the General, described him as one of the most difficult people he had ever done business with.[46]

Part of this, as de Gaulle's superior French officers had already discovered, was simply a matter of character. De Gaulle was always difficult. To this must be added the peculiarly trying circumstances of these early exile years. De Gaulle suffered an acute sense of humiliation at French defeat and capitulation.

He resented his near total dependence on the British, - for money, equipment and diplomatic and physical communications; he did not even have his own aircraft to travel abroad. And there was the strain and loneliness of his self-appointed task, which was heightened by the after-effects of malaria. All this made for some particularly undiplomatic outbursts and unpredictable behaviour. His mood could change with startling rapidity, indeed at one point Eden was questioning de Gaulle's mental stability.[47]

There was, however, also method behind this seeming madness. Defiance was one of the few weapons in the General's very weak armoury, and a man for whom bloody-minded obstinacy came as almost second nature, had no hesitation in employing it with Churchill, let alone lesser figures. It was an essential means of rebuilding French self-respect, as well as defending French national interests against allies who, in the General's acutely suspicious eyes, were taking unfair advantage of a wounded France.[48]

The focus of the General's grievance was Syria and Lebanon, where de Gaulle wrongly believed that Britain was seeking to supplant the French position. It was in the summer of 1941, during the first of what proved to be a series of Levant crises, that de Gaulle shocked his erstwhile champion, General Sir Edward Spears by remarking, 'I don't think I will ever get on with les Anglais...You are all the same, exclusively centred on your own interests and business, quite insensitive to the requirements of others. Do you think I am interested in England winning the war? I am not - I am interested only in France's victory.' When Spears replied that the two were the same, de Gaulle replied, 'Not at all.'[49] Not long afterwards he gave an interview an American newspaper, in which he accused England of being afraid of the French fleet and carrying on a wartime deal with Hitler in which Vichy served as a go-between. It was a remark of supreme tactlessness, which infuriated Churchill.

Then, in December 1941, came the Japanese attack on Pearl Harbour, and the US entry into the war. From now on the United States were to provide an additional source of friction between de Gaulle and the British. But it was the Americans who, almost literally, brought de Gaulle and Macmillan together.

PART TWO:

'YOU HAVE DONE VERY WELL', 1942-44

Chapter 3

The Anglo-Saxon Alliance

Three, General Gavin, the American ambassador to Paris commented in 1961, *apropos* of the then strained state of the Western alliance, 'is always an awkward number - in children, in matrimony and in alliances.'[1] The triangle between Paris, London and Washington which superseded the old *Entente*, and which was to become so closely bound up with the Macmillan-de Gaulle story, has its origins in the same set of events which launched de Gaulle on his political career. France's defeat had marked a parting of Anglo-French ways. The only prospect of re-establishing a European balance of power lay with the United States. Arguing the case for continued French resistance in his broadcast of 18 June, de Gaulle had specifically referred to America's vast industrial resources.[2] The British were even more aware of this potential power, and wooing America quickly became Churchill's highest diplomatic priority. But it was only with Pearl Harbour, described in Macmillan's memoirs as a 'gift from the gods' for Britain, that the Americans became active combatants.[3] Prescient as ever, de Gaulle realised that the war was won. He also believed that British policy would henceforth be subordinate to that of the United States. 'In this industrial war,' he remarked to the aide who brought him the news, 'nothing can resist the might of American industry. From now on, the British will do nothing without Roosevelt's agreement.'[4]

It is a theme to which de Gaulle returns. In his account of a particularly difficult interview with Churchill on the eve of D-Day, the General quotes the British Prime Minister as saying, 'each time we must choose between Europe and the open sea, we shall always choose the open sea. Each time I must choose between you and Roosevelt, I shall always choose Roosevelt.' The memory of this remark, which does not appear in the British record, but which undoubtedly reflects Churchill's sentiments, made an indelible impression on the General. He repeated it on a number of occasions, including his last meeting with Macmillan in December 1962, when he gave notice of his intention to oppose Britain's EEC bid.[5]

No less telling is de Gaulle's account of Churchill's reaction to the proposal which the General put forward in Paris in November 1944, for a post-war Anglo-French alliance. Both Britain and France, de Gaulle argued, would emerge weakened from the war. If they remained divided, neither would be able to exercise real influence. Allied they could 'weigh heavily enough in the world's scales so that nothing will be done which they themselves have not consented to or determined.' Churchill, while accepting an Anglo-French alliance in principle, demurred from this particular bargain, arguing that in politics as in strategy it was better to persuade the stronger rather than pit oneself against him. He preferred to try to restrain the Russians and influence the Americans. What followed was a classic British formulation of the 'special relationship', to which Macmillan would in his turn wholeheartedly subscribe. The US did not always use its immense resources to best advantage. The Prime Minister was trying to enlighten them, 'without forgetting, of course, to benefit my country. I have formed a close personal tie with Roosevelt. With him, I proceed by suggestion in order to influence matters in the right direction.'[6]

While in some respects indeed remarkably close, Anglo-American relations were by no means trouble-free. On the contrary there were a number of serious areas of disagreement, not least divergent views over the future of France and the role of de Gaulle. The Roosevelt Administration had pursued a very different policy from the British since June 1940, maintaining links with Vichy and Pétain. Roosevelt, who took an intense personal interest in French affairs, and according to one senior US diplomat, would discuss the replacement of French officials and changes to French laws 'as if these were matters for Americans to decide', believed that the country had been irredeemably compromised by its defeat and capitulation. France was now a second class Power, and was to be treated accordingly. The American President went so far as to talk about France being disarmed after the war, and the creation of a new state of Walloonia, including parts of north-east France and the Walloon territories of Belgium. There was also American talk, reflecting a typically Rooseveltian mixture of high-minded idealism and calculated American self-interest, of the 'internationalisation' of various French overseas territories, including Indochina and French colonies in the Pacific, as well as the strategically important African ports of Bizerta and Dakar.[7] As to de Gaulle, who at this stage of his career showed no signs of the anti-Americanism which would become so pronounced in later years, the President regarded him as a divisive force, pretentious, unrepresentative, and with potentially fascist tendencies. There was no man, Roosevelt once remarked to his son, Elliott, in whom he had less confidence. His Secretary of State, Cordell Hull, had been known to refer to the Free French as 'polecats'.[8]

Such attitudes put Roosevelt and the State Department at odds with London. However frustrated and angry Churchill might at times be with de

Gaulle, the British were bound to the General, in whom they had already invested much by way of money, as well as honour, prestige and self-interest.[9] Britain could not afford to write France off as a Great, or indeed as an Imperial, Power. At a time when nobody envisaged the creation of NATO or the permanent peacetime presence of US forces in Europe, France was seen as an essential factor in the post-war balance of power.

What brought these issues to a head were the political repercussions of 'Operation Torch'. The Anglo-American landings in North Africa on 8 November 1942 came at a critical turning point of the war. The years of defeat and isolation were now behind Britain. Montgomery had just won his decisive victory over Rommel at the battle of El Alamein, while on the eastern Front, German forces were becoming increasingly embroiled in the battle of Stalingrad. The immediate aim of 'Torch' was to squeeze Axis forces in North Africa from the rear, between the invaders to the west and Montgomery's Eighth Army in Libya. Before that could be done, however, there was a serious political problem to be overcome. The French North African territories of Tunisia, Algeria and Morocco were under Vichy control. Anxious to ensure their cooperation, Roosevelt had insisted that 'Torch' should be under American command, and that the Free French, who had clashed with Vichy troops both at Dakar in 1940 and the next year in the Levant, be excluded.[10] When Allied forces nevertheless met with resistance, which left some three thousand French and a similar number of allied soldiers dead, the local American commanders proceeded to make a deal with one of the most notorious, and Anglophobe, figures of the Vichy regime, Admiral Darlan. 'Darlan gave me Algiers, long live Darlan!' Roosevelt remarked. 'If Laval gives me Paris, long live Laval! I am not like Wilson, I am a realist.'[11]

The British, who had not been consulted, were furious at this act of cynical pragmatism. Eden complained of dealings with 'turncoats and blackmailers', while a Foreign Office telegram to Washington declared that 'we are fighting for international decency and Darlan is the antithesis of this.' North Africa was the first part of France, as indeed of any occupied enemy territory, to be liberated, and important precedents were being set.[12] Public criticism was such that Churchill was forced to defend his policy at a secret session of the House of Commons. At the same time the private minuting on both the British and the American side suggests a more traditional kind of rivalry, as America began to emerge as the senior partner in the alliance. A Foreign Office official commented on the way in which the Americans were 'forging ahead in matters which are of our concern without consulting us or paying regard to our views', a complaint echoed by Eden's private secretary, Oliver Harvey. For their part the State Department complained about the support, believed to be officially inspired, which de Gaulle was getting in the British press. An analysis by the American embassy in London noted that while American policy was to allow the French to choose their own government after the war, the British preferred to see a transitional regime 'which owes its existence to them'. The British, it suggested, were perhaps jealous of America's leading role in North Africa.[13]

These tensions focused British attention onto the need to bolster the political section of AFHQ, Allied Forces Headquarters in Algiers. The allied commander, General Dwight D. Eisenhower, more popularly known as 'Ike', knew little about the local political situation and spoke no French, while the local British diplomatic representative was not senior enough to have the necessary influence.[14] Eden and Churchill initially considered sending out the Permanent Under-Secretary at the Foreign Office, Sir Alexander Cadogan, partly to sort out the immediate North African tangle, partly to restrain the Americans from 'doing stupid things'. This idea, however, foundered when it became clear that Roosevelt would not allow him to raise political questions. On 17 November the Foreign Office forwarded to Washington a proposal to appoint somebody comparable in status to the British Minister in Cairo, who, while working closely with the military authorities, would report directly to the War Cabinet in London.[15] Two days later Roosevelt came up with his own rather different suggestion for the appointment of British and American representatives 'to whom would be given authority not to administer civil functions but to hold a veto power over French administrations, and to direct them in rare instances to follow out certain policies.'[16]

Roosevelt's candidate was Robert Murphy, a controversial State Department official who had spent some ten years before the war in Paris, remaining after the armistice as the senior American representative to Vichy. Catholic, and of Irish origins, this genial and articulate diplomat, whose political sympathies were reputed to be on the Right, had an enthusiasm for causes and a tendency to exaggerate. In September 1940 Roosevelt had instructed him to visit North Africa to make contact with General Weygand, whom the American president saw as the leader of a potential anti-Nazi resistance. The following year Murphy was assigned to Algiers as, in his own later words, 'a sort of High Commissioner for French Africa'. It was Murphy who had been entrusted with the task of trying to ensure that the French military would not oppose the Allied landings.[17]

Roosevelt's choice was not welcome in London, where the American diplomat was regarded as pro-Vichy, anti-de Gaulle and anti-British.[18] On 11 December Churchill put forward his own candidate. 'I would,' he telegraphed the President, 'choose an under-secretary of administrative experience whom Eisenhower might be expected to find sympathetic. For your personal information I had Harold Macmillan in mind.' A separate message noted that like Churchill, Macmillan had an American mother.[19]

A good deal of further negotiation was still required over the new representative's title and status - whether he should be on Eisenhower's staff, and (a matter of particular importance to London) whether he should report direct to the British government. It was only therefore on 22 December that Macmillan was invited to Downing Street. After a long discourse on the North African situation of which Macmillan knew very little, Churchill gradually came to the point, stressing that the new Minister must depend on the influence he could exert on the American commander-in-chief. Here, he told his excited guest:

'was a post of great potential significance. It would bring its occupant into the very centre of world events. Although it would entail secondment from the House of Commons, the chosen minister would keep his seat. It would be an adventure of a high order. The post was at my disposition. It was for me to decide. I replied at once that there was no need to hesitate - I would accept it immediately and gratefully.'[20]

Macmillan had good reason for his gratitude. His war so far had been unspectacular. In February 1942 he had been promoted to be Under-Secretary at the Colonial Office, a post which clearly did not fulfil his ambitions. His frustration occasionally showed. His private secretary, John Wyndham, describes an incident during a car journey when Macmillan 'made a remark, almost to himself, which had nothing to do with what we had been talking about. He suddenly said with great force: 'I *know* I can do it', before lapsing into silence.'[21] When the Colonial Secretary, Lord Cranborne, for whom he had deputised in the House of Commons, was moved in an autumn reshuffle, Macmillan found himself effectively demoted. He contemplated resignation, but was advised to wait by Churchill's confidant, Brendan Bracken.

Even now Macmillan's future did not seem certain. On Christmas Eve Darlan was assassinated. The circumstances were, and remain, murky. SOE involvement was immediately suspected and denied. 'Whatever French may have discovered', the First Sea Lord signalled to Admiral Cunningham in Algiers, 'it cannot incriminate any branch of British Secret Services, who do not indulge in such activities.'[22] No matter what the truth was, Darlan's disappearance resolved the most immediate problem facing the Allies, and greatly simplified Macmillan's mission. At the time Macmillan himself feared that a new minister would not be needed.[23] He need not have worried, although Roosevelt did try to delay his arrival until Eisenhower had arranged the political situation in North Africa to American liking, with the appointment of General Giraud as Darlan's successor as High Commissioner for French Africa and Commander-in Chief. Giraud was the man whom the Americans had originally groomed for Operation Torch; he was also de Gaulle's former pre-war commander in Metz. Churchill, while unable to prevent this manoeuvre, stood his ground.[24] The War Cabinet, he told the President, attached 'much importance to Macmillan's appointment and arrival. We feel quite underrepresented there yet our fortunes are deeply involved and we are trying to make a solid contribution to your enterprise.'[25]

Finally, on 2 January 1943, accompanied by John Wyndham, two typists and two typewriters 'prudently stolen' from the Colonial Office, Macmillan arrived in Algiers to take up the appointment which was to prove his political break-through. He would be attached to Eisenhower's staff, but would not be a member of it. His brief was to report to the government on the political situation and future plans for North Africa, 'and represent to the Commander-in-Chief the views of His Majesty's Government on political matters.' But his functions were purely representative, and Eisenhower retained the final word on everything in North Africa.[26] Macmillan was not accredited to the local French authorities, with whom his relations were intended to be 'of an informal character'. A communication from de Gaulle's French National Committee in London, raising questions about the precedent set by the appointment, and its implications for French sovereignty, was brushed aside.[27]

The mission set off to an uncomfortable start. Macmillan was put up in a hotel where the hot water only worked for an hour in the morning, the bed was hard and there was no fire or heating of any kind. His head of mission, Roger Makins, had not yet arrived, though in his place had come 'a very nice young man', Pierson Dixon, whose knowledge of Balkan politics Macmillan thought would prove useful.[28] The first interview with Eisenhower began on a frosty note. Eisenhower was still smarting from the criticism of the Darlan deal, and, at least according to his own account, had not received any notification of Macmillan's appointment. It was only when Macmillan referred to the fact that his mother had been born in Indiana, in a little town called Spencer, that the American General began to unbend. Macmillan came away from the meeting with the impression that Eisenhower's 'natural antipathy to the idea of a British Minister of Cabinet rank, who might make trouble for him in all sorts of ways, could be overcome. If I would play the game with him, he would do the same by me.' It was a shrewd assessment. Eisenhower had from the outset been a firm believer in Anglo-American cooperation, and he now telegraphed the Combined Chiefs of Staff in Washington that he was convinced that Macmillan would be most helpful, and that he was obviously concerned 'only with assisting me to the utmost'.[29]

The more difficult task was to ensure that Murphy, with whom, along with Eisenhower's Chief of Staff, General Walter Bedell-Smith, Macmillan would primarily deal, regarded him as a colleague rather than an opponent. Macmillan began by establishing his office immediately above the American's in order, as he reported to Churchill, to establish 'complete unity with him'.[30] More important, he treated Murphy, whom he found had a very easy and friendly manner, with complete frankness. He showed him copies of Foreign Office telegrams which the American diplomat, who was kept rather less well informed by the State Department, found useful. And Macmillan was careful not to throw his political weight around. The point was famously made in remarks to the new British Director of Psychological Warfare, Richard Crossman, which have come to epitomise Macmillan's concept of the 'special relationship':

'Remember...when you go into the Hotel St. George, you will regularly enter a room and see an American colonel, his cigar in his mouth and his feet on the table. When your eyes get used to the darkness, you will see in a corner an English captain, his feet down, his shoulders hunched, writing like mad, with a full in-tray and no cigar.

Mr Crossman, you will never call attention to this discrepancy. When you install a similar arrangement in your own office, you will always permit your American colleague not only to have a superior rank to yourself and much higher pay, but also the feeling that he is running the show. This will enable you to run it yourself.

We, my dear Crossman, are Greeks in this American empire.....We must run AFHQ as the Greek slaves ran the operations of the Emperor Claudius.'

(This *bon mot* quickly came to American ears, but at least on Robert Murphy's later testimony, the fact did not stop Macmillan from 'exercising greater influence on Anglo-American affairs in the Mediterranean than was generally recognized.[31])

If, despite the differences between Washington and London, the Americans in Algiers quickly promised to be relatively easy to manage, French politics on the other hand promised nothing but trouble. 1943 was a unique period in the history of modern Anglo-French relations. The British were in effect mediating in a domestic power struggle to determine the shape and complexion of the post-war French government. 'Torch' had brought about a new, and critical, phase in French politics. Until then there had been a relatively simple polarisation between de Gaulle and the Free French on the one hand, and Pétain and Vichy on the other. Now de Gaulle had a new rival in the form of the sixty-three-year old General Giraud. A courageous, straightforward and honest soldier who unlike Darlan, had not collaborated with the Germans, Giraud had a distinguished record in North Africa. Sympathetic to the Allies, his overriding preoccupation was the prosecution of the war. Politically he was quite naïve: Macmillan likened him to the White Knight in *Alice in Wonderland*, since he appeared to live only in the clouds. He outranked de Gaulle, and had a strong sense of his own dignity and seniority. Giraud's remark to Macmillan in early January that he was fully confident of amicable and fruitful relations with de Gaulle, who 'after all served as a colonel under my orders', did not bode well for the future.[32]

The Giraud-de Gaulle conflict was to dominate much of Macmillan's time in Algiers. Both were strong and prickly personalities who spoke of themselves in the third person, and were quite unwilling to subordinate themselves one to the other. As a senior Foreign Office official laconically noted, 'there are two kings of Brentford and neither will give way to the other.' Their mutual animosities and suspicions were compounded by what Macmillan referred to as the 'tapers and tadpoles' in their two camps.[33] But personalities were by no means the whole of the story. Giraud stood for a conservative and traditional view of France which was strongly at odds with the more radical thinking of his younger rival, who was bitterly impatient with the failures of old men whom he believed responsible for France's defeat. It was a clash of ideas and generations as much as of egos.[34]

De Gaulle had wanted to come to meet Giraud immediately after the Darlan assassination to 'study ways that might enable us to concentrate under a provisional central authority', all French forces capable of 'joining the struggle for the liberation and the welfare of France'. But he had been put off by Giraud who suspected a Gaullist hand in the assassination plot. Never one to take a rebuff, the General had publicly complained about the delay. Although the consequent press uproar particularly annoyed Roosevelt, the American president was pragmatic enough to recognise that de Gaulle's aspirations could not be ignored. Murphy was therefore instructed to find a formula for de Gaulle's integration into the Algerian-based French Imperial Council, which Giraud headed.[35]

This was important since it narrowed the gap with the British, who had all along been anxious to work for unity between the French factions. By mid-January Macmillan and the local American authorities had come to a broad measure of agreement on the way forward. Based both on the immediate strategic need to avoid unrest in North Africa which would interfere with the conduct of the war, and the longer-term political desirability of establishing a rather better precedent for future Anglo-American cooperation over the liberation of Europe, it provided for a purge of the local Vichy administration and an early meeting between the two generals. A provisional, liberally-minded French administration, including both politicians and generals, would be established. The initial steps were to be taken at Anfa camp near Casablanca, where Churchill and Roosevelt were about to meet on 15 January for wide-ranging discussions on the future conduct of the war.[36]

The Casablanca meeting has been described as a 'striking, if utility, field of the Cloth of Gold', a reference to the magnificent encounter in 1520 between Henry VIII and Francis I of France. It provided Macmillan with his introduction to the rarefied world of Summit diplomacy, to which he took an instant liking, writing later of such encounters as 'remarkable and romantic episodes, illuminating the routine of life'.[37] With his penchant for classical analogies, he compared the meeting to one of the later period of the Roman Empire, christening the two principals the Emperor of the East and the Emperor of the West. Roosevelt, whom Macmillan had met several times during trips to the United States in the pre-war years, was particularly charming to him, which helped improve Macmillan's standing with Eisenhower. There was a good deal of joking about Macmillan's being publisher to both the Prime Minister and the President. There was also 'a lot of bezique, an enormous quantity of highballs, talk by the hour, and a general atmosphere of extraordinary goodwill'.[38]

The latter did not extend to French affairs. The two leaders were not ready to endorse the more ambitious aspects of the programme for French unity already agreed in Algiers, but they did agree to invite the two French generals to Casablanca. 'We'll call Giraud the bridegroom,' Roosevelt suggested to Churchill, 'and I'll produce him from Algiers; and you get the bride, de Gaulle, down from London, and we'll have a shot-gun wedding.'[39] It was not a tactful idea. The Anglo-Saxon Powers were summoning French leaders to a conference on French territory, something which, as Macmillan had warned when the invitation was being discussed, de Gaulle would particularly resent. It was not just the affront to French sovereignty and dignity; de Gaulle was also rightly afraid that he would come under heavy pressure to compromise.[40] It thus took a good deal of arm-twisting before the General could be induced to accept the invitation, and the cabinet in London had to tone down a message from Churchill threatening that Britain would otherwise break with him. Any suggestion of what one official privately referred to as 'muniching' the General would be strongly resented by British public opinion. There was also concern about the devastating impact which dropping the General would have on the Resistance movement in France, which was beginning to assume increasing importance.[41]

Churchill was therefore forced to wait until 22 January for de Gaulle to appear in Casablanca. By then the conference was virtually over and the Prime Minister had to endure a lot of unwelcome jokes about de Gaulle from Roosevelt. The President believed that de Gaulle and the British shared a common interest in upholding the colonial empires to which Roosevelt was so strongly opposed, and that Churchill was thus deliberately holding him back.[42] Things scarcely improved with the General's arrival. There was no guard of honour. He was met at the airport by an American general and a French colonel, and then lodged in a villa which, like others in the conference compound, was guarded by American sentries and surrounded by barbed wire. In his *War Memoirs* de Gaulle describes it as 'captivity. I had no objection to the Anglo-American leaders imposing it on themselves, but the fact that they were applying it to me, and furthermore on territory under French sovereignty, seemed to me a flagrant insult.' After lunch with Giraud who had arrived without demur five days earlier, de Gaulle deliberately kept to his quarters.[43]

The Allies duly came to him. His first visitor was Macmillan, and it is this Anglo-American Summit which marks the beginning of the de Gaulle-Macmillan relationship, although the two had occasionally met both socially and officially in London.[44] Over the following two days in Casablanca, they were to have a great deal to do with each other. Macmillan began by explaining that, in cooperation with Murphy, he was trying to find a formula for union with Giraud, which could be proposed to them by Churchill and Roosevelt. This was the intervention which de Gaulle had been expecting, and his response was that such an arrangement could only be agreed between Frenchmen.[45]

Later in the afternoon Churchill put to him a plan which would have made Giraud supreme French military commander, with de Gaulle, Giraud, and Churchill's friend, General Georges, as joint chairmen of a governing committee. Other members would include a number of prominent pro-Vichy figures whose names were to become all too familiar to Macmillan over the next few months, notably Marcel Peyrouton, a former member of the Vichy cabinet who had recently been appointed Governor of Algeria, General Noguès, the Resident General in Morocco, and General Boisson. The latter, who was

Governor of Dakar, had been responsible for resisting de Gaulle's assault on the West African port in September 1940. All this was totally unacceptable to de Gaulle, who wanted the establishment of a Provisional Government, and had no intention of submerging his Fighting French, as the Free French movement was now known, in a Vichy-dominated committee under American control.[46]

Little progress was made the next day, during which de Gaulle was subject to pressure from Murphy, and what in his *War Memoirs* he describes as 'a tirade of concern as to the future of Fighting France' from Macmillan.[47] But there remained clear differences between Macmillan and his American colleague. Murphy made no bones of the fact that he regarded de Gaulle as a 'Frankenstein monster', of whom the British should welcome the opportunity of ridding themselves. By contrast Macmillan, who was seeing de Gaulle in action for the first time, quickly realised that he would easily outsmart the politically obtuse Giraud. De Gaulle was clearly the horse to back, and Macmillan found himself in the embarrassing position of constantly seeking to persuade Churchill and Roosevelt to give de Gaulle another chance, which the Frenchman always seemed unwilling to grasp.[48] At a meeting late in the evening of the 23rd, Murphy advocated breaking with de Gaulle. Roosevelt was inclined to agree, but Macmillan, supported by Churchill as well as Roosevelt's confidant, Harry Hopkins, helped dissuade him.[49]

Much of the next morning was spent trying unsuccessfully to persuade de Gaulle and Giraud to accept a formula drafted by Macmillan and Murphy. The two general would proclaim themselves in agreement 'with the principles of the Allied Nations' and announce their intention of forming a joint committee to administer the French Empire during the war. Giraud agreed; de Gaulle did not.[50] An extremely acrimonious interview with Churchill was followed by a final visit to Roosevelt, who proceeded to turn on his charm. De Gaulle was greatly impressed by the American President and anxious not to give an impression of division to the Resistance in France and the French in North Africa. He therefore agreed to issue a joint communiqué which Roosevelt wanted for domestic political reasons, even though, as he told the President, 'It cannot be yours.' Then, when joined by Giraud, Churchill and others, the President made a last request. 'Will you at least agree,' de Gaulle quotes Roosevelt as saying,

> 'to being photographed beside me and the British Prime Minister, along with General Giraud?'
> 'Of course,' I answered, 'for I have the highest regard for this great soldier.'
> 'Will you go so far as to shake General Giraud's hand before the camera?' the President cried.
> 'My answer, in English, was, 'I shall do that for you.'[51]

Macmillan's account has more of a sense of the ridiculous. According to his version, the famous photograph and handshake, which de Gaulle always hated, had been the result of chicanery and pressure. After de Gaulle had repeated his unwillingness to accept the communiqué as drafted, Roosevelt suggested that a final effort be made to get a compromise declaration. Murphy and Macmillan 'did some quick work. I held on to de Gaulle, while he rounded up Giraud.' The two generals then finally agreed to draw up a joint communiqué in the course of the evening after Roosevelt and Churchill had left. To prevent the obvious risk of backsliding, Macmillan took advantage of the arrival of the British and American press corps.

> 'There were some folding doors in the room; as they were thrown open for Roosevelt and Churchill to take their seats on the terrace, Murphy and I almost forcibly pushed out the two generals and made them appear at their side. Two more chairs were hurriedly provided and the Press Conference began. The President and the Prime Minister each made their statements, and then the two generals, in a picture which went round the world, were seen shaking hands with the best approach to a smile that they could manage.'[52]

There was a final, though minor, logistic hitch once the conference was over. De Gaulle's plane was unserviceable and he refused to fly in an American aircraft. Macmillan invited the General and his staff to dinner, where the events of the last few days were not discussed, and the General at last seemed relatively cheerful. Macmillan had made his first mark with de Gaulle. On his return to London the General spoke warmly of the British Minister's role.[53]

Eden too was appreciative.[54] But the Foreign Secretary had an additional reason for being grateful to Macmillan over and above his role in avoiding a breakdown. Roosevelt had not been entirely straight with Churchill. Without any discussion with the Prime Minister, he had signed a document committing both the British and American governments to recognising Giraud as having 'the right and duty of preserving all French interests' until the French people were able to 'designate their regular government'. This would not only have relegated de Gaulle to a secondary role, but also minimised British influence over French affairs, an objective which the President may have been pursuing for some time. It was Macmillan who succeeded in smoking out what became known as the 'Anfa documents'. They caused some anger when they arrived in London, but were subsequently amended under British pressure.[55] Guiding the fractious course of French politics into calmer waters, while trying to maintain harmony in Anglo-American relations, was proving no easy task. But the initial evidence suggested that Macmillan was more than up to it. The next few months would further demonstrate the Resident Minister's diplomatic skills.

Chapter 4

The Resident Minister

Although de Gaulle had won a considerable victory at Casablanca, resisting intense Allied pressure to subordinate the Fighting French to Giraud, he returned to London depressed and pessimistic about the future. His intransigence had alienated Churchill. When an American diplomat asked the Prime Minister about the General, following the famous handshake, Churchill replied, 'Oh, don't let's speak about him. We call him Jeanne d'Arc and we're looking for some bishops to burn him.' Although Churchill did not have resort to bishops, he was looking for ways of reducing de Gaulle's power. Until the end of May, de Gaulle found himself confined to the British capital under what was, in effect, a travel ban.[1]

Macmillan by contrast was now at the centre of the French political action. Casablanca had left the British Minister at least in a relatively more sanguine state of mind. Writing home to his wife, Lady Dorothy, he predicted that the conference would mark the 'beginning, though only just the beginning, of the loosening out of a very complicated situations between the various French peoples.' In a message to the Foreign Office, Macmillan argued that while Casablanca had greatly strengthened Giraud, the latter was willing to come to an understanding with de Gaulle. The right course for Britain therefore would be to press de Gaulle to come forward with reasonable suggestions for a settlement. Before this, however, Giraud needed to liberalise his highly conservative, if not downright reactionary administration, in which most of the former Vichy administrators, as well as the anti-Semitic laws, remained in place.[2]

It was here that the immediate problem lay. Macmillan likened Giraud and some of his colleagues to the oldest and most reactionary members of the

Carlton Club in about 1900, and warned that unless a decent and unified French administration was created in a reasonable time, the outlook was not hopeful. Civil war in France was in any case probable.[3] He returned to this gloomy subject in mid-February in a lengthy despatch to Churchill, which underscored just how high the French stakes were. The country's future, Macmillan warned, would depend very much on the nature of the army of liberation. If its commander were surrounded by men of the Right, the result might be to produce the very situation in France which had led to the Spanish civil war in the mid-1930s. 'Our people will be split by the same bitter divisions of which we had the foretaste in the Spanish affair. It is therefore not only a French but a British interest, on a long view, that there should be a real de Gaulle-Giraud fusion now.'[4]

Macmillan himself had other problems to deal with in February, as well as being laid up for some days by injuries received in an air accident. But he did score something of a diplomatic triumph when he and Murphy sent identical telegrams to their respective governments arguing acceptance of a 'provisional French authority which will speak for all French territories and Frenchmen adhering to the movement of Giraud and de Gaulle.'[5] Tentative signs of movement could also be detected on the French front, with the arrival in Algiers of the advance guard of a de Gaulle's liaison mission. Macmillan, who was sensitive to French feelings, recognised the need to keep in the background. 'I think', he minuted to Roger Makins, who had taken over from Pierson Dixon as chief assistant, 'we must let the French people handle this affair here for the next few weeks without interruption. We can assist by social entertainment and by talking to both sides in a free and easy way and generally jollying them along. But we cannot go too fast. They must go through the proper preliminaries of courtship before the wedding. It was the absence of these preliminaries which spoiled Anfa.'[6]

One other arrival proved important. Along with de Gaulle, Jean Monnet stands out as one of the outstanding personalities of mid-twentieth century French politics. The man who would later come to be known as 'the father of Europe' had been born in 1888 into a merchant family in the brandy-producing town of Cognac. During the First World War, when still in his twenties, he had been French representative on a pioneering Inter-Allied supply committee in London. Subsequently he had become deputy secretary-general of the League of Nations. He was now vice-chairman of the British Supply Council in Washington where, according to the British embassy, 'his work has been of the highest order and he knows all our secrets.' He also had excellent connections with the Roosevelt administration Monnet's *modus operandi* was much closer to Macmillan's than de Gaulle's. He worked exclusively behind the scenes, eschewing drama and concentrating on issues rather than personalities. He had refused to join the Free French and had no political allegiances. Although he had ostensibly come to Algiers to advise Giraud about the shipment of American arms promised at Casablanca, he quickly took a leading role in persuading a reluctant Giraud to liberalise his administration.

. The breakthrough came on 14 March. The scene was a meeting of 'Lorrainers and Alsatians' in Algiers. After a musical performance, followed by the presentation of cakes and bouquets by small children, and with Macmillan and Murphy on the platform, Giraud made a speech in which he suddenly met all the demands which the Allies had been making during the previous weeks. 'The New Deal', as Macmillan dubbed it, included the re-establishment of the democratic laws of the pre-war Third Republic, the ending of political censorship and the proclamation of elections by universal suffrage as the goal once France had been liberated. De Gaulle was invited to Algiers, and immediately accepted. As of the 19th, his arrival was expected within the next week.[7]

Monnet himself made no bones about his part in this *volte-face*, having in his own words negotiated the speech with Giraud 'word for word', a claim confirmed by both Murphy and Giraud. Macmillan's account - in his diary he claimed that the speech had been written by Monnet, Murphy and himself - was somewhat different. His official analysis put greater emphasis on the immediate context: favourable developments against the Germans and Italians on the North African battlefield; the arrival of the de Gaulle liaison mission; and Giraud's growing realisation of the link between the delivery of American arms and liberalisation. 'Then Monnet came - a Frenchman, precise, logical, intelligent; he told the same story, but he had a plan. He arrived, *deux ex machina* (in his case a Liberator aircraft) at the psychological moment. But he was not, as he is disposed to think, the sole author of reform.' [8] There was an additional factor - namely the American shift away from their earlier uncritical support for Giraud, who (as Roosevelt had realised at Casablanca) was a political dud. It was a trend which Macmillan had sought to exploit and encourage.[9]

The way was at last open for substantive negotiations with de Gaulle, and it was now the General's turn to come under pressure to make concessions. Macmillan put the case forcibly to one of de Gaulle's representatives in Algiers, Guy de Charbonnières. The argument, conducted - as Macmillan later admitted - under the influence of whisky, became untypically heated. There was a threat that Britain would otherwise abandon the General, and a declaration, in classically Churchillian terms, that de Gaulle hated England. The next day de Charbonnières received a handsome apology, subsequently becoming one of Macmillan's admirers in Algiers.[10] But though de Gaulle clearly resented Macmillan's pressure, the series of questions he proceeded to address to his liaison team in Algiers suggests that he was fully alive to the new possibilities. What were Giraud's real intentions? What atmosphere could de Gaulle expect when he arrived in Algiers? Would the authorities prevent demonstrations in his favour? Would he have access to radio and freedom to make speeches? Careful preparation must be made, and there was a specific reference to the need create a psychological shock effect.[11]

The negotiations in Algiers were conducted on the Gaullist side by General Catroux, a five-star general who got on with both Giraud and de Gaulle. Macmillan's diary, which provides a highly perceptive and often witty commentary of Algiers life, describes him as 'a good diplomatist; a man of the world; with a very high standard of personal comfort; a French snob (princesses and all that) and yet a broad, tolerant liberal view of life.' Although Macmillan found him refreshingly easy to get on with, the Minister's preference remained to keep out of the negotiations 'and make the French face their own responsibilities. We cannot,' he noted in his diary, 'always be in attendance on them, like nurses.'[12] Two days later, on 2 April, he recorded a 'continual stream of French visitors;

> (a) Giraudists; (b) Gaullists; (c) Neutrals; (d) Giraudists, with sympathy for de Gaulle; (e) Giraudists, without sympathy for de Gaulle; (f) Gaullists, with sympathy for Giraud; (g) Gaullists, without sympathy for Giraud.
> I just sit and murmur from time to time – *"Oui, monsieur - comme vous dîtes, l'union française est indispensable."*[13]

That union, however, still needed time, and de Gaulle's insistence on an early arrival in Algiers was viewed by both Catroux and Monnet as more likely to inflame the situation than facilitate a resolution. The Americans would have liked to have prevented the visit outright, but Macmillan and Catroux argued that it would be more diplomatic for Eisenhower to send a personal request to de Gaulle from one soldier to another, requesting him not to complicate the situation by arriving during the impending battle against the Germans in Tunisia. Macmillan duly drafted the telegram. De Gaulle was furious. Sensing an Anglo-Saxon plot, he recalled Catroux and published a communiqué implying that he had been prevented from coming to North Africa to conduct negotiations for French union by the American commander-in-chief.[14]

It was precisely the sort of reaction which Macmillan had hoped to avoid, and the subsequent strong criticism of Eisenhower in the British and French press did nothing for local Anglo-American relations. General Walter Bedell Smith, with whom Macmillan normally enjoyed excellent relations, expressed his indignation in 'strong and idiomatic language', while Murphy relapsed into his instinctive de Gaullophobia.[15] By 10 April, by which time Catroux had flown to London to see de Gaulle, the crisis was temporarily over. The Americans, Macmillan recorded in his diary, were slowly 'recovering their temper. It's extraordinary,' he continued, 'how sensitive they are, and however much I try to nurse them, they are always near to some emotional exhibition of nerves or temper. Of course, it's really due to some sort of inferiority complex and it takes this form with all people who are not sure of themselves.' But Macmillan's hopes of spending Easter at home had been spoiled by 'these ridiculous Frenchmen', as he now had to stay to wait for the next act in what he described as this 'tragi-comedy'.[16] (The chapter in de Gaulle's *War Memoirs* covering this period is entitled 'Comedy'. The previous chapter dealing with the Darlan episode had been entitled 'Tragedy'.)

Yet progress was being made, with both sides seriously addressing the terms and nature of the proposed union. The issues were fundamental, raising questions of how power was to be shared, whether the military commander would be subordinate to a civilian body, and what arrangements would best ensure against the risk perceived in Algiers, notably by Monnet, of one-man rule and French civil war. Giraud made proposals, de Gaulle made counter-proposals. When Macmillan saw Giraud on 26 April he found the French general in 'stubborn, egotistical and even defiant mood', and he came away depressed.[17] This was particularly worrying, because Macmillan was having difficulties in keeping Murphy committed to the union plan. He had previously described the American as seeming 'without any fixed purpose or plan......affected by every changing mood of local opinion or Washington rumour.' Now he complained that Murphy was back to his old tricks and trying to impede the union without ever consciously admitting to himself what he was doing. Giraud, Macmillan thought, was being stubborn because he believed that he could rely on State Department support. Macmillan's only chance was to get the War Department, notably Eisenhower 'to disapprove and throw a little weight the other way.' But this could not easily be done, especially not overtly.[18]

Fortunately this proved unnecessary. The next day Macmillan was told by a member of Giraud's Cabinet that the mercurial General had completely changed tack. He was now willing to make concessions, including acceptance of the idea that he and de Gaulle should act as equal co-presidents. The fly in the ointment was where the two should meet. Against the background of the growing spread of Gaullist influence in North Africa and reports that large rallies would indeed greet de Gaulle on his arrival in Algiers, Giraud proposed that they should instead meet at one of two airfields: Biskra or more provocatively in a building of the American airport at Marrakesh.[19]

Macmillan now began to put on the pressure. He telegraphed Churchill asking that:

'you and the Foreign Secretary will use all your influence to persuade de Gaulle to accept this invitation without demur.

I feel that this is the last chance of accommodation between the two factions and that though French unity may be achieved in the future through a decline in fortunes of one or other General, or the rise of a third star, persistence of the division of the French camp at the present time is likely to throw a heavy strain on our relations with the United States, whose uncertain and equivocal French policy tends to diverge rather dangerously from our own.

Things have not been easy here in the last few days. My friend Murphy has I suspect been acting with something less than candour...

However Murphy has now fully accepted the position and the plan for a meeting on the present basis and I think he will play along unless de Gaulle makes a blunder.'

'All the cards,' Macmillan concluded, were in de Gaulle's hands. 'He has only to come in order to secure all he can reasonably demand. But if he hesitates I think he is lost.'[20] 'I think' Macmillan wrote in a further message to the Foreign Office, 'de Gaulle retains some pleasant memories of my few official and unofficial contacts with him especially at Anfa. If you wish you may tell him that it is my personal advice to him as a friend not to miss the chance. If he comes I am certain he can swing the issue.'[21]

Churchill saw de Gaulle on 30 April and encouraged him to go to Algiers without delay, while the Foreign Office duly relayed Macmillan's message to René Massigli, a professional diplomat on de Gaulle's National Committee. They had no effect. Giraud might have made some concessions. But he had not agreed to the subordination of the military to the civilian power, and the exclusion of all senior Vichy figures from office, which were key elements of the Gaullist programme. And de Gaulle was intensely suspicious of Giraud's invitation to meet at Marrakesh or Biskra, where, as he wrote to Catroux, with Anfa still very much in mind,

> 'we would find ourselves isolated, without our own means of transport and communication, confronted with people who would on the contrary have every advantage. They could keep us there for as long as they wished on the pretext of prolonging discussions which the Anglo-Saxon radio and press, tendentiously informed, would slant in their own manner. If fed up with the whole thing we accepted the endless compromises which they are prepared to suggest, our position would be diminished and impotent. If we refused, it would be easy to show us up to the gallery as intransigent and reduce us to returning empty-handed to England. Do not forget that this game is being played, not between us and Giraud, who is of no importance, but between us and the Government of the United States.' [22]

Besides, there was no hurry. Moves were afoot to establish a National Council for the Resistance in France, and time seemed to be on the General's side.

In Algiers, Macmillan waited none too optimistically for de Gaulle's answer, believing that the General would either insist on coming to Algiers, or would not come at all. 'He is a difficult horse,' he recorded in his diary. 'He either starts down the course before the gate has been raised, or he won't start at all until the other horses are half-way round.'[23] In the event, de Gaulle's response was rather worse than Macmillan had anticipated. Judging that the moment had come to bring matters to a head, on 4 May he made a blistering personal attack on Giraud in a broadcast on Fighting French radio. Monnet likened de Gaulle's methods to those of Hitler, and privately described the General as an enemy of the French people and their liberties. De Gaulle should be destroyed in the interests of France, the Allies and peace. Giraud threatened to break off nego-

tiations. Catroux, who had told de Gaulle that this was the moment for conciliation, was on the edge of resignation. Massigli told the Foreign Office that he
and others might go too. [24]

'She loves me: she loves me not. She loves me: she loves me not,'
Macmillan wrote in his diary on 5 May. 'Oh dear! today has been a bad day, and
definitely by the end of it, one general does not love the other.' Murphy
described the British Minister as visibly disturbed by events. But his advice at a
meeting with Giraud, Monnet, Catroux and Murphy was sound. For a great
country to remain divided because 'no one could decide whether the negotiation for a coalition should take place in London or Brighton' seemed absurd.
Negotiations should only be broken off over points of principle.[25] When at the
end of a dinner party the next evening Giraud held up his hand and said, 'Calm,
my dear friend, and courage - above all calm', Macmillan felt that somehow he
would get de Gaulle to Algiers after all.[26]

This, however, meant becoming increasingly drawn into the French crisis.
Expecting his views would be sought by the local parties before any further
steps were taken, Macmillan warned the Foreign Office that it would be necessary to give 'rather positive advice' if the negotiations were to be kept going.[27]
The key figure was again Monnet. A diary entry for 8 May reads, '3.pm.
Monnet. Talk, talk, talk.' The next day they were at Tipasa to 'talk it all over quietly'.[28] Macmillan was trying desperately hard to persuade Monnet of the need
for de Gaulle to come to Algiers. The position, he warned, could not be
allowed to drag on. It was injurious not only to French but also British and
American interests. Failure, and here the Minister began to put on the pressure,
would be represented as part of a complicated intrigue in which Monnet's own
position would be compromised. He would be represented 'as a tool, whether
American or British will be disputed. He will certainly be regarded as the "emi-
nence grise"'. In the end it was agreed that the two of them, plus Murphy,
should recommend a reply to Giraud. Asked by Monnet if Britain would support this, Macmillan agreed to advise his government that should de Gaulle
refuse, they should bring maximum pressure bear, to the point of threatening
to disown him.[29]

Yet the immediate problem proved to be Giraud. The Allied victory in
Tunisia, where General von Arnim had surrendered on 12 May, made Giraud,
who was still upset by the de Gaulle's attacks, feel he could stand on his own
feet.[30] In the end a text, largely drafted by Macmillan and Monnet, was
despatched by him, albeit without much enthusiasm. It provided for the establishment of an Executive Committee in Algiers, with a dual presidency shared
by the two generals, and operating on the basis of collective responsibility. It
would function only until a provisional government could be established in
France.[31] No reference was made to the location of the meeting, on which
Giraud had remained obdurate.

Catroux undertook to take Giraud's message to de Gaulle in London. He
was accompanied by Macmillan, who in accordance with his undertaking to
Monnet was anxious to persuade the British Government to take a firm stand.

Union, Macmillan believed, would only come about as a result of a great deal of British pressure on de Gaulle, including the threat to cut off his 'enormous' subsidies. Additional urgency was lent to the affair by the growing danger of incidents between Gaullists and Giraudists troops following the victory over the Germans. At the victory parade in Tunis on 20 May, Gaullist forces had refused to march with Giraud's men, and there were reports that Fighting French forces in Tunis were actively recruiting, with offers of higher pay, advances in rank and other inducements.[32]

But there was now a new complication in the form of the Americans. Macmillan had been right to suspect that Murphy was having second thoughts about the desirability of the union. In a telegram to Washington about de Gaulle's 4 May attack on Giraud, Murphy had argued that de Gaulle would take every conciliatory gesture by Giraud to reduce the latter's power. 'Positive action,' he advised 'preferably in concert with the British Government, should be taken to prevent the situation from further deteriorating, since it is further clear that the National Committee, feeling that it may have the support of the British Government, is making definite efforts to weaken our own position here. In my opinion the time has come when this matter must without delay be thrashed out with London and the necessity of establishing a common policy must be realised by the British Government.'[33]

Shortly afterwards, Churchill, who was in Washington, was presented with a memorandum in which Roosevelt complained that 'the conduct of the "BRIDE" continues to be more and more aggravated. His course and attitude is well-nigh intolerable'. The President went on to suggest that Churchill and he might 'talk over the formation of an entirely new French Committee subject in its membership to the approval of you and me.' As to de Gaulle, Roosevelt suggested, with his tongue only partly in his cheek, that the Prime Minister might like to make him Governor of Madagascar. A large amount of allegedly corroborating material was produced. [34]

Churchill listened. He had his own long list of grievances against de Gaulle, which he poured out in a conversation in Washington with the French diplomat Alexis Léger. The General was 'an egoist, self-regarding, excessively proud, irrational, self-important, he reduces everything to himself. Not very loyal, anti-English, anti-American. He cultivates and furthers a sentiment of Anglophobia everywhere. He does everything to oppose England and America.'[35] On 21 May, the day before Macmillan's arrival in London, the Prime Minister had telegraphed to ask the Cabinet to consider urgently whether they 'should not now eliminate de Gaulle as a political force'.

The answer, as at the time of Casablanca, was again negative. De Gaulle's position in France and North Africa was too strong, replied Eden and Attlee, the deputy Prime Minister. The action proposed by the Prime Minister would turn de Gaulle into a martyr and leave Britain vulnerable to the charge of interfering in French internal affairs. With the prospects of union now growing - and here Macmillan may well have stuck his neck out by suggesting that the chances were better than they in fact were - this was no time for a breach.[36]

Churchill duly withdrew his immediate proposal, declaring it was a new fact to him that de Gaulle was about to meet Giraud. Ominously, however, he did not agree to drop the issue, only to reconsider it in the light of events on his own return to the UK.[37]

The last barrier to de Gaulle's move from exile in Britain to French territory had nevertheless been finally overcome. Macmillan met the General, whom he found calm and benevolent, and did his best to persuade him to accept Giraud's offer. But with de Gaulle having gained most of the main points of principle which he had been fighting for, Macmillan was effectively preaching to the converted. On 24 May de Gaulle sent a friendly message to Giraud accepting his conditions. Two days later Macmillan telegraphed to Makins in Algiers: 'The banns have been called, the ceremony is proceeding and I think all must now forever hold their peace. I have heard from very good sources that when the marriage has take place there is no question of any subsequent divorce.'[38] De Gaulle now made his adieus in London. During his farewell visit to the Foreign Office, Eden repeated his frequent complaint that the General had caused the British more difficulties than all their other European allies together. 'I don't doubt it,' the latter smilingly replied. 'France is a great power.'[39]

Chapter 5

June Crises

De Gaulle's arrival in Algiers on 30 May 1943 was not a grand affair. The scene was a very small landing ground under French control - and away from any welcoming crowds - set in 'a fertile plain; vineyards, olive groves, ripened crops all around, and the mountains as usual embellishing the skyline.' The reception, which this time seems to have satisfied the General, was very different from the one de Gaulle had received four months earlier at Casablanca. He arrived in a French plane, and was greeted by Giraud and a French guard of honour. The 'Marseillaise' was played and the General driven to Algiers in a French car. British and American officials stood carefully *behind* the French.[1] But if the formalities this time were punctiliously observed, the atmosphere was strained and uneasy, and nobody was under any illusions as to the difficulties ahead. The preceding negotiations had served to accentuate rather than diminish the distrust between de Gaulle and Giraud. Giraud was not the only one who suspected the worst of the General. De Gaulle, in Churchill's unsympathetic words, could be expected to ' play the fool'.[2]

It was a mark of the importance of the occasion that the British Prime Minister, who had flown direct from Washington, was now in Algiers. While he had military business in the form of supervising the preparations for 'Operation Husky',(the forthcoming Allied landings in Sicily), he was also anxious to keep an eye on the French power struggle that was about to come to a head. But with his experiences at Casablanca in mind, he had taken the precaution of summoning Eden, whom he described as much better fitted to be 'best man' at the Giraud-de Gaulle wedding. The Prime Minister, who expected 'an unhappy and impermanent' union, was reserving for himself 'the role of heavy father'.[3] On Eden's prompting, and as the Prime Minister made a point of emphasising to Roosevelt, with Macmillan and Murphy working in the closest accord, he kept himself uncharacteristically in the background.[4]

This was just as well, for de Gaulle was in an intensely nervous mood. Jean Monnet, who held a long meeting with him on the evening of his arrival, described the General as varying from comparative calm to extreme excitability. He showed considerable hostility towards the Americans and to a lesser extent the British, referring to the Anglo-Saxon domination of Europe as a mounting threat, which if continued would mean that after the war France would have to lean towards Russia and Germany. (Not long before, he had spoken to Eden of the need for Britain and France to work together in the post-war world, in which they would find themselves situated between the United States and Russia.) [5]

The first meeting between the rival French factions on the following day went badly. Macmillan later noted that the committee of any English village darts club would have put up a better show.[6] Seven men were present - four of them generals, de Gaulle, Giraud, Catroux and Georges. There was no agenda and no secretary. Giraud opened the proceedings by asking whether anybody had anything to say. This gave de Gaulle the opportunity to attack the management of affairs in North Africa and repeat his previous demands for the separation of military and political commands. He called yet again for the resignation of Noguès, Boisson, and Peyroutoun.[7] A subsequent private meeting between de Gaulle and Giraud failed to take things forward.

Outside intervention seemed essential if a crisis was to be averted, and Macmillan quickly showed himself to be in his element. Over dinner he took an embarrassed Monnet to task over his handling of the first formal French session, suggesting how he should call the next meeting and circulate the agenda. He even left Monnet with a text of the proposed resolutions.[8] On the morning of 1 June, Macmillan saw Giraud to persuade him to press ahead with the formation of the French committee as soon as possible. He repeated his advice on meeting management, warned that de Gaulle was playing for position, but that politically the General was on a good wicket in his demands for the resignation of key Vichy figures.[9]

When Macmillan and Murphy saw de Gaulle, the General forcibly outlined his own position. He emphasised that France expected new men for the work ahead, and would not understand a government of what, in an uncomplimentary reference to some of those present the previous day, he described as 'old men associated with defeat'. While giving no indication of any intention of breaking off the negotiations and returning to London, it was clear to Macmillan that the General did not regard himself as committed, 'but spoke of himself as a separate power; and the appearance of his villa was like the court of a visiting monarch'.

On leaving the meeting, de Gaulle took Murphy by the arm, and asked the American diplomat, 'Why do you not understand me? Why do you always interfere with me? It is a mistake. France will not understand why your politics are contrary to me. I represent future France and it will be better for us all if you will support me.'[10] When de Gaulle made the same accusation against Britain, Macmillan replied that he thought that his own position had been regarded as favourable from de Gaulle's point of view, while trying to keep a fair balance and not meddling too much with French affairs. De Gaulle appeared to accept this, but insisted that neither the British nor American governments had recognised the true character of the revolution which had or must take place 'if the soul of France were to be saved'. As after every conversation with de Gaulle, Macmillan commented, one came away wondering whether he was demagogue or madman, but in no doubt that he was the most powerful character on the French political stage. The negotiations, Macmillan correctly concluded, would not be broken off. De Gaulle would as usual get his way, with a formula being found to save face for the others. Murphy broadly concurred, reporting to Washington that de Gaulle had no intention of departing and was convinced of his ability to prevail.[11]

Before that, however, the suspicions and tensions evident since de Gaulle's arrival in Algiers boiled to the surface. The immediate circumstances of the crisis were bizarre. Peyroutoun, who some weeks earlier had indicated his willingness to give up his post, now offered his resignation to both Giraud and de Gaulle.[12] De Gaulle, who claimed not to have known of the communication to Giraud, immediately accepted, and had this announced to the press. Only afterwards did he write to Giraud to say what he had done. Giraud duly replied with two letters of his own. The first, quite reasonably, expressed astonishment at de Gaulle's action. The second accused him of seeking to introduce a political system based on Nazi lines into France and demanded a public disavowal of his pretensions before any further negotiations took place.[13] Giraud feared a Gaullist coup, and declared a state of emergency. Suddenly there were troop movements and rumours of a putsch. In a telegram to the National Committee in London, de Gaulle reported that the affair was beginning to look like an ambush. 'We are in the middle of a tragi-comedy but it could turn out badly.'[14]

It was fortunate that at this point Churchill was out of Algiers inspecting the recent battlefields in Tunisia. Macmillan and Murphy could therefore act without what would otherwise undoubtedly have been vigorous Prime Ministerial interference. They first saw Giraud, and did their best to calm him down. De Gaulle then asked to see Macmillan alone, and at four in the afternoon the two men held what was to prove one of the most remarkable meetings of their long acquaintance. Macmillan, as usual, did some frank talking. He told de Gaulle that he was only saying about the Giraudists what they were saying about him, and that while Peyroutoun had been wrong to send his resignation to de Gaulle, de Gaulle had been wrong to accept it. De Gaulle then said that another attempt would be made to form the new Committee and this gave Macmillan an opportunity to make an appeal to him.

Having asked permission to speak in English - Macmillan's discussions were, unusually for a British politician, normally conducted in French - the Minister began by recalling his own service in France during the First World War and opposition to Appeasement in the 1930s. He then shifted the conversation into a more unexpected direction. Although often accused of right-wing tendencies, de Gaulle had in fact spoken in London of the need for social revolution after the war. Drawing on his own radical record of the interwar years, Macmillan told the General that he thought that their views on social matters were very similar. Both countries had old men who were backward looking. What was needed was young men with young minds. There was a widespread expectation that England's future would be different. Great wealth would disappear and property would be held in trust for the people.

> ' I told him that I had followed all that he had done with the greatest sympathy and admiration; that I realised his impatience on finding old men and old minds still in control; that I understood the difference between my country and his because we had not been subjected to great pressure; we had not suffered a great defeat and the sense of ignominy that followed that defeat. Nevertheless, I implored him to take courage; not to miss his opportunity to join honourably with Giraud in this national administration. I felt sure that as the weeks and months went by he could, without straining the law or acting in any way unconstitutionally, obtain for himself and those who were with him the reality of power.'

De Gaulle was reported to have been deeply moved by what Macmillan privately described as 'this harangue'.[15]

By the next day, 3 June, the crisis, which had left most of its participants either ashamed or exhausted, had abated.[16] A French Committee of National Liberation, the FCNL, was at last formed, based on documents drawn up by de Gaulle. It was to exercise sovereignty over all French territories not in enemy hands and direct the entire French war effort. As soon as France had been liberated, the Committee would hand over authority to a provisional government. De Gaulle and Giraud would serve as joint presidents. It was of course a compromise, and while de Gaulle was not satisfied, he was well aware the game was by no means over. In a move which was picked up by the press but which both the Americans and the British authorities in Algiers appear to have missed, the FCNL was to be enlarged in conditions that would, as de Gaulle put it, 'give it a better complexion'.[17]

Celebrations were called for, and the British held a lunch party, without any American guests, an omission that clearly stung Murphy.[18] The speeches were all in French, Eden's excellent and idiomatic, Churchill drawing widely on both the English and French vocabularies. In his reply to Churchill's toast to 'La Belle France, La France Victorieuse', de Gaulle spoke of his three years in Britain. One judged individuals and peoples more by the way they behaved in bad times than in good. In prosperous times friends were easy to come by, but in times of trouble one found the true value of individuals and countries. He would never forget the inspiration which the British people had given him. When de Gaulle remarked later on the odd coincidence of the Prime Minister's

The celebratory lunch party, 4 June 1943. Left to right sitting. Catroux, de Gaulle, Churchill, Giraud, Eden. Monnet is standing on the extreme left, Macmillan is third from left, Massigli on the extreme right. (Imperial War Museum)

presence, the Prime Minister denied any intention of interfering in French internal affairs, while adding that the military situation compelled Britain to keep track of what was happening 'within this essential zone of communications. We should have had to take steps if too brutal a shock had occurred - if, for example, you had devoured Giraud in one mouthful.'[19]

Macmillan sent notes of congratulations to Giraud, Catroux and, most important, to de Gaulle. 'I have,' the Resident Minister wrote with that mannered flattery which he was to repeat over the years, 'always (sic) valued very highly our acquaintance - or perhaps I may be allowed to call it friendship - and I feel certain that the role which you have played during these three terrible years fits you to play a still greater one in the future. Many grave difficulties and problems lie before you. May God's blessing be upon you in your work for France.'[20] De Gaulle replied in kind, writing that Macmillan's letter had profoundly touched him. He much appreciated the action Macmillan had taken in the name of the British government and valued Macmillan's 'sympathy, which I also venture to call your friendship.'[21] Three days later Churchill announced that all future British dealings, including payments, would be with the FCNL. One object was to cut off de Gaulle's rear. If de Gaulle resigned, he would do so into private life. In thanking Churchill for the decision, which he officially conveyed to Massigli a few days later, Macmillan quoted Scriptures. 'Where your treasure is, there shall your heart be also.'[22]

* * *

The immediate impression, shared by both Macmillan and Murphy, was that things were gradually settling down. The General appeared to both the British and the Americans to be 'friendly and in quite good spirits'. This was welcome news to Macmillan, who was encouraging Murphy keep in touch with de Gaulle and anxious to discourage the idea 'that one General was an American owned and trained horse, and the other was run from a British stable.'[23] In fact de Gaulle was already chafing under the restrictions imposed by the dual presidency with Giraud. He would not allow himself to be paralysed by the manoeuvres of different factions. 'It is not for this that I have come to Algiers,' he told Guy de Charbonnières on 7 June. 'I have come to act. Act, yes act, that is what France expects of me.' To de Charbonnières, de Gaulle seemed a man tormented, even tortured.[24]

The following day the General duly returned to the attack in the FCNL. He opposed Giraud's nomination of General Georges as the Commissioner for Defence, a post he wanted for himself. He insisted once again on the need to separate military and political command, demanding that Giraud must resign as either commander-in- chief or co-president of the Committee. When Giraud refused, de Gaulle withdrew from the workings of the Committee, retiring to his villa in what one of his biographers describes as 'a highly contrived sulk', to await the arrival of new members of the FCNL.[25]

Crisis diplomacy was again the order of the day. Macmillan found Giraud and General Georges to be delighted at the prospect of getting rid of de Gaulle once and for all, and sought to warn them that to accept his resignation at this juncture might risk a complete break-up of the French Empire. When de Gaulle in turn complained that he wanted reform, which meant getting rid of a great number of incompetent and outmoded officers, but was hampered at every point, Macmillan urged patience:

> 'He said, "It is all very annoying. It is *embêtant*." (annoying, boring) I said that I was glad to find that although he had found many Englishmen *embêtant*, he now realised that many Frenchmen were *embêtant* as well. The fact was that one could not get all one's way in this world except by patience and sustained effort on consistent lines. I said I was always at his service, day or night, if he wished to see me.'[26]

Writing to the Foreign Office, Macmillan shrewdly noted that de Gaulle was rather enjoying the commotion he had raised. There was a certain amount of mischief in the General which made him like scenes. De Gaulle could easily have obtained the same results by simpler means, but could not refrain from more brutal methods. The view in Algiers, apparently shared by the Americans, was that there was a good deal of bluff in the crisis, along with physical and mental fatigue, and that left to themselves the French could resolve the matter.[27]

Churchill had initially concurred with this assessment, but he quickly changed his tune in the face of a new attack from the ever-suspicious and hostile Roosevelt. The immediate catalyst of the new crisis was a report from Murphy that de Gaulle was demanding control over French forces not engaged in fighting.[28] 'It may well be better to let him (de Gaulle) go now,' the President cabled to Eisenhower, 'than to have an even more difficult situation in a month from now.' Control by de Gaulle of French military forces in North and West Africa, Roosevelt continued (and the President was particularly sensitive over the future of the French base at Dakar) would seriously endanger the safety of British and American troops.[29] Macmillan was therefore now instructed by Churchill to do everything in his power to enforce the policy advocated by the President, with which the Prime Minister declared himself 'in hearty accord'. A further telegram admonished Macmillan to bear constantly in mind that, were de Gaulle to gain control and mastery of the FCNL, a situation of 'utmost difficulty' would immediately arise with the American government.[30]

The lengths to which the Prime Minister was prepared to go to undermine de Gaulle are clear from the release of a highly critical press circular, parts of which appeared in the next day's *Observer*. If the General continued his displays of intransigence, and failed to behave cooperatively, he would:

> 'soon find himself without friends. He should realise that this is his last chance to retain them. American patience has already reached the point of exhaustion. And nobody is going to allow Anglo-American relations to be disturbed for the sake of a man whose friendliness towards both countries has been no more cordial than he considered strictly necessary. We can do our duty to the people of France in other ways.'[31]

De Gaulle may have had a point when he complained in a letter to his wife, about the 'atmosphere of lies, false news etc., that our good allies and their friends have tried to drown me in.'[32]

This was the background against which Macmillan engaged in another of his more unconventional pieces of diplomacy. An important British personage, codenamed 'General Lyon', had arrived in Algiers. On Whit Sunday, the day the *Observer* article appeared, George VI hosted a lunch party. Churchill had advised the King to go ahead only if the French were behaving well. Told by Macmillan that they were not, the King, who admired de Gaulle, asked what he should do. Macmillan replied that the party might do some good and could do no harm.[33] The Minister then took the opportunity to mention to de Gaulle the attractive character of Tipasa, where he planned to go on afterwards to bathe. The General, who had of course recognised that Macmillan was much more sympathetic to his cause than Murphy, quickly took the hint.[34]

Tipasa had become a favourite haunt of Macmillan's.[35] Monnet, Churchill and Eden had all been shown his own private rocky cove. But the bathing party with de Gaulle, described in the introduction, was unique. Afterwards Macmillan and de Gaulle walked in the ruins of the Roman town, where a small crowd gathered, cheering the General wildly and demanding a speech.[36]

Scattered among their general conversation, was a lot which was highly germane to the current situation. Macmillan found the General very bitter about American and British pressure. He could not understand why Roosevelt and Churchill were so suspicious of him, unless they had 'some malignant design' on French sovereignty. As to his own options, Gaulle felt he had two alternatives. He could try to make the FCNL work. But if he allied himself with 'this show', without real power for himself, he would sully what had previously been a clean record, untainted by association with defeatism or Pétainism. Alternatively, if he resigned before his honour had been tarnished, at some later stage the French people could turn to him as an alternative to the Communists. He might serve France better by keeping himself available for her 'renaissance and reconstruction.'[37]

De Gaulle, Macmillan recorded,

> 'recognised the responsibility of having made the union which I kept pressing on him......I formed the impression that he is still debating in his own mind what he would do. He said it would be more artistic to retire. He is obviously very disappointed that he cannot get complete control, and does not seem to be willing to go through the work of obtaining it gradually.
>
> My policy was to try to discuss both possible lines quite objectively and quite calmly with him, of course hoping that he would play the game and accept any reasonable formula. But I did not try and over-persuade him because I thought it would probably have the opposite effect, and I wanted him to face the realities. He is a little apt to talk rather wildly in order to make an effect and it is not wise to indulge him in this. I was left with the impression that the chances are about five to two in favour of his throwing up his hand and playing the long game. I do not believe that he would have done so if he had not got such an admirable excuse of putting the whole blame upon the Allies.'[38]

Macmillan at this point was effectively fighting on two fronts - with de Gaulle and the French on one side, and Roosevelt, Churchill and to some degree also Murphy on the other. Two days after the bathing party, General Catroux brought the main French protagonists together for tea, but Giraud and Georges proved uncompromising - the result, Macmillan believed, of private American reassurances.[39] In his diary he complained that the Americans, though 'not Eisenhower', were letting their view be known prematurely, giving de Gaulle the chance to accuse the Allies of interference in French affairs. Macmillan's preference was 'to get what we want - if we can - *through* the French, rather than by *imposing* it *on* the French. But it is a difficult hand for me to play.' (emphasis in original) The next day, however, he was reporting to the Foreign Office that the 'strong and undivided British-American front' was beginning to have its effect on de Gaulle. It had been agreed that Eisenhower should see Giraud and de Gaulle, talking to them frankly 'as one soldier to another'.[40]

Murphy was in fact by no means fully onside. He had, or at least claimed that he had, only now found about the expansion of the FCNL, although a Foreign Office official suggested that Murphy had in fact wilfully got it wrong and misled Macmillan. Whatever the truth of the matter, Murphy saw Giraud as having been done down, and the Allies tricked.[41] This was duly reported back to Washington, where Roosevelt reacted in predictable fashion. He told Churchill that he was 'fed up with de Gaulle and the secret personal and political machinations of that Committee in the last few days indicate that there is no possibility of our working with de Gaulle...I agree with you that the time has arrived when we must break with him. It is an intolerable situation. I think the important thing is that we act together.'[42]

This was disingenuous. Churchill had said no such thing, if only because he knew that his cabinet colleagues would not allow him to make such a break. The Foreign Office was horrified. One senior official complained privately of an 'hysterical diatribe' from the president, while Eden noted in his diary that 'we shall be hard put to it to keep in step with the Americans, or rather pull them into step with us, over the French business, and not commit some folly which will give de Gaulle a martyr's crown or control of the French army or both.'[43] It was left to Eisenhower and Macmillan, who was by now under fire from Churchill for not having reported in sufficient detail over the last few days, to defuse the crisis.[44]

18 June therefore saw an intriguing exercise of Anglo-American collusion. Asked by the American Commander-in-Chief 'as a friend' what he thought he should do, Macmillan replied that they might interpret their instructions in their own way. Eisenhower then dictated a message to Washington, to which Macmillan was invited to offer amendments. Eisenhower duly advised the President that he considered the difficulties in Algiers to have been exaggerated, a clear criticism of Murphy, and that the questions of the administration of French West Africa and the future of its Governor, which Roosevelt had raised a few days earlier, were not actual. As to the French military command, he hoped to settle this by the personal meeting with Giraud and de Gaulle.[45]

It was a delicate diplomatic manoeuvre. Eisenhower was sticking his neck out with the President; at the same time, by setting conditions over the way the French organized their military affairs, the Americans and British were making their distrust of their allies all too obvious. It would, as Macmillan noted in his diary, be 'gall and wormwood' to de Gaulle. (Although the Minister added that he thought that de Gaulle had largely brought these problems on himself by making no efforts to earn Churchill and Roosevelt's confidence, and gave insufficient thought to the scale of the effort the British and Americans were making in North Africa.[46]) Nevertheless, in order to hide something of the iron Anglo-American fist, the plan was to emphasise the purely military nature of the interventions. And in an attempt to keep the tone as friendly as possible, the meeting took place at Eisenhower's villa rather than at Allied Forces Headquarters, with only General Bedell Smith, the Chief of Staff, attending the meeting. Macmillan, Murphy and Massigli were on hand in the lobby, in case they were required. De Gaulle describes them as remaining in the neighbourhood 'attentive and audible'.[47]

The meeting lasted one and a half hours. De Gaulle purposely arrived last and spoke first, in what he claimed as his capacity as 'President of the French Government'. Eisenhower politely made it clear that the supply of American arms was dependent on Giraud retaining overall command. This led to a pointed exchange, with de Gaulle asking Eisenhower as a soldier whether he believed that a leader's authority could survive if it rested on the favour of a foreign Power.[48] De Gaulle left first, apparently in a great rage, which Macmillan, who had accompanied the General from the villa, and was well aware of his acting abilities, believed was partly simulated. Giraud left shortly afterwards 'dignified but flushed'. A few days later de Gaulle wrote to his wife, who was still in London, complaining that he found himself confronted by the Americans, and only the Americans. The British, he dismissively - and wrongly - implied, did not count.[49]

By then the crisis had been, at least temporarily, resolved. Instead of a Ministry of Defence, a permanent military committee was established to be responsible for the unification, organisation and training of the armed forces, with de Gaulle as chairman and Giraud as a member. The FCNL would be responsible, as de Gaulle had wanted, for the general direction of the French war effort and overall control of the armed forces. The military command was split, with Giraud commander of the North African army and de Gaulle in command of all other forces in the French empire.[50] This was at best a temporary solution, but it gained time in which the Resident Minister hoped that the civilian elements within the Committee would become strong enough to stand up to the generals.[51] Macmillan, Murphy and Eisenhower all recommended to their governments that the compromise should be accepted. Any attempt to upset the agreement, Macmillan warned Churchill, 'will land us into very deep water indeed and may well compromise our future military plans. You may be assured that this is General Eisenhower's personal view.' And with his Commander-in-Chief thus endorsing the deal, Roosevelt had no valid reason for demanding further action against de Gaulle.[52]

* * *

This had become very much a crisis of the Allies' (particularly of Roosevelt's) making, in which Macmillan had aligned himself with the American military command in order to neutralise presidential and prime ministerial intervention. One catches a glimpse of the strains in the American camp in a letter from Eisenhower to the American Chief of Staff, General George Marshall, in which he wrote that his ablest assistants over the French issue had been 'General Smith and Mr Macmillan. They are both sound, respected by everybody and are not hysterical.'[53]

A more intriguing insight is provided by a very private communication in which Macmillan had told Churchill of Eisenhower and Bedell Smith's concern, expressed to him as a 'trusted friend', about the President's 'autocratic instructions'. Roosevelt, the American generals felt, was inclined to use reasons of military security 'where there is no real danger, for political purposes. A real bust-up here in consequence of measures against de Gaulle or dissolution of the committee would be of much greater military embarrassment to them than any reasonable settlement.' Churchill was unimpressed, expressing shock that the two generals had commented on their differences with Roosevelt. Macmillan was warned not to give encouragement to such moods, 'remembering that the President and I act together in this war and that very great advantage comes to our country and the common cause from our association.'[54] Then, as in later years, the 'special relationship' could operate at several levels.

For light relief at the end of this month of near continuous crises, senior Foreign Office officials dealing with French affairs turned to the *New Statesman*, which published a piece of Shakespearean pastiche:

SCENE A tent in Algiers. General de Gaulle discovered, sulking.
Enter General Giraud
Giraud: General, I say that you have done me wrong.
de Gaulle: I only deal with written grievances.
Giraud: You will not answer letters; I will speak.
de Gaulle: If you speak softly we will give you audience.
Giraud: And who may 'we' be, General de Gaulle?
de Gaulle: We are the President. 'L'État, c'est moi!'
Giraud: We are co-Presidents. 'L'État, c'est nous!'
That you have wronged me must appear in this -
You are conspiring to usurp my place.
de Gaulle: I am elected your superior.
Giraud: Shall I give way to one of lesser rank?
I am commander.
de Gaulle: Under my command.[55]

But the situation in Algiers was settling down. Giraud unwisely departed for a visit to the United States at the beginning of July, thereby, as Macmillan had warned, providing de Gaulle with a splendid opportunity to establish his ascendancy in the FCNL.[56] The war meanwhile moved on. On 10 July the Allies landed in Sicily. Macmillan had, without instructions, since he had thought it wiser not to ask for any or consult anyone, informed de Gaulle the night before. Although the General was still in a suspicious mood, overall the interview went well, Macmillan reporting to the Foreign Office that de Gaulle had been 'personally friendly to me, as always, and half-way between laughing and sobbing. He certainly wanted to impress me with the quiet role he was now playing and the almost saintly character of his patience.'[57]

Much more troublesome was the question of international recognition of the FCNL. While the Foreign Office was sympathetic, Churchill was not. The dispute had been grumbling away for some time. Replying to a telegram from Macmillan of 10 June, which had argued that immediate recognition would be very helpful in at least preliminary form, the Prime Minister had declared - and this was the point where de Gaulle had just walked out of FCNL - that there would be no question of recognition until 'we know what it is we have to recognise'. He cited St.Matthew, chapter vii, verse 16: 'Ye shall know them by their fruits. Do men gather grapes of thorns or figs of thistles?' Macmillan had replied with Revelations, chapter ii, verses 2 to 4, beginning 'I know thy works, and thy labour and thy patience, and how thou canst not bear them that are evil,' and ending, 'Nevertheless I have somewhat against thee, because thou has left thy first love.' It left the Prime Minister speechless with rage.[58]

A few days later Macmillan reported that the State Department was actively considering a formula for recognition, and urged that the matter be taken up with the US government.[59] Churchill remained unwilling to consider the matter until de Gaulle and his 'partisans' had settled down 'to honest teamwork' with the FCNL.[60] On 1 July, after a discussion with General Bedell Smith, Macmillan sent a further telegram to London recapitulating the arguments for recognition, while noting in his diary that to withhold it was 'merely silly and ungracious' and by weakening the FCNL, played into de Gaulle's hands.[61]

The immediate dispute was now in London between Prime Minister and Foreign Secretary. Churchill, as usual, put the future of Anglo-Americans first. Eden argued the need to do everything to raise French morale and promote French self-confidence, even if this meant bearing patiently manifestations of inevitable French sensitivity and suspicious nationalism. And in a passage with which de Gaulle would have wholeheartedly agreed, the Foreign Secretary declared that 'Europe expects us to have a European policy of our own, and to state it. That policy must aim at the restoration of the independence of the smaller European allies and of the greatness of France.' 'In dealing with European problems of the future,' Eden continued, 'we are likely to have to work more closely with France even than with the United States, and while we should naturally concert our policy as far as we can with Washington, there are limits beyond which we ought not to allow our policy to be governed by theirs.'[62]

From Algiers Macmillan tried to keep up the pressure, although careful to acknowledge the reasons of higher policy which might prompt a delay and the need to act 'in this as in all other matters, in harmony with our American allies.'[63] It was one of several instances in July where Macmillan showed himself wary of going too far in crossing the Prime Minister. Nevertheless, when a new French crisis threatened at the end of the month over the divided military command which had been agreed in late June, Macmillan let it be known to the French on his own authority that any reasonable solution would be acceptable to the Allies. This despite an admonitory telegram a week earlier from Churchill not to let 'local ebullitions deflect your judgement'.[64]

On the question of recognition Churchill had by then bowed to the inevitable, and he cited Macmillan's recommendations in the message in which he had at last urged it on Roosevelt.[65] Now it was the President's turn to demur,[66] and the question was only settled when the two leaders met at Quebec at the end of August, by which time thirteen states had already recognised the FCNL. It was in fact an agreement, reached only after what Churchill described as 'prolonged discussions of a laborious character', to disagree. The text of the British recognition was more generous than that of the Americans, and Macmillan was encouraged by Eden to try to prevent the French from under-lining the differences between the two positions. This danger did not materi-alise.[67] Things were going the General's way. He had further managed to strengthen his position as a result of the reorganisation of the FCNL follow-ing Giraud's return from the United States, and now found himself Prime Minister of what was in effect the Provisional French Government.[68]

Chapter 6

Algiers Valedictory

With recognition, Macmillan thought the time had come to bow out. It had been agreed in June that he should remain with Eisenhower when the latter moved his headquarters from Algiers. This had been something of a personal triumph. Washington, Macmillan noted, did not much like the presence of a Minister Resident at AFHQ, and Roosevelt had only given in to the Prime Minister at Eisenhower's request.[1] Macmillan was becoming bored with the French and their affairs, and with the invasion of Sicily and the surrender of Italy in August, he was naturally anxious to concentrate on his new responsibilities. And there was another consideration which he outlined in a letter to Eden. He had 'seen so much of these Frenchmen in their Balkan period, that I feel that it would be better to fade out gracefully now that we have steered them into something like a normal and respectable administration. There will always be the sort of awkwardness one has towards a chap whom one has nursed through an attack of D.T.'[2]

It was not until January 1944 that the former Cabinet minister, Duff Cooper, took up his post as the new British Ambassador to the French Provisional Government in January 1944. Macmillan therefore continued to be intermittently involved in some of the sudden and violent political storms which blew up in the turbulent atmosphere of Algiers.[3] In late September a new crisis developed in the FCNL, when de Gaulle prepared a series of decrees to allow the Committee to appoint a civilian Commissioner of War, to whom Giraud would be responsible. Churchill instructed Macmillan to warn de Gaulle against altering the system of co-presidency, but Macmillan was reluctant. Anything smacking of Allied intervention in French affairs risked reducing the chance of a settlement. On the other hand, of course, if he suppressed the

Prime Minister's message and the affair went wrong he would naturally be blamed.[4] He therefore proceeded to tread lightly. Finding the General to be 'expectantly fishing' for an Allied intervention as an excuse for a patriotic rallying cry, he simply gave it as his personal opinion that a break-up of the Committee resulting in Giraud's resignation would be unfortunate. He reminded the General that he had been a good friend of his all along and that his advice had proved sound, and hoped that he would take it again. Macmillan did his usual rounds of the other key figures, but then left for Italy where on 28 September he received a telegram from his *chargé d'affaires*, Roger Makins, that the crisis was running its 'normal course. Everyone had quarrelled, everyone had resigned and everyone had been reconciled...Giraud claims the victory, de Gaulle has won it.'[5]

De Gaulle seemed at last to be relaxing. Towards the end of October Macmillan, who had deliberately avoided the General for some time, invited him to a small lunch party, which was clearly a success. De Gaulle, his host noted, 'improved' as he obtained power and his sense of responsibility increased.[6] A more formal discussion two weeks later was again friendly. Part of the conversation centred on the need for post-war change, which had just been discussed by the newly formed French Consultative Assembly. De Gaulle had been reading the Beveridge report and was impressed by the fact that such a far-sighted document on social reform had been produced in wartime. Macmillan agreed, saying that he thought that Britain and France would have 'the same problems and the same functions in the post-war world' and suggesting that these should be discussed. If de Gaulle cared to take the matter forward, Macmillan would be happy to give what assistance he could.

Later Gaulle went on to reminisce about his former mentor, Marshal Pétain. When Macmillan asked whether Laval and other Vichy collaborators would take refuge in Germany, de Gaulle replied with a smile that on the contrary they would take refuge in England. 'You need not be afraid that Pétain will be shot. You will give him a villa in the south of England.'[7] These references to Pétain must have sounded rather more uncomfortable to Macmillan than his account suggests. A few weeks earlier the Resident Minister had received a message through an intermediary that the Marshal was willing to leave France. Asserting that there would be no advantage in Pétain's escape, Macmillan had turned the offer down. He had done so, moreover, without having made any attempt to consult higher political authority. Perhaps he believed that it would muddy the French political waters just at the point when he hoped that things were finally settling down. Perhaps, as Charles Williams suggests, he feared that it would undermine his triumph with de Gaulle.[8] In the event, Pétain ended his days in a French prison.

Soon afterwards came more trouble when a new crisis in the FCNL led to the departures of Giraud and Georges. This development does not seem to have unduly worried Macmillan, who was inclined to think that de Gaulle would resist dictatorial tendencies and work within the republican and democratic framework.[9] Much more troublesome for Macmillan was another crisis over the Levant. Like many of his compatriots, the General saw the British manoeuvring to shift Arab hostility from their own position in the Middle East onto the French, as they sought to establish their status as sole suzerain in the region.[10] This was something of a distortion of British policy, which lacked the ruthless ambition attributed to it, but which was certainly concerned about the regional impact of French action in Lebanon and Syria. Elections had been held there in July 1943 which resulted in the heavy defeat of the French candidates. A government hostile to France was formed, which began by formulating a bill declaring complete independence. The local French delegate-general, Ambassador Jean Helleu, responded by arresting the president and ministers and closing parliament. Rioting ensued and there was an outcry among Arab leaders elsewhere in the Middle East.

Macmillan discussed the crisis with Churchill on 15 November aboard the battleship H.M.S.*Renown* off Gibraltar. The Prime Minister was on his way to Cairo before flying on to meet Roosevelt and Stalin in Tehran. He was in characteristically anti-Gaullist mood, resentful of Giraud's recent departure from the FCNL, (although he remained French Commander-in-Chief), and fearful lest these 'lamentable outrages' in Lebanon presaged a Gaullist dictatorship in France hostile to Britain. But Macmillan appears to have found the Prime Minister ready to listen to his argument that the new members of both the FCNL and the Consultative Assembly were not in de Gaulle's hands and were to some extent challenging his authority. Macmillan's strategy was to gain the support of General Catroux, who had been sent to deal with the Lebanese crisis, along with the sympathetic French Commissioner for Foreign Affairs, René Massigli, and a majority of the FCNL, so as to put de Gaulle into a minority.[11]

That meant trying to avoid ultimatums, as well as curbing the activities of Churchill's personal representative in the Levant, Sir Edward Spears, whom de Gaulle and the local French authorities regarded as thoroughly hostile. Saying this to Churchill was brave since Spears was an old friend of the Prime Minister's. But Macmillan felt he had little alternative. Spears, he believed, was determined to elevate himself and degrade the French. 'I will get *all* that H.M.G. requires from the French if I am given a chance,' he angrily recorded in his diary. 'But I want to get it in such a way as preserves and does not destroy the work of nearly a year here and that carries with us the reasonable Frenchmen who are our friends. Spears wants a Fashoda; and I do not.'[12]

Macmillan's immediate dealings were with Massigli. On the morning of 20 November Macmillan showed him an official British note demanding the recall of Helleu and the immediate release of the imprisoned Lebanese president and ministers, and warning that Britain would otherwise declare martial law and occupy Lebanon. But the situation seemed so threatening to the future of Anglo-French relations that Macmillan agreed to Massigli's request not to present it to him formally until after the FCNL meeting later that day. This gave Massigli time to argue the case on its merits without the complication of a British ultimatum. In the event the Committee outvoted de Gaulle and agreed to recall Helleu and release the Lebanese Ministers, although there was now a new problem about their reinstatement. Macmillan protested to London at the failure to withdraw the ultimatum.

On the evening of 22 November, Macmillan and Massigli hatched another plot. Asked whether the ultimatum still applied, Macmillan replied that he did not know, but suggested that it might be better for him not to have an answer until as late as possible. Macmillan then arranged to write Massigli a letter, which would be sent during the next day's FCNL meeting. If Massigli could persuade his colleagues to reinstate the ministers, as Catroux was recommending, he would do so. If asked whether there was a British ultimatum he would say he did not know, since Macmillan's letter would not yet have arrived.[13]

The ruse worked. 'Another British ultimatum, I suppose,' de Gaulle complained as soon as the committee session began, at which point Massigli declared that he knew nothing of this, and that they were there to discuss a telegram from General Catroux.[14] A few days later after the issue had been resolved, Massigli called on Macmillan to deliver a note of protest on the way in which the FCNL had been treated over the affair. The protest was six typewritten pages. 'Tell me,' Macmillan asked Massigli, ' I am not a diplomat, what do I do with this? Must I read it?' 'No,' Massigli replied. 'You need not read it. You must send it through to your government.' 'Fine,' said Macmillan, 'I will. Will you have a drink?' 'Sherry,' said Massigli, 'unless you've got gin.' 'Certainly I have gin - a little vermouth?' 'Please. '[15]

* * *

There was one final incident in December, caused by the arrest and imprisonment of Peyretoun, Boisson and a friend of Churchill in the pre-war days, Pierre Flandin. Churchill was again in the vicinity, this time recuperating in Tunis after a serious bout of pneumonia. It was the familiar story of a crisis created by a combination of Rooseveltian antipathy and distrust and Churchillian anger. Macmillan found himself subjected to a succession of violent calls, with Churchill roaring down the line 'like an excited bull'. Macmillan and the Foreign Office sought to calm matters. The President again sought to 'eliminate' de Gaulle, and instructed Eisenhower to direct the FCNL to release the three men and discontinue their trials.

The reaction in Algiers was one of dismay. Such direct interference in French affairs, Macmillan warned Eden, would create an extremely serious situation. The FCNL, which had ordered the arrests, would refuse and the British and the Americans would then have to use force. A draft telegram to the Foreign Secretary on 23 December expressed anxiety over Churchill's absence from Cabinet colleagues, and warned of drifting into a serious situation which only Eden could help to retrieve. If it were not so tragic, the situation would be almost farcical.[16]

In fact Churchill himself was becoming alarmed at Roosevelt's action, and General Bedell Smith had been persuaded not only to delay implementation of the president's instructions, but to warn Washington that the Americans could not rely on British support in implementing them. The Prime Minister continued to fulminate, telling Bedell Smith to 'Keep Harold up to the mark! He is much too pro-French', and complaining to Eden on Christmas Day that Macmillan had not stated 'our case with sufficient force or zest to Massigli. He was officially appointed as my personal representative but he certainly does not do justice to my views. On the contrary he is too much inclined to whittle away the case. I am seeing him today here at luncheon and will put matters plainly to him.' 'My constant purpose', the Prime Minister continued, 'is the restoration of the greatness of France, which will not be achieved by the persecution mania of the Committee, nor by their violent self-assertion of French dignity, nor will France be helped by De Gaulle's hatred of Britain and the United States.' The FCNL was more likely to be brought to reason by the maintenance of 'a stern pressure' than by 'smooth diplomatic conversations.'[17] Yet when Macmillan arrived in Tunis, he found that the Prime Minister, who was still far from well, seemed rather embarrassed by the matter, at one point saying, 'Well - perhaps you are right. But I do not agree with you. Perhaps I will see de Gaulle. Anyway you have done very well.'[18] And once Roosevelt had withdrawn his instructions, the crisis was over.

It did not quite end there. It was now de Gaulle's turn to be difficult. Churchill's invitation met with initial reluctance, the General complaining that the Prime Minister had lately gone out of his way to insult and thwart him. Churchill then instructed Macmillan to cancel the invitation, saying that it was monstrously undignified to be kept waiting this way. Macmillan had again to see the General, and to his surprise and relief found him in capital humour:

'Before I could say anything, he said he accepted with pleasure. It only remained to fix a date to suit for P.M. and himself. I undertook to telephone this message, and then he kept me for an hour's talk - about France, Russia, Czechoslovakia, Europe in general - not of much intrinsic importance, but in a very expansive and friendly tone throughout. He is certainly a queer man.'[19]

It may have been at this meeting that Macmillan pressed de Gaulle to say what he really thought of the British. 'You British,' the General finally replied 'are so annoying, the Americans so tiring, the Russians so disquieting. I prefer to be annoyed than fatigued or disquieted.'[20] On 4 January 1944, his reputation greatly enhanced, Macmillan formally handed over his functions to Duff Cooper.

* * *

Before leaving Algiers, Macmillan wrote the last of a series of despatches on the situation in North Africa. These had been well received in London, a tribute to the shrewd and clear analysis of the situation they provided, supplemented by sharp, often entertaining pen portraits of the *dramatis personae* of the Algiers scene.[21] By January 1944, Macmillan had had ample opportunity to assess de Gaulle. He was, as already noted, a sympathetic but by no means uncritical observer. A diary entry of 9 June had described the General as a 'modern-minded, ambitious, conceited but clever politician, who makes no pretensions to good manners and has a delight in violent and abusive attacks on individuals, particularly if they are of an older generation.' A few days later, after their bathing trip to Tipasa, Macmillan recorded his belief that the General would always be impossible to work with, being by nature an autocrat, 'just like Louis XIV or Napoleon,' analogies he was to come back to in later years.[22] The despatch of January 1944 was the longest assessment of de Gaulle which Macmillan ever wrote. Nobody, he noted, could deny that:

> 'the General is filled with an intense and patriotic fervour. This takes the form of that peculiar *orgueil* for which there is no real English equivalent. This arrogance makes him from time to time almost impossible to deal with; but it is, as no doubt modern psychologists would agree, the reverse side of an extreme sensibility. I have never known a man at once so ungracious and so sentimental. He has a considerable sense of wit and a certain mordant humour, but really gay and carefree laughter I think he has never experienced...At the same time, he would immensely like to be liked, and the smallest act of courtesy or special kindness touches him with a deep emotion. No Frenchman could at the same time be so unlike the majority of Frenchmen and yet so representative of the present spirit of France. The terrible mixture of inferiority complex and spiritual pride are characteristic of the sad situation into which France has fallen. I have often felt that the solutions here could not be dealt with by politicians. They are rather problems for the professional psychiatrist.'[23]

De Gaulle, Macmillan however continued, no longer 'shouts and bangs the table', the symptom Macmillan suggested, of a family tendency to mental instability, (there was a reference here to his daughter, Anne), and had shown 'a steady progress towards statesmanship'. Aware of the campaign against him personally maintained by London and Washington, de Gaulle was shrewd enough 'to console himself with the reflection that if Giraud has been in fact destroyed by the friendship of the President, he, the General may help keep himself going by the animosity of the Prime Minister. In spite of this, I believe he would sincerely prefer reconciliation to conflict. But he cannot bring himself, of his own effort, to make the first necessary moves.'

> Macmillan concluded: 'It is almost impossible to imagine that he will not be the leader in the first phase of post-liberation France; but it is quite conceivable that the people will soon tire of his dour figure, and if he is thrown aside after his services, he will accept his mar-

tyrdom not merely with resignation but with a certain masochistic satisfaction.'[24]

This was an intelligent if somewhat headmasterly analysis. De Gaulle had come a long way in 1943. In the aftermath of Darlan's assassination, the diplomatic and military advantages - his military superiority to the Fighting French in terms of numbers of divisions was at least five to one - had seemed to lie with Giraud. Yet by the end of the year Giraud had been sidelined, Churchill and Roosevelt had been defied and de Gaulle was firmly in charge.[25] The fundamental reason for the General's success lay in the ruthless and single-minded determination with which he sought to protect French honour and interests, and to establish his own domination of the French political process. This in turn contributed to the growing support which the General was enjoying - in North Africa itself, with the French Resistance, and with public opinion in Britain and the United States. But his victory also owed no small amount to Giraud's extreme political ineptitude.[26] He failed to capitalise on de Gaulle's outbursts, and the irritation and anger that these caused to allies such as Catroux, let alone enemies like Roosevelt and the American Secretary of State, Cordell Hull.[27]

De Gaulle was in many respects his own worst enemy. His intransigence was of course in part calculated. But there remained a compulsive element to his behaviour which made it difficult for him to judge the borderline between the firmness which would gain respect, and the egocentric arrogance which would be counterproductive. A wiser man, noted Oliver Harvey, would have known how to handle Churchill, flatter the Americans as he had in fact flattered Eisenhower, and 'capture the Giraud position by infiltration'. De Gaulle, certainly in the mood he was in during the first half of 1943, could not do so. This made him far more dependent than he may have liked or realised on the support of those who recognised that his failings were outweighed by his strength, and who did not allow themselves to be swayed by the anger and antipathies which affected Churchill and Roosevelt.[28]

Prominent among these was the Minister Resident in Algiers. On leaving, Macmillan received a telegram from Eden which expressed the Foreign Secretary's

'warmest congratulations on your handling of French affairs over these many difficult months. Your tact, wisdom and patience have surmounted many formidable obstacles and have made a big contribution to the cause of Anglo-French friendship which we have so much at heart. You have every reason to be more than satisfied with your work and I am personally very grateful to you.'[29]

These views were shared by senior Foreign Office officials in London, and by Macmillan's own staff in Algiers, as well as by both French and Americans.[30] Although he was at times overly given to flattery and on occasion remarkably high-handed, Algiers sees Macmillan at his best. None of the weaknesses which were to become evident in later years - the tendency to wishful thinking or occasional emotional outbursts – were as yet evident. Where de Gaulle was awkward and angry, Macmillan showed himself subtle and controlled, a clear-headed pragmatist who knew what he wanted and did not allow himself to be deflected from his goal. The assignment played to the strengths of a man who at the age of forty-nine had unexpectedly emerged as an independently-minded character who enjoyed living dangerously. To Richard Crossman Macmillan was 'a dashing man of action, self-confidently poised in his behaviour, gambling on his hunches and, when we lost, as we sometimes did, loyal to his subordinates.'[31]

Macmillan himself liked to claim that he was not a diplomat, but the very unconventionality of some of his diplomacy, along with ability to conciliate and gain peoples confidence suggests otherwise. He certainly established an unusually easy-going relationship with de Gaulle. Which other British, or indeed any minister or official would have taken the General bathing at Tipasa, or told him he was so obstinate that he might be a 'son of the manse'?[32] Macmillan also proved adept at acting as a general shock-absorber and helping contain much of the damage produced by the intemperate words and actions of the various over-sized egos involved in the Algiers drama. As he himself noted at the end of the long succession of June crises, 'what a lot of faces I spend my time saving - and not French faces only, by any means!'[33]

Macmillan's success with de Gaulle himself should not, however, be overstated. As General Catroux once remarked, the only people who had influence with de Gaulle, were those who encouraged him along the path he wanted to tread, which was precisely what Macmillan was mostly trying to do. Macmillan's words may possibly have weighed when the General was in two minds on a course of action, as at Tipasa. But in the light of later events, it is important to note that Macmillan never mastered the art of getting the General to change his mind. Whether he actually saved de Gaulle and place him in a position of power, as Alistair Horne argues, is also debatable. Macmillan was effectively part of a team.[34] Catroux, Massigli, Monnet, Eden, senior Foreign Office officials and on crucial occasions the cabinet in London, as well as Eisenhower, all argued de Gaulle's case. That said, de Gaulle's transition from the leadership of the Free French to the *de facto* head of France's provisional government would have been considerably more difficult without the efforts of the Resident Minister. Certainly there were occasions, at Casablanca, in May 1943 and again during the June crises, when Macmillan helped to sway the outcome in de Gaulle's favour.

De Gaulle was of course by no means the only barrier to French union, and Macmillan's ability to handle Giraud and Churchill was at least as important as his management of the General. Having long acquaintance of Churchill, Macmillan was well aware that the Prime Minister respected those who were willing to stand up to him. He had the advantage of being away from London, where ministers were prone to be overawed. A diary entry in early July following a visit to Britain by Roger Makins, complained that most of his colleagues seemed to be relying on his refusing to obey his instructions from Churchill too literally. 'I really think it is a bit mean of them. They might summon up enough courage to speak up in the Cabinet from time to time.'[35]

More important than distance was Macmillan's success with the Americans. Managing the Americans was after all the task for which Macmillan had been sent to Algiers in the first place, and his success in doing this probably weighed more with Churchill than the Resident Minister's skills in dealing with the General. To some extent Macmillan was lucky. Darlan had been removed from the scene before he arrived in Algiers, and Eisenhower was, in his own words, a 'fanatical' proponent of Anglo-American cooperation. The Americans had their own reasons for backing a Giraud-de Gaulle union, based on the pressure of public opinion, realisation of Giraud's very obvious inadequacies, and their dislike of backing a loser.[36] That said, Macmillan clearly got on with his new American colleagues. Perhaps, as Alistair Horne suggests:

> 'it was the genes of his mother finding an outlet; but in any event the vitality, spontaneous warmth, breezy informality and generosity endemic to the Americans among whom he now lived sparked off something in him. A new Macmillan, relaxed and at ease, more self-confident and less pompous, began to emerge and this in turn undoubtedly contributed to the success of his relations with his US colleagues.'[37]

Murphy's position is particularly important here. Macmillan was probably right in believing that without a change in local US official opinion in Algiers Roosevelt would have succeeded in overthrowing de Gaulle.[38] Murphy's conversion to the General's cause may never have been whole-hearted. But Macmillan had tried hard to counter the American diplomat's hostility to de Gaulle, and as René Massigli argues, left to himself the American diplomat would never have been 'an element of conciliation.' Overall Macmillan did much to contain, if not always defuse Anglo-American tensions over French affairs, re-establishing British influence in Algiers after the eclipse it had suffered in the wake of the 'Torch' landings.[39]

Algiers had a further long-term significance for Macmillan. As 1943 had shown, he was a man who placed great store by the value of personal diplomacy, and Algiers was to prove a place where contacts and friendships which would be important in the post-war world were made. Of his own talented staff, with whom he developed a lasting and reciprocal affection, Roger Makins went on to become ambassador in Washington, before being brought back in 1956 as First Secretary of the Treasury, where Macmillan was currently Chancellor. Harold Caccia, a slightly later arrival in Algiers, succeeded Makins in Washington, and then became Permanent Under-Secretary at the Foreign Office in 1961. Patrick Reilly, another later arrival in 1943, was chosen by Macmillan to be ambassador in Moscow in the late 1950s. He was the senior

Foreign Office official dealing with EEC matters at the time of the first British membership application.[40] But the man who would play the most important part in the de Gaulle-Macmillan story was Pierson Dixon. Although only briefly in Algiers when Macmillan had first arrived, Dixon had impressed Macmillan. When appointed to Paris in 1960, Macmillan told de Gaulle that he and Dixon had been personal friends since their time in North Africa, and that the new ambassador had his particular confidence.[41] The following year Dixon was given the additional responsibility of leading the official delegation negotiating British entry into the EEC.

Of the key American players, Murphy reached the senior ranks of the State Department, where he remained until his resignation in 1959. Eisenhower, who left the Mediterranean to assume command of the D Day landings, became President in 1953. Macmillan was to make ample use of his wartime links with his old friend in his successful attempts to re-establish the Anglo-American 'special relationship.' As early as April 1943, Macmillan had written, 'I cannot help thinking that this experiment in an Anglo-American set-up will have very big results. If we bring it off and make a success of it, it will be a most valuable precedent for post-war cooperation.' Writing years later to Makins, who by then was head of the Atomic Energy Agency, a body which had important American links, the Prime Minister remarked that 'all that you and I have been able to do in the United States is largely based on what we learned at AFHQ.'[42]

The French connections proved more ambivalent. In his memoirs General Catroux described Macmillan as 'a true friend of France', a verdict endorsed by both de Charbonnières, and Massigli, who later became French ambassador in London.[43] The impression which Macmillan made on the French in Algiers is also suggested by Maurice Schumann's encomium in the European Assembly in 1950 that Macmillan had done 'more for France than any man, even including Churchill', and by the number of Frenchmen who wrote letters of congratulation on his appointment as Prime Minister seven years later.[44]

De Gaulle was not among the latter group. Macmillan would later claim that de Gaulle had retained 'an unusual degree of friendship' for him from the war years.[45] But Macmillan features far less prominently in de Gaulle's memoirs of this period than de Gaulle does in Macmillan's. That is perhaps not entirely surprising. De Gaulle was after all far more central to Macmillan's strategy in Algiers than Macmillan was to the General's, though de Gaulle may have not have been aware of how much help Macmillan had given him behind the scenes. What is more striking is that the General's references to Macmillan are considerably less appreciative than those not only to Churchill, but also Eden and Duff Cooper:

'Originally directed by Churchill to associate himself, although with some reservations, with the political actions of the Americans in North Africa, Macmillan had gradually come to the understanding that he had better things to do. His independent spirit and lucid intelligence had found themselves in sympathy with the French group that desired a France without fetters. As our relations developed I sensed that the prejudices he had nursed toward us were dissolving. In return, he had my esteem.'[46]

One reason for this reserve may be the fact that de Gaulle had far less to do with Macmillan than with Eden, Churchill and Duff Cooper. His relations with the two former spanned much of the war; those with Macmillan a matter of months.. But there is more to it than that. However sympathetic and generally well disposed to the French, Macmillan was far less of a Francophile than the other three Britons. He certainly did not have the special affection for France which de Gaulle attributes to the Foreign Secretary.[47] And he was far too pro-American to have endorsed the suggestion in Eden's memoirs that Britain might have done better to have learned from de Gaulle's example of standing up to the US.[48] It was, however, Macmillan's rather than Eden's approach which would dominate British foreign policy in the post-war years when de Gaulle had become president of France.

PART THREE:

A REVERSAL OF FORTUNES, 1944-60

Chapter 7

Suez, Messina and Algeria

After Macmillan left Algiers, he and the General went their separate ways and lost touch. Macmillan's career was a conventional and, at least until 1956, a relatively undramatic affair. He spent the rest of the war in the Mediterranean dealing with the complexities of Italian, Yugoslav and Greek politics, as well as the controversial return in 1945 of Cossack prisoners to the Soviet Union. While his post remained relatively ill-defined, he quietly accumulated great power, becoming in John Wyndham's words, 'Viceroy of the Mediterranean by stealth.'[1]

His return home in May 1945 was an anti-climax. He became briefly Secretary for Air, but in July the Conservatives lost the general election and Macmillan lost his Stockton constituency. Although he was quickly back in parliament, this time for the safe suburban seat of south Bromley, the man who had revelled in wartime action found parliamentary opposition depressing and frustrating, to the point of contemplating leaving politics for full-time work in the family publishing house.[2] When the Conservatives returned to office in 1951, Macmillan was disappointed only to be offered the Ministry of Housing. But building new homes was a Conservative priority, and Macmillan managed to exceed the ambitious official goal of 300,000 houses a year. He was rewarded in October 1954 with promotion to Minister of Defence. Then in May 1955, when the ageing Churchill reluctantly retired, Macmillan became Foreign Secretary. It was the post he had long wanted, and for which his Algiers record suggested he would have real aptitude.

It proved to be a brief, and unsuccessful, appointment. His major problem was the new Prime Minister, Anthony Eden. A long-standing latent rivalry between the two men was reinforced by the Prime Minister's propensity to interfere, something which so independent-minded a minister clearly resented. But Macmillan also found some difficulty adjusting to his job. There was, as the new Foreign Secretary privately noted, 'trouble in every part of the world'. A diary entry of June 1955 refers to 'a bewildering life, one is always mentally behind and trying to catch up'. Eden was privately critical, complaining not only that he took too much on, but that he was 'too woolly generally'.[3] And it was at the Foreign Office that he was involved in the first of two of the Eden government's major mistakes - the decision in 1955 to opt out of the negotiations which were to lead to the formation of the EEC, and Suez – both of which were to have important repercussions for his own career.

The idea of a European union and common market had originally been put forward during a period of Franco-German détente in the late 1920s, by the French Foreign Secretary, Aristide Briand. Although it had come to nothing at the time, the Second World War had given it new impetus, and while still in Algiers, Jean Monnet was already privately outlining some of the ideas which were to crystallise into the European Coal and Steel Community, the ECSC.[4] Like many of his generation, Macmillan's attitude to the post-war European integration movement was inconsistent. As Ann Tusa notes, Macmillan was born 'at a time when the British looked beyond the Continent to the Empire; he was educated in the classics, not modern languages; he preferred a holiday on the moors to a trip abroad; he came from a nation which historically only involved itself in European affairs to restore the balance of power, then willingly withdrew to its island.' He himself once admitted to 'a certain natural and inherited insularity.'[5] Yet he had begun as an enthusiast. Already in the 1930s he had expressed interest in the idea of a European federation. As a committee member of the United Europe Movement established by Churchill in 1947, he attended both the 1948 Hague Congress and the first Council of Europe meeting in Strasbourg the following year. 'We met,' he later wrote, 'in a real atmosphere of spiritual excitement. We really felt convinced that we could found a new order in the Old World - democratic, free, progressive, destined to restore prosperity and preserve peace.'[6]

Yet however keen on the idea of Europe, Macmillan was much less happy about the supranationalist form it took in the early 1950s, with the creation of the ECSC, and the French proposal for a European army and Defence Community, a project to which de Gaulle was even more bitterly opposed. He was certainly much more of a Euro-enthusiast than the majority of his colleagues in the Churchill government, and was anxious for Britain to take a lead in Europe. At one point indeed he was advocating the creation of a European confederation. But his Cabinet interventions on the subject betray a defensive element, which was to become much more pronounced after he had become Prime Minister.[7]

The reason Macmillan believed that Britain needed to take the initiative, was to avoid the risk of a German-dominated Continental bloc which might usurp British influence in Washington. Instead of playing merely second fiddle to the US, 'we might well have to descend to third fiddle, while 150 million Continentals took the second place.' Would not Germany ultimately control a possible European State, he warned in another paper, 'and may we not have created the very situation in Europe to prevent which, in every century since the Elizabethan age, we have fought long and bitter wars? It may be argued that the rise of the United States and Russia have transformed the picture. Yet the inner balance of Europe is essential to the balance of world power.'[8]

In June 1955 came an unexpected and critical development. Foreign Ministers of the six ECSC countries meeting at Messina in Sicily, resolved on radical new steps in the economic sphere. These included the development of common European institutions, the 'gradual amalgamation' of economies, the creation of a common market and the progressive co-ordination of social policies. So bold was this new resolution, that as one of the participants as Messina later wrote, many people thought it unrealistic.[9] This was certainly the view in London. The Chancellor, R.A.Butler, argued in Cabinet that Britain should respond to the invitation to participate in the follow-up conference in Brussels by sending only an observer. Macmillan was characteristically more pragmatic. While accepting that Britain should preserve its full freedom of action and make clear that it was not committed to any bodies which might be set up, 'we might be able to exercise a greater influence in the forthcoming discussions if we were to enter them on the same footing as the other countries concerned.'[10] A diary entry a few days later records him telling officials that while the Foreign Office tradition is hostile to the European movement, 'I favour it - as one of its founders! This has not yet reached the "lower levels."' Yet at the same meeting he also warned along his now familiar line, that 'Europe would be handed over to the Germans.' In the view of one senior official, it was a 'complete thumbs down' to Messina.[11] Thereafter Macmillan took little interest in the Brussels negotiations, indeed by the time the British representative was withdrawn in November, the Foreign Secretary appears to have become actively hostile to the project. A subsequent démarche to Washington and European capitals was aimed at sabotage.[12]

By the beginning of 1956, however, by which time Eden had succeeded in removing him to the Treasury, Macmillan had begun to realise his mistake. In early February he was arguing that it would be dangerous to assume that the Brussels talks would not succeed. Britain now needed to come up with a scheme which would take account of its position as head of the Commonwealth and sterling area. 'I don't want this matter to slide,' he wrote, adding presciently, 'I believe it may be one of the most difficult that we have to deal with in the next few years.'[13] The result, initially devised through the official committee system, was what became unimaginatively known as Plan G - a free trade area embracing Britain, the Six and any other European states which wished to join, in all goods other than foodstuffs. This would avoid problems with the Commonwealth, regarded as one of the key barriers to British involvement in a European Common Market, as well as any kind of political commitment. Unlike the Common Market, it would have neither an external tariff nor institutions. Macmillan, along with the President of the Board of Trade, Peter Thorneycroft, was its main proponent in a sceptical Cabinet, which only finally agreed the plan in November.

By then the government had much more pressing concerns. The Suez operation, aimed at overthrowing the Egyptian leader, Colonel Nasser, and regaining control of the Suez Canal, is the great oddity of post-war British foreign policy. Uncharacteristically, it was a wholly Anglo-French affair, from which the Americans were completely excluded. The French, who were anxious to try to cut off Egyptian support for the Algerian *Front de Libération National,* the FLN, against whom they had been fighting a debilitating colonial war since 1954, were in fact much keener on military action than the British. The French Chief of Staff, General Ely, believed that military operations against Egypt were only possible in cooperation with Britain, and in a move of which de Gaulle strongly disapproved, French forces were put under British command. Relations became close enough for the French Socialist Prime Minister, Guy Mollet, to suggest first a revival of the 1940 wartime project for Anglo-French union, and then that France should join the Commonwealth. The latter suggestion was raised in the context of remarks about nuclear cooperation between the two countries, and his reference to the 'immense hope' in France that Britain would take its place in Europe 'and indeed lead the movement towards closer European unity'.[14]

Suez was also the only point during the difficult quarter century of decline which followed the Second World War when a British government lost its nerve. There was what one of Macmillan's biographers described as 'a mood of almost tribal recidivism, like the moods that sweep through a school, which was not easy to resist.'[15] It was the product of a highly combustible mix, comprising fears over Soviet penetration of the Middle East and the vulnerability of British oil supplies, a rekindling of the memories of Appeasement - Macmillan referred to Nasser as an 'Asiatic Mussolini' - along with a more generalized sense of frustration and anger.[16] In the summer of 1956 retreat seemed to be threatening to turn into a rout. Macmillan, who as the American Secretary of State, John Foster Dulles noted, was 'thoroughly imbued with the tradition of British greatness', believed Britain's position as a First class Power was on the line. Suez was the place to make a stand. Failure to act now, Macmillan emphasised to his old colleague from Algiers days, Robert Murphy, whom Eisenhower sent over to London at the start of the crisis in July, would mean Britain's decline to the status of 'another Netherlands.'[17]

Suez therefore shows a rather different Macmillan from the cool Algiers operator. The tense figure of the late summer and autumn of 1956, who retreated in the evenings to read the classic English novels to keep himself sane, seemed closed to reasonable argument, becoming an older, and also more 'blimpish *persona*'. Macmillan was a leading hawk, and his reasoning is set out in stark, almost apocalyptic terms, in one of his many diaries entries on the crisis. Britain was caught in a terrible dilemma.

If we take strong action agst (sic) Egypt, and as a result the Canal is closed, the pipelines to the Levant are cut, the Persian Gulf revolts and oil production is stopped – then UK and Western Europe have "had it". They get 80-90% of their oil supplies from M East. If we suffer a diplomatic defeat: if Nasser "gets away with it", if Nuri falls and the M East countries, in a ferment, "nationalize oil" and so forth, we have equally "had it". What then are we to do? It seems clear that we shall take the only chance we have - to take strong action, and hope that thereby our friends in the M East will stand, our enemies fall, and the oil be saved. But it is a tremendous decision.' [18]

What this analysis overlooked was the strength of American opposition to the use of force. This was odd, for as Foreign Secretary Macmillan had made a point of renewing his good wartime relations with the Americans, to the clear irritation of Eden, who complained that Macmillan was following Dulles around 'like an admiring poodle'. [19] During Murphy's visit to London, Macmillan had been keen to remind him of their previous close association and his own position, at least as Murphy reported it, as a former adviser and member of President Eisenhower's wartime staff.[20] But while certainly aware that the Americans were 'being very difficult', Macmillan seems to have convinced himself that they would accept a *fait accompli*. This may possibly explain, though certainly not excuse, the Chancellor's failure to pass onto Cabinet Treasury warnings of the danger to sterling if Britain went ahead with military action without US support.[21]

Macmillan's misjudgement quickly became clear when, far from condoning the Anglo-French operation, Eisenhower imposed economic sanctions on his closest ally, and there is a hint of panic in the way Macmillan exaggerated the resultant loss of sterling reserves, and the speed with which he now demanded a cease-fire.[22] The French, who did not share British vulnerability to American financial pressure, did not take kindly to the way in which they were informed rather than consulted about the British decision. Yet with Eden forced almost immediately afterwards to go to Jamaica for health reasons, Macmillan quickly recovered his nerve, giving what one of Eden's biographers describes as 'an admirable performance of calm responsibility under stress, without actually carrying any of the responsibility for explaining the retreat that he had initiated.'[23] Much quicker than Butler to see which way the wind was blowing, he easily outmanoeuvred his rival on Eden's resignation early in the New Year. The sixty-three-year old Chancellor spent a part of the morning of 10 January 1957 at No.11 Downing Street, reading *Pride and Prejudice*. In the evening the new Prime Minister was celebrating with oysters and champagne at the Turf Club. The fact that he had come to power as a result of this most extraordinary crisis, in which his own judgement had been at best questionable, says much about the state of both country and the Conservative Party.[24]

Macmillan's response to the debacle was characteristic. Suez, had been a 'gamble which failed. Now we must go on as if it never happened'.[25] At one level he succeeded. The public and Party were all too willing to forget, the latter subtly egged on by a Prime Minister who spoke of the distinction between pride and vanity in international relations, and told them that historically Britain's greatest moments had been not when it conquered, but when it led. Publicly Macmillan had inveighed against 'any more defeatist talk of second class Powers and of dreadful things to come..Britain has been great, is great and will remain great, provided we close our ranks and get on with the job.'[26]

But if the crude humiliation could be quickly erased from the memory, the aftershocks could not be avoided. Suez helped give a final impetus to the successful conclusion of the Brussels negotiations. The West German Chancellor, Konrad Adenauer, in Paris at the time of the military operations, had spoken of the EEC as France's revenge. Robert Marjolin, a French official who became Vice-President of the EEC Commission, put it slightly differently. He wrote in his memoirs that having long hesitated in the face of the strong opposition from ministers, the civil service and public opinion, Guy Mollet 'felt that the only way to erase, or at least lessen, the humiliation that France had just suffered from the Suez affair was to conclude a European treaty quickly.'[27] Whatever the exact French motives, the signature of the Treaty of Rome on 25 March 1957 was to have more far-reaching effects than the new Prime Minister realised. The days of British-led *Entente*, along with the prospects for British leadership in Europe which he had been so keen to promote, and which Mollet had still been ready to support in September 1956, were now over.[28] Instead Britain found itself faced with a totally new kind of Continental grouping, which it would find remarkably difficult to come to terms with.

An influential minority, including both Eden and the Foreign Secretary, Selwyn Lloyd, had argued in the wake of Suez that Britain should work closer with Europe.[29] Macmillan chose a different path, namely the healing of what he later described as 'the Anglo-American schism'[30] It was not initially easy. Pride had been badly hurt and there was also a great deal of bitterness over American behaviour, which Macmillan made little attempt to hide. 'We felt that we had been let down, if not betrayed, by the vacillating and delaying tactics which Dulles had pursued in the earlier stages of the Suez crisis and by the viciousness with which he and his subordinates had attacked us after the launching of the Anglo-French operation,' he wrote in his memoirs. 'There might come a time when my close ties with America and my former association with the President could be usefully exploited; but I was in no mood to make the first approach.' Fortunately the Anglophile Eisenhower, who was no less anxious to heal the rift, took the initiative, and was willing to make the symbolically important gesture of meeting Macmillan on British territory. The two men met in Bermuda on 20 March.[31]

Here the past was quickly buried, 'spilt milk', as Macmillan put it.[32] The Algiers connection helped. Eisenhower privately described Bermuda as one of the most successful conferences he had attended since 1945, suggesting that the fact that he and Macmillan were 'old wartime comrades and friends of long-standing,' might be the reason for the atmosphere of frankness and confidence in which it was held.[33] But the primary reason was the need to re-establish allied unity in the face of increasing Soviet pressure. The Cold War was an immediate and pressing reality. Powerful as the Americans were, Macmillan had told Eisenhower at Bermuda, 'I don't believe you can do it alone. You need us: for ourselves; for Commonwealth; and as leaders of Europe.'[34]

If the latter seems an odd claim four days before the signature of the Treaty of Rome, the unexpected launching in October of the first Soviet satellite, Sputnik, which as Macmillan privately noted had shaken 'the American cocksureness' provided an opportunity of which the Prime Minister took full advantage. 'If the United States and Britain,' he wrote to Eisenhower, 'could join together to guide and direct the efforts of the free world', they could build up something which might not defeat the Russians but would 'wear them out and force them to defeat themselves'.[35] The Americans readily responded. Macmillan visited Washington, where for the first time since the war a series of highly secret Anglo-American working parties were set up, which the British hoped would institutionalise the 'special', by which they partly meant exclusive, nature of the relationship.[36]

What, however, Macmillan privately referred to as 'the great prize', was the agreement for the repeal of the 1946 McMahon Act, which had unilaterally terminated wartime Anglo-American nuclear cooperation.[37] This promised considerable technical and financial advantages for Britain. It was also to create a new dimension to the 'special relationship', extending the range of issues which the Americans discussed with the British, and thereby making the connection even more important to London.[38] Finally, there was a 'Declaration of Common Purpose', which included two passages which are of particular note in the light of Macmillan's subsequent dealings with de Gaulle. One described western defence arrangements as 'based on the recognition that the concept of national self-sufficiency is now out of date. The countries of the Free World are *inter-dependent* and only in genuine partnership, by combining their resources and sharing tasks in many fields, can progress and safety be found.' The second declared that the two countries' possession of nuclear weapons represented 'a *trust* for the defence of the Free World.' (emphasis added)[39]

It all seemed a remarkably comfortable and satisfactory state of affairs, the advantages of which, both practical and more intangible, flowed both ways. With Macmillan again in office Eisenhower, as two American historians note, was back in his familiar position as 'the acknowledged supreme commander, now in the diplomatic sense, of the world's most important alliance'.[40] Yet this revival of the intimacy of the wartime relationship, which had eluded Churchill during his peacetime premiership, begged several questions which were to become increasingly troubling for the Prime Minister, particularly in his relations with the French.

Although Macmillan was to make much of the concept of '*inter*dependence', the reality was that as a result of the repeal of the McMahon Act, Britain had in fact lost an important part of its nuclear *in*dependence. As the economic constraints on Britain's own nuclear programme became more pressing, the

83

temptation would be to rely increasingly heavily on the Americans. Moreover, having accepted American nuclear know-how and technology, Britain would be constrained from nuclear cooperation with any other Power, since it became increasingly difficult to distinguish British-researched information from that gained from the United States, which Britain was precluded from passing on to third parties. In 1957 this did not seem to be a problem. Indeed when at Bermuda, the Foreign Secretary, Selwyn Lloyd and Dulles discussed a French request for extensive British aid for the French nuclear programme, they agreed that while it would be dangerous to oppose French nuclear plans openly, the two countries should adopt a very cautious policy 'and do very little by way of encouraging or assisting' them.[41] It was not for another four years, that Macmillan was to discover how disadvantageous these agreements would prove.

This exclusion of the French from the intimacies of the Anglo-Saxon club did not escape notice. During the preparations for the October Washington summit, a senior American diplomat had noted the willingness the British had shown to 'toss to the wolves their partner in the Suez adventure....with a cynicism which I doubt the French will easily or quickly forget.' Macmillan certainly had some explaining to do when he in November met the French Prime Minister, Felix Gaillard. His diary records:

> 'All kinds of usual accusations about *perfide Albion*. We and the Americans were accused of (a) trying to dominate NATO, (b) doing the French out of oil exploitation in the Sahara (c) preventing France becoming a nuclear power - etc. etc. However, although it was rather sticky to start with, I think the Paris meeting did good.'[42]

The Prime Minister was shown, but did not comment, on a despatch from Sir Gladwyn Jebb in Paris, in which the British ambassador expressed concern that the 'policy of the Anglo-American Directorate of the type now operating, flattering though it may be to our self-esteem, will be an insecure base for our foreign policy unless it can be fitted into a rather larger framework.'[43] Two months later, Selwyn Lloyd was warning of concern in Europe, especially France, that Britain appeared to be trying to create a two-level Power system, with the British and Americans in charge, and the rest in the ranks. Britain could not afford to 'build up a position as the first lieutenant of the United States in a way which severely damages our position in Europe.'[44]

* * *

But why worry so much about France? Between 1946 and 1958 France, under the Fourth Republic, had fifteen prime ministers to Britain's four.[45] Politically unstable and with low international prestige, the country was regarded as the weak sister of the Western alliance, a cause for concern because of the risk of Communist take-over rather than as a serious rival. For much of this unhappy period de Gaulle had seemed a somewhat peripheral figure. The trajectory of his career had been very different from Macmillan's. On the Liberation of France in 1944, de Gaulle had, as Macmillan predicted, become head of a provisional government of national unity, and subsequently Prime Minister. He succeeded not just in avoiding civil war, but implementing an ambitious social and economic reform programme. But de Gaulle failed to persuade French parliamentarians to accept what he regarded as vital constitutional reforms. Frustrated by the reassertion of the sterile politics of the interwar years, in early 1946 de Gaulle preferred to withdraw, at least temporarily, from the stage. Contrary to Macmillan's January 1944 prediction, de Gaulle seemed to have tired of the French before they had tired of him.[46]

De Gaulle was to find opposition even more frustrating - and much longer-lasting - than Macmillan had done. In 1947 he had founded his own political movement, the *Rassemblement du Peuple Français*, but while initially successful it gradually lost popularity, and by 1954 the General had severed links with it. The following year he announced his retirement from public life, retreating to his country home in the little village of Colombey-les-Deux-Eglises in eastern France, to write his memoirs. 'Finished de Gaulle - a very fine book. I look forward to volume 2, when he gets to Algiers,' Macmillan noted in his diary on 6 March 1955, after reading the first volume, *The Appeal (L'Appel)*.[47] The General's depressed mood in this period, known to Gaullists as 'the crossing of the desert', is reflected in the extraordinary conclusion to *Salvation (Le Salut)*, the last of the three war volumes:

'Silence fills my house. From the corner room where I spend most of my daylight hours, I look out far into the west. There is nothing to obstruct my view for some fifteen kilometres. Above the plain and the woods, my eyes follow the long slopes descending into the valley of the Aube, then the heights of the slope opposite. From a rise in the garden, I look down on the wild depths where the forest envelops the tilled land like the sea beating on a promontory. I watch the night cover the landscape. Then, looking up at the stars I steep myself in the insignificance of earthly things.'[48]

By the time this was published the General was back in power. Macmillan had an unwitting hand in the affair, in so far that some of the seeds of the General's return were sown by the failure of Suez. The immediate cause was the worsening crisis in Algeria. Economic interests, in particular oil and gas, explain only part of Algeria's importance to France. It was the only French colony which came under the direct jurisdiction of the Ministry of the Interior and was therefore at least nominally an integral part of Metropolitan France. It had a French settler community of over a million - the *pieds noirs*. And following their disastrous defeat at Dienbienphu in Indo-China in 1954, the French army were determined not to suffer another reverse. Over the eighteen months after Suez, a view gradually emerged that the problem could not be resolved by the unstable, short-lived governments which the Fourth Republic produced. The alternative, increasingly favourably spoken off in the civil and military bureaucracy, was General de Gaulle.[49]

Algeria, like Suez, was an end-of-empire crisis, which brought about a change of government in the metropolitan homeland. But unlike Suez, for which Macmillan bore a significant responsibility, Algeria was not a crisis of de Gaulle's making. On the other hand, while the transfer of power from Eden to Macmillan had been a constitutionally correct, as well as a reasonably seemly affair, de Gaulle's return to power hovered on the very edges of legality. If the aftermath of Suez had shown Macmillan at his most ambitious and devious, de Gaulle's handling of the 1958 Algerian crisis suggests a ruthlessness of a quite different order. The crisis, which brought France to edge of civil war, had begun in February 1958 when the French had bombed the Tunisian village of Sakhiet, where Algerian nationalists had taken refuge. When the Tunisians demanded UN Security Council action, Britain and the United States sent a 'good offices' mission, including Robert Murphy, to try to resolve the quarrel. Although this achieved little, its very ineffectiveness was regarded as a humiliation in a country which still considered itself to be a Great Power. On 15 April the government of Felix Gaillard resigned, and it would be almost a month before a successor under Pierre Pflimlin was appointed.

By then a rebellion had broken out in Algiers. On 15 May de Gaulle declared himself 'ready to assume the power of the Republic.' In his diary Macmillan noted the General's 'equivocal statement, but one which has terrified the French politicians. It is cast in his usual scornful but enigmatic language. France is in turmoil - no one knows whether it will lead to the collapse or the revival of the Fourth Republic.'[50] What Macmillan does not appear to have been aware of, although the General's supporters were, was 'Operation Resurrection', the plans for which were being hatched in Algiers by a small group of officers. Paratroopers from Algiers and Toulouse would arrive in Paris, and along with tank squadrons based just outside the capital, occupy key buildings in a show of strength designed to force the authorities to accept a government under de Gaulle.[51]

By the end of May, the French government was effectively paralysed. The Minister for Algeria could not go to Algeria, the Minister of Defence was defied by the armed forces and the Minister of the Interior could no longer control the police. When Pflimlin resigned, and the Socialists and Communists threatened to block de Gaulle's path, the General asked the army in Algiers what would happen if the Socialists were to vote against him in the Assembly. Having been briefed in detail on Operation Resurrection, he is reported to have made the supremely enigmatic reply, that it 'would have been vastly preferable for my return to have been achieved by the normal means...Tell General Salan, (the commander-in-chief in Algeria) that what he has done, and what he will do, is for the good of France.'[52] In the event military intervention was unnecessary. On 31 May Macmillan noted in his diary that the General looked like getting enough votes in the National Assembly by constitutional means, which he duly did on 1 June. The night before moving into the Prime Minister's official residence, the Matignon, he went back to his hotel, where the night porter accompanied him respectfully to the lift. The General tapped him on the back and chuckled, 'Albert, I've won.'[53]

De Gaulle's memoirs unsurprisingly skate over the more sensitive elements of this drama. But there is little reason to doubt his claim that having decided to act, he was faced with two alternatives - to restore a semblance of stability and then retire, having given a 'new lease of life to a detestable political system', or to seize the opportunity for radical reform.

> 'Was I to act in such a way that on this basis it became possible to resolve the vital problems of decolonisation, to set in motion the economic and social transformation of our country in the age of science and technology, to re-establish the independence of our foreign policy and our defence, to make France the champion of a European Europe united in its entirety, to give her back throughout the globe, especially in the Third World, the prestige and influence which had been hers through the centuries? This, without the slightest doubt, was the goal that I could and must achieve.'[54]

The man Macmillan would meet for the first time in fourteen years in Paris at the end of June was again a man with a mission.

Chapter 8

The Old Companions

The second act in the Macmillan-de Gaulle drama was to prove much longer, and from Macmillan's point of view, much more difficult than the first. With the shift from the unique wartime preoccupation with internal French politics, to the wider agenda of the post-war international stage, the two men found themselves at odds in a way that they had never done in Algiers. The world had changed almost out of recognition since they had last met in 1944. Roosevelt, Stalin and Churchill were all gone. The international scene was dominated by nuclear weapons and the Cold War. The German problem had not gone away, but with the country divided and Soviet forces entrenched as far west as the Elbe, it now took a new and more manageable form. Western Germany was a fellow member of NATO. It was a member too of a radically new community of six west European countries, which were experimenting with supranational institutions, and were committed by the Treaty of Rome to 'ever closer union'.

A whole complex of diplomatic, strategic and political issues flowed from this new, and in many respects still unstable, situation, criss-crossing and inter-weaving in sometimes surprising ways. De Gaulle had views, usually iconoclastic and outspoken on most of them, and what the General thought had in June 1958 suddenly become of great importance. De Gaulle was by now in his late sixties. While still a commanding figure, he had put on weight and developed a slight stoop. His hair had thinned and greyed, and following a cataract operation, he wore thick glasses.[1] He no longer chain-smoked. Age, along perhaps with the death of his beloved daughter, Anne, had mellowed him. The rawness of the war years - if not always the temper which sometimes still appeared in private - had disappeared. On seeing him again Macmillan was struck by 'a modesty and simplicity of approach which was quite new to me. All the old conceits and prejudices seem to have gone. One felt the same kind of confidence in him as one might feel in talking to a priest.'[2]

This did not, however, as Macmillan also immediately observed, mean that the General had lost his old obstinacy.[3] He was certainly no more open to argument than he had been. 'You go in and, with perfect courtesy,' a French diplomat once explained to his British colleague, 'the General explains his point of view. You then explain your point of view. The General, with perfect courtesy, presents his point of view again, and the interview is over.'[4] But there was a new diplomatic finesse. The crude wartime methods, when he had banged the table and dug in his heels, were no longer in evidence. De Gaulle now knew how to cultivate and flatter, and he was to show himself a master of the arts of equivocation and mystification. 'In the old days,' Gladwyn Jebb noted in September 1958, 'the General seemed to be rude and very precise whereas nowadays he is polite, indeed cordial, and thoroughly vague.'[5] Secretive would be a more accurate word. Like Macmillan, de Gaulle kept his cards very close to his chest, but he went much further than the Prime Minister in terms of keeping everybody else, including his own ministers and officials, guessing. The General's views and intentions often seemed as much a subject of debate among French diplomats as those of any foreign Head of State. Foreign diplomats in Paris were forced to practise a form of French 'Kremlinology'.[6]

With the prospect of working together again, de Gaulle and Macmillan were both naturally keen to draw on old wartime connections, which Macmillan had already been doing to such good effect with Eisenhower. In their respective memoirs of these post-war years, Macmillan and de Gaulle paint an essentially similar picture. 'Since a sense of personal gratitude was by no means excluded from his nature,' Macmillan recorded,

'as long as it was never allowed to conflict with a still stronger sense of national duty, he had retained for me from the war years an unusual degree of friendship. Although I was one of the worst possible examples of 'Anglo-American', being half British and half American by birth, yet I felt somehow exempt from the sweeping condemnation with which he regarded all those unlucky enough to be classed as what he called 'Anglo-Saxons'. Perhaps he recalled sometimes the traditional ties between France and Scotland.'[7]

For his part de Gaulle wrote of the two as having been old friends since Algiers days. 'These memories, combined with the respect which I had for his character, and the interest and enjoyment which I derived from his company, caused me to listen to him with confidence and speak to him with sincerity.'[8] In his first message to the new French Prime Minister, Macmillan had spoken of his great happiness at being able 'to renew our wartime friendship, founded in those days when as President of the Committee of National Liberation you were leading France to victory.' De Gaulle replied; 'I too have the happiest memories of our personal collaboration during the war which Great Britain and France waged together for the freedom of the world. We shall, I know, have much to do together and I look forward to this.'[9] Their letters are respectively addressed 'Dear Friend', and 'Cher ami', a form de Gaulle rarely used.

Yet it is difficult to avoid the impression that both of these skilful practitioners of the art of personal diplomacy were not only exaggerating the extent of their Algiers friendship, but deliberately exploiting it for contemporary political ends. Macmillan certainly makes no attempt to disguise his attempts to make use of his association with the General 'at a most critical moment in his career'.[10] The Prime Minister's letters sometimes have an artificial and ingratiating quality which does not ring true. More telling were the meetings which the two men held together. Superficially these reinforce the impression of old friendship. They were often country house weekends, with most of the formal sessions restricted to tête-à-tête discussions. Macmillan would fly to France, accompanied only by Lady Dorothy, his influential private secretary, Philip de Zulueta, who would take notes, plus a detective and two administrative assistants. Macmillan usually spoke French, although he found the effort of doing so and not making a major error of judgement tiring.[11] But although de Gaulle once visited Macmillan's private country house at Birch Grove in Sussex, the Prime Minister never received the invitation he angled for to visit Colombey-les-Deux-Eglises. When told of Macmillan's suggestion, de Gaulle, who did not like public intrusion into his private home, smiled, and remarked that Colombey was not very comfortable.[12]

The General preferred to receive his guest in the grandeur of a French château. Rambouillet was a favourite for entertaining foreign leaders:

'Housed in the medieval tower where so many of our kings had stayed, passing through the apartments once occupied by our Valois, our Bourbons, our emperors, our presidents, deliberating in the ancient hall of marble with the French Head of State and his ministers, admiring the grandeur of the French ornamental lakes stretched out before their eyes, strolling through the park and the forest in which for ten centuries the rites of official shooting and hunting parties had been performed, our guests were made to feel the nobility behind the geniality, the permanence behind the vicissitudes, of the nation which was their host.'[13]

De Gaulle, as Sir Pierson Dixon once noted, was at his most charming when entertaining shooting parties at Rambouillet, when he put on the cloak of 'the grand seigneur' who enjoyed acting as host on his splendid private estate.[14]

While the hospitality was excellent - the menus still preserved in the Archives Nationales in Paris make mouth-watering reading - the occasions lacked the ease which of Macmillan's meetings with American presidents. Between the formal sessions at Bermuda in March 1957, Macmillan and Eisenhower had 'popped in and out of each other's rooms...sometimes in pyjamas chatting like old school chums'.[15] In a description of Kennedy's visit to Birch Grove in 1963, reminiscent of his account of Casablanca, Macmillan wrote that 'there was none of the solemnity which usually characterises such meetings. After all, we were all friends, and many of us intimate friends; and the whole atmosphere was that of a country house party, to which had been added a garden party and a dance.'[16]

Nor were Macmillan's meetings with the General especially frequent. The Prime Minister would certainly have liked to have seen the General more often, arguing that there was 'no substitute for personal contact; it is the only way of really discussing things frankly and avoiding misunderstandings or misrepresentation.'[17] But, partly because the General was reluctant, partly because of the priority Macmillan afforded the 'special relationship', he had much more contact with Eisenhower and Kennedy. (The General's dislike of diplomatic telephone calls, much used between the White House and No.10, was an additional factor.) De Gaulle in turn had almost twice as many meetings with the West German Chancellor, Konrad Adenauer, than with Macmillan.[18]

None of this prevented some very frank discussion. In his *Memoirs of Hope*, de Gaulle writes of the way in which Macmillan confided his anxiety and perplexity over the future course of British foreign policy. But such confidences never led to agreement, and on no significant issue did either man appear to have changed the other's mind. On the contrary, the records often convey a sense that the two men were either fencing, or talking past each other.[19] Much of the time was taken up in either grand *tours d'horizon*s, or in probing each other's positions. Writing to the Queen after a visit to Rambouillet in March 1960, Macmillan reported that he had been able to find out a good deal of the General's thinking without 'committing myself on British policies'.[20] Lord Home, who succeeded Selwyn Lloyd as Foreign Secretary in July 1960, had a point when he minuted, *apropos* of a suggestion by Macmillan that de Gaulle should be invited to Chequers, 'I don't care for this coming and going of great men with no result to follow.'[21]

At first sight this may seem surprising. Macmillan and de Gaulle had after all a good deal in common. They were allies, threatened by Soviet power and worried about the future of Germany. They led countries of comparable size and ambition. Britain and France were the only two European states which still thought in terms of a global role, actively sought the creation or maintenance of nuclear deterrents, and tenaciously claimed Great Power status of which neither man felt wholly confident. For de Gaulle, like Macmillan, this latter was an article of faith. But his determination to reassert French grandeur was given an edge by the General's personal identification with France, his awareness of its long record of defeats and humiliations, culminating in the disaster of 1940, along with his sense of the historic precariousness of French cohesion and unity. In de Gaulle's eyes France could only be protected from disunity and degeneration by retaining a world role.[22] Since the end of Roman times, he once told an audience in Paris, France had never ceased to be a Great Power. Should it ever renounce this status, France as such would disappear. There would still of course be politicians, cooks, artists, even engineers, peasants and French workers. 'But it would not be France.'[23]

De Gaulle was nevertheless realist enough to admit at least part of the decline which his country had suffered, though it was a realism tinged with bitterness. France, as he said to Eisenhower in 1959, 'had been a great and wealthy country; it was now no longer great nor wealthy, and this knowledge was sometimes difficult for the French to bear.'[24] Macmillan's resentment at British decline was usually kept under control after Suez. But despite the apparent ease with which he had put the debacle behind him, the Prime Minister remained uncomfortably aware that British power was on the cusp, and that his own premiership was in fact something of a rearguard action.[25] In his memoirs Nikita Khrushchev quotes both men speaking to him of their two countries' loss of stature and influence. [26]

The point is worth emphasising, for the spectre of decline stalked Macmillan and de Gaulle. Both pursued overambitious policies, both sought to punch above their country's weight, de Gaulle perhaps rather more successfully than Macmillan. But when it came to the most tangible contemporary expression of decline, Macmillan and de Gaulle both showed themselves to be eminently clear-headed. Withdrawal from empire was a potentially explosive political business. Macmillan worried over the impact on the Conservative Party of withdrawal from the settler colonies of Kenya and Rhodesia, which was to cause so much trouble for British governments between 1965 and 1980.[27] Algeria posed a deadly threat to de Gaulle. It had, in Charles Williams' words, 'all the characteristics that politicians most fear: there was no obviously popular solution; the passions aroused were intense; violence had become commonplace; and positions were so entrenched that there was no identifiable room for manoeuvre.' De Gaulle once described the war, which continued until 1962, as 'a thorn in the foot of France which infects the whole body.' It tied down much of the French army - some 374,000 troops were deployed there in 1960, took up a great deal of the General's time and constrained his foreign policy ambitions. It also threatened his life. According to one estimate Algeria was the cause of as many as thirty assassination attempts on de Gaulle.[28]

Both men reacted in similarly pragmatic fashion. 'It is perfectly natural,' de Gaulle declared in June 1960, 'for people to feel nostalgic for the empire that was, just as we may sigh for the soft glow of oil lamps, the splendour of sailing ships, the charms of the days of the horse-drawn carriage. But alas, no policy worthy of the name can ignore the realities.'[29] In a speech to the South African parliament four months earlier, Macmillan had declared that a wind of change was blowing through Africa, 'and, whether we like it or not, this growth of national consciousness is a political fact. We must accept it as a fact, and our national policies must take account of it.'[30]

Common problems and attitudes do not, however, necessarily make for agreement. Jean Chauvel was French ambassador in London until April 1962, and thus had a ring-side view of much of the second Macmillan-de Gaulle encounter. He put his finger on at least part of the problem in describing the difference in the mechanisms of thinking between the two leaders. London, he noted, dreamed of a new relationship, while Paris sought to loose the shackles restricting its autonomy; London looked for strength, Paris for power. London sought cooperation, Paris wanted control.[31]

But there was much more to it than philosophy or style.. If the wartime vehemence of the General's anti-British sentiment had abated, de Gaulle's personal attitude to Britain was more ambivalent than it had been in 1940. Although the war had created a sense of admiration for Britain and the way it had resisted Germany, it had also added a list of personal grievances to the traditional litany of Anglophobe complaints (Fashoda, etc.) with which the General had arrived in London, and which he made no pretence of having forgotten.[32] When de Gaulle and Macmillan met at Rambouillet in 1960, the talks as the Prime Minister privately noted 'as usual' began with complaints against France's allies during the war. The General, Macmillan continued, resented his exclusion from 'the Roosevelt-Churchill hegemony. He goes back too - in his retentive mind to all the rows about Syria; about D-Day; about the position of the French Army in the final stages of the war; about Yalta...and all the rest.'[33] In addition Macmillan detected an element of resentment that Britain had come out of the conflict so much better than France. Things, as the British Prime Minister later put it, 'would have been easier if Southern England had been occupied by the Nazis - if we'd had Lloyd George for Pétain, then we would have been equal...'[34]

Just how far these memories continued to rankle is suggested by de Gaulle's reluctance to visit the country where he had spent his wartime exile. Jean Chauvel's attempts to persuade him to return Macmillan's visits of 1958 and 1959 were to no avail. The General only returned to Britain 'in majesty', for an elaborate State Visit in April 1960, an occasion to which he had clearly not been looking forward.[35] His apprehensions, along with an acute sense of his own, as of French dignity, are reflected in the difficulties the General made during the preparations. Despite British concerns that flight might be disrupted by bad weather, he had insisted on coming by air rather than sea, which he felt would give too much importance to the trip. Assurance to his hosts that he was confident that there would be no fog caused one official to minute sardonically: 'I can only assume that among the special powers he has now assumed he assumes control of the weather.' When he did arrive, he was displeased to be only met at the airport by the Duchess of Kent, and it had to be explained by the French embassy in London that the only available male member of the Royal family, the Duke of Gloucester, spoke no French. He had refused to stay on for an extra day to stay at Chequers and receive an honorary degree from Oxford. On the British side there was at one point some concern about a lunch in the splendid Great Hall of Chelsea Hospital, which was, however, liberally hung with captured French standards and eagles.[36]

The visit was nevertheless a success, and at the reception at the Guildhall, the General beckoned to Sir Gladwyn Jebb and 'said, quite formally, 'M.L'Ambassadeur, you told me that this would be a success and I did not believe you. But now I declare that you were right.'[37] But he only came twice more to Britain. Once to the talk with Macmillan at Birch Grove, (he appears again to have wanted to avoid going to Chequers), and the last time in 1965 for Churchill's funeral.

Yet the real problem lay not in the past, but in the new phase in the age-old Anglo-French rivalry which the General's return to power heralded, as the two countries increasingly jostled for primacy at the top of the second league. The Prime Minister of course tried to gloss over this. At Rambouillet in 1960 he had told the General that 'we had no empires left - and therefore no rivalries. All those days were past.'[38] But Macmillan's reaction to France's explosion of its first nuclear device a month earlier told a rather different story. France, the Prime Minister recorded in his diary, 'now claims equal partnership with Britain. Yet another problem.'[39] This was much nearer the mark. De Gaulle's feelings are suggested by his response to a minor incident in 1962, when French television obtained some better satellite images than the BBC, 'It is good that France does better than the English. For so long we have been second to the English, and not such brilliant seconds either! Now it must be clear that we are doing better than them. France must be the first in Europe. She can only lead others on this basis.'[40] No less telling is Chauvel's remark that when the General spoke of the 'Big Three', he was referring to the United States, the Soviet Union and France. De Gaulle wanted to overtake Britain in the international power stakes, not simply to achieve equality with her.[41]

Here the General was at an advantage. Britain was still the more powerful of the two countries. In 1956, at the time Mollet had revived the Anglo-French union plan, the Treasury had estimated French national income as seventy per cent that of Britain.[42] Whereas Macmillan already had command over an operational nuclear force, in the form of the 'V' bombers, a trio of remarkably graceful aircraft, the Valiant, Vulcan and Victor, the first bombers of the French *Force de Frappe* would only come into service in 1964. By one, admittedly rough, British estimate, French spending on its military nuclear programme in 1960 amounted to only thirty per cent of its UK counterpart. And Britain retained a capacity for global military intervention which France lacked.[43] But the trends were against Macmillan. While British power was on the ebb, French weakness had bottomed out under the Fourth Republic. De Gaulle had moved promptly in 1958 to bring about political and economic reform, and by 1960 the French growth rate had reached a very healthy 7.9%. This provided a strong base for the vigorous diplomacy which would re-establish the General's very distinctive French voice on the world stage.[44]

More important, and this point was imperfectly understood in London, Britain had lost the ascendancy which she had enjoyed since the early days of the *Entente*. The division of Germany, the emergence of the United States as the prime guarantor of European security, and Franco-German reconciliation, beginning with the European Coal and Steel Community, had all served to reduce the value of the British alliance. True, as late as 1954 when Britain had made a formal long-term commitment of forces to the Continent in order to resolve the crisis created by the French National Assembly's rejection of the European Defence Community, the then French ambassador to London, Macmillan's old wartime friend, René Massigli, had wept unashamedly. For a half a century, he declared, French public opinion had been waiting for this announcement. During the Brussels negotiations leading to the creation of the EEC, the French seemed at several points to be looking for a British lead.[45]

By 1958, however, France was in the EEC, while Britain was not. France, and more particularly its new leader, were to become critical in Macmillan's repeated attempts to come to terms with this new European grouping. The result was to make the Prime Minister a supplicant and *demandeur*, a position de Gaulle was usually very careful to avoid. It was Macmillan who mostly seemed to be running after the General, seeking meetings and initiating nearly all of the extensive correspondence between them. That did not mean the relationship was entirely one-sided. The General continued to look to Britain, which he regarded as one of the few 'serious' nations, for a reinsurance of last resort. When Sir Pierson Dixon presented his credentials in the summer of 1960, the General remarked that the two were close neighbours (in the Faubourg St. Honoré). 'As a good neighbour he would always help me to put out a fire in my house; and he hoped that I would do the same if one broke out in his house.'[46] De Gaulle also sought cooperation on a number of immediate issues, including Africa, relations with the newly independent countries of the Third World, and the development of the French nuclear deterrent. But Britain was never de Gaulle's partner of first choice, indeed according to Maurice Couve de Murville, de Gaulle's long-serving Foreign Minister, London was neither interesting nor important.[47]

If rivalry was the constant undercurrent of the de Gaulle-Macmillan dialogue, disagreement about the Americans was out in the open, indeed it was the Atlantic as much as the Channel which divided Macmillan and de Gaulle after 1958. This was partly a matter of practical necessity, partly of national choice. Due to its greater reliance on world trade and larger number of overseas commitments, Britain needed the United States more than did France.[48] History, common language and culture, helped afford it an access in Washington, which as the events of 1957 had underscored, the French could not come close to matching. There was, for the most part at least, a frankness and trust in Anglo-American relations which extended down from Prime Minister to the wide range of day-to-day diplomatic contacts which the British maintained at all levels of the Washington policy-making machine.[49] Britain shared far less with the French than the Americans, most notably in the critical areas of nuclear technology and intelligence. When in 1961 the French made a request for information on a range of intelligence matters, the Joint Intelligence Committee in London ruled that while the way in which GCHQ (Government Communications Headquarters) fitted into the British organisation could be explained to the French, discussion of the results and the technical aspects of the work 'would, of course, not be permissible'.[50]

Like Felix Gaillard in 1957, de Gaulle resented the fact that Britain got privileged access to American nuclear technology. He also wanted a say over American nuclear decision-making. But contrary to Macmillan's suspicions, the General never sought to duplicate the British junior partnership with Washington. Rather than inveigle himself into Washington's counsels as Macmillan had done, he was determined to keep a noisy distance.[51] De Gaulle had by now developed what one former French official describes an 'invincible distrust' of the United States, which sometimes seemed to take on an obsessive quality.[52] This had only partly to do with the General's wartime experience, when he had come up against the rougher face of American power and fought the Americans hammer and tongs. Much as de Gaulle had indeed resented Roosevelt's behaviour, Macmillan overstates the hatred of the Americans which the war had induced. The critical factor determining de Gaulle's attitude after 1958 was rather a reaction to the sheer scale of American power, which he once likened to a physical phenomenon such as a tidal wave or the eruption of an volcano. De Gaulle rebelled against this hegemony by calculation as much as temperament. For the General, the acute imbalance of power between the US and its European allies was dangerous; his *War Memoirs* already contain a reference to 'the heavy servitude of an alliance with giants.'[53]

The basic facts were clear enough. In 1960 the US spent some $45.3 billion dollars on defence, compared with Britain's $4.6 billion and France's $3.8 billion.[54] Some indication of the technological gap is suggested by the astonishment expressed by the Chief of the French Air Staff, on a visit to the United States in 1961, at American developments in the field of rocketry and satellites. (But when on his return to France he tried to explain what was happening, he found that nobody was willing to listen.) In October 1962 when the former American Secretary of State, Dean Acheson, briefed de Gaulle about the Cuban missile crisis, the General had to control his astonishment at the quality of the US pictures of the Soviet missile sites. Told that the photographs had been taken from 65,000 feet the General started to say, 'We don't have anything...', then caught himself and remarked that he was not familiar with such photography.[55]

Macmillan had his own occasional doubts about the dangers that Britain might become an American satellite, and the long-term sustainability of an increasingly unequal relationship. He sometimes complained of American ruthlessness, and his angry outbursts when things went wrong betray the junior partner's underlying sense of insecurity.[56] But the Prime Minister had made his career on the assumption that Britain *could* retain its independence within the undefined concept of 'interdependence' which had emerged at the time of his October 1957 visit to the United States, and that the 'special relationship' would provide an essential means of cushioning, if not actually staving off, further decline. (The British, de Gaulle once remarked, consoled themselves for their decline by saying that they shared American hegemony.) For Macmillan, as for Tony Blair forty years later, America was an essentially benign Power. The Americans might need advice and influence. But 'au fond' the Americans were 'the good boys'.[57]

De Gaulle thought otherwise, being of too instinctively suspicious a disposition to put the kind of trust in the Americans which Macmillan was willing to do. 'When the outer leaves of the artichoke, the benevolence and economic aid and desire for European unity, are peeled off,' Sir Pierson Dixon wrote in February 1962, 'there remains the central core of determination to retain power for themselves. He does not blame them. He would do the same himself in their position.'[58] The General saw the North Atlantic alliance not as a permanent partnership, but rather the reflection of a classic temporary coincidence of interests. He himself might enjoy cordial personal relations with Eisenhower and later Kennedy; the United States might be a democracy. But Great Powers instinctively tended to deprive weaker ones of freedom of action. The General's notion of international relations has been likened to the operation of a planetary system, in which every planet had its own gravitational pull. Medium sized planets must stay out of the gravitational fields of larger ones or become satellites.[59] Or, as the President of the French National Assembly, Jacques Chaban-Delmas once elegantly put it to Kennedy, America's pre-eminent position 'may lead to the temptation for the United States to take the position that major decisions belong to the United States alone. This would amount to being tempted by the devil.' De Gaulle had no doubt that the Americans had succumbed.[60]

US power posed an additional affront to de Gaulle - it stood in the way of the freedom of diplomatic manoeuvre which was the lodestone of his foreign policy. Having won the war, the British could accommodate with at least relative ease to the inevitable, accepting junior partnership in what was after all an 'Anglo-Saxon' alliance, and acknowledging that the notion of national self-sufficiency had become an anachronism. Independence, as Macmillan remarked to de Gaulle in December 1962 was a means rather than an end.[61] De Gaulle instinctively rebelled against acceptance of this position. France (or indeed Britain) could not claim Great Power status, he believed, if it was incapable of independent action. And if the French lost their sense of self-reliance, and no longer felt in control of their destiny, then they would lose confidence in themselves. The very survival of the state would then be in question.[62]

An odd incident occurred in Downing Street in 1962, five years into the Macmillan premiership, when the possibility of joint Anglo-French nuclear targeting was under discussion. Macmillan's secretary, Philip de Zulueta, who wrote many of his position papers on Anglo-French matters, told the Prime Minister that British nuclear plans were fully integrated with those of the US and that he believed an independent British nuclear plan did not exist, only to be contradicted almost six months later by the Ministry of Defence. That could never have occurred in the Élysée.[63]

Against this background it is hardly surprising to find that Macmillan and de Gaulle had such divergent approaches to alliances. If Suez had shown that Macmillan could on occasion treat his allies in a cavalier fashion, the Prime Minister was nevertheless essentially a team-player. British foreign policy was alliance policy, and the reference to the Americans as partners was more than simply manipulative rhetoric. De Gaulle by contrast was a strategic, as well as individual, loner, who was philosophically and temperamentally disinclined to the kind of compromise essential to partnership in friendship or alliance. While accepting the basic need for alliances, he had no scruple in seeking to maximise French advantage at the expense of the general good, or to make himself an almost, but never a totally, impossible ally. 'In serious crises we can always talk and co-ordinate our action. In normal times, we go our own way.' Or, as he once more bluntly put it, 'war is against our enemies, peace is against our friends.'[64]

So substantial a catalogue of differences could only make for trouble. But it was Macmillan who would prove the main loser. So far the Prime Minister had been remarkably successful in repairing the damage done by Suez. With the General's return, life was about to become more difficult.

Chapter 9

In Search of Lost Friendship

'I'm off to see de Gaulle which will be rather amusing,' Macmillan light-heartedly wrote to a friend on 28 June, though in reality he did not travel to Paris in a particularly confident mood. De Gaulle's unexpected return to power was bound to arouse mixed feelings in London, Washington and other allied capitals. France had been on the edge of civil war, and the prospect of a leader who could bring political stability, tackle the country's precarious financial situation and solve the Algerian problem, was obviously welcome.[1]

At the same time the General had a wartime track record in his relations with the 'Anglo-Saxons' which was scarcely likely to command confidence. More specifically the immediate prospects were clouded by his known nuclear ambitions and hostility to NATO. The Americans were worried that de Gaulle, who had a long-standing interest in a Franco-Soviet agreement, might be tempted to make an independent approach to the Soviet Union.[2] Macmillan's primary concern was with the way de Gaulle's return might influence the evolving political and economic institutions of Western Europe. 'With the coup d'état (sic) in Paris', he later wrote,

'It seemed likely that all the previous discussions so carefully prepared and carried on with such detail and patience would fall to the ground. Both the European Community of the Six and the larger concept of the Free Trade Area would depend upon the unpredictable decisions of the new rule of France. I had to confess to myself that the prospects did not seem very favourable..It would indeed be difficult to lead him away from the nostalgic concepts of

France's position in Europe towards the new picture of what a United Europe might mean in a changed and changing world.'[3]

There were thus two immediate priorities. The first was to find out exactly how the General's mind was working on the principal issues of the day - his views in retirement were not after all necessarily a good guide to the policies he would pursue in office.[4] The second was to ward off trouble. Macmillan was anxious to make de Gaulle feel that, in the words of a Foreign Office minute, 'we and the Americans accept him as a friend and ally and to prevent him embarking at once on policies which may be distasteful to us.' Or, as the same official also put it, 'If we make the French feel cosy with us, that might have the effect of making them moderate their pretensions.'[5]

Hence the speed with which Macmillan moved to remind the General of their old wartime association, and his attempt to try and arrange an early meeting. Ideas of flying immediately to Paris, or of getting the Americans to invite de Gaulle to Washington which Macmillan was about to visit, were rejected. Macmillan went ahead with his American trip, but bearing in mind the General's anti-American prejudices, he felt it wise to tell de Gaulle of his plans rather than let him hear about them indirectly. It may not, however, have been so tactful to have reminded the General of his American ancestry by explaining the visit as primarily a private trip to receive a degree at the university where his maternal grandfather had attended.[6] It would certainly not have been tactful to have briefed him fully of the result of the Washington visit. According to British records, it was agreed that there could be no question of admitting France into the new Anglo-American partnership established the previous year. Given, however, de Gaulle's likely sensitivities, they should proceed on a tripartite basis on those issues such as Germany and preparations for an East-West summit, where the French had an historical *locus standi.*[7]

De Gaulle had domestic priorities, and Macmillan only arrived in Paris at the end of June: the first foreign leader to do so. He was met at Orly airport by the General, whom he found 'all affability and charm', along with a very large crowd. Dinner after the first session at the Matignon was 'simple and excellent', and afterwards the two men walked in the garden before resuming their conference. [8] The pleasantries over, including a reprise of the General's affection for Britain, which the French ambassador, Jean Chauvel, had already conveyed to Macmillan, the prime ministers got down to a set of informal but wide-ranging talks.[9] These included two issues which would come to dominate the new de Gaulle-Macmillan agenda - nuclear weapons and the British relationship with the EEC. And at the very outset there was a misunderstanding. De Gaulle mistakenly believed that Macmillan was suggesting a deal in the form of a trade-off between British help with France's nuclear programme in return for French help on the Free Trade Area negotiations (FTA.) 'This manner of doing business did not in any case seem surprising or shocking' the General recorded in a note attached to the French record, 'its proper purpose being to clarify the cost of the concessions it would be necessary to make.'[10]

It sounded like an obvious trade-off. The FTA was a priority for Macmillan. This was the old Plan G which the Prime Minister had helped to push through a reluctant British cabinet in 1956. But the negotiations with the Six had made slow progress, and well before de Gaulle returned to the scene it had been apparent that French opposition made the prospects for a successful outcome of the negotiations doubtful.[11] The French, who were traditionally protectionist in trade, feared the effects of exposing their industry and economy to further external competition, without the compensatory safeguards provided for by the Treaty of Rome. They worried that agreement on a free trade area might encourage some of their new EEC partners to renege on concessions they had made during the Brussels negotiations, most notably the implementation of a common agricultural policy about which the Germans had never been enthusiastic. And they thought, not perhaps without justice, that this was an unbalanced deal. Britain would gain access for its industrial goods to Continental markets, without giving comparable freedom to European agricultural producers to sell in Britain. At the same time British manufacturers would have the cost advantage of cheap Commonwealth food and raw materials. Britain was trying to get the best of both worlds, seeking 'to win at both tables' ('jouer gagnant sur deux tables').[12]

If Britain needed French help over the trade negotiations, de Gaulle wanted British help with France's nuclear programme, which the General had accelerated immediately after his return to office.[13] Although he often talked about the deterrent value of France's projected small nuclear *Force de Frappe*, like Macmillan de Gaulle's primary interest in nuclear weapons was political. Nuclear weapons were a *sine qua non* of an independent foreign policy, as well as a vital status symbol. 'Hurrah for France!,' de Gaulle declared when France finally exploded its first atomic device in 1960. 'From this morning she is stronger and prouder.'[14] France had finally put an end to what de Gaulle had earlier described as the 'position of chronic and overwhelming inferiority', *vis-à-vis* Britain, the United States and the Soviet Union. British aid might not be critical to the French, any more than American aid was critical to the British nuclear programme, but it would save valuable time and money.

Macmillan however was neither able, nor indeed disposed, to help. It was only a year since Britain and the United States had agreed at Bermuda to do nothing to advance French nuclear ambitions. Also the amendment of the McMahon Act facilitating the formal resumption of Anglo-American nuclear cooperation, was about to be passed by Congress. This, the official brief for the Paris meeting noted, 'makes it very difficult for us, even if we really wanted to, to give much help in this field.'[15] Talking to Chauvel, before his Paris visit, Macmillan had sought to discourage the General's nuclear ambitions, with the somewhat disingenuous remark that it was ironic that de Gaulle should wish to enter the atomic race, just at the point when Macmillan was anxious to leave it. The cost of producing all these weapons was quite crippling. Making these bomb, the Prime Minister noted, was not like making a car or a bicycle; there was no end to what was needed. However, the Prime Minister would not say this to General de Gaulle![16]

When the nuclear question was raised in Paris, Macmillan was discouraging, but not totally unambiguously so. He sought to deflect any French request for nuclear help by urging de Gaulle to talk to the Americans. The French record quotes Macmillan as saying that Britain wanted France to be a nuclear power, but that it was important that the expansion of the nuclear club stopped at some point. Told that the French couldn't conduct their first nuclear test until 1959, Macmillan warned that the position would be difficult to hold for much longer in the face of the ongoing East-West test ban talks in Geneva. De Gaulle, Macmillan went on to say, ought to see whether he could make some kind of an experiment as soon as he could 'in order to qualify'. (sic) [17]

This enigmatic rider may have reflected Macmillan's realisation that de Gaulle was going to go ahead with his nuclear plans whatever Britain said, and that it would be unwise to oppose him directly. But assuming there were no further unrecorded exchanges, (and the records can never be fully relied upon), it is nevertheless difficult not to explain de Gaulle's reading of a FTA-nuclear trade-off into Macmillan's words, other than as a matter of wishful thinking on the part of a practitioner of classic *Realpolitik*. De Gaulle thought he heard what he expected, or perhaps wanted, to hear.[18]

Having eschewed this nuclear deal, Macmillan was left a very weak hand over the FTA. His objectives were admittedly limited. He was not trying to negotiate but rather to encourage the General to take a 'positive' and 'helpful' interest in the negotiations, the success or failure of which would now depend on the instructions which he gave to his officials.[19] The course Macmillan opted for was both dramatic and risky – linking the trade talks with the existing British defence commitment to Europe. He had outlined the argument a few days earlier in a memorandum to the Foreign Secretary, Selwyn Lloyd and the Chancellor of the Exchequer, Derick Heathcoat Amory. Noting that Britain was apt not to press its point too strongly in the early stages of negotiation, and then to be accused of perfidy when it took a definite position once a crisis occurred, Macmillan argued that Britain should now make clear to its friends that if the 'Little Europe' of the Six arose without parallel developments of the free trade area, it would have to reconsider the whole of its political and economic attitude towards Europe. Britain should:

> 'fight back with every weapon in our armoury. We would take our troops out of Europe. We would withdraw from NATO. We would adopt a policy of isolationism. We would surround ourselves with rockets and we would say to the Germans and the French and all the rest of them: "Look after yourselves with your own forces. Look after yourselves when the Russians overrun your countries."'[20]

These were defiant words which the Prime Minister was to repeat on a number of occasions, and which defy ready or rational explanation. They were certainly more than just a tactical device to apply pressure, and highlight the political importance of what Gaulle might otherwise see as a purely technical and hence secondary issue. Europe was beginning to bring out something of the apocalyptic streak in Macmillan's thinking evident during Suez. (He had already warned cabinet colleagues in July 1957, that Britain must not be bullied by the activities of the six members of the EEC, but 'must take the lead, either in widening their project, or, if they will not cooperate with us, in opposing it.')[21]

Frustration in the face of the obstacles Macmillan was finding in his attempts to work out an acceptable British relationship with the EEC, may explain part of the Minister's response. Anti-German sentiment was also a factor, heightened by the Macmillan's annoyance over the foreign exchange costs Britain was incurring for the maintenance of the British Army of the Rhine. Above all, there was a real fear, already evident in his warnings from the early 1950s (quoted in chapter six) of the consequences of the emergence of a new Continental grouping, from which Britain would be excluded. His critics would argue, with some justice, that the Prime Minister's thinking, which drew heavily on traditional British concerns with the maintenance of a European balance of power, had been rendered obsolete by the EEC. 'Anachronistic nonsense' was the term used by a senior American official, George Ball, to describe Macmillan's later assertion that should France and Germany go down the road to European unification, Britain would have no alternative but to lead a peripheral alliance against them. But his belief was sincerely held.[22]

The immediate trouble for the Prime Minister in June 1958 was not, however, so much that his ideas were out of date, but that the threat wasn't credible. Britain could not afford to 'sulk in its island'. The withdrawal of British troops from Germany, as Selwyn Lloyd noted with typical British understatement, would have 'disagreeable consequences all round'. American forces would be likely to follow, with West Germany going neutral or even accommodating itself with the Soviet Union.[23] And empty threats, as Macmillan should have been aware, were unlikely to have much impact on the General.

When the Paris discussions turned to the free trade question, de Gaulle, who had indeed not yet had a chance to give much attention to the question, and appeared to be sticking rigidly to his brief, outlined France's long-standing and deep-rooted reservations.[24] He had nothing in principle against a wider form of cooperation than the EEC, but it was not easy to put into practice, and the FTA, to which French opinion was unfavourable, could cause them great difficulties unless they took proper precautions. The French would gladly listen to British proposals but 'could not enter lightly into any agreement on this subject'.[25] Macmillan now issued his warning. 'The Prime Minister', the British record reads,

> 'said the negotiations had gone on too long. We were still waiting for the counterproposals of the Six..If the negotiations broke down altogether the effect would be very bad. If France were traditionally

103

protectionist, Great Britain was traditionally isolationist. It had been a great effort and departure from tradition for us to keep four divisions on the continent. If we were to be threatened with a trade war by the Six we would be driven back on ourselves and would have to seek our friends elsewhere. He and General de Gaulle must so steer things that the experts got the negotiations started. Otherwise Europe would break up.'[26]

He also said, though this point is glossed over in the British record, that failure to establish the FTA would have serious political consequences for himself.[27]

De Gaulle was clearly struck by this attack, to which he was still referring years later, and on at least one interpretation suspected that it masked a British project to establish political control of Europe.[28] But while he gave no ground, his response demonstrated his new diplomatic skills. Several weeks earlier, de Gaulle had told the crowd of French settlers in Algiers that he had understood them. 'Je vous ai compris.' Now, this master of the arts of politico-linguistic ambiguity, used the same formula to try to calm his English guest. 'J'ai compris votre position - I have understood your position. Do not believe that we will reply negatively. That is not because of what you have said about NATO...but because of our desire to cooperate with you.' When Macmillan replied that if Europe united its efforts it could become richer than the Americans, de Gaulle responded that like Churchill in 1946, Macmillan was also very European. 'We will not seek to oppose you in this evolution.'[29] Macmillan was under no illusions. He knew that he had failed to make an impact, and left 'a very strong' letter on the subject, grumbling in his diary that de Gaulle 'like so many soldiers of his type cares nothing for "logistics"', and worrying that the new Minister for Finance, M.Pinay, disobligingly described as 'a small man with a small mind', was entirely dominated by the *patronat*.[30] On 4 July Macmillan worried that 'the whole of this great effort will break down, foiled by the selfishness and the insularity of the French'.[31] De Gaulle's reply, which arrived the same day, was couched in what Macmillan described as the General's 'rather vague style', but promised that the General would personally follow the matter 'in the spirit of close friendship which characterised our conversations'.[32]

* * *

In his memoirs Macmillan included a photograph of the two Prime Ministers coming out of one of their meetings in Paris. Outwardly, reads the caption, 'everything seemed friendly and the omens hopeful.'[33] The picture, reproduced on the cover of this book, shows de Gaulle holding his glasses, with a slightly quizzical expression, looking to the left, while Macmillan, grim-faced, is marching straight ahead. Just over two weeks later, Anglo-French relations were in overt difficulty. Among the other subjects which had been discussed in Paris was a simmering crisis in the Lebanon, the scene of some of the worst of Franco-British wartime disputes. Although that country had long since gained its independence, the French retained considerable interests there. In the spring of 1958, against a background of rising nationalist agitation in the Middle East, tension between the Christian and Moslem communities reached the point where the Lebanese President, Camille Chamoun, requested British and American military assistance. When de Gaulle asked his visitor what the British intended to do, Macmillan replied that military intervention might perhaps have been possible at the beginning of the crisis, but that now it was too late.[34] What he did not add, although the British ambassador, Sir Gladwyn Jebb had previously hinted at the fact, was that neither the British nor the Americans wanted French involvement should military intervention become necessary.[35] The war in Algeria, along with the close French connection with Israel, made France a political liability in the rest of the Arab world.

Then on 14 July came devastating news. The royalist regime in Iraq was overthrown, and the King, along with one of Britain's staunchest Middle East allies, Nuri as Said, was assassinated. The British embassy in Baghdad was looted and burned. The Middle East seemed to be on the brink of the slide into the Nasserist control which Macmillan had feared in 1956. At Suez, Britain had acted with France. His fingers badly burnt, Macmillan's instinctive response now was to look to the Americans, with whom the British had already been making contingency plans. Macmillan was again in one of his more emotive moods. The trouble, he told Eisenhower, would probably 'destroy the oilfields, and the pipelines and all the rest of it, and will blaze right through. We shall have to go through with it. We may well be ruined. It is not much fun getting nothing back. But I am all for it if we are determined to see it through'.[36] Eisenhower, however, was not prepared to launch a major military operation in the Middle East. American troops would only be sent to the Lebanon, and he was markedly unkeen for British troops to accompany them. The British therefore confined their military intervention to support for the Anglophile King Hussein of Jordan. The French were not only left out, they had neither been consulted nor properly advised in advance.[37]

To de Gaulle, this was all too reminiscent of Anglo-Saxons' wartime methods, and he made no attempt to disguise his displeasure. The French Fleet was sent to the Mediterranean with orders to act independently and not to exchange courtesy visits with the British or Americas, while an unusually frosty note was despatched by the Quai d'Orsay to the Foreign Office and State Department.[38] From Paris Gladwyn Jebb warned that unless de Gaulle's concerns with tripartite consultation were met the General might revert to his 1940 methods which would 'a tragedy after such a good start.'[39] More ominously, the message quickly reached London that the General believed that he had been deceived by both Macmillan and Dulles, who had visited Paris a few days after the British Prime Minister. De Gaulle suspected a long-standing plot involving Britain, Turkey and the United States for the military occupation of the Lebanon and Jordan, which his British and American guests had concealed from him.[40] This was untrue, and on Foreign Office advice Macmillan wrote a toughly worded letter to de Gaulle denying that there had been any attempt to mislead him. In classic Macmillan fashion he explained that he was writing so frankly 'after some thought' and because of the importance he attached to 'my own friendship with you and because of my desire that there should be full confidence between us.' The reply pointedly failed to accept the Prime Minister's assurances, but the Paris embassy reported that the General's entourage believed that the correspondence had been beneficial. Somewhat optimistically Macmillan minuted, 'Not too bad!' [41]

The Prime Minister might have been more perturbed had he known details of the talks which de Gaulle had held with the Italians on 7 August, when the General had called for cooperation between Italy, France and Germany. Although they should not act against the Anglo-Saxons, the Europeans should make their voices heard. United, the three European Powers could play a much more important role than they could individually.[42] It was a straw in the wind, an early indicator of de Gaulle's interest in creating an autonomous European bloc as a counterweight to existing international power structures, from which Britain would, at least in the short term, be excluded.

What Macmillan did know was that de Gaulle was creating difficulties over a possible East-West Summit. On 19 July Khrushchev had called for a meeting to discuss the Middle East situation. Macmillan, who felt that this was unavoidable, but recognized that it was important to take the initiative away from the Russians, wanted the discussion to be held at the United Nations.[43] De Gaulle, whom the British were now careful to consult, disagreed. Instead he called for a Summit in Geneva, where there would be less much less scope for propaganda and mischief-making by what the French Foreign Minister, Couve de Murville, described as 'spectators'.[44]

Couve de Murville was to prove a figure of some importance in the Macmillan's dealings with the new France. A member of the FCNL in Algiers in 1943, as a young man he had been briefly engaged to teach French to the sons of Harold Nicolson and Vita Sackville-West. Nigel Nicolson later recalled him as a shy youth 'brittle as a biscuit.' As Foreign Minister he was to prove himself an aloof, but immensely skilful negotiator, who though always operating within the bounds set by de Gaulle, never gave the impression of being only his master's voice. Like de Gaulle he was said to admire and envy the institutions and continuity of British political life.[45]

Couve's role in this July crisis was to prove a harbinger of future difficulties. The Prime Minister was under pressure from domestic public opinion, his troops in Jordan were in a very exposed position, and he badly needed some kind of exit strategy. But the French Foreign Minister had turned down an invitation to visit London, while de Gaulle's position, as some members of the Quai d'Orsay privately admitted, had opened the way for Soviet wedge-driving between the Western Powers.[46] Once again, the Prime Minister let off steam in his diary. 'In spite of all my efforts with the French Government,' he wrote on 27 July, 'de Gaulle had insisted on replying in a totally different way to us and the Americans. He had swallowed the Soviet bait hook, line and sinker. He accepted a Summit meeting of five, at Geneva. This is partly his dislike of U.N.; but chiefly the desire for a European meeting where he can play a larger role and make France (in the absence of Germany) the recognised leader of Continental Europe.'[47]

Soon afterwards, reading a biography of Palmerston, Macmillan noted how neither Russian nor French policy had changed since the 1850s. 'De Gaulle is Prince President. It is not so much the duplicity as the vanity of the French which is so alarming.'[48] Yet only the previous day Macmillan had written the General with technical information on the operation of nuclear reactors 'of which I understand your scientists may not be aware. 'I hope,' he somewhat clumsily concluded, 'that you will not think that my sending this is an interference, but after careful consideration I came to the conclusion that it was right to send this to you out of our long friendship.[49]

At the same time, in line with his remarks to de Gaulle in Paris, Macmillan was anxious to protect French interests in the face of American proposals for a moratorium on nuclear tests. Care must be taken, he wrote to Selwyn Lloyd, not to let the French feel:

'that we and the Americans have betrayed them. We must consider most carefully what to do, especially in relation to de Gaulle. There is much at stake there including the economic structure of Europe. The important point is for the Americans to decide what they are prepared to do to help the French and what stage the French must reach in their atomic programme to qualify for American help.'[50]

Writing shortly afterwards to Eisenhower, who now wanted to announce the abolition of tests as of 1 October, a proposal which also raised problems for Britain's own nuclear programme, Macmillan described himself as seriously troubled.:

'I feel that after all our difficulties with de Gaulle over recent events, while he is still suspicious of our intentions towards him, it would be a serious mistake to force the French Government into a position of dissociating itself from our proposals…We really must consult them fully and give them time to come to a conclusion.'[51]

Managing de Gaulle, and keeping a balance between the French and the Americans, was proving a more challenging task for Macmillan as Prime Minister than it had been when he was Resident Minister in Algiers.

Chapter 10

The General Strikes Out

The focus of diplomatic attention now shifted back to the European arena, with the initiative passing to de Gaulle. The General had wasted little time after his return to power in planning his own, highly ambitious diplomatic agenda. He had lost nothing of his wartime taste for drama and the *coup de théâtre*. This was now focused on developing the Franco-German reconciliation, which had begun with Monnet and Robert Schuman's initiative for the creation of the European Coal and Steel Community eight years earlier. De Gaulle's aim was to build his own 'special relationship' with Konrad Adenauer, and elevate this new Franco-German axis into the key element of French European policy.

The General was deeply preoccupied with the country with which France had fought so many wars. His suspicion and dislike of Germany never disappeared. The well-informed American commentator, John Newhouse, reports him as describing the Germans as 'maléfique' (unnaturally pernicious). Sir Patrick Reilly heard the General refer to the Germans with the 'utmost contempt' and on at least one occasion his language was so extreme that the British diplomat thought it wise not to record it.[1] Yet fear and admiration were inextricably mixed. De Gaulle spoke German well and knew German philosophy and literature, often quoting from Nietzsche, Hegel and Kant. He admired the bravery and the organisation of the German army and once publicly described the Germans as 'a great people'.[2] Although he had originally opposed the creation of the Federal Republic, he was pragmatic enough to accept a *fait accompli*. Already in a speech in Bordeaux on 25 September 1949, he had declared that 'the unity of Europe must, if possible and despite everything, include the Germans.' 'If Europe is to acquire shape,' he wrote in the last volume of his

War Memoirs, 'then the cooperation of the two enemies of yesterday is the necessary precondition.'[3] He was now about to turn these ideas into reality by hosting Adenauer in France.

Unlike Macmillan's low-key journey to Paris, the German Chancellor's visit on 14 September could justifiably be described as a turning-point. It was de Gaulle who had taken the initiative for this meeting, and unlike Macmillan, the Chancellor was being afforded the singular honour of an invitation to Colombey-les-Deux-Eglises. The atmosphere of a family home, de Gaulle on this occasion believed, 'would be more striking than the splendour of a palace.'[4] Adenauer was in many respects an obvious partner for the General. A Catholic Rhinelander who disliked the Protestants and Prussians of the east, the West German Chancellor shared something of de Gaulle's distrust of the German people. He had a strong democratic record, and an acute sense of Germany's responsibility for the Second World War.[5] He had, however, initially been highly suspicious of the General's policies, and had been reluctant to come to France. Once there, he was quickly won over by his host's modesty, courtesy and naturalness.[6]

More important, the Chancellor was also much impressed by what de Gaulle had to say. France, the General reassured his worried guest, *would* go ahead with the EEC, (something de Gaulle had already implied to Macmillan in June), on condition that agriculture was included. The General had been at best sceptical towards the EEC while out of power. 'What are all these treaties?' he is said to have remarked. 'We will tear them up when we are in office.' This scepticism would never entirely dissipate. He frequently referred to the EEC as simply a commercial treaty, and shortly before his retirement in 1969 suggested that the EEC might be transformed into a looser form of free trade area.

But on his return to power in 1958 the General had been quick to appreciate the Community's potential value for France. The EEC seemed the only acceptable compromise between a system of protectionism which had become incompatible with France's economic development, and the uncontrolled opening of French frontiers to international competition. Diplomatically, it would help what for de Gaulle was the all-important task of tying the Federal Republic of Germany, the FRG to the West. Besides, de Gaulle had quite enough difficulties on his plate, including the new constitution establishing the Fifth Republic and of course the Algerian problem, to want to precipitate a major diplomatic crisis by calling French EEC membership into question. If anything, the EEC might help the process of withdrawal from Algeria by offering the French a European future to replace their colonial past. In marked contrast to the gradual British retreat from empire, France could feel itself to be 'coming home' to Europe. [7]

No less important to the West German Chancellor, de Gaulle was willing to draw a line under the past. 'What we see today is a new Germany. I take note.'[8] France looked to this new Germany as its privileged partner in Europe, indeed the General spoke of the need for the two countries to form 'a permanent and organic contact.'[9] None of this, or so the General again claimed, was geared against the 'Anglo-Saxons', who after all remained important allies against the Soviet Union. As in his earlier discussions with the Italians, however, de Gaulle was keen to emphasise the need for Europe to pursue a policy independent of the United States. 'The Americans remain the Americans. I do not speak of Britain which constitutes a secondary problem and remains an island.' Adenauer recorded the remark slightly differently. 'The English are not Europeans; precisement ce sont des Anglais.'[10]

The implications for London were disturbing. The German 'glue' which had held the *Entente Cordiale* together was being weakened. From now onwards, it was Germany rather than Britain that would be France's ally of first choice, indeed the de Gaulle-Adenauer idyll would, in the words of one French newspaper, become for Macmillan, a 'liaison dangereuse'.[11] But, characteristically of de Gaulle, this was not an alliance of equals. The General had not said anything to confirm the Chancellor's fear that France would claim the leadership of Europe However, much of the attraction of the new alliance lay precisely in the fact that Germany was at last chastened, as well as divided, and thus for the first time since 1870 weaker than France. As de Gaulle once privately put it, Germany 'a les reins casses' - its back was broken.[12] The point was bluntly underscored in autumn 1958 by his failure to say anything to Adenauer about a second major initiative he was about to take on 17 September. This took the form of a letter proposing radical changes in the organisation of NATO, addressed only Eisenhower and Macmillan.

De Gaulle had already warned Macmillan during their June talks that he would be making proposals for the reorganisation of NATO, to which he attached great importance.[13] The General was a long-time critic of the Alliance, founded during the early years of the Cold War in 1949, in which the Anglo-Saxons had much too much influence for his taste. France currently only held two senior commands, against Britain and America's three, and did much less well at the lower level. De Gaulle was quick to question why Britain should have both Channel commands; 'la Manche' was after all as much French as British.[14] More importantly he regarded NATO as 'a system of security whereby Washington controlled the defence *and consequently* the foreign policy and even the territory of its allies.' (emphasis added)[15] For the General it was no more acceptable that the defence of a great nation such as France should depend on a foreign general than that its destiny be left to the nuclear decisions of other countries, however friendly.[16] Above all, and here one can again detect the long shadow of French history, he believed that NATO's integrated command system denationalised, and thus undermined, France's defence efforts.[17]

De Gaulle's memorandum of 17 September, however, addressed a different issue. The focus of the Cold War had shifted away from Europe, to which NATO's geographical remit was then confined, to the Middle and Far East. Crises such as the one which had just taken place in Lebanon, and a Chinese threat against the off-shore Taiwanese islands of Quemoy and Matsu, which had been grumbling during the summer of 1958, involved a risk of nuclear escalation. The General naturally wanted a say in these decisions, which were currently primarily in American, and to a much lesser extent, British hands. In future, therefore, he proposed that the alliance should be placed under what in his memoirs he called 'a triple rather than a dual direction'. Put in less diplomatic language, the General was seeking to break into the exclusive Anglo-American relationship which Macmillan had sought to build up over the previous eighteen months, and was bidding for some form of involvement in the planning for, if not the actual use of, nuclear weapons. Germany would remain outside this directorate, because, (or at least so de Gaulle told Gladwyn Jebb) of its division, the complications of the Berlin situation, and its lack of any extra-European role.[18]

The result, as the General had intended - de Gaulle had taken care to ensure that his letter would be leaked within the alliance - was consternation.[19] The Americans had no intention of treating France as an equal, or giving de Gaulle a veto over the use of their nuclear weapons, while the other European members of the Atlantic Alliance were horrified at the idea of establishing a formal tripartite directorate from which they would be excluded. The British ambassador to NATO, Sir Frank Roberts, quoted his Belgian colleague as summarising de Gaulle's intentions as seducing the Great, outwitting the middle-rank, and ignoring the small Powers.[20] The Germans saw de Gaulle bidding to 'speak for Europe' in the proposed directorate from which they would be excluded, and after the promises of Colombey, Adenauer felt betrayed. Macmillan, who visited the German Chancellor on 8 October, took some pleasure in increasing his hosts suspicions of the General, while appearing to try to calm him down. 'I had a much longer experience of de Gaulle than almost anyone. He was apt to treat his friends with this curious ineptness and rudeness. It was because of his mysticism and egoism.' But, and here Macmillan appears to have been thinking back to his diplomatic strategy of Algiers days, the Prime Minister 'felt sure that the best way to deal with this, before it went too far and caused real trouble in NATO, was to get the General to write another memorandum, leaving out the offensive parts, which could be circulated and discussed in NATO.'[21]

That, however, begged the question of de Gaulle's intentions. Did he really expect to get what he asked for? Or was he deliberately overbidding in order to establish a bargaining position to enhance France's position in the alliance? More ominously, was he putting down a marker to justify the long-term withdrawal from the hated integrated command structure? Macmillan was by no means the only one who failed to foresee this latter possibility. But the hypothesis is supported both by subsequent events - France left the integrated command structure once the Cold War had abated somewhat in 1966 - as well as de Gaulle's own testimony in his *Memoirs of Hope*. 'I was looking for a way of leaving NATO and regaining the freedom of action which the Fourth Republic had surrendered. I asked for the moon. I was sure I would not get it.'[22]

That, however, was not the whole of the story. De Gaulle certainly wanted to enhance France's international prestige by being openly acknowledged as one of the West's 'Big Three'. France, he told the Conseil de Défense in January

1959, would play two games - one with the other two Western Powers, the other with 'les petits puissances' (the small Powers) of Europe. He had every interest in trying to rein in the United States which seemed increasingly to be going it alone, and gaining the kind of leverage over American policy which had long been one of the prime objectives of the British 'special relationship'.[23] Wartime memories may have been an additional influence. According to Hervé Alphand, France's ambassador to Washington, de Gaulle had never forgotten the tripartite wartime relationship between Roosevelt, Churchill and Stalin from which he had been excluded. What he wanted now was a similar relationship with Eisenhower and Macmillan from which Khrushchev was excluded.[24] De Gaulle's intentions are perhaps best suggested by François Seydoux, the French ambassador to Bonn, who had been summoned back to Paris in September 1958 to be briefed on the initiative. The General gave him the impression of not being confident of the success of his project, 'but he was enjoying himself. If he succeeded, fine. If he failed he would have embarrassed the American President and the British Prime Minister, who could not later complain of his wanting to fly with his own wings.'[25]

* * *

Over the next couple of years Macmillan was to come to see tripartism as an element in a Anglo-French deal over Europe. His concern in the autumn of 1958 was more limited - to avoid diluting the 'special relationship', while at the same time not snubbing the General who might otherwise create difficulties over the crucial FTA talks. (A Foreign Office telegram of 22 October defined the British objective as keeping de Gaulle 'in as friendly a frame of mind as possible, to avoid a rift between France and the United States, and above all to prevent us being blamed by either the French or the Americans if there is trouble between them.'[26]) During the summer prospects for the FTA had briefly appeared to improve. By early July the new French government was focusing attention on the problem, with French experts reportedly being summoned back from leave.[27] The subject was discussed at Cabinet level, where according to the account Couve de Murville gave to the chief British negotiator, Reginald Maudling, there had been a battle between the Ministry of Finance and Industry, which wanted to stop the negotiations, and the Quai d'Orsay which wanted to go ahead. The Quai had won, and according to Couve again, Macmillan's letter to de Gaulle had been the decisive factor.[28]

In fact the changes in policy appears primarily to have been of a tactical nature, designed to ease the pressure which the French had for some time been feeling from their negotiating partners.[29] By September Maudling was complaining that French officials were once more obstructing the negotiations in every possible way, and in mid October Macmillan asked the Foreign Secretary and Chancellor to consider what to do if the talks broke down, again raising the question of withdrawing British troops from Germany.[30] 'I have already said something pretty stiff to de Gaulle but then he will have forgotten it by now. I said the same to Adenauer the other day. He was shocked but impressed.[31] On the 26th Macmillan described the outlook for the free trade area as bad. The French were determined to exclude the United Kingdom. De Gaulle was 'bidding high for the hegemony of Europe. If he could get peace in Algeria and hold on to the Sahara oil, he might achieve it.' The Cabinet agreed that if the French were unwilling to make progress by the end of November, the talks should be broken off. [32]

What this British analysis overlooked was the extent to which the French felt themselves pressurised. A Note by the Quai d'Orsay, written in early October, described French isolation in the larger OEEC negotiating forum as complete. Believing that the negotiations had reached a critical stage, and that the creation of a large and loose free trade area would place the existence of the EEC in jeopardy, it was thus the French government which broke off the negotiations.[33] De Gaulle 'visibly winced' when on 6 November Gladwyn Jebb raised the FTA question, and with good reason.[34] Couve de Murville was currently in London for talks in which he made it clear that France would no longer continue with the negotiations.

The news was not well received. Selwyn Lloyd spoke of 'perhaps the most critical development in Anglo-French relations since 1940.' Macmillan took a larger historical view, with an allusion to the Peloponnesian war. 'It depressed him to feel that the French Government had decided that Athens and Sparta must quarrel. The Russians were getting stronger all the time and here was the free world voluntarily weakening and dividing itself. History would regard this as a tragic decision and the crowning folly of twentieth century Europe.'[35] If this sounded melodramatic, a Note written the same day in the Quai d'Orsay endorsed at least part of the Prime Minister's verdict, arguing that any division between the six EEC countries and the eleven other members of the OEEC would lead to a crisis within the Atlantic alliance, from which only the Soviet Union could benefit.[36] The discussions, Couve noted in his memoirs, were difficult and the disagreement complete. Macmillan referred in his diary to a painful discussion with an old friend. [37]

Typically, however, the Prime Minister was not yet ready to take no for an answer. After all, although Couve had been rigid, this might have been simply part of a bargaining process intended to secure the maximum advantage for France.[38] The next day, and against the advice of the Chancellor of the Exchequer, who felt it unwise to show too much anxiety about the French attitude, Macmillan sent de Gaulle a long and strongly-worded letter.[39] The Prime Minister took direct issue with Couve's claim that the free trade area would undermine the Common Market, which if really true would mean that 'we have been negotiating at cross purposes.' He again warned of the risks of political division in Europe, pointedly stating that France was operating on a conception 'quite different from that of her partners in the Six, who generally welcome the FTA for its political sake alone. Nobody,' he declared, 'has striven harder than I to put Europe in its rightful place in the world. Nobody has made greater efforts to find the means whereby Britain can be brought closer to

Europe.' He begged the General not to regard this as a technical matter, which de Gaulle by this stage certainly did not do, and expressed himself as confident that the General would not mind his 'taking advantage of our old friendship to speak quite frankly to you.'.[40]

It was to no avail. A week later the French Minister of Information, Jacques Soustelle, publicly declared that the talks were dead. The wording was terse. It was:

> 'not possible to create a Free Trade Area as wished by the British - that is, with free trade between the Common Market and the rest of the OEEC but without a single external tariff barrier round the seventeen countries, and without harmonisation in the economic and social sphere.'[41]

It was Macmillan's first major foreign policy reverse.

* * *

Unlike the later British EEC application bid, de Gaulle had inherited the FTA negotiations. Elections for the National Assembly were due in late November; de Gaulle himself would stand for election as president of the new Fifth Republic a month later. But if domestic politics clearly militated against concessions, the General also suspected that 'les Anglais' were again up to no good. Their real purpose was to torpedo the EEC by submerging it within a wider and looser economic grouping, which would be of much less economic or political value to the French. [42] Well aware of the traditional British preoccupation with balance of power politics, by which Macmillan set such store, de Gaulle was instinctively suspicious of British European motives. Speaking in 1956 about the need for a European federation, to be preceded by a Franco-German arrangement, he anticipated British opposition designed to maintain a disequilibrium on the Continent. He spoke in similar vein to NATO's Secretary General, Paul-Henri Spaak, in September 1958. Press comment in France and other EEC countries the previous year, as well as the files in the Quai d'Orsay, suggest that the General's suspicions of Britain's European motives over the FTA were widely shared.[43]

The FTA veto bears many of de Gaulle's hallmarks - French unilateralism, the uncompromising statement and the willingness to break deadlock through radical action - in his *Memoirs of Hope*, de Gaulle writes of his government having 'broken the spell'.[44] The readiness to say 'no', and defy allies, familiar to the British from the war years, would become familiar to his EEC partners. In contrast to the later British EEC bid, however, de Gaulle left the execution of his policy to his ministers. This was a high risk strategy. In 1958 the French felt themselves in a much weaker position than they were to do in 1963. Killing the two-year old FTA negotiation involved real dangers for France, and the country's precarious balance of payments situation meant that the French franc would be likely to become the first casualty of any economic war in Europe.[45] Some very rapid and skilful French diplomatic footwork was therefore now necessary. Paris badly needed to shift the blame for the breakdown onto the British in order to mitigate tension with their EEC partners and try to gain German support.

Here the French enjoyed two strokes of good fortune. The first reflected a British tactical mistake. The decision by Reginald Maudling, who chaired the seventeen-nation committee conducting the FTA negotiations, to suspend the talks following Soustelle's announcement, helped the French to divert attention from their own role in precipitating the crisis. A telegram to French diplomatic posts from the Quai disingenuously described Maudling as having acted in a fit of temper to Soustelle 'who was not in charge of the negotiations and who in any case had said nothing new.'[46]

A more unexpected source of help came from Moscow, where on 10 November, Khrushchev suddenly began to put pressure on the Western position in Berlin. At their next meeting, held at Bad Kreuznach on 26 November, de Gaulle, who was making his first official visit abroad since his return to power, was quick to reassure Adenauer of French support in the new Berlin crisis. He also told the West German Chancellor that France would go ahead with the implementation of the Treaty of Rome without recourse to any safeguard clauses, and asked in return for German support over the free trade area.[47]

Whether a deal was actually made is still disputed, but there seems little doubt of the importance of German acquiescence, and some years later de Gaulle claimed that the FTA negotiations were broken off once it was clear that France was sufficiently close to Germany. At the time one British diplomat was struck by the extraordinary sense of confidence regarding their ability to ride out the crisis which the French delegation had brought back from Bad Kreuznach. The French now felt they could rely on unqualified German support, and that there was nothing that anybody else could now do. No less striking was the way in which a senior French official read out to his British colleague the passage in de Gaulle's *War Memoirs* in which the General described how to deal with crises with the British. The conclusion of this was that provided the French stood firm, the British would sooner or later make up the quarrel. And with the Berlin crisis on the boil, the French diplomat continued, Britain would not be so irresponsible as to start an economic war in Europe.[48]

Tempers, however, were fraying. Anger in London had by no means been confined to ministers, whose fierce talk caused concern within the Foreign Office.[49] There had also been strong press criticism. *The Times* published an editorial entitled 'France the Wrecker', which accused the French, not (as was privately admitted within the Quai) without some justice, of having wrecked the negotiations single-handed, after wasting many precious months in sheer prevarication.[50] On 15 December a heated Anglo-French exchange had taken place at a meeting of the OEEC ministerial council. The President of the Board of Trade, David Eccles, had threatened 'defensive measures' if EEC trade quota remissions, due to come into effect on 1 January 1959, were not reciprocally applied to all OEEC members. A furious Couve de Murville had declared that France would not negotiate under threat. At a reception held afterwards at the Quai d'Orsay, the French Foreign Minister was described by Gladwyn Jebb as 'quivering with emotion...he looked exactly like a sort of cat who'd been brutally assaulted by a bulldog and who had just gone on quivering.'[51]

The problem for London was not simply the immediate threat to British trade, which was at least partially alleviated by the EEC's decision to reduce quotas on imports into the Community when the Treaty of Rome came into effect on 1 January 1959. Nor was it what Maudling had once referred to as the 'grim' prospect of facing '160 million people under German leadership'.[52] The German threat was largely a figment of British imagination which underestimated the caution and constraint which characterised Bonn's post-war policy. The real problem was that with the collapse of the FTA talks, Macmillan's government was left without a European policy. There was, as Maudling had noted three months earlier, no satisfactory alternative. Something might be done in terms of establishing a counterweight, and minds in Whitehall were already turning to a grouping known as 'Uniscan', consisting of Britain and the Scandinavian countries. This was the forerunner of what became the seven-nation European Free Trade Area, inelegantly known as EFTA. But this was very much a second best, promoted on the grounds that half a loaf was better than none.[53]

The General himself was careful not to rub salt into the wound. At the French Cabinet meeting on 12 November he had said that something had to be done quickly for the British, and this point was also made, albeit not quite so directly, to Adenauer at Bad Kreuznach.[54] When Selwyn-Lloyd visited Paris on 17 December, the Foreign Secretary was given a personal message for the Prime Minister; 'Tell M. Macmillan that I think very often of him, that my good wishes go to him entirely personally, but if M. Selwyn-Lloyd will permit me to say so, rather less to his policies.' Later in the talks the General promised to do all he could to avoid a trade war and promote the widest possible exchange of goods. He would do nothing to aggravate the situation, and believed that the French press would follow his lead.[55] It was easily said. Holding the General to these expressions of goodwill,was to prove another matter.

* * *

From Macmillan's point of view, 1958 had not been a good beginning. De Gaulle might indeed have mellowed, but Macmillan was finding him much more difficult to deal with than before. In 1943 he had had the advantage of being an intermediary between de Gaulle and Churchill. Now as Prime Minister and thus principal, it was his turn to bear the full burden of Anglo-French tensions. Personal diplomacy had yielded the Prime Minister little. The General returned Macmillan's compliments and made the right noises about their wartime association. But he had quickly gone off in his own directions, and on the one question which really mattered to Macmillan, the FTA project which he had personally promoted for the last two years, national interests had clashed and the General had turned the Prime Minister down.

But if de Gaulle was being every bit as difficult as the Prime Minister feared, Macmillan in turn lacked the flair he had shown in 1943. His diplomacy had been essentially exhortatory, a matter of letters and threats. This failed to give the General a clear idea of the Prime Minister's motives. Partly perhaps because of Macmillan's unguarded remarks in June, de Gaulle appears to have given more credence to domestic rather than foreign policy pressures on the Prime Minister, while underestimating the importance of Commonwealth concerns.[56] More important it had failed to impress. Macmillan had done nothing to make what the French had all along seen as an unpalatable arrangement more attractive to the General. De Gaulle had not suggested a deal, but he had certainly thought about one. Macmillan of course was precluded from making a nuclear offer by his ever closer relations with the United States, which he had been careful to reaffirm in Washington immediately after de Gaulle's return to power. But the failure even to consider such a possibility suggests a misjudgement of the General quite unlike the Macmillan of Algiers days.

What the failure also reflects is an underestimation of the scale of the threat which de Gaulle's reappearance posed to British interests. The General would have been greatly gratified had he lived to read the verdict in Gladwyn Jebb's memoirs, that until the FTA veto, 'we had often taken the French for granted. Now it became clear that she might no longer be a difficult, though essentially rather subservient, partner. On the contrary a quite formidable adversary was about to emerge.'[57] The Prime Minister, however, does not yet appear fully to have shared this view. He certainly showed far more signs of frustration with de Gaulle than he had done during the war, when his diary comments suggest an amused tolerance which was now conspicuously absent. But he still 'felt *hopeful*', as he later wrote in his own memoirs, 'that in the long run one could appeal to the General's high conception of world drama as well as to his sense of honour. He might thus be *persuaded* to allow, and even promote, the emergence of a Western Europe in which Britain could play an equal part in every sphere of endeavour.'[58] (emphasis added) Hope and persuasion were to prove key words in Macmillan's future strategy for trying to manage the General, a sure sign of the underlying weakness of the British Prime Minister's hand.

Chapter 11

Forcing the Way

Worrying away at the problems left by the failure of the FTA talks, Macmillan sometimes argued that the economic threat from Europe was greater than that posed by the Soviet Union. Being bankrupted seemed a greater danger than being blown up.[1] Yet at the end of the 1950s, the risk of nuclear conflict could not be dismissed out of hand. The Cold War was entering into one of its most active and dangerous phases. The immediate cause was Nikita Khrushchev. The most colourful and exuberant of all Soviet leaders, Khrushchev had made his political career under Stalin, eventually succeeding, and then in his famous 1956 'secret speech', denouncing him. Macmillan had first met Khrushchev a year earlier at an unsuccessful East-West Summit conference at Geneva, where the Soviet leader had made a powerful but distinctly unfavourable impression. Macmillan described him as 'an obscene figure; very fat, with a great paunch; eats and drinks greedily; interrupts boisterously and rudely.' How, he wondered could such a man really be the 'head - the aspirant Tsar - of all these millions of people and this vast country?'[2]

Bad manners were not the only problem. Khrushchev was a peculiar mixture. A self-made man, determined to be honoured as the leader of a world Power, he nevertheless feared contempt and felt insecure. He had much curiosity, yet little knowledge of a world which he saw as sharply divided into two hostile ideological camps. Khrushchev had no doubt that the 'correlation of forces' was shifting decisively in Socialism's favour, a confidence boosted by recent Soviet technological achievements in the field of rocketry, as well as hopes that newly independent countries in Africa and Asia would gravitate to the East.[3]

At the same time the Soviet Union was still a poor country. In his valedictory despatch when leaving Moscow in 1960, Sir Patrick Reilly described watching two women, some thirty miles outside the capital, shouldering ox yokes with dangling buckets, trudging five hundred yards to a river where they broke the ice to draw their household water. Unlike the United States, the Soviet Union could not afford both guns and butter, and Khrushchev needed East-West détente in order to finance his ambitious seven year plan. Détente was also the logical direction for a man who had a genuine hatred of warfare, born of his experiences following the German invasion of 1941. He once said that when he first learned the facts of nuclear weapons he was unable to sleep for several days. 'Then I became convinced that we could never possibly use these weapons, and when I realised that I was able to sleep again.' Rather less reassuring was the fact that Khrushchev was also an impulsive figure and something of a gambler. While he had no intention of using rockets, he had no scruples about rattling them, which he had done against Britain and France during the Suez crisis. It had been sheer bluff, but Khrushchev had drawn the dangerous, and erroneous, conclusion that it had worked.[4]

His immediate target in the late autumn of 1958 was Berlin. Khrushchev variously described the former German capital, which then lay behind the Iron Curtain, as a thorn, a cancer and a bone in the throat.[5] The arrangement, originally intended to be temporary, went back to the period towards the end of the Second World War when it was still assumed that Britain, the United States and the Soviet Union would be able to establish some kind of long-term modus vivendi. That optimistic assumption had quickly proved false, and in an earlier attempt to put pressure on the Western position, Stalin had unsuccessfully blockaded land communications to the city in 1948. By the mid 1950s two German states had emerged - the Federal Republic and the rival Communist German Democratic Republic, the GDR. The subsequent western refusal to negotiate any long-term settlement on the basis of 'peaceful coexistence' between the two Germanies infuriated and worried Khrushchev. According to his son, Sergei, the main objective of the Berlin crisis was to force the West to the negotiating table.[6]

Khrushchev's methods were belligerent and crude. Shortly after comparing Adenauer's September visit to Colombey-les-Deux-Eglises with Hitler's 1934 meeting with Mussolini, on 10 November 1958 Khrushchev warned that if the West did not recognise the GDR, the Soviet Union would hand over control of the access routes to Berlin to the East Germans; any subsequent attack on the GDR would be regarded as an attack on the Soviet Union.[7] This was followed by an official Soviet note which informed the Western Powers that the Soviet Union considered the existing Four Power arrangements on Berlin as null and void. But it was prepared to negotiate for the establishment of West Berlin as a 'demilitarised free city', and there would be no changes in existing procedures for military traffic between West Berlin and West Germany for six months.

Berlin presented the Western allies with a peculiarly difficult problem. Nobody was sure of Khrushchev's intentions, or how far he was ready to press the crisis. What was clear was that even if they had been certain of their legal position, which the British were not, the Western Powers had no easy options. Another airlift would be much more difficult to mount than it had been in 1948, while militarily Berlin was indefensible by conventional means. Any attempts to defend, or force the access routes, risked an unpredictable process of escalation which might all too easily end in nuclear war.[8] This was the risk on which Khrushchev seemed to be capitalising. The alternative, which raised complex diplomatic and political difficulties, was negotiation.

From the outset the allies were divided, with de Gaulle and Macmillan at particular odds. At Bad Kreuznach the General had, as already noted, assured Adenauer that the French were unreservedly with the Germans. De Gaulle believed that the nature of the Soviet challenge, along with the exposed Western position in Berlin, required a position of absolute Western resolution. Only by standing firm and refusing to be intimidated could conflict be avoided. 'The best is to let the Russians get on with their diplomacy without getting agitated and seeming to worry about things which may not happen.' De Gaulle was rightly convinced that, unlike Hitler, Khrushchev was a man who made a lot of noise, but did nothing. The Soviet Union's bluster, as the General put it in a letter to Macmillan, was a reflection of weaknesses which would 'prevent him from overstepping certain limits'[9]

Where de Gaulle was ready to call Khrushchev's bluff, Macmillan was decidedly not. Unlike his main Western allies, the British Prime Minister did not believe the future of the Western alliance was at stake in Berlin. He saw the Soviet aim as essentially defensive - the maintenance of the European *status quo*, in order to consolidate and expand the Communist position *behind* the Iron Curtain. The Soviet position could be summed up in the phrase 'where the tree falls, let it lie'. While believing that Berlin was really on the eastern side of the line, the Russians were prepared to make special arrangements to protect it.[10] The question of whether the Russians or the East Germans 'approve the bills of lading or punch the railway tickets' was not therefore an action of great symbolic importance, and could certainly not be made into a *casus belli*. The essential thing was that civil and military supplies should reach Berlin. From the outset, therefore, the Prime Minister had been ready for talks. He was also ready - and here he parted even wider company from his allies - to explore alternative security arrangements in central Europe.[11]

These divergences are certainly not to be explained in terms of any fundamental difference about Germany, towards which Macmillan and de Gaulle shared a common distrust. 'Of course', the British record of an exchange in December 1959 quotes the Prime Minister as saying, he

'liked some Germans. Dr.Adenauer for example was a good man. President de Gaulle agreed that Dr Adenauer was good. The Prime Minister said that with some other Germans one could not be quite sure. President de Gaulle agreed that one could never be sure with the Germans.'[12]

Where the two men parted company was that Macmillan felt little compulsion to disguise his feelings. As his son-in-law Julian Amery once noted, he 'didn't really look upon the Germans as full partners'. His experience in the trenches, reinforced by his reading of German history, meant that he shared the British public's disinclination to run undue risks for a people who had 'tried to destroy us twice in this century.' Dislike, in other words predominated over the concern repeatedly voiced by de Gaulle, and unlike the General, Macmillan saw little reason to court the Chancellor. Indeed at the end of 1958 there was a strong sense of having been betrayed by Adenauer over the FTA.[13]

This, however, was a dispute about nuclear crisis management as much as about the Germans, and here de Gaulle and Macmillan parted company even further. De Gaulle's claim that Khrushchev was bluffing conveniently allowed the General not to have to admit that France's military inferiority left with him with few practical alternatives. Macmillan by contrast not only possessed a nuclear deterrent, he was also worried by a strong anti-nuclear movement in the form of the Campaign for Nuclear Disarmament.[14] The man who had publicly mocked Neville Chamberlain after Munich as 'Umbrello' was certainly no appeaser. But Macmillan was haunted by his memories of the trenches in a way de Gaulle had never been, and was deeply conscious of the vulnerability of a small island to thermonuclear war. In talks with Eisenhower in March 1959, Macmillan was described in the American record as becoming 'exceedingly emotional.' He could not take his people into a war without first trying a Summit. Eight bombs could kill 20 to 30 million Englishmen.[15]

To one with de Gaulle's iron nerves, this seemed a reflection of weakness. Yet Macmillan had reason to worry about the parallels with the summer of 1914, and the danger of a drift to war through equivocation.[16] What made Khrushchev dangerous was that, as his son Sergei admitted, he had not thought his Berlin strategy through. In a world in which the rules of the nuclear game had still to be established, there was a danger that the Soviet leader might call the Western bluff, leaving it with the stark alternatives of war or diplomatic humiliation. The risk was of the 'pretence of strength followed by a final shrinking from the ultimate decision'.[17]

It was Macmillan who therefore first moved centre stage in the Berlin crisis, and the first half of 1959, when the Prime Minister emerged as the most persistent Western proponent of an East-West Summit, is primarily, if only temporarily, Macmillan's story. The idea of a Summit meeting, which had originally been championed by Churchill following the death of Stalin in 1953, was to become something of an obsession for Macmillan. The Prime Minister's motives were a complex blend of the idealistic and opportunistic, of hardheaded calculation and emotion, which his allies found difficult to fathom. Macmillan's interest was not in the Summit as a one-off event but rather the establishment of a negotiating process built around a regular series of high-level meetings and personal diplomacy.[18] The immediate objective, as far as Berlin was concerned, was 'to entangle the bear in the net of negotiations'. Or, as Macmillan once put it to Chauvel, 'rather like social life in England, if there was a prospect of grouse shooting after the pheasant season had ended you were less likely to quarrel with your hosts.' His long-term aim, however, was East-West détente. The West could not 'live forever in this sort of twilight world between peace and war'. There needed to be a shift from Cold War to a more civilised code of international conduct based on 'a readiness to discuss and negotiate...a return to that flexibility without which the conduct of human affairs becomes almost intolerable'.[19]

There were of course other considerations. At the beginning of January 1959 Macmillan, who had been reading a life of Disraeli, wondered what Dizzy would do if he had to deal with Khrushchev? How would he play the hand, now that the USA and the USSR were so powerful?[20] Summitry provided an answer to more than the problem of Mr Khrushchev. It would institutionalise Britain's (and coincidentally, though this was certainly not Macmillan's main objective, France's) position at the top table. Britain would have a role and a place as the world's peacemaker. National pride would be boosted by this demonstration of British leadership, while the Prime Minister would be staking his claim to a place in history.[21] Last and by no means least, a general election was looming. The Conservative Party had been trailing behind Labour in the opinion polls, and a summit meeting would be electorally popular.[22]

His starting point was deliberately dramatic. When Macmillan had first suggested a trip to Moscow in early 1958, ostensibly returning a visit Khrushchev and Bulganin had paid to London two years earlier, he had met with Cabinet opposition. The Berlin crisis, and the resultant Pentagon military contingency planning which greatly worried the Prime Minister, made the idea more opportune, and indeed urgent.[23] It was a classic Macmillan initiative - imaginative, adventurous, an attempt to seize the lead in the face of what he saw as Western indecision. 'A visit from a British Prime Minister at a period when Britain's power in the world was still formidable and her prestige following the Second War still undiminished,' Macmillan wrote in the early 1970s, by which time a US-Soviet détente was well under way and Britain's status substantially diminished, 'would be no mere conventional courtesy, but rather a startling and almost sensational event.'[24] The Prime Minister was, however, reasonably realistic in his expectations. He did not expect any kind of breakthrough. This was an exploratory mission designed to probe the Soviet position, premised on the assumption that while personal contacts might not of themselves solve international problems, they could at times contribute to a solution.'[25]

If Suez had already demonstrated Macmillan's occasional capacity to try to hustle his allies, the early stages of his 1959 Summit diplomacy suggest a unilateralism more characteristic of de Gaulle. The Americans had been consulted, and their objections, including the possibility that the French and Germans might follow suit, were brushed aside. Macmillan's diary claim of 22 January that the Americans had in effect said that they 'have complete confidence in me and I must do whatever I think best', is at best an oversimplification, at worst disingenuous.[26] The Cabinet along with the French and the Germans were only informed after the initiative had been taken.

'The French, (who I thought would be upset by the visit to Moscow),' Macmillan noted in his diary on 5 February, 'are not at all concerned. Adenauer is rather put out.' In fact de Gaulle regarded the visit as 'unnecessary and unhelpful'. In talks with the Germans, the French Prime Minister, Michel Debré, complained that the visit weakened Western unity, while Couve de Murville remarked that in this kind of crisis, the worst thing was to show anxiety.[27] The West German Chancellor was more than put out at what he saw as a breaking of Western ranks over Berlin.[28] Bulldozing allies in this way was potentially dangerous. It brought latent suspicions to the surface, and set precedents. As David Bruce, the American ambassador in Bonn put it, 'being power conscious, the Soviets have long made it manifest they would like to treat bilaterally with us. Faithful to our alliances, we have refused to do so. Prime Minister Macmillan has not been so scrupulous. Might we not, at some point, consider practising the same technique?'[29]

In his own memoirs Macmillan devotes some one hundred pages to the Moscow visit which began on 21 February. His Soviet hosts were much less generous. The former Soviet Foreign Minister, Andrei Gromyko, has only eighteen lines, Khrushchev does not even mention it, while writing in detail of his own subsequent meetings with de Gaulle and Eisenhower.[30] But the visit was clearly welcome. Foreign visitors were still a rarity in the Kremlin. Khrushchev wanted negotiations, and here was the second most senior Western leader in Moscow wanting to do just that. According to Sergei Khrushchev, his father went out of his way to try to establish informal, personal contacts with his guest beyond the bounds of official protocol.[31] But little common ground could be found on disarmament, in which both men were interested, and on Germany and Berlin there was some very hard, and at one stage, very offensive talking. Khrushchev engaged in some rather crude wedge-driving, while Macmillan warned that 'a very dangerous situation was in prospect' and that Britain would stand by and cooperate with its allies.[32]

It was a tense moment, and the Prime Minister considered abandoning the rest of the trip. But hard-talking did him no harm with his allies, whom he was careful to keep closely informed, or indeed with Khrushchev, who soon regained his composure. He was now willing to defer the date of the ultimatum. It could be or 27 June or 27 August; the date didn't matter very much. He was also willing to accept the idea of a prior Foreign Ministers' conference. He liked the idea of regular meetings. The British delegation returned home after their gruelling eleven day trip very well satisfied. In a telegram to Washington, Selwyn Lloyd spoke of 'one of the turning points of history', while the Cabinet minutes recorded that 'effectively, the leadership of the Western world now rested with the United Kingdom Government.'[33]

While this was a piece of wishful thinking, diplomatically as well as domestically, the trip had certainly served many of the Prime Minister's purposes. There was merit in trying to establish direct contact with a hostile and isolated Soviet government. ('In those days,' writes Sergei Khrushchev of his father's visit to America later in the year, 'each trip abroad resembled a landing on an unknown planet.'[34]) Whether Khrushchev's commitment to negotiations was really the result of Macmillan's initiative, as the Prime Minister claimed, or whether it would have come in any case, may be open to doubt. But Sergei Khrushchev writes of his father having taken advantage of the opportunity Macmillan's visit provided, adding, 'of course he retreated. The whole world saw him retreat.'[35]

It was small wonder therefore that the Moscow visit reinforced the Prime Minister's determination to press forward with his summit diplomacy. Believing that while Khrushchev was determined to avoid war, he was nevertheless determined to go ahead with a peace treaty with East Germany, Macmillan felt that a Summit was imperative if a summer crisis was to be avoided. Britain must therefore convince its allies of the need for 'a realistic response' to the Soviet willingness to negotiate.[36] And to promote this end, as well as both to brief, and mend fences, with his allies, the Prime Minister set off on a new round of visits, starting on 9 March with Paris.

In the Quai d'Orsay's view the talks, initially with Debré, then with de Gaulle, who in January had become President of the newly-established Fifth Republic, went some way towards clearing the air.[37] The French were not opposed to a Summit, and accepted that some modus vivendi would eventually have to be found. But de Gaulle could not resist the temptation of alluding to the Prime Minister's electoral motives, or the fact that when France had wanted a Summit at the time of the 1958 Lebanese crisis, Macmillan and Eisenhower had been opposed.[38] More seriously, there was unease in Paris about the prospects of any change to the *status quo* over Berlin, as too about British tactics. The British were seen as over keen to negotiate and tending to play their cards too soon.[39]

The impact of all this on West Germany clearly worried Macmillan's hosts. The Germans, de Gaulle warned, were 'very unhappy and lost and worried. In particular the position over Berlin had destroyed the illusion in which they had been living that Germany had recovered its position of greatness. Now they realised they were dependent on others.' Adenauer was currently on the side of the West. But if he came to feel abandoned, 'no one could tell how his thinking would change. It was very important not to have Moscow on the Rhine.'[40] Great French emphasis was put on the need for Allied firmness and unity.

Macmillan was unmoved. Still smarting from the FTA veto, he saw the French as trying to pretend that they were being tough and the British weak and defeatist, in order to impress Adenauer and keep his support for 'their protectionist attitude towards European economic problems'. The Prime Minister therefore sought to call French bluff by stressing the need to prepare against possible failure of negotiations, by calling up reservists and bringing troops back from Algeria. He talked of measures 'to prepare England for the shock of bombardment since the major attack would fall on the United Kingdom'. An enquiry of de Gaulle about what he proposed to do in support of the hard line he was advocating elicited the response that 'France possessed no atomic weapons, at any rate at the moment, and could therefore not take many precautions. It was mainly a question for the United States.'[41]

Macmillan's next stop, on 12 March, was Bonn. Although the Prime Minister thought that he had convinced Adenauer of the need for a Summit, he had underestimated the lasting damage the Moscow visit had done to Adenauer's confidence in him. The Chancellor, who was particularly unhappy about British ideas for military disengagement in Central Europe, reportedly told a colleague afterwards that it was high time that Britain learned that it was 'no longer the leader of Europe - Germany and France are the leaders now.' 'The old man,' the British ambassador, Sir Christopher Steel reported at the end of March 'seems finally to have made up his mind that British policy is fundamentally perfidious. He refers to us in private conversations as 'Verraeter.' (betrayer). Adenauer, who was temperamentally even more suspicious than de Gaulle, believed that Macmillan and Khrushchev had reached a secret agreement in Moscow, a suspicion which the French later claimed to have tried unsuccessfully to dispel.[42]

Six days later in Washington, Macmillan again found himself under attack, this time from John Foster Dulles, who was dying of cancer. The Allies and the Third World must not be given the impression that the Soviets were 'in the driving seat'. The American Secretary of State was opposed to a Summit premised only on the hope that it might produce something positive. The West would be under almost irresistible pressure to make concessions, with no commensurate pressure on the Soviet Union. There was more frank talking when Eisenhower and Macmillan met at the presidential retreat at Camp David, where Macmillan skated over his differences with Adenauer and de Gaulle. The French, he claimed, had 'agreed with them on everything'. But while Eisenhower insisted that he would not be 'dragooned' into a Summit, he was prepared to go if there was 'even slight progress'.[43] Macmillan, who had a tendency to put a favourable gloss on such events, described the President his diary as '*very* reasonable' when left to himself. The President 'wants to help. He especially wants to help me...No doubt,' he added, 'the French (and perhaps the Germans too) will make trouble, because they always dislike an Anglo-American agreement.' (emphasis in original.) But the French embassy may have been nearer the mark when it reported a malaise in Anglo-American relations after Camp David, and that Eisenhower had found greater support from Paris than London.[44]

* * *

Despite the objections, Macmillan's determination and obstinacy nevertheless seemed to be paying off. His allies might not be enthusiastic, and charges of appeasement were such that the Prime Minister felt it better for Britain to take a lower profile, and make rather less of the flexibility which was so central to his policy.[45] But the idea of a Summit was gaining ground. At a press conference on 25 March de Gaulle had announced that France would participate if it were held in a peaceful atmosphere and if the proposed Foreign Ministers' conference established elements of agreement on major points. France, the

General declared, making a virtue out of non-nuclear necessity, felt particularly qualified to speak at a Summit with clarity and serenity. It had no animosity towards the Russian people and, unlike the other participants, would not be haunted by the possibility of having to use nuclear weapons. France, and here de Gaulle may have been seeking to distinguish himself from Macmillan, could thus judge the present crisis with 'lucidity and even impartiality'.[46] Five days later the Soviet Union accepted the Western proposal for a Foreign Ministers' meeting, which opened on 11 May in Geneva.

Initially there was some tension between the British delegation and the French and the Americans. (The French and the Germans, Selwyn Lloyd reported on 21 May, were putting it about that the British were soft, ascribing French motives to 'a little bit of natural dislike, the Common Market controversy, irritation that the General was forestalled on the road to Moscow, and resentment at our nuclear power and of our special relationship with the US.')[47] But while the worst of this was quickly overcome, it was soon clear that progress was likely to be slow to non-existent. Khrushchev's only real interest in Geneva was as a preliminary to fixing the date and procedure for a Summit. The Foreign Ministers, Khrushchev had earlier complained, would talk indefinitely, and nothing much would come of it. He would be obliged to pay Mr Gromyko for nothing.[48]

'I expect like me,' Macmillan had written to de Gaulle on 5 June, 'you feel a certain sense of detachment at the moment. The negotiations seem to drag on at Geneva and it seems still very obscure what will happen.'[49] But while de Gaulle was indeed calm, the Prime Minister was to show himself anything but detached. When four days later the Soviet position hardened with the presentation by Gromyko of a new set of proposals which effectively amounted to a new ultimatum,[50] Macmillan began to worry that the Summit would be lost. This fear, amounting almost to an obsession was to stay with him for the next six weeks.[51] It made him an impatient and at times infuriating ally.

The Macmillan of June and July 1959 has little in common with the popular image of the 'unflappable Supermac'. 'We must', he insisted to Selwyn Lloyd on 10 June, 'have a Summit...I feel all this so strongly that if a Summit does not take place I should have to express my feelings in public even at the cost of separating myself from the other Three.'[52] Proposals either to adjourn for two or three months, during which Macmillan feared that the Soviet Union would preserve its monolithic front while the West would be thrown into 'a Babel of confusion', or break off *sine die,* heightened his concern.[53] But there seemed to be a possible way out. Though privately critical of the British fascination with a Summit for its own sake, the new American Secretary of State, Christian Herter, had rather unwisely thrown out the suggestion that Macmillan might invite the three leaders to an 'informal' Summit to discuss Berlin.[54] When the idea was discussed in London, de Gaulle was seen as the most likely obstacle. The General, Selwyn Lloyd warned, might dislike the idea as evidence of British weakness and another piece of British initiative, 'but there might be ways of persuading him. Dr Adenauer would certainly dislike it, but he could be ignored.'[55] Macmillan suggested to that he might visit de Gaulle to explain the idea to the General, but received a bluntly discouraging response from Gladwyn Jebb in Paris. The ambassador rightly believed that the General would be unimpressed by the Prime Minister's arguments.[56]

In the event it was Eisenhower who killed the suggestion. Like Herter, the President was irritated with Macmillan's relentless pursuit of the Summit. Although the pill was sugared with flattery, a frustrated Prime Minister was left continuing to worry about the dangers of 'merely drifting on', which he felt that his allies did not appreciate, and being faced by a sudden Soviet fait accompli. But he would not give up.[57] A letter to Eisenhower (dated 23 June), supporting a recent Western proposal for an interim agreement on Berlin, concluded by wishing that they could meet and talk. 'It is so difficult to put on paper all that one feels.' 'History will never forgive us', he wrote a few days later, 'if we do it wrong. And as you know it all rests on you and me.' De Gaulle and Adenauer, he recorded separately, were 'just hopeless'.[58]

What the Prime Minister failed to appreciate was that in pressing his old American wartime friend so hard, he was in danger of finding himself upstaged. Already on 16 June Eisenhower had mentioned an idea that he had been considering for some time: he might invite Khrushchev to meet him alone, in order to prevent Macmillan from seizing the initiative again.[59] That was not of course quite how he put it to the Prime Minister. 'Assuming no objection on the part of our allies,' Eisenhower, as he wrote to Macmillan the next day, would be willing to meet Khrushchev should the Soviet leader by any chance come to the Soviet exhibition being held in New York.[60] On 13 July Herter told Selwyn Lloyd that Eisenhower had been impressed by the British argument that the West could not go to the brink of war without every effort for negotiations having been made. He was now thinking of a Summit in Quebec, a venue which it was believed might appeal to de Gaulle, to be held around 1 September. It would be preceded by a Heads of Western Governments meeting in Paris around 20 August. The President, Selwyn Lloyd also reported Herter as saying, was 'very conscious of our (electoral) timetable and anxious to do anything that he could to fit in with that.'[61]

Eisenhower had, however, not dropped his long-standing condition that the Summit, as Macmillan put it, was 'a sort of post-graduate course, which the boys can only take if they first graduate with honours (at Geneva).' Macmillan again quickly began to show signs of impatience. 'We cannot', he telegraphed to Selwyn Lloyd on 22nd, 'let things run, because I feel sure that they will get worse..If we had the power, I would now call for a Summit myself, but we must accept that only the Americans have the power to do this.'[62] 'Shall I,' he reflected in his diary the following day, 'make a public statement, dissociating Britain from the allied position? A great responsibility. But so it is to drift along with the tide - with a-half crazy Adenauer, a cynical and remote de Gaulle and a weak President. Shall I ask to go immediately to Washington for a further talk?'[63] Herter tellingly described a draft Macmillan letter to Eisenhower which he had been shown as 'almost hysterical'.[64]

Then came what for Macmillan was a bombshell. Khrushchev was being asked to the US, albeit as the result of a botched invitation. Eisenhower's intention had been to invite Khrushchev to talks prior to a Summit in Quebec, though in keeping with his long-standing view, the invitation was to be contingent on progress at Geneva. The President would then visit the Soviet Union in October. But due to a misunderstanding with the State Department, Robert Murphy had omitted the critical condition from the invitation. Khrushchev accepted with alacrity.

Overwrought and with the election looming closer, Macmillan was furious with 'this foolish and incredibly naive piece of amateur diplomacy'. His diary entry for 26 July is eloquent. Over and above the prospect of losing the Summit, which it appeared might now be postponed until the New Year, the Prime Minister's own position would be greatly weakened.

> 'Everyone will assume that the two Great Powers - Russia and the U.S.A. - are going to fix up a deal over our head and behind our backs. My whole policy - pursued for many years and especially during my Premiership - of close alliance and cooperation with America will be undermined. People will ask, "Why should U.K. try to stay in the big game? Why should she be a nuclear power? You told us that this would give you power and authority in the world. But you and we have been made fools of... U.K. had better give up the struggle and accept, as gracefully as possible, the position of a second-rate power."'[65]

To make matters worse, Eisenhower was planning a foreign tour which did not include Britain. Macmillan, who had been angling for an American visit for electoral reasons for some time, was furious, complaining in his diary of an insult 'to the Queen and our whole nation which will never be forgiven.'[66]

In this frame of mind, the Prime Minister's reply was scarcely tactful. It included a request for a Summit at the end of August, and an expression of concern that the President might otherwise have difficulty in avoiding discussions of substance with Khrushchev. 'You would probably find this embarrassing. It might cause considerable suspicion on the part of the French and Germans, nor would my public position be very easy to explain.'[67] This went down badly. The Prime Minister, Eisenhower complained, seemed to have fixed his election date for late October and was now 'caught by these dates'. Macmillan was trying to manipulate the President's activities much too closely and the Americans should be more reserved with the British. Macmillan's concerns about the Khrushchev visit, Eisenhower went on to note with some justification, came with ill grace given the Prime Minister's Moscow trip.[68]

Nevertheless 'in view of the extreme pressure' from the British, Herter was subsequently told that it probably would be necessary to accept a Four Power meeting provided the Soviet Union accepted the American view of its rights in Berlin.[69] While rejecting Macmillan's request for an immediate Summit invitation, Eisenhower was now ready to talk about a meeting in November or December, with a so-called 'Western' Summit, involving Britain, France and the US in August. Macmillan duly accepted this proposal, though he found it politic to deny that he had ever wanted a Summit 'for its own sake...What I have wanted is a settlement,' and this could only be reached at Summit level.[70] It was no doubt what Macmillan himself believed, but it was scarcely the whole truth.

Chapter 12

'The most tragic day of my life'

The Anglo-American mini crisis proved a storm in a teacup. Eisenhower decided to visit Britain, there was no public outcry against Macmillan's policy and, as the Prime Minister quickly realised, the Russians were unlikely to take unilateral actions over Berlin while Khrushchev was 'surfing in Florida' or Eisenhower 'duck-shooting in Siberia'. From the point of view of the electoral time-table, things had now reached the stage where the Summit would be more of an asset as a future prospect.[1] But it was a telling incident, an uncomfortable reminder of the ease with which Macmillan's Summit strategy could be upset by unexpected events, and a symptom of a foreign policy seeking to punch not so much above, as beyond, Britain's weight. The Prime Minister had lost the initiative. This would have happened sooner or later since Britain, though Macmillan was loath to admit the fact, was ultimately only a secondary player.[2] But by pressing the Summit case too hard, the Prime Minister had overplayed his hand. Eisenhower had now taken over the running, while the focus of the European side of the diplomacy was about to move to Paris.

Characteristically, and indeed wisely in the Prime Minister's view, de Gaulle was opposed to a 'Western Summit' before the Khrushchev-Eisenhower meeting. Selwyn Lloyd suggested that he did not want to give the American president 'plenipotentiary' powers to negotiate for the West.[3] Macmillan once again discussed the possibility of going to see de Gaulle in Paris, but was discouraged by the Foreign Secretary. As the details of the President's European trip were being sorted out, Macmillan began fretting about a new problem. The General might ask Adenauer to Paris to meet the American President. Such a Franco-German summit without Britain would have 'a most deplorable effect', and he might have to ask Eisenhower to refuse.[4] But the Prime Minister seems again to have worried unduly. Eisenhower came to Britain where he hosted a dinner at the American embassy for old comrades from Algiers days, which Macmillan attended as 'ex Minister Resident', rather than Prime Minister. In his latter capacity Macmillan pleaded with Eisenhower to be more sympathetic to de Gaulle over Algeria. 'Without him France might collapse into anarchy or Communism.'[5] In Paris Eisenhower and the General found themselves in broad agreement on both Berlin and a Summit, while de Gaulle expressed regret over British attempts to oppose the new Franco-German alliance which he portrayed as providing a new element of constraint on Bonn.[6] In mid September Khrushchev visited the United States. On 8 October the long-await-ed British general election proved a triumphant success for Macmillan, with the Conservatives increasing their lead over Labour from 67 to 107 seats. It seemed a far cry from his appointment in January 1957 when Macmillan had only expected the Government to last a few weeks.

There was now, however, a new obstacle on the road to the Summit. De Gaulle was concerned that the forthcoming new stage in East-West relations might be dangerous for France. Eisenhower and Khrushchev might not be about to divide up the world: neither man, he privately commented, had the stomach for that. But they might come to agreement on some issues which would be harmful to French interests.[7] Officially the French cited the risks of either a Summit failure resulting in a worsening of the international situation, or Western concessions which would undermine the Alliance. De Gaulle's con-cern, however, was not to prevent the meeting but to postpone it until the fol-lowing May or June. The General wanted his own bilateral meeting with the Soviet leader to put him in a position of equality with his allies. (This argument had its merits in British eyes: a Khrushchev visit to Paris, the Foreign Office condescendingly argued, 'may help to diminish the feeling of inferiority which colours their attitude to so many problems.'[8]) No less important, the General did not want to be the only non-nuclear Power at the Summit, which would therefore have to wait until after the first nuclear test in the New Year.[9]

The Americans now turned to the British for help. Herter asked whether Macmillan could telephone the General or send a message, but the Prime Minister preferred to get British and American thinking into line first. When he did write on 17 October he made no impression, and the first Macmillan heard of de Gaulle's readiness to accept a 'Western Summit' was allegedly from the newspapers.[10] Macmillan floated the idea to Chauvel of going to Paris for 'a sort of Camp David' meeting with President de Gaulle at which they could talk together privately and frankly as they used to do in Algeria.[11] A week later Macmillan was telling the Canadian Prime Minister, John Diefenbaker, that for the time-being his policy was to let the Americans make the running, and to avoid making the French and the Germans suspicious.[12]

Although Macmillan did not have his French 'Camp David', Selwyn Lloyd made what he regarded as a successful visit in mid November, reporting that he had brought the French 'back to thinking of us as her main ally and of Germany as a country that must be looked after for the general benefit.'[13] The first half of this judgement, as with so many British assessments of Anglo-French relations at the time, was over-optimistic. During talks with Adenauer two weeks later, the French again made it clear that they regarded the 'Anglo-Saxon' position on Berlin as too accommodating, while stressing that Franco-German unity was the core of the EEC. Ties should be multiplied at different levels. 'Our people must get used to this.'[14]

The 'Western Summit' just before Christmas was another reunion, the first time in sixteen years, as de Gaulle pointed out, that he, Macmillan and Eisenhower had met together. But this time, although he was of course too polite to say so, he was the gracious host rather than a defeated and awkward supplicant. Macmillan was clearly impressed. The General had conducted the occasion with 'extraordinary dignity and grace, but very much in his own manner.' Despite his attention to historic ceremony he had a 'great and attractive simplicity'. He was 'proud but not vain'.[15]

The three men - Adenauer appeared for only some of the sessions, an exclusion which Macmillan described de Gaulle as managing with a 'combination of exquisite courtesy and complete assurance' - had an extensive agenda. This included the tripartite consultations which de Gaulle had raised in his memorandum of 17 September 1958, and the European trade question, which was still very much on Macmillan's mind.[16] But the most immediate business concerned East-West relations - Berlin, Germany and the Summit, which as de Gaulle put it, it was now impossible to avoid. 'Tout le monde', Macmillan records him as saying, 'accepte la thèse du Premier Ministre Britannique.' Having fixed the question of date for the end of April, despite Macmillan's suggestion that Khrushchev would not want to be out of Moscow on May Day, the leaders turned to the venue. De Gaulle angled for Paris. Geneva was not 'tres gai. Le lac. Et puis toute cette histoire de ce Monsieur Calvin. Non...'[17] This suited Macmillan, who disliked Geneva and saw Paris as a means of committing de Gaulle more wholeheartedly to the new enterprise. All were now agreed this should be the first of a series - the advantage from the French point of view being that it would reduce the risk of a choice between 'dangerous concessions' and failure. The Prime Minister could therefore look forward to being the host in London on a subsequent occasion.[18] When it came to substance, however, the differences between France and the Anglo-Saxons were again evident, with the French going out of their way to express the potential impact of the Berlin crisis on Germany.[19]

In bilateral talks with Macmillan, de Gaulle made no attempt to hide his belief that the Prime Minister was too much of an 'enthusiast' for a Summit. But this exchange had an informal quality reminiscent of Algiers days, with Macmillan being invited for 'une tasse de thé' in the private apartments of the Elysée palace. There he found the General in a most friendly and solicitous mood.[20] Surveying the long-term future, the two men agreed that it would one day be possible to make a real arrangement with the Russians. In a letter to the Queen, Macmillan described de Gaulle's view of the future of the Soviet Union as having been put 'shyly and tentatively, obviously thinking that I would regard them as rather fantastic. Actually they are views which I have held for a long time.'[21] More telling perhaps in the light of subsequent events, was de Gaulle's emphasis on Western Europe unity. The more the Soviet Union saw Europe 'was together, the more reason they would have to come to terms with it'. And as Europe gained economic strength and regained political stability, it would have less need of the United States.[22]

* * *

In retrospect 1959 seemed to have been a satisfactory year. Macmillan had succeeded in 'pointing the way', the title he used for the volume of his memoirs covering the years 1959-61.[23] Despite earlier setbacks and the continued reservations of allies, the Berlin crisis was on hold and the Prime Minister's ambitious East-West policy seemed on track. For the next few weeks Macmillan undertook a lengthy African tour. But he was at Rambouillet for a tête-à-tête with de Gaulle in mid March, which the Prime Minister saw as successful in revitalising their old friendship.[24] By the end of March high level diplomacy in preparation for the Summit was in top gear. Both Macmillan and, much more unusually, de Gaulle went to Washington, where the General was described by the American columnist, Walter Lippman, as the chief spokesman of the Western alliance.[25] De Gaulle next made his largely ceremonial State Visit to London. Most important of all, and an encounter to which Khrushchev attached particular importance, the Soviet leader came to Paris.[26]

De Gaulle impressed Khruchshev far more than Macmillan had done. The Soviet leader was struck by his host's air of authority, self-confidence, and firmness of will.[27] But the unconventionality of this encounter, during which Khrushchev conspicuously did not repeat the scene he had made with Macmillan in Moscow the previous year, was primarily of de Gaulle's making. There was a bizarre incident on a rowing trip at Rambouillet, when de Gaulle suddenly began singing the Volga boatman's song, with Khrushchev joining in.[28] There was also the deliberate coincidence of France's second nuclear test. 'I understand your joy,' Khrushchev responded on being told the news by de Gaulle. 'We felt it not so long ago.' Then after a moment, 'But, you know, it's very expensive.' Khrushchev was in fact worried. A nuclear test moratorium was currently in force, and the Soviet leader was concerned that these might be American tests in French guise.[29]

When it came to the long private conversations between the two leaders, the main issues were Europe and Germany. Krushchev expressed his bitter distrust of the Germans, while hinting that the West Germans might one day come to an agreement with Moscow.[30] De Gaulle was resolute in defending the Western position on Berlin. But he did not disguise his opposition to German reunification, nor did he totally disagree with Khrushchev's hostile view of the Germans. 'As far as Germany is concerned,' de Gaulle told his guest, 'if you think I have great confidence in her, you are mistaken.' France's policy towards her was based on practical considerations rather than trust. But Germany, the

General argued, while a considerable economic power, was divided, without a capital and dependent on others, and hence not an immediate threat.[31]

Up until this point there was no fundamental difference between the Paris talks and those Macmillan had held in Moscow. But while the Prime Minister's main aim was to defuse the tensions and dangers of the Cold War, de Gaulle was playing a rather different game. The General looked to the end of the Cold War as a means of reviving France's freedom of diplomatic manoeuvre. As he had once remarked during the Second World War, he did not want 'a policy of permanent alliances. I want France to play a balancing role in the world, sometimes leaning to Russia, sometimes to England, etc.'[32] What France now sought was a Europe 'qui soit en equilibre'. This, he told Khrushchev, would provide the basis for real détente with the Soviet Union, which would in turn facilitate a resolution of the German problem. Under such circumstances France would not need NATO, which had 'a circumstantial character', or the United States.[33] Nuclear weapons would allow France a European policy which was not necessarily that of the United States.

If Khrushchev was nonplussed by all this, de Gaulle came away from the meeting with the impression that there was a chance for peace in the world and a future for Europe, and that something 'of profound importance' had occurred in Franco-Soviet relations.[34] But he certainly showed no great optimism about the prospects for the Summit, from which he expected few positive outcomes. 'Peaceful coexistence' was too recent, and the German question was not yet ripe for a solution. The most that could be hoped for was that the Summit did not break down in failure.[35]

In the weeks before the Summit, Macmillan's mood seesawed. 'All the omens are good,' he noted in his diary following a friendly and positive letter from Khrushchev on 19 March, but a month later he was complaining that very little advance was contemplated by most of his colleagues, and that 'if there is to be a breakthrough, we shall have to do something ourselves.'[36] Britain's two objectives, de Zulueta noted on 6 May, were to 'defuse' Berlin, at least temporarily, and agree a nuclear test treaty. Ideally both, but either would do.[37] The subsequent evidence suggests that both Eisenhower and Khrushchev wanted to reach agreements on Berlin and disarmament, though Khrushchev seems to have been becoming increasingly sceptical about whether this was actually possible.[38]

Luck, however, was against Macmillan. On 1 May, Soviet air defences had finally succeeded in shooting down an American U2 reconnaissance plane, deep over Soviet territory. The high level U2 flights were an Anglo-American project (about which de Gaulle was only briefed on the eve of the Paris conference), which provided the two countries with a vital intelligence sources on the state of the Soviet missile programme. With the Summit approaching, Macmillan, always sensitive to the way in which the military tail might wag the political dog, had ordered the cancellation of the British flights. The Americans were planning to do the same, but Eisenhower had been assured that the U2 was out of the range of Soviet air defences, and reluctantly agreed to authorise an additional, and in the event, fateful mission.[39]

Khrushchev's initial response was to play hide and seek with the Americans. He would not report immediately that the U2 had been shot down, but wait until the Americans had concocted a story and only then expose them in order to pay them back for the years of humiliation during which the U2s had infringed Soviet airspace.[40] The Americans duly fell into the trap. Against the advice which Macmillan had discreetly passed to Washington through Robert Murphy, Eisenhower admitted personal responsibility for the affair.[41] This placed Khrushchev in a serious dilemma. While he continued to want détente, he felt that Soviet prestige was on the line.[42] How could Moscow expect newly emerging countries in the colonial world 'to count on us to give them a helping hand if we allowed ourselves to be spat upon without so much as a murmur of protest?' And the trust he had developed in Eisenhower after his American visit had been destroyed. Khrushchev had already been making pessimistic noises during discussions with the French ambassador in Moscow on 4 May. By the time he arrived in Paris, the Soviet leader had decided to abort the Summit.[43]

The prospects of confronting a very angry Khrushchev had not eased the strains within the Western camp.[44] At an unproductive tripartite session with Eisenhower on 15 May, there were some pointed exchanges between Macmillan and the General. When de Gaulle declared that if the West lost Berlin it would have lost a great deal morally and politically, Macmillan responded that while Western morale would be harmed, it would be still worse to *say* we would defend Berlin, and then find that we could not do so. At another point de Gaulle turned to the British Prime Minister and according to the American record asked, 'How far will you go on Berlin and how far will you not go?' but got no reply.[45] After dining quietly at the embassy, the Prime Minister went to bed 'with rather a heavy heart but not without hope.'[46]

The next day, 16 May, was to prove one of the most agonising and exhausting Macmillan had ever been through, except perhaps, as he later revealingly wrote, in battle.[47] The preliminary morning session was tense and angry. Macmillan describes Khrushchev trying to 'pulverise Ike (as Micawber did Heep) by a mixture of abuse, vitriolic and offensive, and legal argument.' He wanted not only a public apology, but an assurance that there would be no such U2 flights in the future and that those responsible would be punished. The Summit must be postponed for six to eight months, by which time Eisenhower would have left office; an invitation for the President to visit Russia was cancelled. Eisenhower barely managed to contain his anger. Macmillan argued the need for the participants to give themselves time for reflection. In his *Memoirs of Hope* de Gaulle unsympathetically describes the British Prime Minister as exuding 'anxiety and distress'.[48] The General sought unsuccessfully to calm the proceedings. But in pointing out the inconsistencies of Khrushchev's position by noting that France was now being constantly orbited by a Soviet satellite, he only succeeded in rubbing salt into Khrushchev's wounds. The American had previously announced their intention to launch their own reconnaissance satellites, which Khrushchev knew he had no means of preventing.[49] As

Eisenhower walked out at the end of a session in which he had been humiliated, de Gaulle touched him on the shoulder, saying, 'Whatever happens, we are with you.'[50]

Although it was clear to the General that a rupture was inevitable, Macmillan would not, and could not, give up.[51] He tried, unsuccessfully and not very tactfully, to get Eisenhower to make some statement which would have got Khrushchev off the hook. (The President, he said many years later, 'wasn't well, he was getting old and he was surrounded by people giving separate advice.') Then, and against the advice of Selwyn Lloyd, he held a private meeting with Khrushchev, which lasted two and a half hours. But the Prime Minister's emotional appeal to the Soviet leader not to break up the Summit - 'the peace of the world and the future of mankind were in Mr. Khrushchev's hands' - made little impression. The Soviet leader was 'polite, but quite immovable'.[52]

On the morning of the 17th de Gaulle sent out invitations for the Summit to begin its formal work later in the day. When the Russians failed to turn up for the opening session, Eisenhower and de Gaulle wanted to issue a statement declaring the conference over; Macmillan pleaded for one more effort to save the Summit. Eisenhower was initially disposed to support the Prime Minister, but de Gaulle, speaking in an icy and contemptuous tone, killed this initiative. Towards the end of the session, at which he did at last manage to persuade his colleagues to agree to wait until the next day before taking a final decision, Macmillan spoke of 'the most tragic day' of his life. If Khrushchev did not change his mind, public opinion in Britain should be prepared for a 'grave situation'.[53]

Khrushchev paid a farewell visit to de Gaulle and Macmillan. The General made a firm defence of Eisenhower, reminding Khrushchev of the American president's wartime role. 'He deserves respect not only because of the past, but also because of the present.' And while making no reference to the possibility of another Summit, he did hint back to his April earlier discussions with the Soviet leader, when he expressed his belief that it would not in future be impossible to find a common way for cooperation in Europe.[54]

Macmillan told Khrushchev that he hoped it would be possible to press forward in a few months 'when the dust had settled'. In his Memoirs, the Soviet leader claimed that he could tell that the Prime Minister 'supported our position'. More striking, Khrushchev quotes Macmillan as saying that England was

> 'no longer able to take an independent stand on issues of international politics. It used to be that Great Britain was the ruler of the seas and could determine policy towards Europe and the whole the world. But that era has passed. Now the two mightiest states in the world are the United States and yourselves, the Soviet Union. Therefore many things depend on you now.' [55]

While these words do not appear in the British record, they are certainly consistent with the Prime Minister's mood. They are also consistent with the comment made many years later by de Zulueta, who was present at the encounter, that Paris was the moment when Macmillan 'suddenly realised that Britain counted for nothing; he couldn't move Ike to make a gesture towards Khrushchev, and de Gaulle was simply not interested. I think this represented a real watershed in his life.' The bottles of rare claret which Gladwyn Jebb had bought to celebrate an agreement remained undrunk.[56]

* * *

The Summit had started as Macmillan's story, but it was the much more sceptical de Gaulle who had come out of the affair with his reputation enhanced. Eisenhower's subsequent letters to his two allies are telling. 'You did everything that you possibly could to bring about a degree of civilised behaviour in the arrogant and intransigent man from Moscow,' he told Macmillan, while saluting de Gaulle for 'the staunch determination that you and your countrymen have shown'.[57] De Gaulle was clearly pleased with himself. In his *Memoirs of Hope* he writes of 'a chorus of praise and thanks addressed to me by all the participants', and in a broadcast two weeks later he spoke of the Summit demonstrating how much international influence French determination could exercise.[58] If the style, notably the cool and courteous way in which he had chaired the Summit, was very much the man, the fact was also that the General had invested much less than any of the other three in the Summit process. De Gaulle's primary skill, however, had been in the way he had exploited the whole Berlin crisis to France's diplomatic advantage without seriously straining his relations with his allies. Though by no means inflexible, he had pursued a policy of firmness, albeit of course one based on American rather than French power. As during the Second World War, the General had again shown a remarkable capacity to make the best of a weak hand.

Macmillan emerged as the main loser from the debacle. This was not primarily because of the impression he had made at Paris, where the Prime Minister had clearly been in a highly emotional state which worried the American delegation, and which at least one British diplomat had incorrectly ascribed to alcohol. Macmillan himself later said he had a sensation like a blow to the chest and thought that he might have had either a heart attack or a stroke. De Gaulle privately referred to a 'lamentable performance of lachrymose munichism', and there is some suggestion, which Eisenhower was subsequently anxious to deny, that the President was disappointed at the lack of the Prime Minister's support.[59]

The real problem was more fundamental. Summit diplomacy, which epitomised the personal diplomacy by which Macmillan set so much store and the means by which he sought to keep Britain at the 'top table' with the superpowers, had reached the end of the road. In a letter to Commonwealth Prime Ministers immediately after the Summit's collapse, the Prime Minister characteristically refused 'to abandon hope that progress may yet be made and if there is any chance of a movement I shall try to seize it.'[60] But there was no prospect of this during Eisenhower's remaining few months in office, and while Macmillan occasionally returned to the idea in later years, Kennedy was much less interested in Summit diplomacy, and did not want Macmillan acting as an intermediary. Kennedy's only meeting with Khrushchev in Vienna in 1961 was kept as a strictly bilateral affair.[61] The Paris failure was a personal blow which the Prime Minister felt much more acutely than de Gaulle's FTA veto. To a number of observers, including Chauvel as well as de Zulueta, the 'Summit manqué', as the French sometimes called it, marked the watershed in his premiership. Until then the Prime Minister had played his hand with authority, imagination and 'not without audacity'. Thereafter, Chauvel notes, he appeared hesitant, and more uncertain of his way.[62]

Macmillan had been unlucky. Without the U2, the Paris meeting might perhaps have started a process of regular high-level East-West contacts, which while unlikely to have resulted in early détente, might have made it easier to prevent the miscalculations which two years later resulted in the Cuban missile crisis. That said, the continued Western disagreements over Berlin on the eve of the meeting had not boded well for the conference, while the whole U2 incident underscored the depth of mutual East-West distrust and incomprehension which made the Prime Minister's pursuit of the Summit so ambitious an undertaking. Macmillan had tried too hard. Like the other main Western protagonists in this more complex of crises, Macmillan saw only part of the picture. Perceptive of dangers which de Gaulle oversimplified or ignored, he had been reluctant to recognise the extent to which his diplomacy undermined Western unity, and seemed to play into Khrushchev's hands.[63] While the Prime Minister saw his policy as one of being 'firm but flexible', the French had some reason for fearing that the flexibility was often in danger of obscuring the firmness.[64] The impression he sometimes gave of seeking to achieve, and later save, a Summit at any price do not suggest a diplomat of the first rank.

The Summit demonstrates a final point: for most of 1959, France was still not regarded by the British as an equal. The British attitude towards the French had been a peculiar blend of fascination, at least as far as Macmillan's view of the General was concerned, condescension and irritation. If part of the latter was understandable - de Gaulle's position had been opportunistic and in the early stages at least obstructive, the lesson was also clear. British policy would have to take de Gaulle into greater consideration in future, even if it was not prepared to pay Adenauer the same compliment. In a revealing comment to the Queen following the December 'Western Summit', Macmillan noted how the General had 'treated Adenauer almost as a satellite, and the Germans were very quiet, even deflated. This made me feel that, in the present state of Europe, if we are to reach agreements helpful to this country, so long as de Gaulle remains in power, the French are the key.'[65]

PART FOUR:

'NE PLEUREZ PAS, MILORD',
1960-63

Chapter 13

Grand Designs

De Gaulle wasted little time in following up the advantage he had gained in Paris. The tensions generated by the collapse of the Summit - there was a real fear that Khrushchev would now renew the Berlin crisis - and the uncertainty over American policy in the remaining last few months of the Eisenhower Administration provided both impetus and opportunity for the General to launch the major European initiative, which would be central to his foreign policy over the next few years.[1] He had already spoken of the need for the countries of Europe to unite their policies in the face of Soviet power in 1946. In the early 1950s he had, like Macmillan, put forward the idea of a European confederation. There had been a reference to a recurrent and 'organic' council of heads of government seeking common policies in the political, economic, cultural and military fields.[2] Within weeks of his return to power in 1958, de Gaulle was dropping hints of his political ambitions for Europe, and to some obvious British concern, the Six had since January 1960 begun to consult on foreign policy.[3]

In his French television broadcast after the collapse of the Summit, the General spoke of the creation of a West European union, which could 'one day' create a European entente between the Atlantic and the Urals. Such a Europe would again become 'le foyer capital de la civilisation', hastening the development of Africa, Asia and Latin America, and although he did not name the country, even influencing China. 'Le but est grand,' the General declared. 'The goal is great...the task is hard. But among the disturbances of the world, see, Frenchmen and Frenchwomen, how weighty can be the will of France once more.'[4] More details were spelled out when Adenauer visited Rambouillet in July 1960. There would be regular meetings of Heads of Government, a small permanent secretariat and a European assembly, although with a purely consultative role. Ratification by referendum was designed to underline popular support. Cooperation would be focused on education and culture, finance, defence and foreign policy, where the aim was the establishment of common positions which could extend to global issues and international organisations.[5]

The motives behind the rhetoric are not difficult to discern. In January 1959 de Gaulle had, as already noted, spoken at the Conseil de Défense having two games to play, the one with the other two Western world Powers, the other with 'les petits puissances'. Each would reinforce the other, and France as the head at the French-African Community, the group of former West African colonies to whom de Gaulle had just granted independence, would be at the point of intersection between the European and Atlantic groupings.[6]

To students of British foreign policy, this may hint at a French version of Churchill's three Circles - Britain at the intersecting point between the Commonwealth, the English-speaking world and Europe.[7] But while Churchill was unashamedly pro-American, de Gaulle was becoming increasingly preoccupied with the need for a European counterweight to the two 'mastodons', the great superpowers between whom hr feared that France and Europe risked being crushed. Without Europe, he told the Dutch Foreign Minister, Josef Luns, 'nothing would remain but the two superpowers confronting one another and the prospect of a general cataclysm.' De Gaulle looked forward to a Europe which would surpass the United States economically. The friend of the United States, while also open to the Soviet Union, this Europe could become an arbiter on the international scene. A united western Europe, as he had already suggested to Macmillan, might hasten détente, and even, an idea rarely considered at this point of the Cold War, hasten the dissolution of the Soviet bloc.[8]

There was of course another critical strand to de Gaulle's thinking, which comes out in a private remark recorded by his Information Minister, Alain Peyrefitte. 'The Six together could do as well as either of the superpowers. And if France can manage to be the first of the Six, which is within our grasp, she could act like an Archimedes screw. She could lead the others. Europe is the means by which France can become what she has not been since Waterloo – the first country in the world.' Macmillan had a point when, in one of his moments of frustration with the General, he complained that de Gaulle spoke of Europe, but meant France.[9]

How much of this remarkably ambitious programme the seventy year old de Gaulle actually expected to achieve, certainly within his own lifetime, must be open to question. 'The realist in de Gaulle,' writes John Newhouse, 'saw as clearly as anyone that Europe's organisation would emerge only slowly, painfully and in stages. But the romantic in him made claims for France for which the realist could entertain no hope.' What was clear from the outset was that none of his EEC partners was happy with the idea. They did not share his ambitions for Europe, and were less concerned at the prospect that it would be permanently eclipsed. There was worry, particularly in Germany, about the dangers of weakening the American security guarantee to Europe, while small states, notably the Dutch and Belgians, suspected France's motives and feared that the union would be dominated by the French and Germans. Hence their concern to ensure British involvement.[10]

De Gaulle did not rule out this latter idea over the long-term, but he made little attempt to disguise his lack of enthusiasm. 'England must become European,' he told the Luxembourg Prime Minister in September 1960,

> 'but we cannot force her to do so. If we make Europe, British coop-
> eration is of the first importance. But we must recognise that Great
> Britain will not come to us. The English distrust Europe. They tend
> to exaggerate the importance of the Commonwealth. Moreover they
> believe that it is good policy to cling to the Americans. We too must
> not separate ourselves from the Americans, but we must try to have
> our own independent existence. We must take the English as they
> are. If we make Europe successfully, it is possible that their views
> will alter. The English are the English; that is not our fault.'[11]

A note written in the Quasi d'Orsay, spelled out more bluntly the risks of British participation without its relationship with the EEC having been settled. The British might emerge as arbiters, undermining the cohesion of the new grouping, and promoting their old idea of a free trade area.[12]

* * *

Seriously upset by the Paris debacle, and much less sure now of his own future foreign policy directions than the General, Macmillan took time to respond to the collapse of his Summit strategy. It was only over the Christmas holiday that, led by 'that fatal itch for composition which is the outcome of a classical education' as he later elegantly put it in his Memoirs, the Prime Minister sought to devise a strategy to tackle the complex set of interrelated and highly intractable problems facing Britain and the West in the 1960s.[13] The immediate spur was the changing of the guard in Washington. In a letter to Eisenhower immediately after the presidential election in November, Macmillan had written that while he would seek to keep Britain and America on the same course, 'I cannot of course ever hope to have anything to replace the sort of relations that we have had.' The new President, John F. Kennedy, was some twenty years younger than Macmillan. Unable to draw on the shared links of wartime memory and friendship which he had successfully utilised in his cultivation of Eisenhower, Macmillan looked to appeal to the new man through ideas. It was partly to this end, partly to clear his own mind, that he now put pen to paper.[14]

The result was a wide-ranging document which inaugurated the second, and more defensive foreign policy phase of Macmillan's premiership. Known within Macmillan's private office as the 'Grand Design', it offered a very different vision of the future from the one which de Gaulle had just been propounding. International rather than European in focus, it focused on the Cold War, which the Prime Minister saw as now entering a new phase in which economic and political cooperation would be as important as the military side of the Western alliance. But where de Gaulle's European strategy looked to an optimistic French future, 'the Grand Design' was premised on that sense of growing British weakness which the Prime Minister had discerned when the Summit had collapsed. With all her experience, Britain had neither the economic nor the military power to take the leading role. The country was:

'harassed with countless problems - the narrow knife-edge on which our own economy is balanced; the difficult task of changing an Empire into a Commonwealth...the uncertainty about our relations (with) the new economic, and perhaps political, state which is being created by the Six countries of continental Western Europe; and the uncertainty of American policies towards us - treated now as just another country, now as an ally in a special and unique category.'[15]

There is a third and crucial divergence between Macmillan and de Gaulle's ideas in late 1960. While Britain had no immediate place in de Gaulle's thinking, the General was at last becoming central to Macmillan's preoccupations. This latter point comes out clearly in the summary of 'The Grand Design' made by Philip de Zulueta.:

'1. The Communists have been doing too well for the last eight years.
2. At the same time the free world is more divided than it was - this is mainly because of the revival of Europe.
3. The free world is in danger of dividing itself in the same sort of way that Europe did in the 19th century.
4. To stop this we must have unity in diversity: -
(a) Get the banking system of the free world right.
(b) Get the trading system right - this means first with the Six and the Seven and then move to Atlantic Union.
(c) This makes us strong enough to win the uncommitted countries by trade and aid.
5. In all this the French, as represented by de Gaulle, are the key and Britain is the lynch-pin. De Gaulle's Europe is not strong enough to be a third force without Britain. He wants us in, but only after we have 'chosen Europe' instead of the United States. We must somehow persuade him that this idea of choice is false and out of date. Unity is the only way.
6. Until we find a way to convince him, we must never give him bits of what he wants. It must be the whole Grand Design or nothing.'[16]

By emphasising the need for greater Western unity, Macmillan hoped to kill two birds with one stone. A genuine necessity in the face of a growing

Communist threat, it also promised a means of pressurising de Gaulle into resolving the economic problems between Britain and the EEC without having to make the choice between Europe and America. A year earlier, in the wake of the 'Western Summit' in Paris, the Prime Minister had confided to Selwyn Lloyd, that he had already for some time 'been puzzled as to how to use my old friendship with de Gaulle and how to restore our old relations with the French *without disloyalty to the Americans*. It is this,' he continued, 'which has made me so uncertain in recent weeks, and even months.' (emphasis added) The theme of drift was one to which he returned over the next twelve months.[17]

The immediate cause of Macmillan's troubles was the fact de Gaulle had done little to resolve the problems left by the collapse of the FTA talks, indeed the General made no secret of the fact that he thought that the Prime Minister was exaggerating the difficulties. This was not entirely fair. The EEC was an important market, accounting for some fourteen per cent of British exports. Also worrying was the prospect of increased global competition, as the EEC improved its competitiveness in world markets. That said, de Gaulle did have a point in so far that Macmillan continued to be highly emotive about Europe.[18] When in September 1960 a Franco-German row appeared to loom in NATO, and the British ambassador to the alliance, Sir Frank Roberts, sought to steer a middle course, the Prime Minister forcibly demurred. Only when the Six fell out, he argued, was there any chance for the seven EFTA countries to come into their own. 'I do not think Sir Frank Roberts realises that we are a country to whom nothing at this moment matters except our export trade. Without our revival our strength disappears. The Six have entered into a plot to injure us and yet are still trying to hold us to defend them at immense expense to ourselves.' 'Exclusion from the strongest economic group in the civilised world, *must* injure us,' he noted in the 'Grand Design'. (emphasis in original)[19]

Underlying these anxieties was of course the Prime Minister's inability to fashion a new European policy. EEC membership was unacceptable to the Cabinet, while Macmillan himself, although happy to exploit difficulties among the Six, had ruled out the possibility of deliberately disrupting the Community. To do so would, he believed, unite against Britain all the Europeans 'who have felt humiliated during the past decade by the weakness of Europe', would upset the United States, and would play into the hands of the Russians. The Prime Minister's only real alternative therefore was a settlement with France, which some senior Foreign Office officials doubted was possible. The trouble, as Gladwyn Jebb saw it, was that whereas Gaulle could give Britain something it wanted, the British could give the General precious little that *he* wanted.[20]

The Prime Minister disagreed. He had learned the lesson of the FTA failure that Britain would have to pay a price for an agreement, and believed that French concern over Germany might make the General more amenable to a deal. Moreover, unlike Jebb, Macmillan believed that Britain might in fact have something important to offer the General. Elevating France 'out of the ruck of European countries, including Germany', and putting her in a 'different category', in Macmillan's view were the main reasons why the General was pressing for tripartite consultations with Britain and the United States. If Britain could use its influence and good offices with the United States to facilitate this aim, then might it not be in a position to demand a price in Europe from the General?[21]

Macmillan had first become seriously interested in this idea at the 'Western Summit', where Eisenhower had suggested that the three countries might establish tripartite machinery on a 'clandestine basis' to discuss questions of common interest. The Prime Minister had been surprised and excited. In his account to the Queen, he reported that de Gaulle believed that the President's initiative had been the result of British pressure, 'and was correspondingly grateful.' Thanks to Eisenhower Britain's chances 'of getting closer to the French and the French government has been considerably enhanced.' 'I must,' he wrote to the Chancellor of the Exchequer, Derick Heathcoat Amory, play this to the full to get an economic quid pro quo.'[22]

It had not worked out. As Macmillan feared, the Americans had subsequently rowed back on Eisenhower's initiative, and while various ideas continued to be floated, there was no sign of the US conceding the strategic consultations on the use of nuclear weapons which the General wanted. The Foreign Office, fiercely pro-American and still much less exercised than Macmillan over the European problem, was worried that tripartism must inevitably mean a diminution in Britain's privileged position in Washington.[23] No less troubling, and never clearly answered, were the questions raised by the Cabinet Secretary, Sir Norman Brook. If Britain admitted France into tripartite consultation with the Americans, would she not have to rely on the argument that France was speaking for Europe? If so, on what basis would Britain go into Europe? 'Should we be willing to place ourselves, even in Europe, under the leadership of France?'[24] Undeterred, Macmillan who had been pressing the tripartite card during 1960, regarded it as an essential element of the 'Grand Design'.

The Prime Minister had another, and even more controversial string to his bow - the nuclear cooperation which the General had mistakenly believed in June 1958 to be Macmillan's quid pro quo for an FTA bargain. Well aware that it would be impossible to get anything from de Gaulle by orthodox means, Macmillan had gradually come to believe that nuclear aid represented the most promising card in his hand.[25] The case for a nuclear deal had been argued in the strict privacy of No.10 by Frederick Bishop, Macmillan's former private secretary who was now the deputy Cabinet secretary. He had first raised the matter in late 1959, following it up seven months later in a paper entitled 'Joanna Southcott's box', named after a nineteenth century religious eccentric who claimed to be a prophetess. Macmillan had been interested. 'I can see what they (the French) want,' he minuted, 'and I have always thought it worth doing. Support them in their general attitude towards NATO, give them the Bomb, perhaps some V-bombers, and generally support the idea of a confederation of Europe instead of a Federation.'[26]

By then, however, Macmillan and de Gaulle had already broached the nuclear issue. March 1960 when the two men met at Rambouillet, was the month in which Britain cancelled its Blue Streak missile, which had been intended to succeed the current generation of V bombers. It was also the month, immediately following the first French nuclear test, when the French government was deciding to go ahead with its own missile programme.[27] Nuclear matters were thus very much on both men's minds. Macmillan, while careful to emphasise the limits imposed by the McMahon Act, hinted at the possibility of cooperation, particularly in the area of missiles, where Britain was not tied by any agreement with the Americans. 'As delicately as possible,' he wrote in his diary, 'I put the idea in his mind that we might be able to help him either with American agreement or connivance.' De Gaulle was interested, requesting nuclear assistance 'even with means of delivery only'. But he was also sceptical about what the British could provide, and there is no suggestion here that the General was offering any kind of quid pro quo.[28] When the British and French Defence Ministers, Harold Watkinson and Pierre Messmer met in April, the latter noted that for the first time there had been an exchange of views 'confident and generally open'. The British, he continued, might not rejoice at French nuclear progress, but their traditional pragmatism led them to draw the consequences.[29]

The possibility of a nuclear deal featured prominently in the 'Grand Design'. In Macmillan's view France's exclusion from the nuclear club was the measure of France's inferior status. It was 'particularly galling' for de Gaulle that *Britain* should have an independent nuclear capacity; the United States was accepted as being in a different category. Could Britain therefore provide France with British techniques, bombs 'or any share of our nuclear power' on terms which were prudent and publicly defensible, and which the US would agree to? At first sight, the Prime Minister acknowledged, the prospect seemed hopeless. But, he continued, since this seemed the one thing which might persuade de Gaulle to accept a European settlement, it was worth serious consideration. The problem was the McMahon Act, which prevented the sharing of nuclear information or technology with countries other than Britain. In Macmillan's view, however, the Act was widely drawn and permissive.

> 'My experience of the Americans - in private as in public affairs - is this. If they *want* to do a thing, they find a way round. If they *don't*, the laws offer an insuperable obstacle.
>
> It might, however, be easier both for America and for us to avoid a straight deal with the French by which we just 'gave' them the nuclear weapon.
> Could we make it more respectable (and more acceptable to general public opinion) in some other way?
>
> Could Britain and France form a nuclear force - sharing the cost, production etc.. - as European trustees for NATO?

> Could we devise a formula for joint political control by us both? Failing that, could we at least have some arrangement for consultation about its use, on the analogy of President Eisenhower's private understanding with me?...
>
> Could we thus give France the satisfaction of a nominally 'independent nuclear force' while subjecting them to at least the same kind of moral restraints which the Americans have accepted in their understanding with us?' (emphasis in original)[30]

In seeking to answer this formidable set of obstacles, the Prime Minister faced two immediate problems. The first came in the form of opposition in Whitehall. Official concern was reflected in the withholding from the Prime Minister of a memorandum from Sir Pierson Dixon, who had now succeeded Gladwyn Jebb in Paris. For Dixon was also making the case for a grand bargain, albeit with the significant caveat 'that we did not too obviously appear to be trying to get the best of both worlds, European and American'. And when officials and ministers met to discuss strategy at Chequers in January 1961, Macmillan was warned against offering concessions to France which would weaken the Western alliance and cause difficulties with the United States.[31]

The second problem was of a more tactical nature. The Prime Minister wasn't to meet Kennedy until April. The discussions with de Gaulle, due at the end of the January, would therefore have to be conducted with the maximum of discretion. For while the Prime Minister was anxious to sound the General out regarding the 'Grand Design', he certainly did not want the new American President to get the impression that he had tried to fix things up in advance with de Gaulle. The French, or so the British feared, had a strong interest in doing precisely that.[32]

Returning to Rambouillet after less than a year, the Prime Minister found that he once again had the same rather romantic suite in the François Premier tower. This time, however, the creature comforts of the imposing French château were rather better than they had been in March 1960. The rooms were heated, the bathwater was hot, and there were sufficient bedclothes.[33] When the talks opened, the Prime Minister duly made his pitch around the theme of Europe to be united politically and economically, but France and Britain, the only two European states with nuclear weapons and world interests, to be so recognised by the United States. Close relations between the United States and Britain, declared the man who had gone out of his way since 1957 to revive the 'special relationship', 'were perhaps no longer enough in these changed circumstances. It would be desirable to bring France into the picture.' France with its Community in Africa on the one hand, Britain with its Commonwealth on the other, 'ought to come to an understanding as European and world Powers and speak to the New World as the true representatives of the Old.' The Prime Minster raised the possibility of 'some arrangement' whereby Britain, France and the US might become 'trustees' for nuclear weapons, (a vague, and in one

British official's view an 'inevitably slightly hypocritical term'). It was possible, the Prime Minister went on to suggest, that a part of the French *Force de Frappe* need not be under NATO command, and there could be some system of target allocation with tripartite arrangement on consultation. This would probably not take a definitive juridical form but there would have to be agreement first with the US.[34]

The weakness of this approach was that it did not take account of de Gaulle's view of nuclear weapons as 'un gage d'indépendance', which must under all circumstances remain under French operational control. Indeed the General made no response to Macmillan's proposal. Nor was he much more encouraging to a second proposal put forward by the Prime Minister. Britain's economic difficulties with the Six, Macmillan suggested, might be solved by some form of association, and the acceptance of the common external tariff, 'subject to certain exceptions to allow for the import of Commonwealth raw materials and temperate foodstuffs.' Although reluctantly agreeing to expert discussions on the subject, the General advised his guest that Britain should 'take its time and move little by little'. At the same time de Gaulle was anxious to reassure Macmillan that Britain had nothing to fear from the discussions on European union. There could be 'no Europe without England. The political arrangements would only be a beginning and France would keep in the closest touch with the UK.' (Several years later Pierson Dixon noted that whenever de Gaulle said there was nothing for Britain to worry about, he usually meant the opposite.[35])

Despite the cool response to these two important proposals, the Prime Minister had been encouraged by Rambouillet, believing that de Gaulle had been genuinely attracted by his main themes. This was overoptimistic, for although it was certainly a friendly encounter, there had been no meeting of minds. The two men were pursuing different agendas. De Gaulle wanted Anglo-French cooperation, but *outside* Europe; and he wanted to woo the Prime Minister away from the Americans, rather than allow him to find a middle way between Europe and the United States. The General had sought to make the most of Macmillan's concerns about the change of Administration taking place in Washington. 'For some time at least,' he warned, 'it could be that solidarity would not be respected and the US would pursue a policy more American than Western. It is especially important that the entente between Britain and France be as intimate as possible.' Later he wondered if in future it might always be necessary for Britain 'to follow exactly in the wake of the Americans.'[36] Speaking shortly afterwards to Adenauer, de Gaulle remarked that Britain seemed to be moving closer to Europe because of Macmillan's concern about the new Administration in the United States. A day would come perhaps where it would be possible to do something in common. Personally the General did not think this would come soon, but if a proposal was made, he would be the first to rejoice.[37]

When Macmillan travelled to North America in April to promote the 'Grand Design', he argued what he at least saw as the General's case. France would not continue to accept what de Gaulle considered to be subordination to Anglo-Saxon leadership, or behave as a fully cooperative ally until it was treated as a world Power. 'The pride of General de Gaulle and of other determined men in Europe demanded that they should have some further share of control over the nuclear strength of the West. They would not tolerate a position in which their future was determined by others. They were determined to put Europe back on the map.'[38]

What gave added importance to this presentation was an unexpected development in British European policy. 'The Grand Design' had made no mention of Britain joining the EEC. Now, Macmillan told the Canadian cabinet that the British government was 'contemplating the possibility of some form of close association with the Six.' George Ball records Macmillan in more forthright mood. 'We're going to join Europe,' he told the American Under-Secretary of State. 'We'll need your help, since we'll have trouble with de Gaulle, but we're going to do it.'[39]

Chapter 14

The $64,000 Question

W hen the possibility of British membership of the EEC had first been seriously raised in Whitehall in the Spring of 1960, Frederick Bishop had warned the Prime Minister of 'a reappraisal which might well be very agonising indeed'.[1] Joining Europe represented much more than a reversal of the policy first adopted by the Attlee government in 1950 in response to the proposed creation of the ECSC, and reaffirmed by the Conservatives in 1955 following the Messina initiative. It was a break with one of the central traditions of British foreign policy, the long-standing determination to keep aloof from Continental affairs, intervening only to maintain the balance of power. Even when the formal commitment to maintain the troops in Germany had been made in 1954, Eden had declared 'ours is above all an island story. We are still an island people in thought and tradition, whatever the modern facts of weapons and strategy may compel.'[2] 'Although I agree that the political arguments in favour of joining the Community are strong,' Sir Frederick Hoyer-Millar, the Permanent Under Secretary at the Foreign Office, minuted in the summer of 1960, 'all my instincts are against doing so. Although one's mind thinks one ought to join, one's heart is against it.'[3]

The Cabinet had duly balked at the decision in July 1960, but by the following Spring it was firmly on the agenda.[4] Macmillan couched the argument for membership within the larger framework of his 'Grand Design', in particular the need encourage Western unity in order to win the Cold War. Britain had an opportunity to take the initiative and help bind Europe within the wider Atlantic community; it was the 'bridge' between Europe and America. And once in 'Europe', with skill and good management Britain could, as Macmillan once put in a letter to the Queen 'dominate or at any rate lead.'[5] But his main motive was more defensive, harking back to arguments he had put forward in the early 1950s. If Britain stayed out as the Six continued to consolidate, it would enter into a period of relative decline in which industry, agriculture, and international influence, not least with Washington, would suffer.[6]

All this, however, begged two critical questions. Would it be possible to negotiate entry on acceptable terms for British agriculture and the Commonwealth? Second, and of course closely related, how would France react to a British application to join a club which the French were finding increasingly profitable and politically useful? The auguries were not encouraging, although a certain note of ambiguity appeared to have entered the picture in 1960. Pressed by Macmillan for a resolution of the trade problem during his State Visit to London in April, de Gaulle had asked whether Britain could not contemplate joining the EEC, and received the probably not unexpected answer that unfortunately this was not possible.[7] In June he had told Lord Mountbatten that he was anxious that Britain should be in the EEC. In September the French ambassador in London quoted de Gaulle as saying that if Britain wanted to join the EEC, he thought that this could be arranged, but assumed Britain would prefer association. Yet only a few weeks later the General told the new British ambassador in Paris, Sir Pierson Dixon, that it was 'obvious' that Britain, which was an island with global connections, could not come into Europe. Matters had gone so far with the Six that it was difficult to see how any modification could be made which would enable Britain to join.[8]

The first meeting in February 1961 between British and French officials, which de Gaulle had sanctioned at Rambouillet, produced a delphic exchange during a car journey, between the head of the Treasury, Sir Frank Lee, and Olivier Wormser. Wormser, who was Director of Economic Affairs at the Quai d'Orsay, was a key figure in the Anglo-French European duel. He had been in Britain during part of the war, when he had had a 'decorous affair' with the young Iris Murdoch, and many years later had led the French delegation during the FTA talks. Described by one British official as a polymath, he was said to know almost instinctively what de Gaulle and Couve de Murville would allow him to do. His papers show him to have been as anything but well disposed to the British bid.[9] Replying to Wormser's comment that it would make a great difference if Britain would say she would join the Six, Lee asked whether this meant that Britain would be able to join and get its essential conditions for the Commonwealth and agriculture. Wormser 'smiled and said, "That of course is the $64,000 question" - by which time they had arrived at their destination.' It was, Lee concluded, 'an agreeable conversation, but I felt I had rarely seen a more consummate display of playing all the bowling with a deadbat.'[10] It was the beginning of what may be called the French mystification of the British, a process which was to continue until almost the end of the EEC negotiations. Despite good diplomatic contacts, as well as having managed to break the French diplomatic ciphers and thus being able to read cable traffic between the French embassy in London and the Quai d'Orsay, British ministers and officials were constantly left having to guess French intentions.[11]

The signs continued to be contradictory. In London Chauvel told Heath that he 'did not want it to be thought that France was hostile to Britain joining the Six; she merely thought it was not possible', while in Paris Pierre Maillard, diplomatic counsellor at the Elysée, told a British diplomat that de Gaulle did not believe that 'at this moment' Britain could come into Europe 'without damage to herself and consequently Europe'. He cited the Commonwealth rather than the 'special relationship'.[12] By early April a rather more encouraging tone seemed to be coming from the French capital. During the second round of expert discussions, Wormser declared that having checked in 'every quarter', he could say that reaction in Paris to a British bid would be one of 'unreserved welcome'. A few days later Couve de Murville told the French Foreign Affairs Committee that 'we have always said that there was no other solution for Europe than the adhesion of Great Britain to the Common Market.' Whether such remarks could be taken at face value, was another question. As a Dutch diplomat remarked to his British colleague, 'it was difficult to quite know where one was with the French', a remark borne out by the fact that a few weeks later Couve told Adenauer that Britain would never agree to join the EEC as a full member, and that France might have to break off any new negotiations as it had in 1958.[13]

French equivocation at this stage was not simply a matter of tactics. Although certainly reluctant to reveal their hand while still unsure of British intentions, the French had been taken by surprise by the growing signs in early 1961 that Britain was now seriously contemplating EEC membership, and appear to have had decidedly mixed feelings about the prospect. British entry posed a major dilemma for French policy-makers. Keeping Britain out would not be easy, and on strategic grounds would not in the long term be desirable. Wormser told the Minister of Agriculture, Christopher Soames, that the French government was divided on the question, and that de Gaulle's attitude was schizophrenic, 'sometimes wanting us in, sometimes fearing that with our Anglo-Saxon habits we should prevent him getting what he wanted to get out of it.'[14]

This is less surprising than it may at first sight seem. The General had after all ambivalent feelings about Britain, for whom he had more respect than his other EEC partners, and whose hostility to the prevailing supranationalist ideas in the Community chimed well with his own.[15] Both during and after the war, de Gaulle had hoped that the contraction of British power would bring about a shift towards Europe. In the wake of the 1963 veto he privately attributed his early reservations about the EEC to concern that it would embroil France with Britain, without whom he could not conceive Europe.[16] Britain was critical to providing the military – in the first place nuclear capability, without which it would be impossible for Europe to play the international role de Gaulle dreamed of. According to Pierre Maillard, the General did not believe that the Six could play an effective role in world affairs unless Britain was 'associated with it'.[17]

153

The problem was - and this was a dilemma de Gaulle never seems to have resolved - that British membership would be very much at France's expense. French officials expected Britain to exercise great influence once in the EEC.[18] The Community of the Six had become a French sphere of influence. That would inevitably be undermined once the EEC was enlarged. In place of the Franco-German entente, the Quai d'Orsay warned, there would at best be Anglo-French rivalry. Germany would support the British position on many issues.[19] In de Gaulle's view Britain, along with its 'cortège' of satellites, the Danes, Norwegians and Irish, all of whom were also interested in joining, would reopen questions already resolved by the Six, but this time with a majority who would not want to construct Europe in the same spirit as the Six. 'Each one would cease to participate.' Europe with Britain, the General also feared, would speak English rather than French.[20]

De Gaulle's doubts about British membership were further strengthened by Britain's Atlanticism, and his longstanding awareness of its strong insular traditions. Back in Algiers in 1943, when talk had once turned to the possibility of some kind of post-war European grouping, de Gaulle had commented to Jean Monnet and Hervé Alphand that Britain would not join, pulled as it would be between Europe and the empire.[21] Nearly twenty years later he referred to the difficulty of knowing whether Britain would give priority to Europe or 'au grand large' - the Open Sea which led towards the Commonwealth, and above all the United States - as 'the eternal question'.[22]

Although the case against British entry had probably not been fully formulated in Paris in the spring of 1961, there was sufficient anxiety to ensure that the General himself said nothing after 1960 to encourage an application. Both Adenauer and Kennedy came away from meetings in late May and early June with a negative impression of the General's attitude to British membership. De Gaulle told the German Chancellor that he did not believe that Britain was ready to join the EEC, but if it did the British would have to make a choice between the Commonwealth and the Common Market. They could not have both.[23] He made much the same point to Kennedy, who came away with the impression that 'de Gaulle prefers the present situation in which he is the dominant figure'.[24]

A good deal of this got through to London. A memorandum written for the Prime Minister in March referred to recent reports, (sources unspecified), confirming the view that the French opposed UK membership, and noting how, 'all along the French have emphasised as being important those points on which they judged the UK was not prepared to negotiate at the time.'[25] Talking with American officials in early May, the British ambassador in Washington, Sir Harold Caccia, remarked that there was considerable doubt that France would have the UK on any terms.[26] That was certainly the message which some British diplomats, as well as the veteran of the FTA negotiations, Reginald Maudling, drew from a hard-line paper circulated by Wormser on 1 June in anticipation of the next round of Anglo-French talks. Wormser was quite deliberately setting out to dispel any British illusion that the French were prepared to make any changes at all to the workings of the Treaty of Rome.[27]

Macmillan too became more pessimistic over the spring and early summer. Speaking in Cabinet on 20 April, the Prime Minister was still hoping that de Gaulle might accept British membership of the EEC 'if he could be brought to see that the West as a whole could not prevail against the Communists unless its leading countries worked together towards a wider unity in the free world as a whole.'[28] A variant of the 'Grand Design' sent shortly afterwards to Kennedy included the incentive of nuclear aid for France in return for a French commitment to develop a nuclear capability, which was seen as a contribution to the Western deterrent rather than an independent force, and more by way of tripartism. There was also a new element in the form of a review of NATO command structures and of the distribution of senior commands. A covering letter made clear that Macmillan was anxious for Kennedy to sound out de Gaulle out about a British application during his forthcoming visit to Paris. What the British needed was an assurance that France would welcome British entry into the EEC, that it understood the British need for special arrangements for the Commonwealth and EFTA and would enter negotiations in good faith. 'We do not want needlessly to upset our friends and partners by making new declarations if in fact the French intend to reject any reasonable arrangement.'[29]

The Prime Minister was to find himself doubly frustrated. Kennedy had shown himself generally helpful during their talks in early April, and was anxious for Britain to join the EEC. But he had subsequently decided against any relaxation of American nuclear policy towards France, thereby denying Macmillan the nuclear carrot which had been a key element of the 'Grand Design', and incidentally, underscoring de Gaulle's points about the limits of British independence.[30] And although Jacqueline Kennedy had taken Paris by storm when the couple visited the French capital in early June, her husband had proved no more able to move the General than anybody else. Macmillan's bitterness comes through in his diary. De Gaulle, he noted, on 11 June, had been

' very avuncular, very gracious, very oracular and very unyielding. He would take all the plums - Tripartism, new arrangements in NATO, and help with the technique of missiles and bombs (other than the actual nuclear content) with cavalier profligacy. But when it comes to *giving* anything in return - e.g. Britain's desire to enter Europe on reasonable terms, having regard to Commonwealth and British agricultural structures - then the General was in his most austere mood. So far as I can see (unless the General was just playing the hand *very* close to his chest) my great plan has failed - or, at least, failed up to now. But at least we have got a completely new American attitude to our efforts.'[31] (emphasis in original)

Two weeks later the Prime Minister recorded that the Europeans, especially de Gaulle, are 'hardening against us'.[32] More revealing is the diary entry for 22 July, shortly after the Cabinet had finally approved the EEC application, and the day after de Gaulle had told Dixon that British membership would 'take

155

some time', a phrase the General was to repeat frequently. 'I should judge', Macmillan recorded, 'that the chances are *against* an agreement, unless - on political grounds- de Gaulle changes his mind. For I feel he is still hostile and jealous.'[33] (emphasis in original.) Writing a week later to the Lord Privy Seal, Ted Heath, who was to lead the British delegation at the negotiations in Brussels, Macmillan argued that the outcome would depend on two points. First whether de Gaulle, whom the Prime Minister described as 'becoming more and more Napoleonic and self-centred, really wants us in or not', and whether even if the General wants to settle, 'we can work out terms which seem reasonably fair to all concerned.'[34]

Yet at no stage in the intensive debate about EEC membership, which took place in Whitehall in the spring and summer of 1961, were the implications of potential French opposition seriously addressed.[35] The Cabinet, which was now closely involved, showed little interest in Maudling's blunt warnings of the futility of tilting at the Gaullist windmill, focusing rather on the highly sensitive political problems which EEC membership raised. At issue was a potentially highly combustible mix of tradition, emotion and interests, especially agriculture, always well represented in Conservative Party ranks, not least by the Chancellor, R.A.Butler, who had represented the rural Saffron Walden constituency since 1929. But the question which overshadowed all others in cabinet discussion, was the Commonwealth.[36] Although its economic and political importance were in decline, sentiment and honour - the Commonwealth's contribution during the two world wars were still fresh in memories - demanded that the Commonwealth interests must be fully protected. Canada, Australia and New Zealand, which Macmillan himself referred to as 'an English farm in the Pacific', all depended heavily on access to the British market for temperate foodstuffs such as grain, lamb and dairy produce.[37]

Macmillan himself was under no illusions about how much was at stake. He believed the EEC had the potential to split the Conservative Party - he sometimes recalled Sir Robert Peel's fate over the Corn Laws in 1846. He believed too that public opinion was uncertain, and that the whole project could be overthrown by a last minute appeal to emotion.[38] But it was the Prime Minister's job to ensure that all aspects of the problem – foreign policy as well as domestic - were duly taken into account. He knew de Gaulle far better than any of his Cabinet colleagues, and had recent experience of the General's ways. At the end of April Macmillan had asked de Gaulle to postpone the fourth French nuclear test in the Sahara by a few days until after 1 May, to avoid it's coinciding with the Sierra Leonean independence celebrations. Having been very supportive of France in the face of opposition at the United Nations to the French nuclear testing programme, despite the damage this might do to Britain with new African Commonwealth countries such as Nigeria, the Prime Minister had good reason to ask a political favour. In characteristic fashion the General had ignored Macmillan's request; his reply on 2 May had simply expressed his pleasure that the Sierra Leonean celebrations had not been affected by the French explosion.[39]

Policy-making is usually a segmented business. What goes on in Africa does not necessarily make much impact on those dealing with Europe. And this was of itself a minor incident. Nevertheless to de Gaulle-watchers it was a useful reminder that the General was not a man who repaid favours. On the contrary, he remained capable of a brutality which might have caused the Prime Minister to question the assumption, never perhaps fully spelled out, that while he might be opposed to British membership of the EEC, he would be unlikely to translate such opposition into a veto.

The rationales behind this conveniently benign line of thinking were strikingly disparate. Sir Pierson Dixon did not think that the General would keep Britain out simply because he wanted to remain 'cock of the walk in Europe'.[40] Others believed, or hoped, that the official signals of discouragement from Paris might be tactically-inspired, designed to strengthen France's position in the tough negotiations which lay ahead. Even if this was not the case, the General's own position was by no means secure. In late April 1961 a military coup in Algiers threatened to spill over into France. De Gaulle declared a state of emergency, and broadcast in uniform to the nation, ending with the dramatic and almost desperate appeal, 'Françaises, Français, aidez-moi!' ('Frenchwomen, Frenchmen, help me!') A month later the British passed on intelligence to Paris of another coup attempt, this time involving the police in Metropolitan France.[41]

Two other factors should be taken into account to explain why French opposition was not taken more seriously at this critical stage. One was the disposition of the Prime Minister, who combined an increasingly pronounced penchant for wishful thinking with great persistence and a continued disposition to take risks. The second was the sense that the options were narrowing. By the middle of 1961 the dangers of failing to resolve Britain's EEC problem appeared to justify the risk of a failed negotiation which he had so far been anxious to avoid. The point was put with considerable frankness in a letter to the Australian Prime Minister, Sir Robert Menzies, at the beginning of July. Britain, Macmillan wrote, had been unable through informal discussions to get the French to give an indication of what would be acceptable to them without putting more cards on the table. Since therefore 'it is not possible to clarify the position in advance, we feel that the risk of a breakdown might have to be accepted.'[42]

And yet as the decision to apply for membership came closer, nobody at the heart of government knew how to tackle the General. On 7 June the Cabinet Secretary, Sir Norman Brook, had written to the Prime Minister to say that he believed that before a final Cabinet decision, it would be necessary to reach some understanding with de Gaulle about the object of the negotiations, which only Macmillan could do. 'This will have to be done,' Macmillan replied, 'but *how* I am not sure.'[43] (emphasis in original) Officials debated the pros and cons of an approach. EEC entry was not something which was in de Gaulle's gift, and it was not in British interests to make him feel that it was. But it was also argued that once a decision had been taken, there might be some advantage in consulting de Gaulle about the best method of approaching the Six. A sense of clutching at straws come from a note by de Zulueta a few days later, describing British support for NATO tripartism as 'the one card' left in Macmillan's hand, on which the Prime Minister minuted 'yes - indeed.'[44]

In the event, the General was only given three days' warning of the official announcement of the British application. Remarks made a few days earlier by the French ambassador to Heath, suggesting that the application would come as an unpleasant surprise in Paris, had raised concern in the Foreign Office. This timetable was considered to be consistent 'with the need for reasonable notice but late enough to prevent the French from raising serious last-minute objections.' A more personal message passed to Chauvel in London may have been intended to mitigate some of the inevitable effects.[45] But the lack of confidence is revealing. With the 'Grand Design' dead, Macmillan was entering a negotiation to which he knew that de Gaulle was at best unsympathetic, without a strategy for overcoming his opposition. Macmillan had now little to offer the General. It was a dangerous move: putting oneself in the General's hands rarely came out well.

Chapter 15

Not Persuading the General

The decision to make a formal application 'for negotiations with a view to joining the (European Economic) Community, if satisfactory arrangements could be made for the special needs of the United Kingdom, of the Commonwealth and of the European Free Trade Association', was announced by Macmillan in the House of Commons on 31 July 1961, just ahead of the parliamentary recess. It was an uninspired performance. The Prime Minister seemed tired, and the French embassy in London reported that he had read the declaration in a low and monotonous voice. They also noted that he had done his utmost to dispel the impression that his government was going to Canossa.[1] But however cautiously phrased and conditional, the importance of the announcement was clear to MPs. 'No issue which has come before this House in my lifetime,' declared the Labour MP, Jennie Lee, 'has been of greater importance.' The former Conservative minister, Sir Derek Walker-Smith, spoke of great issues which 'concern our constitutional practices, our national institutions and our future as a sovereign state.'[2]

Most official international reaction to the announcement was positive. The Italian Prime Minister, Amintore Fanfani, was reported by the British ambassador to Rome to have been 'really delighted'. His Luxembourg counterpart 'expressed his warmest approval of our decision', while the Dutch Foreign Minister, Joseph Luns, promised 'fullest support in all negotiations that lie ahead.'[3] Kennedy was also enthusiastic. The US Administration was keenly anxious for British membership, which it saw as essential to Europe's long-term stability. 'An enduring European edifice,' wrote George Ball, 'could never be built merely on a Franco-German rapprochement, yet an enduring structure was essential. Germany must be incorporated into a European framework to neutralise aberrant forces generated by the irridentist desire for reunification. So long as the United Kingdom remained outside the Common Market, it was like a giant lodestone exerting uneven degrees of attraction on individual member states of the Six, and even on individual factions within member states.'[4]

But there was also a less altruistic consideration. 'Politically,' as Macmillan noted after his April discussions in Washington, the Americans 'hoped that if we were in the Six we should be able to steer them, and influence them, whatever might be the political personalities.'[5]

These were hardly motives likely to appeal to de Gaulle, who showed himself distinctly vexed when informed of the application, repeating his earlier warning that 'it would take a long time for the many difficulties to be settled.'[6] As the Foreign Office had predicted, the General had been taken by surprise by the British application, which he saw not as a serious bid but rather as a wrecking move. Having failed to strangle the EEC at birth, the British, he wrongly believed, were seeking to paralyse it from within.[7]

De Gaulle, however, faced a problem. Once installed at the negotiating table, the British would be very difficult to dislodge.[8] At the same time it would scarcely be possible to prevent negotiations taking place. Quite apart from the fact that the French were on record as advocating British membership, outright hostility would create major difficulties with the other EEC countries at an extremely awkward moment for France. Negotiations on the Common Agricultural Policy, vital to French interests, were still in the balance, while talks on de Gaulle's no less important plans for political union were at a very delicate stage. The relationship between the EEC and Francophone African states was also due to be renegotiated. On the domestic front the centrist MRP, the Mouvement Républicain Populaire on which the government depended, tended to support British entry. There was nothing to be gained by early elections, which would be fought on an issue on which the MRP was more in step with public opinion than the government. And there was also the Algerian factor. Elections might disrupt talks between the French government and the Algerian FLN which were now under way.[9]

That said, it would not be difficult for the French to create trouble for Britain in the forthcoming entry negotiations. The British government was trying to square a circle. It needed a quick agreement because, as Macmillan had already told Jean Monnet in October 1961, the longer the negotiations dragged on, the more domestic opposition and pressure groups would grow in strength.[10] But it was also seeking extensive exceptions and derogations from the Treaty of Rome. It wanted exemption from the common external tariffs for no less than twenty-seven Commonwealth products, as well as the assurance of 'equivalent outlets' elsewhere in the EEC to compensate the old

Commonwealth for diminished agricultural export opportunities to Britain. There was also a request for a long period of transition, (a period of twelve to fifteen years was sought initially sought) before the full application of the Common Agricultural Policy to Britain.[11]

With the best will in the world, all this would have been difficult to negotiate in a Community in which the '*acquis communautaire*', the body of Community decisions and regulations already agreed on by the Six, was still new, fragile, and therefore jealously guarded. It certainly could not, as Macmillan had wanted, be negotiated quickly. Here, as Macmillan quickly recognised, was France's opportunity.[12] Acting in the name of the guardian of the *acquis*, it could drag out the negotiations and force up the price Britain would have to pay for membership. The attractions of this tactic was clear. It would protect France's extensive economic interests in the event of an agreement being reached. Alternatively, and this was the French preference all along, it might encourage the British government to realise that it would be unable to gain an acceptable deal, and withdraw its application. 'The English,' de Gaulle is reported to have told the French Council of Ministers, 'will not be able, for the most honourable reasons, to play the game of the Treaty of Rome. But we shall be too polite to tell them so.'[13] And, by speaking in the name of the EEC, insisting that the Community maintain its fundamental character as a regional European customs union, and that its rules must not be transformed to the

Papas's view of the EEC negotiations, Guardian, 9 November 1961. (Centre for the Study of Cartoon and Caricature, University of Kent.)

point where the exceptions became the rules and the rules exceptions, France could protect itself from trouble with its EEC partners who were anxious for the negotiations to succeed.

The French could not of course disguise their position entirely.[14] To British negotiators, French tactics seemed at times to come close to outright political warfare. One member of the British team later recalled how the delegation came to expect intervention by Couve de Murville 'whenever agreement on an issue under discussion had been reached and the president was about to move on to the next item on the agenda. The interventions were frequently introduced with the phrase, "Monsieur le President, je crains qu'il n'y ait une petite equivoque." After that would come a lengthy exercise in obfuscation.'[15] French obstructionism was equally evident to other EEC countries. But the French could always respond, as Couve de Murville did to the Italians in September 1962, that the real question was not whether France accepted Britain in the EEC, but whether Britain accepted the EEC 'as it is.' Despite changes which the Couve and the General were careful to acknowledge, Britain remained too different; it was still insufficiently 'European'.[16] This diagnosis, while no doubt genuine in French eyes, admirably served the purpose of seeking to discredit the British bid and deflect responsibility for difficulty and possible failure from Paris to London.

* * *

The formal negotiations between Britain and the EEC began on 10 October, not in Brussels where all the subsequent discussion would take place, but rather in Paris, where the real power of decision lay.[17] This latter point was also implicitly acknowledged by the unusual, and subsequently much criticized, appointment of Sir Pierson Dixon as head of the British delegation, in addition to his Paris duties. The former post, as Macmillan privately noted, required a man of 'great intelligence, diplomatic skill and high standing. Bob Dixon has all of these qualities.' The Prime Minister also hoped that the choice would please the General.[18] Yet it could scarcely compensate for the fundamental difficulty that having been deprived by the Americans a few months earlier of the possibility of trading British support for France's fledgling nuclear deterrent for a European deal, Macmillan was now forced back on argument and persuasion. As he was well aware from his earlier acquaintance, these were doubtfully effective arts where the General was concerned. Their limitations were certainly made evident in November when de Gaulle made one of his rare visits to England.

The talks had originally been suggested by the General before the British application, and at his request they took place in the informal setting of Macmillan's private country home at Birch Grove in Sussex. Here, as de Gaulle artfully put it, the two men could talk as 'vieux copains - old friends'.[19] Birch Grove was not the most convenient of venues to entertain a Head of State, least of all one whose Algerian policy made him subject to repeated assassination attempts. A place had to be found to store the blood supplies which the General carried with him - he belonged to a rare blood group; the Macmillans' cook protested at the use of the refrigerator or the deep freeze. The Prime Minister's game keeper was so incensed by the way in which the security men were disturbing the pheasants, that he interrupted what Macmillan later described as 'one of the General's enthralling pontifications on the world situation and the American influence', in order to protest. The General was not amused. Lady Dorothy had her own problems about entertaining Mme. de Gaulle, complaining that she wouldn't 'go to the hunt, nor the cripple' craft school, nor even...the Pavilion at Brighton.'[20]

While these various logistic difficulties were eventually resolved, the political problems proved more intractable. To Harold Evans, Macmillan's press secretary, who had never previously met the General, de Gaulle seemed aloof and preoccupied, with never a smile to be seen. Ted Heath, who was also meeting de Gaulle for the first time, found him quietly spoken, reserved and almost shy. Macmillan too paints a more complimentary portrait of his guest. De Gaulle 'behaved throughout with exquisite good manners and exerted to the full his remarkable powers of charm.' But there was a sting in the tail. De Gaulle, he went on to note, 'was a man who was never rude by mistake'.[21]

Birch Grove was in fact the most difficult set of talks Macmillan had yet held with de Gaulle since Algiers. One area of disagreement was again Berlin. Khrushchev had reignited the crisis earlier in the summer, and in mid August had started building the notorious wall, in order to staunch the flow of East German refugees to the West. At the time de Gaulle had tried unsuccessfully to persuade his allies to agree military action to remove the barrier. (He later claimed that he had been unable to contact Macmillan because the Prime Minister was away on the grouse moors.) The immediate issue at Birch Grove was the British and American view that there should now be negotiations with the Russians. De Gaulle, who thought that British policy was to quit Berlin as quickly as possible, feared that once talks began, the Western position over Berlin would rapidly erode, and that Germany would go neutral.[22]

Neither man could convince the other. At one point during the talks Macmillan covered his face with his hands and appeared to go to sleep (both his secretary and the French ambassador believed he actually did so), although he came to life in time to explode, 'Oh well, let's have a war then.' 'Of course,' Macmillan complained in his diary,

> 'de Gaulle's policy is clear and has never changed. He does not want war. He does not believe there will be war. But he wants to pretend to the French and the Germans that *he* (de Gaulle) is the strong, loyal man. He will not 'do a Munich'. But he only dares take this line, devoutly praying that the British and Americans will get him out....naturally his main purpose is to see that France gets the credit for loyalty, and that the Anglo-Americans are made responsible for the betrayal of Germany.'[23] (emphasis in original)

This was not just annoying but worrying because according to the official British brief for the talks, which drew heavily on Pierson Dixon's assessment, Berlin was now closely connected in the General's mind with the British relationship with Europe. The Foreign Office recognised that the General was not yet convinced that Britain and the Commonwealth could easily fit into his vision of a French-led Europe. Much would depend on whether he believed that if Britain did join, it would work to weaken Europe's growing unity or work with him to bind Germany as tightly as possible to the new Europe. Failure to persuade de Gaulle on this score at Birch Grove inevitably therefore threatened to compromise Macmillan's attempts to overcome the General's known reservations on the British bid, and persuade him to give to give instructions to French officials to settle the matter as soon as possible.[24]

De Gaulle, who had more pressing priorities, seems at this point still to have been unsure what the British were up to. 'What is all this about?' he asked Heath at one point. 'Is it serious or is it just a game?' But the brief provided by the Quai d'Orsay suggested that Macmillan had staked his own, and his Government's political future, on a successful outcome of the negotiations. It also anticipated most of the Prime Minister's arguments. The General was advised to keep the Prime Minister guessing as to France's intentions regarding the outcome of the EEC negotiations. If Macmillan got the impression that they would succeed, France's negotiating position would be weakened. If, on the other hand, he came away believing that France was hostile, it would be easy to create trouble not only with France's five EEC partners, but also the US and other European and non-European countries. France would thus be able to keep its options open and make a decision at a later stage. But the general impression, both from the clear list of the disadvantages to France of a successful British bid, and the suggestion that the agricultural problems, which had not yet been raised in Brussels, might provide an opportunity to draw the negotiations in the sands, was negative.[25]

Macmillan duly made his pitch, emphasising the historic opportunity which presented itself while the General and Adenauer were still in power, as well as the points of agreement between the two sides. Britain liked the Fouchet plan, as de Gaulle's proposal for European political union was now known; it shared French concerns about Germany. And the Prime Minister indicated views, vision is too strong a word, of Europe and its relations with the United States, which he might have hoped would have attractions for his guest. Although there was no reference to defence, an omission which de Gaulle remarked on, Macmillan did say that Europe could 'not forever' rely on the Americans. Addressing one of the General's specific concerns - the impact of further enlargement of the EEC beyond Britain - the Prime Minister suggested that Europe might be organised in concentric circles with a political and military core, around which there would be an economic organisation. Smaller European states might be associated with this, and there might be special cultural associations. But Europe must also look outwards. It should aim to become the most powerful trading bloc in the world. Britain with its important

Commonwealth connections would 'broaden the base and provide added strength'.[26]

De Gaulle in turn combined tactical astuteness in keeping the Prime Minister guessing, in line with the Quai's advice, with a frankness which reflected the underlying equivocation of his own personal position. He liked Macmillan's idea of concentric circles, and talked about the need to bring the four main European states - Britain, France, Italy and West Germany - together. It was Europe's 'last chance, or at least her last chance but one, because the final chance was Russia joining with Europe.' If Britain came into Europe this would 'add a certain flexibility and suppleness to political thought which was lacking among the French and the Germans.' He was also ready to acknowledge that the French 'could not contain Germany and even Italy by themselves, and that Europe had everything to gain by letting serious-minded people like the British in. British membership was certainly in the common interest. It would hold Europe together and add enormously to its influence in the world.'[27]

But while the General expressed himself towards the end of the conversation as 'optimistic' about the future and British membership, the underlying message was negative. The EEC was still new and fragile, and the General had difficulty in seeing how Britain would fit into this 'beginning of Europe'. How, moreover, could the UK join if the Commonwealth were 'excluded, and how, if they were included, could the US be kept out'? Europe would then lose itself, and be 'drowned in the Atlantic'. There was 'no great hurry' and 'one should not be pressing, more time was needed'. Macmillan's warning that if the negotiations failed a reaction would set in Britain against the EEC, and all possibility of agreement would be lost for a generation, made no impact.[28]

The British sought to put a positive gloss on the talks. According to the French embassy in London, the favourable press reporting was partly the result of a Foreign Office handout. 'In the intimate weekend atmosphere of an English country home, the two statesmen were able to talk freely and forthrightly on the great problems of the day.'[29] In his account to Commonwealth leaders, Macmillan tried to accentuate the positive. De Gaulle 'was not unsympathetic' on the EEC question, and appeared to believe that it 'would not be impossible' to devise satisfactory economic arrangements to meet Commonwealth interests. The Prime Minister got the impression that the General would 'like to see a solution if he could adjust his mind to what must be, to some extent, a new and more constructive view of the relations between the Old World and the New.'[30]

In private, however, Macmillan was much more pessimistic and the Prime Minister's diary reflects greater frustration with de Gaulle than at any previous point in their relationship.

'The Emperor of the French (for he is now an almost complete autocrat, taking no notice of any advice and indeed receiving little of independent value) is older, more isolated, more sententious, and far more *royal* than when I saw him last. He is well informed, yet remote.

His hatred of the 'Anglo-Americans' is as great as ever. While he has extraordinary dignity and charm, is nice to servants and children and so forth, he does not apparently listen to argument. I mean this almost literally. Not only is he not convinced, he actually does not listen. He merely repeats over and over again what he has said before. And the doctrine - almost dogma - is based on intuition, not ratiocination. He talks of Europe, and means France. The France of Louis XIV (as regards its religion, boundaries and power), of Napoleon (as regards the fanatical loyalty of its Army). He allows a little of Napoleon III, as regards the management of a so-called parliament.'

'The tragedy of it all,' Macmillan concluded,

'is that we agree with de Gaulle on almost everything. We like the political Europe (*union des patries* or *union d'états*) that de Gaulle likes. We are anti-federalists; so is he. We are pragmatists in our economic planning; so is he. We fear a German revival and have no desire to see a revived Germany. These are de Gaulle's thoughts too. We agree; but his pride, his inherited hatred of England (since Joan of Arc), his bitter memories of the last war; above all, his intense 'vanity' for France - she must dominate - make him half welcome, half repel us, with a strange 'love-hate' complex. Sometimes, when I am with him, I feel I have overcome it. But he goes back to his distrust and dislike, like a dog to his vomit. I still feel that he has *not* absolutely decided about our admission to the Economic Community. I am inclined to think he will be more likely to yield to pressure than persuasion.'[31] (emphasis in original.)

If Birch Grove had served to confirm Macmillan's doubts as to whether de Gaulle's opposition to British membership could be overcome, over the next year the Prime Minister's mood would nevertheless veer between pessimism and a very human hope, which often seemed to verge on wishful thinking. The Embassy in Paris cited official French sources as saying that de Gaulle found himself 'very much in agreement' with what Macmillan had said on Europe. 'Some of his suspicions about our desire to bring the Commonwealth in with us,' it reported on 28 November, 'are said to have been allayed.' Just before Christmas de Gaulle sent Macmillan a signed photograph 'in testimony of their friendship since the war'. 'A similar token on your part,' he wrote, 'would give me great pleasure.'[32]

This display of friendship carefully masked the fact that de Gaulle had not been moved. Macmillan, the General told Adenauer in early December, had made 'a great and sentimental drama' at Birch Grove.[33] Writing to the Prime Minister after this meeting, de Gaulle struck a guarded note. He and the West German Chancellor had reaffirmed their intentions to advance matters, and hoped that Britain could 'one day' join the EEC on the same conditions as existing members.[34] Two months later when Adenauer and de Gaulle again met, the General remarked that if it were a question of 'admitting an aged Britain into our union without privileges, on the same basis as ourselves, I concur. But if it means allowing her to enter with all of her retinue, Canada, Australia, India, the whole character of our Union would be altered…We must not allow ourselves to soften.'[35]

Chapter 16

Château de Champs

The uncompromising position which de Gaulle had outlined to Adenauer, was duly reflected in the lack of progress in the negotiations in Brussels In February 1962 Heath recorded his suspicions that the French were trying to drag the negotiations out, though he was unsure whether the motive was to kill them off, or get a better deal for France[1] Around the same time, Sir Pierson Dixon described de Gaulle's attitude as still an enigma. The General's mind, he believed, was 'open to the possibility' of the negotiations succeeding. 'Neutral rather than hostile would be the word to use now if one wished to find a word.'[2] Macmillan was no less perplexed, and much more nervous. The fortunes 'and probably the life of the government', he noted in April, depended on the success of the bid. But would de Gaulle ' "smile and smile and smile" but betray us after all? No one knows. I feel rather overwhelmed by the responsibility on me and rather lonely.'[3]

At this point, however, de Gaulle had more immediate problems to worry about than the British bid. The ending of the Algerian war - a formal peace agreement was signed in Evian in March - had coincided with a crisis in the General's European strategy. Unwilling to accept the compromise essential to secure a deal with his five EEC partners, de Gaulle had overplayed his hand. He had personally redrafted a text for a political union which had been agreed by officials and Ministers of the Six, including Couve de Murville, cutting out all reference to both NATO and the Treaty of Rome. Subsequently the General had rowed back somewhat on this unsustainable position. But suspicions about his long-term purposes, among countries strongly committed to the Atlantic alliance and the supranationalist institutions of the EEC, had been heightened. Although the British were not directly involved in this affair, the fact that the talks broke down over Dutch and Belgian insistence that Britain should be consulted about the proposed treaty can have done nothing to improve the British case. The impression in Paris was that the Dutch delegation had been acting with British encouragement.[4]

When two days later, on 19 April, Macmillan saw Chauvel, who was finally leaving London, the Prime Minister sought to underscore the community of Anglo-French interests in support of a *'union des patries'* by likening the existing European integration to a 'political esperanto', in which all the useful elements were diluted and neutralised. The phrase was repeated to the new ambassador, Geoffrey de Courcel, on 9 May, and found an echo during de Gaulle's press conference six days later. Europe, the General declared, could not be a living reality 'without France and her Frenchmen, Germany and her Germans, Italy and her Italians.' Dante, Goethe and Chateaubriand, he continued, 'belong to Europe in the same way as they were respectively and eminently an Italian, a German and a Frenchman. They would not have served Europe much if they had been non-national and if they had thought and written in some form of Esperanto or Volapuk.' There was no reference in this literary context to Shakespeare, or indeed to the British bid.[5] Although the Foreign Office was concerned about the latter omission, Macmillan professed to de Courcel that he was not worried by it.[6]

It was at this point that Dixon sent a paper in which for the first time he argued that it was 'only safe to assume' that the General would like the negotiations to fail, although Dixon still believed that it was possible to reach a successful outcome in Brussels. Several officials in the Embassy had been pressing this case for some time, but the ambassador wanted to be sure before forwarding such an unwelcome assessment.[7] This was still very much a minority view in Whitehall, and the Prime Minister believed that de Gaulle remained torn between emotion and reason, and had not yet made up his mind.[8] Nevertheless, the question clearly weighed on Macmillan's mind, and when one of his grandchildren asked why he was rereading Tolstoy's *War and Peace*, the Prime Minister replied, only half jokingly, that it was instructive to see how another French general was defeated.[9]

On 22 May Dixon had an interview with de Gaulle which only served to confirm the ambassador's pessimism. In his view the General's objections - the Commonwealth, the domestic problems Britain would have in adjusting to membership - were those of a man who wanted to make difficulties rather than find solutions.[10] A sympathetic senior member of the French delegation in Brussels, who was asked around the same time whether his instructions were to 'slow everything down', replied that 'unfortunately they were worse than that'.[11] Small wonder if a few days later Macmillan's diary records 'an increasing impression that de Gaulle does *not* repeat *not* want us in Europe. (Although it seems as if Couve de Murville accepts our adhesion as "a historic fatality.")' The French, he feared, might:

'insist on terms so harsh for our farmers and for the Commonwealth that we shall be forced to withdraw. This, of course, is a dangerous game. French hegemony in Europe (or a part of Europe) may be maintained for a time. But the future will be insecure. What will Germany do *after* Adenauer? What will France be *after* de Gaulle?'[12]

It was against this unpromising background that on 2 and 3 June, Macmillan and de Gaulle held their second discussion about the British EEC bid. The French view was that after six months of fruitless discussion in Brussels the time had come for a frank exchange between the two principals. The venue was Château de Champs, an elegant eighteenth-century house of modest size to the west of Paris, which had once belonged to Madame de Pompadour. It had what the Prime Minister described in his diary as a 'wonderful garden...in the classic style - avenues of cut limes, statues, fountains, etc., etc. The furniture is good and the rooms reasonably comfortable.' De Gaulle was as ever a charming host. In his memoirs Macmillan describes the small family dinner after the first set of talks, with de Gaulle 'in the role of a stately monarch unbending a little to the representative of a once hostile but now friendly country.'[13]

Macmillan was well aware that this might be the last opportunity to convince de Gaulle of the desirability of British membership.[14] The Prime Minister still believed that the key to a solution lay in a nuclear deal. A strong hint of this was given in a farewell interview in April with Chauvel, when the Prime Minister raised the question of European defence. There was of course, Macmillan insisted, no question of giving up NATO or reducing its effectiveness. But from the day Europe would constitute a unique entity with capabilities matching the US, 'things would take another turn.' Macmillan went on to speak of a possible Franco-British understanding on making nuclear armaments, so as to reduce dependence on American supplies which were 'expensive to obtain and whose sale could be contested'. The Prime Minister returned to these questions when he saw de Courcel on 9 May. The reorganisation of Europe must be based on 'a close Anglo-French understanding' as a new version of the *Entente Cordiale*. This of course required British entry to EEC, a subject which in turn led on to defence. Insisting that he was only speaking privately, Macmillan raised the possibility of France and Britain holding their nuclear power within NATO 'as trustees for Europe'.[15]

Macmillan clearly made an impression on the new ambassador, who reported that 'The care with which he (Macmillan) took to develop his ideas, the warmth of his tone, the friendliness of his manner lead one to infer that during his visit to Champs he will deploy all his powers of persuasion.' But as so often with the Prime Minister's grand designs, there was a fly in the ointment. When de Courcel had enquired whether Macmillan's ideas were compatible with existing Anglo-American agreements, the Prime Minister's response had not been very clear.[16] This was scarcely surprising, for however much the Americans wanted Britain in the EEC, opinion in Washington remained hostile to any Anglo-French nuclear deal. The British, as a senior White House official had put it, 'would be appeasing the French with our secrets, and no good would come of it for Europe or for us.' [17]

In talks with Kennedy in late April Macmillan had been circumspect, saying that while he would not be precluded from dangling the idea of an Anglo-French nuclear contribution to NATO before de Gaulle's eyes, 'it would be a mistake to come to an agreement now. He would merely take, and pay nothing for it,' a view with which the President strongly agreed.[18] Three weeks later, by which time the Prime Minister had had his interview with de Courcel, Kennedy felt it necessary to reinforce his opposition. Although there had by now been press speculation about a possible Anglo-French deal, the Americans appear to have been tipped off by the Foreign Office, where there was once again concern that the Prime Minister might be jeopardising Anglo-American cooperation. Clearly irritated, Macmillan instructed the British ambassador to Washington, David Ormsby-Gore, to tell Kennedy that he had no intention of doing anything foolish at Château de Champs. The issue was unlikely to arise. 'If it does I shall be very careful.'[19] By then Macmillan had been advised that de Gaulle, who saw the Prime Minister's suggestions as a means of bringing the French nuclear programme under American influence, was not interested. It was characteristic, if not particularly courteous, of de Gaulle, that he raised the matter with Dixon by reference to the press speculation, rather than Macmillan's overtures to the French ambassadors.[20]

To Dixon the message was unambiguous, making it 'unnecessary.... for the Prime Minister to give any further thought to the possibility of referring seriously to nuclear matters in this connection.' The Foreign Office brief for Château de Champs, which effectively summarised the substantial amount of thinking which had taken place in Whitehall over the past few weeks, had repeated the by-now standard line that there was 'very little' which Britain could offer de Gaulle because of 'our American ties'.[21] Macmillan, however, was still not deterred. Just how far he went at Château de Champs remains uncertain. According to Couve de Murville, the subject may have been raised during lunch conversations, but was not a 'topic for discussion.' De Courcel was more specific, insisting that an offer of nuclear cooperation as an implicit quid pro quo for British EEC entry had been made.[22]

The official British and French accounts make clear that a carrot was indeed dangled, although the Prime Minister confined himself to hinting at the long-term nuclear opportunities, albeit with the unspoken if quite obvious condition that Britain must first be admitted to the EEC. Developing themes from previous conversations, Macmillan talked of the Atlantic alliance having two pillars, a structure which would strengthen both the alliance and Europe's voice in it.

> 'Without going into details he felt that after Europe had been created there must be discussions about the political and defence aspects and an attempt made to create a European world position. There was the question of reserve armies to support Europe's defence and

there was the nuclear question. There was a feeling that the deterrent forces of the United States and the Soviet Union had now become so large that they might cease to be credible. If there was an attack against Europe at some future date the United States might perhaps hesitate to use her nuclear forces. Some European deterrent was therefore perhaps necessary.'[23]

De Gaulle, who did not have to worry about American sensitivities, was much more direct. France and Britain seemed to him to have similar ideas about nuclear weapons; the General thought that Britain envisaged their deployment the same way as France. If Britain and France decided to make Europe, they must pool their forces and develop a common plan. It might be useful if the two countries were to have further discussions. He left it to his Defence Minister, Pierre Messmer, to make the specific proposal of Anglo-French cooperation on a submarine-launched ballistic missile system, when he met his British counterpart, Peter Thorneycroft a few days later.[24]

The main thrust of Macmillan's presentation at Château de Champs, however, was directed at tackling the points of disagreement about the British bid, which were holding up the Brussels negotiations. The most immediate of these was agriculture. French farmers were a powerful lobby. De Gaulle privately described agriculture as the most serious problem facing France after the settlement of the Algerian problem, and the possibility of rioting by French farmers and social turbulence were a matter of real anxiety. Addressing French concerns over the impact of British entry in terms of possible delay in the implementation of the CAP, and of cheap agricultural imports from Britain and the Commonwealth was thus a matter of urgency.[25] As to the Commonwealth link, on which the General found it so convenient to harp, Macmillan assured his host that the younger generation 'felt much more European than the older people who had been brought up in the days of Kipling with their idea that their work in the world lay inside the British empire.' The General later paraphrased this as 'The England of Kipling is dead.' Whatever the exact words, Macmillan's sentiments were very different from the ones he had been expressing to the Australian Prime Minister, Robert Menzies.[26]

De Gaulle had again received the same advice from the Quai d'Orsay as before Birch Grove, - not to give any indication of French intent - and while at times somewhat condescending, was careful to balance encouragement and discouragement.[27] The British record, while sometimes differing in details from the French, captures much of the flavour of the penultimate de Gaulle-Macmillan meeting. After elaborating his reasons for promoting political union, de Gaulle noted that although it was indeed conceivable that the Common Market should be enlarged,

'Britain was not quite in the same position as the Continental countries; she was not quite so menaced by the Russians. It was perhaps true that in reality the Channel was not much of a protection but it made a psychological difference to the people of Britain. Then again, Britain was much more open to world influences than Europe and saw things differently from people on the Continent. Finally, there was the British liaison with the United States. This was naturally close because of common language, common habits and joint engagements. Britain could join the Community but it would then become a different sort of organisation. Of course, Britain would bring considerable economic, political and military strength and would make the Community a larger reality but it would also *change everything*. That was why France had to look at this matter carefully.' (emphasis added)[28]

Having thanked de Gaulle for his frankness, Macmillan went on the emotional offensive. He recalled the damage which had been done by lack of Anglo-French unity before the two world wars, and warned of the dangers of isolationism in Britain. 'If Britain was left outside the Community she would pursue some policy or other; this might or might not be to the liking of the Six but it would in any case be an independent policy. This would give great opportunities to the Russians for driving wedges between the different allies. If there was a close European union closely knit, this would not happen.' The General, he noted:

'had said that British entry would embarrass the other six; this was a hard thing to suggest after all the history of the last 50 years. *President de Gaulle* said that there was no need for Britain to feel hurt because it was not true that she was not wanted. There was no question of not maintaining the alliance. It would perhaps be better if Britain did join the Six but he wondered if it would then be possible to have a common policy on such matters as Berlin and defence questions. *The Prime Minister* quite agreed that if the alliance remained as it was, a common policy on these matters would be difficult, but if the system changed so would the possibilities. *President de Gaulle* said that he was an old Frenchman. It was hard for him to make arrangements with Germany and even with Italy but in the face of the Russians it was necessary, and in addition it was essential to make an organisation which would be independent of the United States and not just an American satellite. In this respect he wondered if the Prime Minister felt the same way as he did.'[29]

The burden of this message, which might be summarised as 'Perhaps, but', succeeded admirably in keeping his guest guessing. The British, as Dixon later commented, were 'rather baffled' by the Château de Champs meeting. 'As so often before,' Macmillan wrote in his Memoirs, 'I found it difficult to fathom the character of this strange and enigmatic man,' though he did believe that for the time being at least, the risks of a veto had been avoided. In a letter to

Kennedy he described the meeting as 'fairly satisfactory'. 'I do not know that I convinced him that the advantages (of British membership) outweighed possible disadvantages. But I do think that he accepted the seriousness of our purpose in entering into negotiations with the Six.'[30]

This was a fair assessment. Macmillan had certainly made a stronger impression than at Birch Grove. De Gaulle had been struck by how much Macmillan's attitude to the EEC had changed since their meeting in June 1958, and was impressed by the sincerity with which his visitor had spoken. A senior member of the French embassy in London quoted de Courcel as saying that de Gaulle had previously regarded the prospects of failure at Brussels as ninety per cent; he now regarded the prospect of success as sixty per cent. When a month later the French ambassador to Washington, Hervé Alphand, met de Gaulle, he also noted a change in the General's thinking on British entry. The General no longer seemed to rule the prospect out entirely, though he continued to deplore it.[31]

But if Macmillan had for the first time given de Gaulle pause for thought, he had not converted him. There was after all as yet no concrete evidence to suggest that the British were prepared to offer the substantial price necessary to compensate France for the political disadvantages of British membership mentioned, though not spelled out in one of the French briefing document produced for Château de Champs. The Prime Minister might talk of a double-headed alliance. But he had also at one point in the discussion referred to himself as half-American, and had given no sign that he was ready to *prefer* Europe to the United States, which is what de Gaulle wanted. As to the hints of nuclear cooperation, these were very vague. Was this really a quid pro quo for British membership, or were the British trying to blackmail the Americans into giving additional help at a time when the French believed that the British nuclear programme was in difficulties?[32]

Small wonder therefore if the favourable impact of Château de Champ proved short-lived. There was certainly no indication of any change of heart on de Gaulle's part regarding the British application when he met Adenauer in early July. Could the Six, he asked, absorb Britain with all its problems. 'Perhaps, but not certainly.'[33] When, a few days later, the American journalist, C.L. Sulzberger visited London, he found British ministers very much on the defensive. Asked what would happen if Britain did not get into Europe, the Prime Minister looked at his interviewer 'with mild horror like a handsome bloodhound', declaring that he had always made it a rule in life 'to avoid fall-back positions. When you have a fall-back position, you always fall back...There was no fall-back position in the battle of Britain. After all, if we had used pure reason in 1940, we might have sought a compromise peace.'[34]

Before the Brussels talks adjourned for the summer recess at the beginning of August, French ministers reviewed the progress - or rather lack of progress. The French position was summarised by the Prime Minister, Georges Pompidou. If the EEC collapsed, he argued, apart from Italy, France would be the main loser. But the French also had an interest in ensuring that the British application did not succeed. If Britain were to enter, she must break with the Commonwealth. 'It was not desirable that France should take responsibility for the breakdown of the negotiations. It would be better to try and let them run into the sands. After a time a preferable alternative to British entry, such as association, could probably be found.'[35]

As the French duly dragged out the ensuing negotiations, Macmillan gave vent to his anxiety and frustration. In a bitter diary entry on 4 August, the Prime Minister mused that this was the forty-eighth anniversary of the beginning of the First, and almost the twentieth anniversary of the beginning of the Second, World War. 'In both the French let us down and now they are trying to let us down again. News from Brussels is trickling in. Not much progress. The Five are friendly but seem strangely mesmerised by the French.' In the event there was no breakdown and the talks were adjourned, leaving the Prime Minister feeling 'not too depressed.'[36] The British negotiators, he optimistically told the Queen, had emerged if not with complete success, then at least with a great moral triumph. He hoped that world public opinion would gradually force the French along the lines of an acceptable agreement.[37]

The Brussels adjournment round has sometimes been seen as a lost opportunity. Had Britain signed up on the dotted line, France would have found it difficult to prevent a successful outcome of the negotiations.[38] This option, however, was never seriously considered. Ministers remained much more concerned about the prospect for a special and potentially very difficult Commonwealth meeting due to meet in London the following month, than about the danger of a French veto. Nor indeed was this an immediate danger. The General was not yet ready to take responsibility for a breakdown of the Brussels negotiations. At the same time, however, he had no intention of giving way. At a meeting of the French Council of Ministers on 8 August, he reiterated the crucial importance of the EEC in giving impetus to French agriculture. If Britain was not ready to accept this, the Common Market would have little interest for France. As to the Commonwealth, the Conservatives wanted the EEC to enter the Commonwealth; Macmillan by contrast was ready to enter the EEC without conditions, but he faced a very difficult political situation. 'We do not wish ill to Macmillan, who is a sincere ally of France,' de Gaulle declared. 'But we cannot sacrifice a fundamental French interest to this sympathy. We will not change our position.'[39]

Chapter 17

Autumn Gales

At the beginning of August de Gaulle had still been willing to stay his hand, and let his negotiators try to draw the Brussels negotiations into the sands. By the end of the year, when he and Macmillan met for the last time at Rambouillet, the General was ready to drop the mask and declare France's opposition to the British bid. The doubts he had briefly entertained at the time of Château de Champs had long since evaporated, and for the first time de Gaulle felt confident enough to bring matters to a head. His own fortunes were on the rise, while Macmillan's were in decline.[1]

Writing in February 1962 to the Australian Prime Minister, Sir Robert Menzies, Macmillan had suggested that the end of the Algerian war would mean that de Gaulle had outlived his welcome, 'and the politicians will get charge again. Alternatively the army will make a coup, and there will be first an extreme right-wing government followed by an extreme left-wing government.' When two months later a ceasefire was finally agreed, the Prime Minister thought this would be helpful, since 'the Algerian revolt touched a most delicate chord in his sensitive character.'[2] Macmillan had misjudged. The ending of the Algerian war greatly strengthened the General's position, allowing him to turn much more of his attention to foreign policy, beginning with his European grand design. If the small Powers, Holland and Belgium, for which the General had so much disdain, had thwarted his immediate initiative for European union, he would now refocus his diplomacy around what he had always regarded as its Franco-German core.

Macmillan's inconclusive encounter with the General at Château de Champs had thus been followed by a very high profile state visit by Adenauer. Intended as a demonstration of solidarity with Germany over Berlin in the face of what de Gaulle privately called the 'madness' with which the Anglo-Saxons were forcing themselves to the negotiating table with the Soviet Union, the extraordinary attention lavished on his German visitor also reflected de Gaulle's wider ambitions.[3] This was to be the formal reconciliation between hereditary enemies, which the General regarded himself, as Germany's most implacable wartime adversary, as uniquely qualified to bring about. (Alain Peyrefitte quotes him as saying, 'It is from me that they await absolution for their war crimes.') The climax came in a solemn ceremony at Rheims cathedral, overlooking the great battlefields of the First World War, and a joint parade by French and German troops at Mourmelon, where as the historically ever-conscious de Gaulle privately put it, our armies 'were so embroiled' and where the battle of the Marne saved France in 1914.[4]

Adenauer was both impressed and helpful. The Chancellor agreed to the General's suggestion to relaunch his European union scheme around a Franco-German core, should planned attempts to revive the Fouchet project fail because of continued Dutch and Belgian insistence on British involvement. And he made no bones about his lack of his enthusiasm about the British EEC membership bid. The British application, Adenauer declared, 'should not be approved with three cheers', and he mischievously went on to claim that Macmillan had offered economic union with the US, which Kennedy had refused.[5] Adenauer made clear his objections to British membership to the German cabinet in early August, adding that the negotiations had turned 'into a Franco-British duel...in a certain way France has won it (the leading role in Europe) now, and England doesn't like that. If the two would now agree on our costs, (sic) that would be the very worst.' He had previously expressed concern about Britain becoming the arbitrator of Europe.[6] A month later the Chancellor was asking how France could host a parade of German armoured vehicles 'in the Great Parade ground of Mourmelon, whereas German armoured vehicles are not seen with favour in England?' - an allusion to British protests against the training of German units in Wales.[7]

When de Gaulle paid a return visit to Germany in September, he went out of his way to make an impression. He spoke in German - he had spoken in French during his State visit to London two years earlier - and it was on this occasion that he declared, 'you are a great people'. His reception was over-whelming. No one, as Adenauer's biographer Hans-Peter Schwarz notes, had addressed them like this since Wilhelm 11 and Hitler. In an enthusiastic letter to his sister, de Gaulle wrote of the visit having multiplied French prestige.[8]

The General's hostility to British membership on this occasion was undis-guised. As reported back by the British embassy to London, de Gaulle made it clear to leading members of the opposition parties that he disliked the idea of additional members of the EEC, which would make the EEC unwieldy and make it difficult to reach decisions.[9] Europe, with Britain, its Commonwealth 'and its junior partners,' he told President Luebke, 'is the abandonment of a European policy. It is Europe subjected to American policy.'[10] Adenauer repeat-ed several times that he had not actually reached a decision on British membership; the British bid enjoyed considerable support within the Bonn government. But it must by now have been clear to de Gaulle that he need expect little trouble from the Chancellor should he opt for more brutal methods against Macmillan's bid.

His hand was further strengthened by developments on the French domestic front. The General had sought to consolidate his position by a constitutional amendment providing for the direct election of the president. This was a highly controversial move, which was voted down in the National Assembly. De Gaulle responded on 10 October by dissolving the Assembly, announcing a referendum on the bill, to be followed three weeks later by new elections. Musing in his diary on the likely outcome of 'all this commotion', Macmillan wondered whether it would make the General more or less difficult to deal with over Europe, and feared the former.[11]

The referendum was duly approved, and in the second round of the elections, de Gaulle gained an absolute parliamentary majority, one of the greatest political triumphs of his career. With his administration securely in power, and most of his bitterest critics defeated, de Gaulle had come into his kingdom. The Paris embassy warned that he now had 'carte blanche for all his policies, domestic and international.'[12] Macmillan too sensed at least some of the danger. Describing the General in the privacy of his diary again as a mixture of Louis XIV and Napoleon, on 5 December the Prime Minister expected him to be

'more mystical and remote, pontificating in general terms. At the same time, to protect the material interests (and short-term interests) of French agriculture and commerce, he will bargain as hard and as selfishly as any old French housewife in the market. The Brussels negotiations are dragging - but I suppose the crunch must come in February or March, at the latest.'[13]

* * *

Macmillan himself was now in visible difficulty. The Conservatives had been in power for a decade. Time was now against them, and there were increasing indications that Macmillan's tired appearance was becoming less a studied pose and more a reflection of reality.[14] The government's loss of popularity was reflected in a series of bad by-elections results, and Macmillan further undermined his own position in July through a botched governmental reshuffle. A third of the cabinet, including the Chancellor, Selwyn Lloyd, were sacked in the 'Night of the Long Knives'. This failed to stop the rot, indeed shortly before the Prime Minister met de Gaulle in December at Rambouillet, a bad opinion poll forced him to tell the Conservative Party's 1922 Executive Committee that he would be willing to resign the Party leadership if this would help. It was, as he noted in his diary, indicative of the seriousness of the position that he had to use this weapon.[15]

All this had of course been picked up by the French, who were constantly speculating about the Government's strength and the date of the next election.[16] But something else was also happening - the erosion of Britain's international position was visibly accelerating, giving rise to public unease and disillusion. The chairman of the Conservative Party, Iain Macleod, had touched on the subject in April, when addressing the Party's National Union Executive Dean Acheson's remark at the end of the year about Britain having 'lost an empire and not yet found a role' was pithily paraphrased by one MP as 'this country was no longer a Great Power and did not know where it was going.'[17]

To make matters eeven worse the 'special relationship' was also coming under strain. Although Macmillan had succeeded in forging a genuine personal friendship with Kennedy, the old wartime Anglo-American links were dissolving. At the Pentagon, the Secretary of Defence, Robert McNamara, was publicly attacking independent nuclear deterrents as 'dangerous, expensive, prone to obsolescence and lacking in credibility', a criticism which while ostensibly aimed at France in fact also targeted at Britain. At the State Department there were calls to down-grade the relationship with London, and give France equality of treatment with Britain.[18] There were disagreements over a wide range of questions, including arms sales, where the British felt that the much vaunted concept of interdependence with the US was becoming something of a 'one-sided traffic'. Macmillan became particularly angry about American tactics over the sale, in competition with a British weapon, of Hawk anti-aircraft missiles to Israel. Playing fair, he wrote to the Defence Secretary, Peter Thorneycroft, on 4 September, 'is beyond their capacity..If only we can "get into Europe", we shall, of course, have a much stronger position.'[19]

More bad blood between London and Washington was caused by Cuba. The US had for some time been pressing Britain to impose trade sanctions against Fidel Castro's Communist government.. On 2 October Macmillan minuted to the Foreign Secretary, Lord Home, that there was 'no reason to help the Americans on Cuba.' On the 20th he was expressing concern to the Queen about the American threat to British shipping interests in connection with Cuba. Two days later the Caribbean island was headline news, but for very much more serious reasons. The story of the Cuban missile crisis - the World Crisis, as Macmillan called it - has been likened to a wildly implausible sequel to Graham Greene's *Our Man in Havana*.[20] This, however, was scarcely the 'entertainment' which Greene's book had been. Cuba was the one point in the forty-year-long Cold War, in which the possibility of nuclear conflict suddenly seemed acute. Men as hardheaded as McNamara and Thorneycroft wondered 'whether this really is it'.[21]

The crisis had begun on 14 October when American U2 aircraft spotted Soviet medium range ballistic missile sites under construction on Cuba, Khrushchev wanted to protect Fidel Castro's revolution against US attack. But aware that the Soviet Union was falling behind in the strategic arms race, he also believed that he had found an easy means of shifting the balance of global strategic power in Moscow's favour. He had therefore gambled on being able to install the missiles fewer than a hundred miles from the Florida coast, without detection, as on American willingness to accept so flagrant a breach of the informal conventions which had hitherto characterised the nuclear stalemate as a fait accompli.

The Americans took their crucial original decision for a blockade, rather than an invasion or air strike, on their own. When the question of consulting allies was first raised Kennedy remarked that he didn't 'know how much use consulting with the British has been. They'll just object. Just have to decide to do it. Probably ought to tell them, though, the night before.' Although British officials were in fact tipped off on the intelligence network, official notification indeed only came a day before the public announcement of the blockade on 22 October, when Kennedy briefed David Ormsby-Gore. Macmillan was briefed by the US ambassador in London, de Gaulle and Adenauer by Dean Acheson. The President, as one of his aides Theodore Sorenson later put it, did not feel that in matters of pressing importance, the approval of the allies was a primary consideration.[22]

Macmillan and de Gaulle both reacted robustly to the Soviet move, although the General with rather more style than the Prime Minister. However difficult an ally in normal times, de Gaulle was always careful to align himself unambiguously with the Americans when real danger threatened. Having told Acheson that there would be no war, he concluded an interview with the Soviet ambassador, Sergei Vinogradov, who had come to warn him of the consequences of siding with the United States, with the words, 'Alas, Mr Ambassador, we shall die together. Good-bye, Mr. Ambassador.'[23]

Macmillan had no doubts that, unlike the Berlin crisis, a trial of wills was in play, and that US credibility was on the line. Writing to Menzies, Diefenbaker and the New Zealand Prime Minister, Keith Holyoake, he drew the lesson of Appeasement that it was important 'not to become so alarmed by a particular crisis that we settle it at the expense of being a point or two down in the larger struggle.' But Macmillan was again no out-and-out hawk. Unlike de Gaulle, he had to worry about public opinion which he knew would be sceptical of the US claims about the Soviet missiles, and was thus anxious to ensure publication of the American photographic evidence. In Cabinet he spoke of the need to find a 'middle course' between a settlement which would lower the Free World's resistance to aggression and the dangers of driving those who felt they had been victims of aggression to desperation.[24]

The alliance diplomacy of the crucial next few days was nevertheless a lopsided affair. There was formal contact between Macmillan and de Gaulle, who had immediately exchanged messages stressing the need to keep closely in touch. When Dixon saw the General on 23 October, the latter repeated many of the points he had previously made to Acheson, including the need for 'immediate and continuous consultation', should Khrushchev make any move against Berlin. There was a further exchange of messages on the 25th and 26th., the General writing, 'As we see it, you and I, we are really very close to each other.'[25] Two days later the crisis was over. Franco-American exchanges were even sparser. After the Acheson briefing, there was no further high level American contact with de Gaulle, whose standing challenge of American leadership did not go down well in Washington. At the same time Kennedy was in continuous touch with the British, either through his close personal friend, David Ormsby-Gore, to whom some of the President's remarks were so frank that the British ambassador was reluctant to report them, or by phone direct to Macmillan.[26]

Macmillan was very anxious to publicise these conversations, and protested vigorously when the Cabinet Office tried to dissuade him from going into detail when he came to write his memoirs.[27] Whether in fact they tell quite the story Macmillan wanted to convey is open to question. These were as much conversations between friends as formal discussions between allies. One member of the Kennedy Administration later explained the calls as being more a matter of the President seeking 'to touch base' than of his really wanting to know what Macmillan thought about a thing.' Another has spoken of 'the sense of reassurance' Kennedy gained from talking to 'an old professional political leader for whom he had great respect'. The President himself spoke of feeling 'at home with Macmillan because I can share my loneliness with him. The others are all foreigners to me.' That perhaps justifies the verdict of two American historians, Ernest May and Philip Zelikow, who edited the White House tape recordings of the affair, that Macmillan and Ormsby-Gore became de facto members of Excomm, the committee which Kennedy had set up to manage the crisis.[28]

Being consulted, however, is not the same thing as being influential. Macmillan rarely offered direct advice, and Kennedy only once asked for it. This was over another '$64,000 question' - whether to invade Cuba, to which the Prime Minister replied that he would like to think about it. (With self-deprecating humour, in his diary Macmillan compared the dialogue with 'a review called *Beyond the Fringe* which takes off the leading politicians.')[29] But the Prime Minister was discouraged from visiting Washington, and his proposal to immobilise medium-range Thor missiles in Britain as a way of helping the Russians save face, was brushed aside. May and Zelikow believe that by 26 October, in other words only four days into the crisis, Kennedy had become sceptical of the quality of Macmillan's advice.[30]

That message did not get back to the Prime Minister, who felt reassured that despite the recent Anglo-American difficulties, he remained the Washington insider.[31] Writing to the Cabinet Secretary, Sir Norman Brook, Macmillan expressed himself satisfied at the way in which 'Anglo-American cooperation and confidence in each other' had stood up during the crisis. In his diary he likened the whole episode to a battle and 'we in Admiralty House' (where the Prime Minister was temporarily living) felt 'as if we were in the battle H.Q.'[32] Macmillan had stayed up into the early hours of the morning to take Kennedy's phone calls. The General by contrast had conspicuously refused to change his normal habits, going down to Colombey-les-Deux-Eglises during the weekend of 27-8 October, when the crisis came to a head, and refusing an offer for a briefing there from the American ambassador, Charles Bohlen.[33]

Subsequently de Gaulle mixed self-satisfaction with complaint. He told the French cabinet that while the French position had been clear, Macmillan had written to him several times contradicting himself. At the same time he was understandably unhappy about the lack of consultation. He had been careful to ascertain from Acheson that he was being informed rather than consulted about the blockade, and he subsequently made a point of harking back to the arguments he had put forward in his September 1958 memorandum.[34] In de Gaulle's eyes, far from strengthening allied confidence in the US, as the Americans claimed, Cuba had shown that the US put its own security interests first, and those of its European allies second. He would doubtless have agreed with the verdict of Sir Frank Roberts, now British ambassador in Moscow, that Cuba had made clear that the future of the world lay in the hand of the superpowers, and various other states, great or small, counted for relatively little.[35]

Too much should not perhaps be read into this strange incident. Unusually for the Cold War, this had been a bilateral superpower affair, which remained confined to the Western Hemisphere, an area of traditional American sensitivity. There would have been much more contact with allies had a resolution not come so quickly or had Berlin been threatened. As it was by 27 October Kennedy was showing concern to get back in touch with de Gaulle.[36] But if de Gaulle was instinctively over-pessimistic in the conclusions he drew from the affair, which tended to reinforce his own anti-American prejudices, Macmillan was in turn over-sanguine about British influence in Washington. The 'special relationship' was not yet out of the woods.

* * *

Once it was all over, Macmillan's mind turned to personal diplomacy. He wanted to see Kennedy, but was also anxious for a prior meeting with the General, to forestall suspicions of some Anglo-Saxon plot at European expense.[37] While the post-Cuba situation would obviously feature in the French talks, the EEC bid remained the more pressing issue. The auguries were not promising. Although he had managed to defuse a revolt at the September Commonwealth Summit, the Labour Party had now come out against the EEC, and the opinion polls showed a steep decline in support. In Brussels, where the negotiations had now moved to the highly sensitive agricultural question, there was stalemate.

The French suspected the British of dragging out the talks in the expectation that de Gaulle might lose the forthcoming legislative elections. The British meanwhile received negative reports from Paris. According to an intelligence report which Macmillan read in mid September, de Gaulle was determined Britain should not join the EEC. In an interview with Dixon two weeks later, the General 'made no effort even for the sake of politeness to convey any impression other than that he had no intention of being helpful and that if we

had to come in he would at least do his best to ensure that France made a financial killing.' In his diary Macmillan described de Gaulle's mood as having been
'gloomy, cynical and harsh - in his worst Algerian form.' Just before the Cuban
crisis the General had seemed a little more encouraging, although in reporting
this Dixon warned that it was always difficult immediately after the event to be
certain what interpretation to place on de Gaulle's remarks.[38]

During the preparation for the Anglo-French talks, which had been fixed
for Rambouillet in mid December, the Foreign Office had argued that there
was no point in Macmillan's raising the EEC question, This was opposed by
Dixon who countered that de Gaulle would otherwise argue that Britain was no
longer interested in membership.[39] But while it was duly agreed that the British
bid must be raised, in marked contrast to Château de Champs, the aim this time
was confined to damage limitation. As de Zulueta put it, the Prime Minister
'starts from the idea that he must primarily avoid doing any harm to the negotiations in Brussels and that any positive good that he does will be as it were an
uncovenanted bonus.'[40] Writing in his diary on 1 December Macmillan referred
to the French opposing the British by 'every means, fair and foul' and terrify-
ing their five EEC partners by 'their intellectual superiority, and spiritual arrogance, and shameful disregard of truth and honour.'[41] In his memoirs he
described the object of the visit as to make a final appeal to de Gaulle to withdraw his opposition to the British bid.

Before we reach the final Macmillan-de Gaulle encounter, it is worth paus-
ing over two documents. The first was produced by the British embassy in
Paris. Noting that de Gaulle was on the crest of a wave after his electoral triumph, it went on to argue that he:

> 'probably believes that we are in pretty poor shape, facing econom-
> ic difficulties and having no particular policy at the moment except
> to join the Common Market.
> The General does not want us to join the Common Market.
> On the other hand, the General has a long established relationship
> of friendship with the Prime Minister, has a respect for Britain as a
> historical phenomenon, may be becoming disillusioned with
> Germany as a partner, and is not averse to picking up some advan-
> tage for France wherever he can...
> The General is not one to be flattered, certainly not one to be
> appealed to...,and respects those who state their position with some
> bluntness.....
> We need to show ourselves confident and if necessary combative.'[42]

The second document was also written in Paris, but this time within the
Quai d'Orsay. It was a briefing paper by Olivier Wormser, advocating a crucial
change in French tactics from those employed at Birch Grove and Château de
Champs. Wormser predicted that the Brussels negotiations were likely to reach
a crisis in January or February 1963, and that it was up to France to take the

initiative to ensure that the outcome was favourable to French interests. Wormser was worried that the tactics the French had hitherto pursued, of defending the letter of the Treaty of Rome, were creating increasing tension with the Five, and could even threaten the cohesion of the EEC. France therefore should aim to get Britain to withdraw from the negotiations. Macmillan was under pressure from both the Labour opposition and his own Party, and there was also, or at least so Wormser claimed, disagreement within the Cabinet. If the Prime Minister returned from Rambouillet 'without having been strengthened', he would disengage himself from the negotiations. Some alternative solution, much more amenable to French interests, could then be found.[43]

De Gaulle was to take at least part of Wormser's advice. This third Rambouillet encounter, held on 15 and 16 December, was to be the last meeting between the two men, the private prelude to the public drama of the General's press conference and the ensuing veto in Brussels. Couve de Murville describes the conversation as 'uneasy, even nervous on the English side, philosophical and disabused on the French.'[44] It was the only meeting between the two men where de Gaulle unambiguously held the upper hand; it was also the only meeting which resulted in a decisive outcome. Macmillan could protest and remonstrate, but there was nothing he could do to appeal against the sentence which de Gaulle pronounced. Nor was there a great row; Macmillan only refers to a 'wrangle'. Churchillian anger was not in the Prime Minister's style, and the General had no interest in inflaming a difficult and potentially dangerous argument.

The occasion had begun pleasantly for the Prime Minister with an elaborate pheasant shoot, in which Macmillan was credited seventy-seven birds. The General, who did not shoot, came out to watch the last stand. When the official conversations opened, de Gaulle seemed in expansive mood. They could speak at leisure. Time, he declared did not press, neither for them, nor their two countries. Yet by the end of the afternoon session, which focused on the larger international scene, Macmillan was sufficiently worried by what the General had said on the EEC to summon Dixon back from Paris.[45] The next day he insisted on an interpreter to be sure that no nuance of what he said might be lost, and it was now that de Gaulle finally came to the point, declaring that it was not possible for Britain to enter tomorrow, and that arrangements within the EEC might be 'too rigid' for the UK.[46] Macmillan declared himself to be 'astonished and deeply wounded' at what the General had just said, (the French text quotes him as describing it as a great disappointment), and became somewhat emotional in his description of the ideals and passions behind the European Movement originally founded by Churchill, whose object was 'to end the old quarrels and establish a system of European independence and interdependence.' If as Macmillan claims, the General was taken slightly aback at this counterattack, he certainly gave no ground.[47]

The arrival of advisers for the next session did nothing to reduce the tension. Macmillan was stung by the General's condescending remarks, made 'in the tone of a headmaster addressing an intelligent but somewhat pushing boy', that it was important that Britain should 'get nearer Europe, and that France was very pleased that she had come so far. The progress made hitherto was entirely due to my leadership.'[48] The Prime Minister made a last effort to sketch the European future which British entry might offer. If the process did not begin soon the moment would be lost. 'This would not be a disaster and life would no doubt continue, but it would be a tragic failure to match the level of events.' De Gaulle recalled Churchill's alleged comment on the eve of D Day, that if forced to choose between Europe and the Open Sea, he would always opt for the latter. Slightly startled, Macmillan noted the necessity Britain had been under at the time, pointedly adding that when Britain had had the choice in the Second World War, she had stood alone to defend the independence of Europe. This, Macmillan records de Gaulle acknowledged 'rather ungraciously', although the official record does quote him as saying that Britain had never been so European as she was in 1940.[49]

Heavy as the shadow of history fell at Rambouillet, de Gaulle's primary motivation was reflected in the present and future – his preoccupation with European independence of the US, and his frank admission that as the EEC was currently constituted 'France had some weight and could say no even against the Germans'. Once the British and the Scandinavians joined, 'things would be different'. An enlarged EEC would eventually become a kind of world free trade area and cease to be European. At this point there was a pause, broken by the Prime Minister's declaration, made with some heat, that the General had just made a most serious statement amounting to:

'a fundamental objection in principle to the British application. If this was really the French Government's view, it should have been put forward at the very start...*President de Gaulle* said that this was not the case. France desired British entry into the Common Market. M.Pompidou observed that it was a question of dates.
The general discussion then ended and General de Gaulle said that he understood that Lord Home wished to raise a point to which he would be glad to listen.'[50]

Pompidou and Couve seemed embarrassed. Not so the General. In his briefing note Wormser had argued that it would be injudicious to give Macmillan a purely negative impression. The problem of Britain's position *vis-à-vis* Europe would remain even if the Brussels negotiations broke down. The British were after all allies and had a right to France's friendly help to solve an important problem. Besides, too negative a French attitude would be unwise in view of Kennedy's support for British entry. This may help to explain why, after the talks, de Gaulle told Dixon that he had been glad to have had discussions with the Prime Minister. It was 'of the greatest value' that the two should meet at regular intervals, and as a result of the Rambouillet talks he felt he could say that the *Entente* was 'still in full vigour'. He wrote in similar, if sombre, vein to the Prime Minister a few days later.[51]

Macmillan seemed close to tears when he briefed the British embassy staff on the talks, although on his return to Britain was overheard saying, 'I'm damned if I'll go there again.'[52] In his diary he described the European parts of the talks as having been 'as bad as they could be'. The brutal truth had been 'cleverly concealed by all the courtesy and good manners which surrounded the visit in all its details'. The only glimmer of hope lay in French unwillingness 'to be held up to all the world as having openly wrecked our entry and having never really tried to negotiate seriously.'[53] This, however, was precisely what de Gaulle was no longer concerned about. And something at Rambouillet seems to have rankled. There were later complaints from the French side that Macmillan had been rude; Dixon suggested that de Gaulle had been angry at finding himself out-argued by the Prime Minister. Perhaps it was after all embarrassment, or indeed a bad conscience.[54] Whatever the reason, de Gaulle made some particularly uncharitable remarks to the French Council of Ministers on 19 December, some of which were immediately leaked to the press. According to the version given later by the Information Minister, Alain Peyrefitte, de Gaulle said that both men had been melancholy at Rambouillet. 'We prefer the Britain of Macmillan to that of Labour, and would like to help him to stay in power. But what could I do, except sing to him Edith Piaf's song: *Ne pleurez pas, Milord* !' When, as the historian Philip Bell asks, had a French statesman spoken so disparagingly about a British Prime Minister?[55]

After the Council of Ministers' meeting, de Gaulle talked privately with Peyrefitte, authorising him to announce a press conference for 14 January 1963. The flaw in Wormser's strategy lay in the belief that Macmillan would be sufficiently discouraged at Rambouillet as to make him give up. De Gaulle knew the Prime Minister better and recognised that more decisive action would be necessary in order, as he put it, to settle the issue of British entry into the EEC. 'In reality,' the General bluntly continued, echoing Acheson's sentiments,

> 'England's back is broken. She does not know what she wants. She always hangs on to the dream of the Commonwealth. And at the same time she dreams of cracking the Common Market by entering with its retinue. But if we accept these conditions, it is not England which will enter the Common Market, but the Common Market which will enter the Commonwealth.'[56]

Once the EEC had been firmly established in a way conducive to French interests, things might be looked at again. ('alors nous verrons.') At his press conference he would certainly 'ferai un coup de chapeau' to Churchill, Britain's role in the Second World War and his friend Macmillan. But 'I will close the door. This has gone on long enough. At such a moment if one has not the courage to say no, one will end up being ensnared.'[57]

Chapter 18

Trouble with Missiles

T he day after his return from Paris on 16 December, Macmillan flew to
Nassau for what promised to be another extremely difficult meeting,
this time with Kennedy. Not only was the Prime Minister threatened
with British exclusion from the EEC, the future of Britain's 'independent'
nuclear deterrent and the 'special relationship', were also in doubt. The Nassau
Summit, which had originally been intended to review the post-Cuba world,
had become overshadowed by the Pentagon's decision to cancel the Skybolt
missile. The Americans, who had several much more effective systems available, did not need what was proving to be an expensive and unreliable weapon.
The British, however, desperately did and had no reinsurance against the even-
tuality of Skybolt's cancellation or failure.

Britain had made a relatively successful entry into the atomic business in
the 1950s as the world's third nuclear power. But the British-designed and
British built V bombers were quickly threatened with obsolescence by Soviet
air defence. The original plan had been to replace them with a British-built missile (albeit one based on an American design), Blue Streak, but this quickly
proved vulnerable to pre-emptive Soviet attack. After much discussion - and
the expenditure of a considerable amount of money - the weapon was abandoned in 1960.

The choice of alternative was effectively made by default. Although determined to stay in the nuclear club, Britain could only afford the minimum sub-
scription.[1] The French missile programme was still at an early stage, and there
was no interest in exploring the possibility of missile cooperation with France,
which de Gaulle had proposed when Macmillan visited him at Rambouillet in
March 1960. The easiest, indeed only, solution therefore was to opt for an

American weapon. The air-launched Skybolt had a number of advantages, not least the fact that the Americans were willing to sell it without political strings; and they were not asking for a British contribution to the research and development costs. On the other hand it was the most complex system the Americans had ever attempted: an error of one foot per second at firing translated into one thousand feet at target.[2] Nobody at this stage, as Macmillan privately admitted, knew whether it would work, indeed the formal memorandum of agreement between the two countries specifically stated that the offer was dependent on the successful and timely completion of the development programme.[3] The political implications were spelled out in a memorandum by the Minister of Defence. For all practical purposes, Harold Watkinson warned, 'we should be dependent on American goodwill: no promise by an American administration could be a guarantee of the future. We should be seen by the world to be dependent.'[4]

The Skybolt decision did not, as some of those involved at the time complained, reflect particularly well on the government. The Chancellor of the Exchequer, Derick Heathcoat Amory, saw 'great disadvantage in making such a commitment on the spur of the moment, with no examination of the merits of the alternative courses,' and warned that the government would be seen as 'plunging wildly from one weapon to another.'[5] The Prime Minister's diary entry - not quoted in his memoirs - that if the missile didn't work, 'we don't buy it', reinforces the impression of a government which found itself politically and strategically on the defensive. and which had not fully recognised what it was doing.[6]

Evidence of the dangers of putting all Britain's strategic eggs in Skybolt's still distinctly fragile basket was not long in coming. As early as October 1960 Watkinson was warned by a senior Pentagon official that the costs of Skybolt were turning out to be much greater than expected. But while Macmillan talked of the need to consider available alternatives, nothing came of this.[7] Subsequent warnings that the project was in trouble were ignored, and the government thus allowed itself to be taken by surprise when on 8 November 1962, McNamara informed David Ormsby-Gore that cancellation of the project was all but certain. This was very bad political news. To lose one strategic missile system might be regarded as a misfortune, (although not all the government's critics had been quite so charitable at the time of Blue Streak's cancellation). To lose a second within two years, looked suspiciously like carelessness. Cancellation of Skybolt would expose Britain's nuclear nakedness; it could even, or so some ministers believed, threaten the future of the government.[8] 'We must treat it calmly,' Macmillan had cabled to Ormsby-Gore shortly before the Nassau meeting, 'but it is no use trying to ignore facts.' If a realistic agreement for an alternative means to continue the British independent deterrent could not be found, 'an agonising reappraisal of all our foreign and defence policies will be required.'[9]

Ideally Macmillan would have preferred to play Skybolt for another twelve to eighteen month to avoid political difficulties at home.[10] But with the missile's technical defects being increasingly widely publicised, this was not a realistic option. The trouble was that the alternatives now were even more limited than they had been two years earlier. The prospects for developing and building a British submarine-launched missile were not good. In addition to difficulties with guidance and underwater firing systems, Britain had lost the technique of solid fuel rockets. To build up the necessary knowledge and develop the industrial infrastructure would be time-consuming and involve a formidable rearrangement of the country's industrial and technical effort.[11]

Nor did the prospect for an Anglo-French option seem promising. In the wake of the Château de Champs meeting, Macmillan had asked a committee of senior civil servants, including two former members of his Algiers staff, Roger Makins and Harold Caccia, to consider the prospects of Anglo-French nuclear cooperation assuming that Britain's entry into the EEC, as well as American approval had been secured. The result had been wholly negative. Given de Gaulle's determination to ensure the complete independence of the French nuclear deterrent, the point which Macmillan had never been willing to take fully on board, the committee had been unable to see any fruitful possibilities for Anglo-French cooperation. Skybolt's imminent cancellation does not appear to have prompted any kind of reassessment. The view in Whitehall was that even combined, the two countries lacked the technical means to produce a credible alternative which would be available before the V bombers finally became obsolete later in the decade. And there was a natural reluctance to make any nuclear deal with the General in advance of a successful outcome of the Brussels negotiations.[12]

Macmillan had, however, been careful to brief de Gaulle at Rambouillet on the Skybolt problem. He had done so reluctantly, assuming with some reason that the General would take pleasure at this evidence of Anglo-American difference, although the General was naturally much too polite to allow this to show.[13] The Prime Minister had pitched his arguments in the manner most likely to appeal to de Gaulle, emphasising the importance he attached to the possession of an independent British deterrent, since 'without it, however friendly Britain might be with the United States, she would not preserve her moral independence and this would be bad, not only for Britain, but also for Europe.' Independence was essential 'if it was ever to be possible to make the united Europe which was his dream.' If the US was unwilling to provide an adequate replacement for Skybolt, Macmillan insisted that Britain would have to make her own system, even though this might require economies in other areas of defence.[14]

The General was in fact already well informed on Skybolt's problems, and French officials believed that its cancellation might finally open up the prospect of Anglo-French nuclear cooperation. De Gaulle's briefing papers included a long list of hints and references to the possibility by British ministers and officials. This may explain a a misunderstanding at Rambouillet reminiscent of the one which occurred when they met in June 1958. The British record quotes Macmillan as saying that there was no objection to cooperating on making weapons 'if they could then be bought outright. Once bought, they passed into the possession of the buyer, in the same way as conventional warships.' The French record reads slightly differently. 'Cooperation between our two countries,' Macmillan is quoted as saying, would be useful to create an effective deterrent. De Gaulle seems to have read rather more into this than Macmillan meant, and when the General went on to make his own proposal for nuclear cooperation, Macmillan had not responded. Although the General did not pursue the matter, he duly noted his visitor's silence. In conversations with Adenauer in January 1963, de Gaulle claimed that the reason he had been very cold at the end (sic) of the Rambouillet meeting was that he sensed an American nuclear deal was in the offing.[15]

This was premature. Macmillan was in fact far from sure that the Americans would provide the replacement he wanted – the Polaris submarine-launched missile -, and had been careful not to mention the possibility at Rambouillet. The American attitude to Britain's deterrent had hardened since 1960. In Eisenhower's time, the British nuclear force had been seen as a strategic asset. The Kennedy administration was far more confident of America's nuclear superiority over the Soviet Union. It worried more than its predecessor had done about the risks of nuclear proliferation. And it was much more interested in developing nuclear war-fighting strategies which might be complicated, or even threatened, by the existence independent nuclear deterrents.[16] Already in April 1961, the month Macmillan had first raised the prospect of Anglo-French nuclear cooperation with the Americans, a National Security Council Policy Directive had referred to the desirability of phasing Britain out of the nuclear deterrent business over the long run. If the development of Skybolt was not warranted for American purposes, the directive stated, 'the US should not prolong the life of the V bomber force by this or other means.'[17]

Although not much had subsequently been done to implement this policy, Skybolt's cancellation was seized as an opportunity by some senior State Department officials. George Ball was determined 'to have the British get out of the feeling that they were a Great Power because they had an Empire, which they no longer had, and they had nuclear weapons which the others didn't have, and they had a relationship with the United States which nobody else had. This seemed to me not very healthy even from the British point of view.' Indeed during the Nassau conference the French embassy in Washington reported that White House advisers believed that possession of an independent deterrent provided a bad example for the Continent, and that Britain must 'return to the ranks'.[18]

The Nassau summit therefore opened on a very strained note. The Prime Minister was visibly tired, and the British delegation angry, though whether, as George Ball believed, the playing of 'Oh, don't deceive me' by the Bahamas band when Kennedy arrived on Air Force One was deliberate, is questionable.[19] The opening session did not go well. The Americans offered to sell an alternative air-launched missile called Hound Dog, which the British argued was unsuitable for the V bombers. Alternatively they would continue development of Skybolt with the costs shared equally between the two countries. But they did not accept the Prime Minister's argument that the much more sophisticated Polaris, which would extend the life of the British deterrent well beyond 1970 when Skybolt was expected to become obsolescent, was simply a substitute for Skybolt. To make this additional commitment to the British deterrent would cause serious trouble in Europe. It would complicate Britain's EEC bid and reinforce de Gaulle's arguments, which, according to Kennedy, 'he used to some effect round Europe about the US intention to dominate Europe.' Emphasis was also put on the knock-on effect of the British and French deterrents on German nuclear ambitions.[20] Polaris would only be supplied if British submarines were committed to a multilateral force, under NATO command. This was a very different deal from the one which Macmillan had negotiated with Eisenhower for Skybolt back in 1960, an all-too-uncomfortable a reminder how Britain's position had slipped in only two years. The independence, which Macmillan had defined to de Gaulle at Rambouillet as having forces 'under the control of United Kingdom Ministers' would be publicly compromised.[21]

Nassau sees Macmillan in his most Gaullist vein; wounded British nationalism had not been on such overt display since Suez. 'No one in England,' the Prime Minister insisted, would accept the position of there being only two nuclear powers, the US and Russia - with no other effective nuclear force. The American proposals gave the impression that 'the US only wanted "to keep the little boys quiet."' De Gaulle would say the UK had sold out.' The Atlantic alliance would never succeed except on a pooling of equal pride and honour.[22] Nuclear weapons might be only a status symbol, 'a question of keeping up with the Joneses', but the UK did not want to be 'just a clown or a satellite'. An independent nuclear deterrent was essential if Britain was to 'remain something in the world'.[23] As to the idea of a multilateral force, Macmillan echoed de Gaulle's complaint about NATO's integrated command structure. A British admiral of the Fleet must be in a position of issuing commands, 'otherwise the units would have no life of their own.'[24]

In confronting his American audience, the Prime Minister had a number of advantages he had not enjoyed at Rambouillet. In the first place he was not with an ally-rival, but among friends. At the personal level, the President was much more susceptible to the kind of emotional appeal which Macmillan was so good at, but which had no impact on the General. Alistair Horne describes how as the two leaders 'strolled together, disregarding the rough edges of their staffs, talking not only about the Skybolt crisis and politics, but also about their shared interest in history and the things that both found ridiculous or funny, or deadly serious, the whole atmosphere began to change from above.'[25]

At the same time Macmillan knew how to play on American fears. His own political weakness, which de Gaulle saw as an opportunity for French diplomacy, could be put to British advantage at Nassau. However dubious some of the rhetoric of 'interdependence', the Skybolt underscored the fact that the Americans were in some senses dependent on Macmillan. Over and above their concerns about the prospects of a Labour government, which seemed likely to pursue much less pro-American policies, they could not afford to be seen to be double-crossing their oldest and closest ally.[26] 'We have to have somebody to talk to in the world,' Rusk had told State Department colleagues a few days before Nassau. 'We can't talk to de Gaulle or Adenauer; do you want to take Macmillan away and leave nobody? Do you want to leave me with nobody but Harold Wilson?'[27] Macmillan's threats of an 'agonising reappraisal' of British policy, of a 'deep rift' with the United States, had therefore a much greater impact on the Americans than his frequently repeated threat to withdraw British forces from the Continent ever had on de Gaulle. A threat of nuclear cooperation with the French may also have helped.[28]

By the end of the conference a compromise was therefore agreed. Britain would get Polaris and commit the submarines to NATO, but there was a vital escape clause; the force could be withdrawn where 'Her Majesty's Government may decide that supreme national interests are at stake.' Just what this hastily and ambiguously drafted phrase meant was not clear. But it allowed the Prime Minister to claim to have preserved the 'independence' of the British nuclear deterrent, while the Americans could point to a British commitment to a multilateral nuclear force.[29]

* * *

The *Beyond the Fringe* team had fun with Nassau.

Kennedy, Peter Cook's Prime Minister told his audience, had kindly shown him some beautiful photographs of Polaris, taken by Karsch of Ottawa, no less. Britain would be very proud to have these pictures - the actual missiles would unfortunately not be available for some years. Meanwhile Britain would have to keep very quiet and try not to upset anybody.[30]

Like the Cuban missile crisis, Nassau can be read different ways. Macmillan had done an effective salvage job. He had largely neutralised the US attempt, admittedly only half-hearted, to rein in the British nuclear deterrent. Polaris, which was being obtained on remarkably favourable financial terms, was an infinitely superior weapon to Skybolt, and the Nassau agreement effectively secured the future of the British deterrent for the rest of the century. When the time to replace Polaris came in the early 1980s, the American decision to substitute Trident went through 'on the nod'. Some two decades later, when the question of Trident's replacement was under consideration, President George W. Bush told Congress that it remained in US interests to continue assisting Britain to maintain a credible nuclear force. All this was a vindication of the Prime Minister's personal diplomacy, as of the 'special relationship'.[31]

At the same time the crisis had dramatically illustrated the risks of the nuclear overdependency culture on the Americans which had developed during the Macmillan years. If Macmillan had managed to demonstrate that Britain was no satellite, the case for *independence* was now more difficult to make, indeed the Permanent Secretary at the Ministry of Defence thought the deal would put Britain 'in the American pocket' for the next decade.[32] Nassau had gone as far as, if not further than, was politically endurable in Britain, and some ministers, as Macmillan privately admitted, believed that Britain had been 'degraded from a "special position" to that of a European Power.'[33] Last, and by no means least, there was the impact of the agreement on de Gaulle and Britain's by now very shaky prospects of joining the EEC.

The spectre of the General had hovered over the Nassau meeting. Fearing that Rambouillet would play into the hands of American opponents of the 'special relationship', Macmillan had managed to withhold news of what had happened, insisting that the effect of a new agreement on the Common Market negotiations would be 'frankly, absolutely none'. France's reaction nevertheless remained a matter of serious concern to the Americans.[34] So much so that Kennedy had decided to offer Polaris to France on the same terms as Britain. This was not quite the new departure it seemed. During the Cuban missile crisis, a reluctant State Department had been instructed by Kennedy to reverse the long-standing policy of nuclear non-cooperation, although following the speedy resolution of the crisis, nothing had been done to implement the policy.[35] Now, the American ambassador to Paris was instructed to tell the French that the Polaris offer implied a willingness to recognise France as a nuclear power 'and to bring substantially to an end the exclusive quality of the US-UK relationship'.[36]

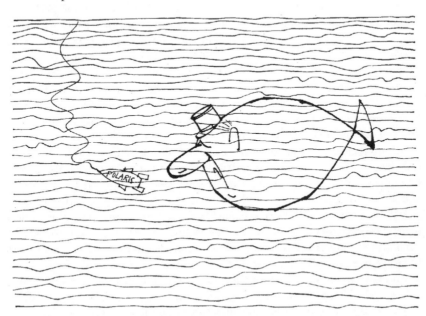

Atlantic with bait and skeptical fish
Paul Flora, Ach du liebe Zeit ii, (Copyright 1964 Diogenes Verlag AG Zurich)

Nassau thoroughly muddied the European waters. The president had given little prior consideration as to whether the French - who had neither the submarines nor the warheads - had any use for Polaris. Nor was much thought given as to how a deal stitched up hurriedly at an exclusively Anglo-Saxon summit might be made palatable to the General. At one stage there was talk that Macmillan or Kennedy might fly to Paris, but this got lost amidst the distractions of the last-minute work on the communiqué.[37] But the fundamental problem with the proposal was neither technical nor presentational. De Gaulle had no interest whatsoever in an offer tied to a multilateral force, which he viewed as an attempt to camouflage American hegemony, an issues over which he had become increasingly preoccupied since the end of the Algerian war. Unlike Macmillan, he was unwilling to accept an ambiguous compromise about the conditions under which national control could be reasserted.[38]

That, however, did not mean that the General was indifferent to what had happened. His suggestion to Adenauer that Macmillan's refusal of the offer of Anglo-French nuclear cooperation had affected the outcome of the Rambouillet talks was disingenuous. The decision to oppose the British bid pre-dated Rambouillet. De Gaulle was simply taking advantage of the Nassau affair to impugn Macmillan's European credentials, never very difficult where Adenauer was concerned, and justify his intended veto.[39] Nevertheless, the General's further remark to the West German Chancellor, that he found it singular that Macmillan should be making special nuclear arrangements with the United States without discussing the subject with its European allies, has a ring of truth to it.[40] So too does his more rhetorically emotive question to Peyrefitte, 'How can we allow a country to enter Europe which has at this moment made allegiance to the Americans?' By opting for Polaris, Macmillan was in de Gaulle's eyes backtracking from the hints he had dropped at Château de Champs, thus confirming all the General's suspicions about the Prime Minister's instinctive Atlanticism. In the process he was also rendering impossible the prospect of a European nuclear force so central to the General's European design. Macmillan, the General told de Courcel, 'has let me down, and you can tell him so'.[41]

The General's disdain had been evident from the outset. Although he had only finally revealed his hand at his 14 January press conference, he had shown little interest in the deal when briefed by Sir Pierson Dixon on 21 December, and the ambassador subsequently warned that this initial negative reaction would be maintained.[42] In a separate letter surveying the post-Rambouillet scene, Dixon advised that an EEC veto was now possible. De Gaulle would prefer not to be blamed for failure, 'but I now think he might consider a success to be worse from his point of view than would be the attribution of blame.' There was nothing, in the ambassador's view, more to be done with the French, though it might be marginally worth attempting to mobilise the Five, by convincing them that the British were being 'better Europeans' than de Gaulle [43]

Macmillan, however, could not afford to be so hard-headed. He knew that on both the EEC and Nassau counts the odds were against him. A Boxing Day memorandum entitled 'Tasks Ahead' referred to the need to consider how the Brussels talks should be broken off if this became necessary. 'We do not expect much from de Gaulle except obstinacy and non-cooperation,' he noted in his diary on 31 December, '*but we must try.*' (emphasis added)[44] Giving up was never in Macmillan's style. In Philip de Zulueta's words:

> 'When one is in a negotiation one simply cannot know how it will come out until it is over; to conclude prematurely that one is bound to lose, is to disarm one's self. The Prime Minister, characteristically, is very much aware of that. His stance as a negotiator is never to let down until the bell, and never above all to *show* that one is giving up... De Gaulle had never really been *friendly*; at Rambouillet he was merely *colder*, but that's relative. He had changed his tack before, he might again. Besides, there were the Five. No matter, the worse it looked for us the *more* important to give him the sense that we were going on, straight on, despite him...To let him sense anything else would have been to play into his hands.'[45] (emphasis in original)

And the Prime Minister had still not despaired of a nuclear deal. France would face many difficulties in accepting the US offer, he told a ministerial meeting on New Year's Eve, 'and it might be that we could help them in a number of ways,' for example with the development or construction of a missile.[46]

Or, indeed, warheads. Shortly after Nassau, Kennedy is quoted as telling Ormsby-Gore that if de Gaulle 'accepts this deal - and I don't think he will - warheads lie at the end of the road - yours.'[47] Macmillan had subsequently raised this highly sensitive issue in a letter to the British ambassador. Might the President agree to Britain supplying France with warheads on the understanding, which would not, however, be part of a written agreement, that France would bring the Brussels talks to a successful conclusion? 'It sounds rather a crude deal,' the Prime Minister wrote, 'but it is not. It is an attempt to bring off during 1963 what would really be the foundation of a very sound system. Without the French, and that is to say without Europe, I fear we shall all be forced back into isolationism of one kind or another.'[48] In discussion in London with Dixon on 31 December, Macmillan instructed him to explore an Anglo-French deal to cooperate independently of the US on Polaris. If the ambassador found the General to be unreceptive, he was authorised to raise the stakes and discuss Anglo-French cooperation over a warhead.[49]

The New Year began badly for the Prime Minister. The Americans were trying to help. Kennedy had invited the French ambassador, Hervé Alphand, onto his yacht at Palm Beach, where he had dropped hints that ways might be found of overcoming the French problem about launchers and submarines. He had also taken the opportunity of applying a little pressure over British membership of the EEC, expressing serious concern about Macmillan's political future and talking of the risk of a Labour government which would recognise East Germany and be accommodating to the Soviet Union. The future of the

EEC negotiations, the President suggested, would play an important role in determining the Prime Minister's fate. But American advocacy of this latter kind was at best counterproductive in de Gaulle's eyes. And *pace* the President's reported earlier comments, Ormsby-Gore's did not believe that Kennedy would sanction British help with warheads.[50] From Paris Couve de Murville, ridiculing the notion of a multilateral force, was reported as saying that in the past it was normal for states to hire and pay for mercenaries. Now the Americans were trying to persuade their European allies to serve as mercenaries who would themselves pay for the privilege.[51]

The same day Dixon saw de Gaulle again and found that, as the ambassador had expected, reflection had only confirmed the General in his hostility. He impugned the whole notion of a multilateral force, in ways which Dixon described as not just critical but very disparaging of the Americans. De Gaulle expressed scepticism about the Nassau escape clause, doubting whether 'anyone, even ourselves, who subscribed to this idea, would in practice be able to withdraw their nuclear contribution for national purposes. The command structure, the habits of work, etc., would sap the will to act in a national way.' Finally, Dixon reported, 'the General mumbled acidly that he quite understood why, with all our tradition, we had not found it possible to tell the Americans that the terms of their offer of nuclear help were unacceptable, and turn instead to cooperate with European nuclear defence.'[52]

Dixon asked whether the General was thinking of making any public statements about French views in the near future. The General replied that 'he had no present intention of doing so'. As the ambassador was leaving, however, de Gaulle said that he would no doubt be asked questions about Polaris at his press conference in about a week's time: 'he would be very prudent.' De Gaulle had still not finished. Were the British, who had suggested Anglo-French talks on the use of missiles, prepared to help France over construction, including warheads and 'the motors' for nuclear submarines? 'He thought not, under our arrangement with the Americans. I said he would appreciate that I could not give him an answer to such a question. However, I felt sure that explanations about next steps with the Americans and the technical implementation could not fail to be to our mutual interest.'[53]

Dixon, who described the General as having an extraordinarily oversimplified view of the problems of building a nuclear deterrent, had played his hand with great caution. The ambassador had dropped hints of possible cooperation which he had no doubt that the General would have picked up, but gone no further. Given what he described as de Gaulle's 'bitter anti-American prejudices', the ambassador did not believe that a warhead deal would tip the balance in favour of acceptance of the American offer, or dispose him to agree to British EEC membership. The risk was that de Gaulle would swallow the nuclear bait without taking the EEC hook, in effect picking Britain's nuclear brains in order to continue pursuing his own independent policy.[54] Yet neither this advice, nor warnings from Charles Bohlen, the American ambassador in Paris, against the British going beyond the techniques of the use of Polaris in their proposed talks with the French, would put Macmillan off. While accepting that it would be a mistake to pursue the idea of nuclear cooperation without a certain quid pro quo, the Prime Minister still believed 'that we might now go this small degree further in indicating that once Brussels is out of the way we shall be ready to have frank discussions with the French and shall not just try to push these back under the rug.'[55]

Dixon's reticence was amply justified. De Gaulle was in self-confident mood. France, as he wrote to de Courcel, was beginning the New Year with several trumps in hand.[56] At the French Council of Ministers' meeting on 3 January, the General underscored his hostility to the Polaris deal. France must keep its hands free, which was precisely what the Americans wanted to prevent its doing. They did not want their allies to have an independent strategy or policy. This was a fair judgement. At a meeting in Washington McNamara had suggested that providing nuclear equipment to Britain and France would 'make them more dependent on us as a source of supply, thus enhancing indirectly our power to control final policies.'[57]

The broader thrust of de Gaulle's thinking is suggested by remarks made after the meeting to Peyrefitte. Before his return to power, the General said, Britain had lived with the idea that she was the privileged sister. She did not have an independent nuclear force, but she was the only one to have a finger on the American trigger. This gave her a dominant position in Europe, and an ability to play off Continental rivalries. Now, however, France was gaining her own independent force, while Britain had put its deterrent in a multilateral force under an American commander, and become an American satellite. If she entered the Common Market, it would be only as a Trojan horse for the Americans, which would mean Europe losing its independence. When Peyrefitte asked whether this is what de Gaulle would say, at his press conference, the General replied, 'Not like that!'[58]

On 8 January news reached Dixon that the General had decided to reject the Polaris deal. The next day the new British Cabinet Secretary, Sir Burke Trend, warned Macmillan of the need to speed up the EEC negotiations, because of an erosion of public support for Europe. On 10 January *Le Monde* published an article, based on an off-the-record Elysée briefing, which accurately predicted the contents of the press conference.[59] George Ball who was in Paris, in connection with the Nassau deal, duly tackled Couve de Murville, who denied that a veto was imminent. Edward Heath posed the same question at the end of a lunch where there had been an interesting discussion about French literature. The understated language of the British official record is eloquent.

'In answer to a remark by the Lord Privy Seal, M. Couve indicated that he did not expect General de Gaulle at his press conference on Monday to make statements which might have the effect of bringing the Brussels negotiations to a halt. The Lord Privy Seal asked M. Couve whether the French political objections to our coming into

Europe at the present moment meant that even if we were able to solve the economic problems of Brussels this would mean that the French would still oppose our entry. M.Couve replied with some emphasis that if the economic problems could be solved nothing could prevent our acceding to the European Economic Community. The Lord Privy Seal said that this was an important statement of which he took note.'[60]

Foreign Ministers, while often economical with the truth, do not normally lie outright, and over the preceding months Heath had established a good working relationship with Couve. As he records in his memoirs, the Lord Privy Seal returned to London feeling 'rather satisfied'. The Prime Minister too retained his resolute optimism. French propaganda, he noted in his diary on the 12th, 'is developing on familiar lines. I am not discouraged. They often do this as a prelude to an agreement.' 'A good week,' he commented a day later, reflecting on the sixth anniversary of his premiership. Two days later in a classic example of what French officials called 'le jupiterisme' - government by thunderbolt - the storm broke.[61]

Chapter 19

Jupiterism and After

With his press conference on 14 January 1963, de Gaulle changed roles. Gone was the skilful diplomat who had long sought to keep Macmillan guessing. In his place was the master of political theatre, the man who had no compunction in defying all his allies in his determination of promote French interests and ambition. He had spent the previous three weeks preparing for the event, with all non-essential engagements cleared from his diary. The case against the British - or English, as the General put it - application which he presented publicly, perceptively enumerated the underlying differences between Britain and the countries of the EEC. Britain was:

'insular, she is maritime, she is linked through her exchanges, her markets, her supply lines to the most diverse and often the most distant countries; she pursues essentially industrial and commercial activities, and only slightly agricultural ones. She has in all her doings very marked and very original habits and traditions. In short, the nature, the structure, the very situation that are England's differ profoundly from those of the continentals.'

Blame for the impending failure of the talks was placed on Britain's failure to transform herself sufficiently to become part of the European Community, 'without restriction, without reserve, and in preference to anything else', a veiled reference to both the Commonwealth and the Americans.[2]

The condescension of tone, which Macmillan had already noted at Rambouillet, was perhaps primarily a matter of style. But it also suggests a conscious turning of Anglo-French tables, if not a settling of historic scores. De

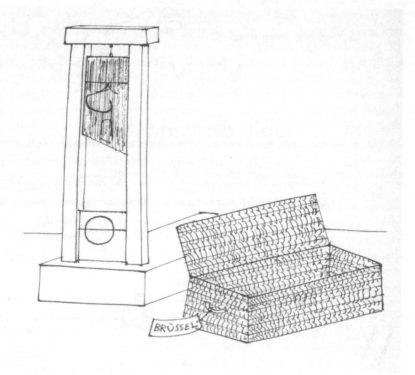

Paul Flora, Ach du liebe Zeit, ii, (Copyright 1964 Diogenes Verlag, AG Zurich)

Gaulle had not forgotten the many occasions in which the British had worsted the French; there was a specific reference in the press conference to the frequent Anglo-French conflicts. Nor can he have been unaware that he was speaking almost exactly twenty years after the Casablanca Summit, where he had felt so humiliated by the Anglo-Saxons. According to one French official, although it was the British who had borne the brunt of the General's attack, he had really been aiming at the Americans; the General had also rejected Kennedy's Polaris offer and the proposed NATO multilateral force. The point, however, is at best moot. Both Anglo-Saxon Powers had been publicly defied, with the British sustaining by far the most serious damage.[3]

The reaction to this extraordinary performance fully lived up to the General's expectations. De Gaulle had achieved the surprise and shock he had sought, and clearly enjoyed the ensuing scandal. 'Strange times, gentlemen,' one of those present records him as saying at the next Council of Ministers' meeting, 'when one cannot say, without provoking I do not know what kind of hullabaloo, that England is an island and America is not Europe.' It was his only remark on the subject, and came right at the end of the session.[4]

The anger and indignation at the contempt which the General had shown for partners, allies and opponents were widespread. Kennedy phoned the

British embassy in Washington and delivered himself of what Ormsby-Gore diplomatically described as 'some crisp and highly critical comments'. In Brussels, the Italian Foreign Minister warned that Italy and the other members of the EEC couldn't be 'treated like colonies.' The outspoken Dutch Foreign Minister, Joseph Luns, drew unflattering parallels between the General's behaviour and Soviet treatment of their East European satellites. After Couve had accused the Dutch of having always been lackeys of the English, Luns replied, 'Yes, I suppose you could say that in the sense that you could talk of you French as always having been the raw material of their victories.'[5] Although the response in France was mixed, several years later the British embassy admitted that in their hearts few Frenchmen dissented from the General's decision.[6]

Macmillan naturally shared in the international indignation, telling Kennedy on the 19th that the General had 'gone crazy - absolutely crazy.' His initial response to what one British newspaper had described as 'the Olympian excommunication,' had, however, been calmer. It was important, he wrote to ministers the day after the press conference, to 'keep our nerve and not be dragged into speculation, still less into a battle of words...(we) should let the pressure and anger develop now from the Five and not from Britain. If at the end of it all a measure of agreement can be reached in a practical way over a wide field, then de Gaulle's philosophical observations will look a trifle absurd.' De Gaulle might have hoped that Britain would break off the talks in Brussels, Macmillan told the Cabinet on the 17th; instead Britain's objective should be to maintain the negotiations and unite the Five, though it was not certain that they would have the strength to resist French pressure.[7]

This would prove uncomfortably near the mark, but France's EEC partners enjoyed an immediate tactical advantage in that French officials and ministers in Brussels had been taken as much by surprise as everybody else by the press conference. The unfortunate French Agriculture Minister, Edgard Pisani, was acutely embarrassed to find himself in the middle of a negotiating session in Brussels when the news came. Olivier Wormser was overheard saying, 'If only he'd told me beforehand I could have done it so much better.' Couve de Murville seemed uncertain how to bring the negotiations to an end.[8] Faced with the threat of retaliation against French interests, including future progress towards the all-important Common Agricultural Policy, the French Foreign Minister was forced to postpone a final decision until the next ministerial meeting on 28 January.[9]

At Couve's suggestion, and apparently without de Gaulle's knowledge, the French Foreign Minister subsequently held a private meeting with Dixon. The British record is again eloquent. Couve, Dixon reported

'started by saying stiffly that it was painful for the French Foreign Minister to see the British ambassador in such unfortunate circumstances. He went on to speak in an apologetic way about the situation which had now arisen. He understood how shocked we must have been by General de Gaulle's statement at his press conference.'

Much of the conversation focused on defence and Nassau. The whole question, Couve noted, 'was really about Europe in its political and defence aspects. Perhaps the French government at an earlier stage should have discussed the political aspects with us frankly.' De Gaulle had been disappointed by the Prime Minister's failure to say anything about defence cooperation and building Europe up as an effective entity vis-à-vis the United States at Rambouillet, and British press comments about Nassau had shown no instinctive desire to turn to Europe as an alternative. 'It was the psychological effect of all this on the General which mattered.' An unimpressed Dixon commented to the Foreign Office that he thought 'it would be going a little far to suggest that the General see a psychiatrist.' At the end of the session, when Dixon had asked whether there was any prospect of a change in the French position in Brussels, Couve shook his head.[10]

Couve's embarrassment was evident. He had after all given Heath the assurance that there would be no veto. And while agreeing with the General's policy, as a professional diplomat he was not at ease with the General's highly undiplomatic methods. The General in turn seems to have been dissatisfied with Couve's performance at Brussels. According to a British embassy source, the Foreign Minister 'had his head washed' for failing to terminate the talks before an important visit by Adenauer to Paris. De Gaulle had another *coup de théâtre* in the offing, in the form of a Franco-German treaty.[11] De Gaulle's press conference was putting Adenauer under intense domestic and international pressure to try to change de Gaulle's mind over the British EEC bid. A telegram from the Foreign Office to Bonn spoke of the need to make it clear to Adenauer that there would be 'a political row of the first magnitude' if he acquiesced in Britain's exclusion from the EEC. Macmillan duly urged Kennedy to put 'a little bit of fear' into the Chancellor's mind.[12]

De Gaulle, however, knew his man. While recognising the political need to do something 'to calm down spirits in Brussels', the Chancellor, who like the General had iron political nerves, was unwilling to go any further.[13] Reconciliation with France was for Adenauer an historic act, the crowning point of his career. It offered a critical reinsurance against the pressure from the East, as well as additional international leverage for the FRG.[14] As the Chancellor himself put it, acting with France, Germany, 'can exert greater influence in international affairs; without France, we cannot.' Against this Macmillan, who was paying the belated German price for his earlier Summit diplomacy and general neglect of the Chancellor, could not compete. Shortly after the veto the British embassy in Bonn reported somebody close to Adenauer commenting that far from stretching out the hand of friendship, Britain had been 'cold, reserved and strictly practical'. At the same time there was also reported to be a good deal of sneaking German sympathy for de Gaulle's view that Britain was not yet ripe for collaboration with Europe.[15]

The British question was not therefore allowed to stand in the way of the signature of the Franco-German treaty on 22 January. Adenauer made no protest over the press conference or de Gaulle's failure to consult beforehand, nor did he complain about the political difficulties the affair had caused him. And when he raised the British application towards the end of the second day of the talks, he did little to argue the British case. The German ambassador in Paris, Herbert Blankenhorn, depicted de Gaulle as having sought to put the British in a very bad light, although for his part de Gaulle said little to Adenauer about the British bid which he had not said before. He did, however, deny a suggestion which Macmillan had just publicly made, that France did not want Britain in the EEC. If that had been true, the General somewhat disingenuously remarked, the French certainly wouldn't have negotiated for fifteen months. The danger was that by making concession after concession, one would completely distort the EEC.[16]

Coming little more than a week after the press conference, the news of the Franco-German treaty proved a considerable shock. When the Cabinet met in London on 22 January, Macmillan was in one of his most apocalyptic moods. The General had shown his intention to work for the inward-looking Europe, necessary for the removal of American forces and the break up NATO. He might see the attractions of a deal with Moscow, possibly leading to German reunification and neutralisation. There was little that Britain could do to influence events in the EEC in the immediate future - 'these great issues would probably be settled without us.' The Prime Minister described the Franco-German treaty as an instrument by which de Gaulle hoped to 'subject the course of German policy to his own views and to the aggrandisement of France.' The failure of the negotiations would have political and commercial consequences 'of the gravest kind.' Britain might have to re-examine its commitment to maintain its forces on the Continent, since the circumstances under which it had been made had radically changed.[17]

A day later the Belgian Foreign Minister, Paul-Henri Spaak, spoke to the British ambassador in Brussels about the need to stop dictators at the beginning of their dictatorship, a theme rapidly picked up by Dixon.[18] The language of a telegram from Paris was reminiscent of that used by Churchill and Roosevelt during the war.

'The situation in Paris is gradually deteriorating. Many of the Gaullist faithfuls, in and out of the Elysée and the U.N.R., are getting beyond the embryo Fascist stage. The lying propaganda campaign mounted by de Gaulle's machine is extremely disagreeable. The Minister of Information, (Peyrefitte), who perhaps sees more of the General than any other Minister these days, is regarded by decent Frenchmen as despicable. Provincial editors are reproached by prefects if they write anti-Gaullist editorials. Our friends in the Quai d'Orsay do not hesitate to say, and not only to us, that the General is, in fact, a maniac when it comes to power. France is not yet, of course, a police State but the telephones are widely tapped and in the last few weeks people have begun to grow cautious. The Nationalist drum is constantly beaten. There is a real danger that chauvinism may take hold in this country if de Gaulle continues to succeed and that the important minority of reasonable internationalist Europeans in positions of influence may be submerged.'[19]

When the General had said at his press conference that Britain could join the EEC one day, the embassy continued, he was thinking 'of a moment when Britain herself would have been humiliated and brought to her knees and will only be too glad to come crawling to a French-led Europe.' The General saw the Franco-German alliance as a step towards a reversal of alliances. 'If not defeated de Gaulle may become really dangerous.'[20]

While this was grossly overstepping the mark, the General's wartime interest in a Franco-Soviet pact, and the general atmosphere bordering at times on near hysteria which de Gaulle had generated since 14 January, were making policy-makers in London and Washington particularly receptive to alarmist intelligence reports. The one about a possible French deal with Moscow appears to have originated with the British. But the Americans were sufficiently concerned for Kennedy to instruct that intelligence resources should be concentrated on finding out 'everything we can' about discussions between the French and the Russians.[21] In fact the rumours were completely unfounded, and Moscow was strongly opposed to the Franco-German treaty. The Soviet paper *Izvestia* described it as 'stuffed with military articles like lamb with garlic', and a strong Soviet diplomatic protest was lodged in Paris.[22]

De Gaulle took the pressure in his stride, though some of his ministers remained more nervous. At the Council of Ministers held on 24 January, Couve expressed concern about the solidarity shown in Brussels between Britain and the Five, and warned of the possibility that the *Bundestag* might refuse to ratify the Franco-German treaty if the French insisted on German support. There were, Couve suggested, two alternatives: 'une crise brutale', the General's choice, or a more diffused termination of the negotiations by asking the Commission to draw up a report in order to gain time, which the Foreign Minister preferred. The General contented himself by concluding that the Anglo-Saxons, along with their friends in the press and in French political circles,were making 'a quite unimaginable racket.'[23] Couve's continued unease is suggested by a second private meeting with Dixon, two days later, at which the French Foreign Minister talked of the 'terrible mess' which things now were in. Although France might be temporarily isolated, he believed that in the long term it would find itself in better shape than Britain. More surprising was Couve's reference to the need to 'look ahead to a time when present personalities were no longer there'. Such veiled references to de Gaulle were rare from his loyal Foreign Minister.[24]

The British, however, were not interested in the long term. Their preoccupation now was simply with ensuring that the French took the blame for the impending failure of the negotiations.[25] Macmillan's initial sangfroid had disappeared. The impending veto was only one of a series of problems, including the impact of a bitterly cold winter on power supplies, unemployment and the attacks on the Nassau agreement, which brought the Prime Minister close to despair. It was, he wrote to a friend on the 28th, the worst time he had been through since Suez. In his diary he referred to Peyrefitte as 'the new Goebbels', and Adenauer as 'the Pétain of Germany.'

> 'All our policies at home and abroad are in ruins. Our defence plans have been radically changed, from air to sea. European unity is no more; French domination of Europe is the new and alarming feature; our popularity as a Government is rapidly declining. We have lost everything, except our courage and determination.'[26]

The press was far less self-pitying. The *Daily Mail* complained that de Gaulle had been 'stringing Britain along until he could conveniently stab her in the back', while the *Daily Herald* described Britain's bid to join Europe as having been blocked by de Gaulle's blind obstinacy and his arrogant ambition to see France dominate Europe. This upset the French embassy in London, which complained that while the more serious papers were keeping their expressions of resentment against France within acceptable bounds, the popular press was calling the Five for a 'crusade against the ungodly', with Napoleon, Hitler, Agincourt, Waterloo and Fashoda being reportedly evoked pel-mel.[27]

The *coup de grâce* was delivered by a nervous Couve in Brussels. Heath was defiantly dignified, declaring that Britain would not turn its back on Europe, of which it was a part by 'geography, tradition, history, culture and civilisation'.[28] At the end of the session, he went round to thank ministers and officials from the Five and the Commission. Couve and Wormser went into a corner and turned their backs. In his memoirs Heath ascribes this to embarrassment. Macmillan's response at the time was less charitable. Couve, he wrote, had behaved 'with a rudeness which was unbelievable'.[29]

The atmosphere in London the following day, as described by the French embassy, was very heavy; the English were consternated.[30] In a broadcast made in a tone of suppressed anger, and which the embassy claimed was distributed in thirty-three languages, Macmillan described the breakdown of the negotiations as 'bad, bad for us, bad for Europe, and bad for the whole Free World.' He attacked de Gaulle's European policy as backward-looking and misguided. France and her government seemed 'to think that one nation can dominate Europe and, equally wrong, that Europe can or ought to stand alone. But Europe cannot stand alone. She must cooperate with the rest of the Free World, with the Commonwealth, with the United States in *an equal and honourable partnership.*' (emphasis added)[31]

Injured national pride - the veto had followed swiftly on Acheson's remark about Britain having lost an empire and failed to find a role - which had raised a storm of protest the previous month, mixed with a resurgence of francophobia. 'At home,' Macmillan noted in his diary on 4 February, 'there is the return of the old feeling "the French always betray you in the end."' This had the immediate advantage of obscuring the scale of the reversal which the

Prime Minister had suffered. As one American observer remarked, next to getting into the EEC triumphant, there was no better political posture than being kept out by the French.[32] The hard fact was, however, that the EEC bid had been Macmillan's last big initiative. He had gambled heavily on what he had known from the outset would be a very difficult set of negotiations, and having lost he was, as after the collapse of the FTA negotiations in 1958, once again without a European policy. Since de Gaulle's press conference, there had been some discussion about the creation of a new grouping of the Five plus Britain, possibly to be launched at a conference in London. The very fact of holding it in the British capital, Dixon argued, would be such a defeat for de Gaulle that it would be hard to see that he could survive. But even assuming that the Five had been willing to take such a step, London had quickly got cold feet on account of the Five's commitment to a supranational Europe, and the possibility of additional European defence commitments being demanded of Britain.[33] Having no fall-back position, Macmillan was politically vulnerable to Harold Wilson's charge that he lacked the capacity or ideas to chart a course out of the 'Sargossa sea' in which the government felt themselves becalmed.[34] Macmillan was too tired to turn the crisis into a Dunkirk-style victory. Nor, as after Suez, could he pretend that nothing had happened.

The implications for the Conservatives" already uncertain electoral prospects were obvious, not least in Paris where de Gaulle expected Labour to win the next election, but predicted that British membership of the EEC would only come after the Conservatives' subsequent return to power.[35] But there was also a more personal factor. Macmillan was devastated. At a meeting in Rome in early February, he astonished his Italian hosts by declaring that he was not interested in the technical trade details under discussion; he just wanted to make clear that the events of the past week had been a complete disaster, and he did not know what to do. Heath had 'terrible difficulties' with Macmillan after the veto. 'He wouldn't do anything, wouldn't concentrate on anything. This was the end of the world.' Lord Home's private secretary, Sir Oliver Wright, described the veto as a blow 'political, psychological and physical' from which the Prime Minister never really recovered.[36]

* * *

De Gaulle was not, however, to have it all his own way. Macmillan's diary reference of early February to nobody knowing what de Gaulle would do next - 'it is terribly reminiscent of the late 1930s - waiting on Hitler', seriously exaggerated the General's power.[37] De Gaulle was not about to stride the European scene like a colossus. Although he had correctly judged his EEC partners' reactions - as one French official crudely put it, they had 'big mouths' but were bad at sustaining action - de Gaulle would have to pay a price for his unilateralism.[38] The January crisis had exposed his aims and methods to unprecedentedly hostile scrutiny, generating a fund of suspicion and ill-will which would handicap the General's future European diplomacy. There is no evidence to suggest that serious attempts were made to prevent the ratification of the Franco-German treaty, a possibility which the British and American embassies in Bonn had discussed at the end of January. But the *Bundestag* did write an important qualification into the preamble, reaffirming the FRG's commitment to the existing European communities and to NATO. By the time de Gaulle next visited Bonn in July, the bloom was already off the Franco-German relationship. Treaties, the General remarked, 'are like young girls and roses; they last as long as they last'.[39]

Anglo-French relations made a slow recovery following an ill-judged, and much criticised, cancellation of a visit to Paris by Princess Margaret. The French were naturally anxious to try to minimise the damage. When in April Lord Home attended a reception at the Elysée for ministers from member states of the South East Asia Treaty Organisation, de Gaulle enquired after Macmillan, and then, without waiting for an answer, went on to say that he knew that the Prime Minister was angry with him. 'He had no real cause for this. The General's warm feelings of friendship for Mr Macmillan had not changed nor had his warm feelings towards England. If difficulties had arisen between them,' he enigmatically continued, 'it was perhaps because they had both basically had the same ideas but the ideas had come together at the wrong moment.'[40]

Macmillan's view, as expressed in early March, was that the British attitude towards the French should be one of 'wait and see.' Others, however, were keen to see whether something might not yet be saved from the wreckage. The Minister of Defence, Peter Thorneycroft, who in 1955 had co-sponsored Plan G in a reluctant British cabinet, produced a paper arguing the case for Anglo-French nuclear cooperation. Macmillan duly demurred. He did not see what Britain could get out of such an approach and did not think that it would be wise 'to appear to be running after the French when they have after all behaved so badly'.[41] The suggestion of a nuclear deal in return for EEC entry was next raised by the Minister of Aviation, Julian Amery, shortly before a visit to London by the French Defence Minister, Pierre Messmer. Macmillan now seemed attracted, but Heath and Home were opposed, and on 17 July Thorneycroft was instructed to confine the discussions to technical issues. If the French Defence Minister raised wider issues, Thorneycroft could 'not refuse to listen', but should merely take note.[42]

The next day Thoneycroft duly reported that Messmer had indeed raised wider issues. He had come to discuss cooperation on strategic missiles which could form part of a package deal which would include settlement of the EEC question and joint targeting of nuclear weapons both separately with Britain, and with Britain and the United States together. If these represented de Gaulle's views, which certainly cannot be ruled out, wrote Thorneycroft, they would present 'some important possibilities'.[43] The French account is rather different. According to de Courcel, it was Thorneycroft who raised the possibility of a deal to include Britain's supplying France with nuclear information, the reform of NATO, the co-ordination of the British and French deterrents, particularly in the area of targeting, and British entry into the EEC. While surprised by the suggestion, de Courcel found it difficult to believe that the plans had not had Macmillan's prior approval, and quoted 'a close collaborator' of Macmillan's who had read Thonrneycroft's account of the talks, as saying that important developments could be expected after the signature of a nuclear test ban treaty.[44] Having been expressly forbidden to raise the issue himself by Macmillan, Thorneycroft appears to have put his own ideas into Messmer's mouth.

The testing of nuclear weapons in the atmosphere, symbolised by the now largely-forgotten mushroom cloud, had been one of the most sinister features of the earlier years of the Cold War. Over and above their environmental effects, nuclear tests had been a source of international tension and public fear, and negotiations for a test ban treaty had been going on since the late 1950s. Like the Summit, this was a cause very close to Macmillan's heart. For the Prime Minister it was an issue of human decency and survival, rather than simply a question of domestic political expediency, and he had repeatedly pressed both Eisenhower and Kennedy for an agreement.

It was the shock produced by the Cuban missile crisis, which finally helped clear the way for what became the first arms control agreement of the Cold War. When news of the signature of the treaty banning tests in the atmosphere reached London on 25 July, Macmillan was deeply affected. In his diary he records having to go out of the room. 'I went to tell D(orothy) and burst into tears. I had prayed hard for this night after night.'[45] But it was not an unalloyed triumph. Britain, as *The Times* noted, 'was in Moscow as a third man', while Lord Hailsham, who led the British negotiating team, described the occasion as 'the last time that Britain appeared in international negotiations as a great power.'[46]

And then, as so often, there was the problem of de Gaulle, who resolutely refused to alter his long-standing policy of remaining aloof from the treaty. France had yet to complete its nuclear test programme and the General saw arms control as a contrivance by which the superpowers sought to maintain their nuclear monopoly.[47] In an attempt to persuade him to change his mind, Kennedy unexpectedly proposed a further reversal of American nuclear policy. He would, as Macmillan somewhat bitterly put it in his memoirs, 'release the vital nuclear information which had been so long and so jealously withheld, first from us and then from the French', with the sole condition that France abstained from tests. 'Had the Americans armed me with this powerful weapon six month before,' Macmillan continued, 'it might have made the whole difference to Britain and to Europe.'[48] But the Prime Minister's hopes had been raised - his diary speaks of the possibility of reviving 'Europe (Common Market, etc.) and a new and hopeful movement to straighten out the whole alliance.'

These themes were taken up in his reply to Kennedy. On the immediate question of tests, the Prime Minister was concerned to stop de Gaulle destroying 'at least the moral effect of any test ban' by making intemperate remarks immediately after an agreement was initialled, possibly at his next press conference due at the end of the month. France should be invited to private talks with Britain and the US to see what help could be provided to obviate the need for further French atmospheric tests. Meanwhile the British and Americans should discuss the price they might ask for such extensive nuclear aid.[49]

There was a final diplomatic flurry, as London and Washington went through the by now familiar and fruitless motions of trying to avoid being thwarted by the General. Immediate concern focused on the contents and timing of the messages which Macmillan and Kennedy would separately deliver to de Gaulle. Macmillan had advised against a joint démarche bearing in mind the General's suspicions of Anglo-Saxon collusion. In London he rejected Thorneycroft's suggestion that a hint of an EEC deal should be included.[50] From Paris, the embassy advised that in order to throw the General off balance, the message should be delivered only just before the press conference. The embassy's reasoning says much about how bad Anglo-French relations now were. One of the main props on which de Gaulle's support in France rested, it argued, was the belief:

> 'that he has raised France's international standing. And one of the main props of this myth is the appearance he manages to convey, in Europe generally as well as in France, of being able to dumbfound the World and control the destinies of the nations by means of pronouncements delivered twice a year at Press conferences. If we can contrive to make this next one go off at half cock by timing our actions right we shall help to cut him down to size in Europe.'[51]

The suspicion and anger, however, were by no means one-sided. Adenauer was deeply uneasy about a Soviet proposal for a non-aggression pact, and Ormsby-Gore reported from Washington that the French were said to be 'pouring out a stream of poison to anyone who will listen'. Kennedy had been told that the French ambassador in Moscow was advising de Gaulle to do a deal with the Soviet Union to obtain nuclear information to rid himself of the Atlantic links.[52] Whether or not this was correct, Britain's role in the Moscow talks certainly went down badly in Paris. An inspired article, which the embassy believed might actually have been written by the French Prime Minister, Georges Pompidou, complained that in Moscow Britain had given its approval to the 'enslavement' of Europe. If only Britain would join with France and Germany, the US would be forced to allow Europe real partnership within the Atlantic alliance.[53]

True to form, de Gaulle did not bend. At his news conference on 29 July, the General declared that he would not associate France with any arrangements which might be schemed up over her head and which might concern Europe, in particular Germany, while Couve de Murville was quoted as saying that France was not to be bought.[54] The phrasing of the key section of de Gaulle's reply to Macmillan's letter dealing with the offer of tripartite talks was classically enigmatic, and a good deal of time was spent in the Quai d'Orsay, as well as London and Washington, in trying to fathom out just what he meant.[55] Writing to Kennedy, Macmillan argued that the General seemed to be saying that if he got nuclear technology and not the weapons he would still have to test to see that the weapons worked properly, but if he gets weapons he is afraid he might be asked for a quid pro quo.[56]

While there seemed little chance of de Gaulle giving way, the Paris embassy did argue the tactical case for making de Gaulle a nuclear offer on the grounds that a large section of French public opinion would withdraw their support if they knew that the General had refused even to discuss an offer which would reduce the costs of the French nuclear programme.[57] De Zulueta, who had been instructed by Macmillan to draw up yet another paper on the French nuclear conundrum, sought to wrestle with the question of whether there was a price which 'we want, the French would give, and the Americans would not dislike'.[58] The most which seemed feasible was an American offer to help France with technology on the conduct of underground tests if de Gaulle would sign the Test Ban treaty. 'But of course,' Macmillan noted sourly in his diary on 20 September, 'he won't.'[59]

* * *

And there the Macmillan-de Gaulle story effectively ended. Seriously weakened by the Profumo security scandal which had broken in the summer, Macmillan was contemplating resignation. 'The real issue is simple,' he had noted in a diary entry on 29 August, which had begun by referring to France under the General remaining in sullen isolation. 'Can I get the next move in the détente with Russia under way, or will Franco-German opposition be too great? If there has to be substantial delay, I cannot wait and had better rest content with what has been achieved.'[60] Three weeks later he told Lord Home that there needed to be a change in the Paris embassy. 'For no fault of his own, Bob Dixon can have no influence. While de Gaulle remains in power, there is little to be done.'[61]

But it was Macmillan who was to leave office first. Struck down by sudden illness, he resigned on October 9th. De Gaulle wrote Macmillan a note of good wishes. At a diplomatic shoot at Rambouillet a few days later, the General appeared much preoccupied with the Prime Minister's disappearance, noting that all the men who had held office in major states during his own active life were now dead or out of power. The departure of his old friend from Algiers days had brought intimations of his own mortality. He made a point of telling Dixon that despite all that had happened, his feelings for Macmillan remained unchanged. 'I wish you to believe this,' he told the ambassador. 'What I say is meant in all sincerity. I wish Mr Macmillan well both today and in the future.' Cynical as Dixon by now was about the General's assurances, on this occasion the ambassador was inclined to believe that the sentiments were genuine.[62]

Macmillan and de Gaulle kept in occasional touch. The General wrote on the death of Lady Dorothy in 1966. Macmillan sent de Gaulle a copy of the volume of his Memoirs dealing with the war years and their time in Algiers.[63] His personal bitterness towards de Gaulle rapidly subsided. Any anger he felt towards de Gaulle, writes Alistair Horne, was always mingled with admiration. His verdict in retirement was generous and fair. De Gaulle was a 'great and brave man, and he saved France.'[64] Dixon stayed in Paris until February 1965. 'I like General de Gaulle very much as a person', he wrote in his valedictory despatch, 'but as a statesman I regarded him as misguided at best and danger- ous at worst.' Dixon died a few weeks after retirement, his health undermined by the strains of combining the Paris embassy with leadership of the British EEC negotiating team in Brussels.[65]

De Gaulle himself remained in office for another six, and very eventful, years. They included a major crisis with his EEC partners in 1965, withdrawal from NATO's integrated command structure, an attempted opening to the East with a visit to Moscow in 1966, recognition of Communist China, and his famous salutation of 'le Québec libre' during a visit to Canada in 1967. Although Britain and France began cooperation on a number of civil and mil- itary aircraft projects, including the supersonic airliner, Concorde, the General's relationship with 'les Anglais' never recovered. British policy, the new Foreign Secretary, R.A Butler, argued in May 1964, could only be one of waiting out the storm, which would gradually subside after the General's disappearance. 'We must go on treating him as a tricky kind of ally, but we can no longer think in terms of an *Entente Cordiale*.'[66] The Labour government, which came to office in the autumn, decided it could not wait out the General, and a second EEC application bid was made in 1967. This time de Gaulle was careful to ensure that his veto pre-empted any negotiation.

A few months before leaving office, de Gaulle seemed to change course. Shaken by the 1968 French student revolt, anxious about growing German strength, and perhaps too by now aware that France was not strong enough to organise Europe without Britain, the General reverted to his wartime idea of a Franco-British alliance. His interlocutor was the new British ambassador to Paris, Churchill's son-in-law, Christopher Soames. In an interview on 4 February 1969, de Gaulle told Soames that he would like to see the EEC change into a looser form of free trade area, with arrangement for each coun- try exchanging agricultural goods, and with an inner circle consisting of Britain, France, Germany and Italy. He proposed secret Anglo-French talks to explore the possibility, and see whether Britain and France could resolve their differ- ences.[67]

By now it was too late. Suspicion of the General had reached such a peak that the Foreign Office's only concern was to avoid being tricked. Until the British told the Five, the Foreign Secretary, Michael Stewart minuted,

'we are exposed to the risk that the French will leak their version of these conversations at a moment and at a manner calculated to benefit their interests and harm ours. We know from bitter experience that the French will never scruple to act in this way. Our experience also teaches us that once any tendentious French version of an Anglo-French conversation gets out, we never really catch up...These proposals will be anathema to the other five governments, and the sooner we tell them what their partner is up to the better.'[68]

The information was duly leaked, and a brief but bitter Anglo-French row ensued. It was not good, the French Foreign Minister, Michel Debré, told Soames, for Britain to base its policy on the death or departure of General de Gaulle. It may seem regrettable, de Gaulle privately noted, that Britain had made direct talks with France impossible. 'But perhaps on the contrary it is better that the uncertainty about Britain's real intentions is thus dispelled.'[69]

The 'Soames affair', as it became known, stands as epitaph as much as epilogue to de Gaulle's long and fraught relationship with 'les Anglais' which had caused Macmillan so much trouble. Less than four months later the General resigned. The following year the Conservatives, led now by Ted Heath, returned to power. Heath was more instinctively pro-European, as well as much more sceptical of the 'special relationship' than Macmillan, and within less than a year he had managed to reach the understanding with de Gaulle's successor, Georges Pompidou, which had eluded Macmillan and the General. By the time Britain formally acceded to the Treaty of Rome in January 1972, de Gaulle was dead. Macmillan outlived him by sixteen years.

Chapter 20

'At the End of the Day'

The de Gaulle-Macmillan story constitutes one of the strangest modern chapters in the ever uneasy relationship between France and Britain. Rivals as much as allies, Macmillan and de Gaulle sought to chart a course at two periods of great international change and upheaval. At issue in 1943 was the future of France. When they next met in 1958 the Cold War was at its height, and the political culture of western Europe was being radically recast. For de Gaulle Europe was France's opportunity. His problem was with the power of the United States. For Macmillan Europe was the problem, and the 'special relationship' the opportunity. These very different perspectives on the nature of American power, apparently benign yet potentially domineering, are instructive for the contemporary world to which both men looked forward, in which trans-Atlantic relations have come under heavy strain, and the great imbalance of power at the heart of the Atlantic alliance about which both worried, has become a source of increasing difficulties.

Whether the course of trans-Atlantic, let alone Anglo-French history, would have been fundamentally different had Macmillan or de Gaulle been killed in either World War may be open to doubt. Their strategies were first and foremost an expression of divergent national interests, broadly supported within their respective governments. But their characters, styles and ideas, as indeed their prejudices and illusions, especially de Gaulle's, imposed a strong personal imprint on the alliances which they sough to mould and manipulate. If Anglo-French relations lacked the high drama of the de Gaulle-Churchill years, during the de Gaulle-Macmillan period they had an ambivalent and ultimately elusive quality which fascinates precisely because it defies simple summary or interpretation.

It is for instance tempting to see the events leading up to the eventual breach between Macmillan and the General in terms of France achieving the upper hand over its historic rival, or even indeed of de Gaulle's revenge for Fashoda and his wartime grievances against the Anglo-Saxons. De Gaulle's sense of history, his pride or (to Macmillan), his vanity for France, and his consciousness of Anglo-French rivalry all point in this direction. But that had not stopped the General proposing an alliance to Churchill in 1944 or an Anglo-French understanding to Christopher Soames a quarter of a century later. Writing of the last Rambouillet Summit, Burin des Roziers, de Gaulle's chief of staff describes de Gaulle as seeing France and Britain parted by divergent currents and distancing themselves from each other with regret. Heart and reason, says des Roziers, led the General to view Britain as France's privileged ally, and the melancholy farewells in December 1962 reflected the disillusionment of two men of goodwill who had failed to form a destiny together.[1] They had tried often enough, and if they shared one thing in common by early 1963, it was frustration.

De Gaulle had once complained to Macmillan that while agreeing in principle, Britain and France seldom did the same thing in practice.[2] That had certainly been true over the Berlin crisis, where de Gaulle had found Macmillan's policy at best ill-judged, at worst dangerous. He had made absolutely no headway in his attempts to woo the Prime Minister away from Washington, while nothing had come of Macmillan's repeated hints of nuclear cooperation. Whatever France had suggested, whether it was joint targeting or cooperation on making missiles, the British had had objections. Either the French had too little to offer, or the 'special relationship' stood in the way. In the end Anglo-French nuclear cooperation was limited to RAF training of navigators for the French *Force de Frappe*.[3] In opting in December 1962 for Polaris instead of agreeing to develop an Anglo-French missile, Macmillan had finally scuppered de Gaulle's hope than an Anglo-French force might form the basis for an independent European defence and political identity. Although this would never have occurred to Macmillan, it is perhaps small wonder that the General felt that the Prime Minister had let him down,

De Gaulle's difficulty was that he had never come to grips with his 'English problem'. He had never developed an English strategy, in the sense that he had a European strategy, or a strategy for dealing with Germany. He certainly never offered the Prime Minister a deal, though the possibility had constantly seemed to loom behind the arras, in Paris as well as London. Had Britain decided to come into a European nuclear force, Couve de Murville claimed after the breakdown of the EEC negotiation,

'it would have proved Britain's desire to have become truly European. Then, in that context other problems would have been more easily solved - such problems as wheat, mutton - and we could even have made transitional arrangements to help the British out. And we would have been ready for compromise. It is hard to envisage a European atomic force without British participation.'[4]

French unwillingness to spell out a proposal was partly a matter of tactics; de Gaulle always tried to avoid putting himself in the position of *demandeur*. It was up to his negotiating partners to come up with suggestions and then have to pay the price for the necessary French 'concessions'. But it also reflected the General's inability to fit the off-shore Power into his overambitious and fundamentally unrealistic European strategy.

Britain was a rival in a way West Germany was not. Whatever Macmillan might say about the England of Kipling being dead, the country still looked instinctively to Churchill's 'Open Sea' rather than to the Continent. The Prime Minister was seeking to shore up Britain's international position by adding a new European dimension, rather than choosing Europe. Nor was it realistic to expect him to do otherwise. It was certainly not in British interests to be allow itself to be weaned away from the all-powerful American connection which it had originally been forced to pursue in the wake of the collapse of France in 1940. France's subsequently recovery might have brought her back to the centre of west European diplomacy, but it was not in the same strategic power league as the US, a fact clearly underscored by the ongoing debate about missiles. Talking to ministers and senior officials in the wake of Nassau, Macmillan noted that the Americans were developing a system of firing coveys of warheads to fox Soviet anti-missile defence, some of which would be decoys. 'Had the French', he wondered, 'even begun to think about these highly advanced techniques?'[5] If de Gaulle never elaborated an Anglo-French deal, the reason had thus much to do with the fact that none was possible, at least on terms acceptable to him. He naturally preferred, at least while Adenauer was in office, to work with his more tractable and weaker West German partner, while postponing his 'English problem' to an indefinite future.

For his part Macmillan had found the General at best an opinionated nuisance, at worst a serious threat to his foreign policy. De Gaulle had frustrated a succession of the Prime Minister's initiatives - the FTA negotiations back in 1958, the 1961 'Grand Design' and finally the Common Market bid. He had thus made it impossible for Macmillan to establish a satisfactory relationship with the EEC, and move British policy away from the overdependency on the US which had developed in the first year of his premiership, to a more balanced relationship between western Europe and the United States. The bridge which the Prime Minister had wanted to operate between the two continents had remained firmly barred.

Yet if the sense of frustration was ultimately mutual, it was Macmillan who was the main looser and whose personal diplomacy raises the most questions. Should we admire the persistence and ingenuity with which the Prime Minister sought to resolve the obstacle de Gaulle posed to the resolution of Britain's EEC dilemma? Or should we rather deplore his tendency to take high risks, and to pursue a policy in which the line between persistence and wishful thinking, which had become more marked as Macmillan grew older and the options open to British foreign policy contracted, is often impossible to draw? Was Macmillan right to keep seeking common ground with the General, or did his constant attempt to blur and minimise the differences reflect a fundamental reluctance to acknowledge the division of purpose between them?

The European dilemma facing the Prime Minister by the beginning of the 1960s was, in part of course thanks to his own mistakes over the post-Messina negotiations five years earlier, an unenviable one. While there was no immediate crisis, the underlying pressures on British foreign policy were beginning to build up ominously. The continual slippage of Britain's global position dramatised by the breakdown of the 1960 Paris Summit, underscored the dangers of failing to come to terms with the new Continental grouping, which seemed to be taking on political as well as economic substance under de Gaulle's leadership. Macmillan's problem was that while recognizing that thanks to de Gaulle, the odds were against a successful membership bid, he could not afford to outwait the General. Nor, of course, was he inclined to do so. Macmillan was an activist. It was not in his character to tread diplomatic water indefinitely and wait for the General to disappear.

Holding a weak hand, it was unfortunate therefore that after 1958 Macmillan also seemed to lack the sureness of touch in handling de Gaulle which he had shown as Resident Minister in Algiers. While all too well aware that the General could be difficult, as Prime Minister, Macmillan seems never quite to have grasped his capacity to evade concession and resist compromise. The point had not escaped the Foreign Office. A brief prepared at the time of the General's 1960 State Visit to Britain, minced no words about the difficulties of dealing with him. While accepting that de Gaulle was susceptible to personal flattery and acknowledgement of himself as the personification and incarnation of France, the Foreign Office believed that

> 'he will take this as his due and must not be expected to be more cooperative and forthcoming as a result. *Per contra*, if we do not give him what he regards as his due, he may easily become less cooperative and forthcoming. It will probably become increasingly difficult to give him even the amount of support which has so far been possible, and the future of Anglo-French relations seems likely to be unhappy.'[6]

Part of the reason why Macmillan did not share this Foreign Office pessimism was his failure to register the intensity of the emotional drives behind de Gaulle's foreign policy. Macmillan got much of the picture. He had a good feel for de Gaulle's Great Power and European ambitions; he was well aware of the General's sense of Anglo-French rivalry and his resentment of his wartime treatment by the Anglo-Saxons. But Macmillan never fully grasped the obsessive quality which de Gaulle's suspicion of post-war American purposes sometimes assumed. Having succeeded in establishing good wartime relations with both de Gaulle and the local American authorities in Algiers, the Prime Minister did not appreciate the extent to which after 1958 he was now compromised in de Gaulle's eyes by the 'special relationship'. As Kennedy admitted to Macmillan after the veto, a good deal of the Prime Minister's difficulties had resulted from 'your country's historic association with the United States and your own strong support for the alliance'.[7]

Nor, in his preoccupation with finding a means of drawing closer to France without disloyalty to the Americans, had the proponent of the 'middle way' recognised that the General would never allow Britain to have the best of both the Atlantic and European worlds. Himself adept at having his diplomatic cake and eating it, de Gaulle was not going to allow Britain the advantage of 'winning at both tables'.

There were two other aspects of the General's foreign policy which Macmillan did not get fully in focus. A Prime Minister who saw an unqualified notion of independence as an anachronism found it naturally difficult to appreciate the importance which the idea played in de Gaulle's thinking about both France's *Force de Frappe* and Europe. In consequence the Prime Minister failed to realise how little some of his ideas of nuclear cooperation were likely to appeal to the General. Finally Macmillan underestimated de Gaulle's ruthless uncollegiality, his essentially exploitative approach to alliance relationships; the kind of appeal for long-term Western unity on which Macmillan's 'Grand Design' was based was always destined to fall on deaf ears.

Having underestimated his differences with de Gaulle, Macmillan compounded his problem by overestimating his ability to manage the General. Here the Algiers experience was more hindrance than help. Precisely because he had been successful in dealing with the General in 1943, as Prime Minister Macmillan seemed overconfident in his ability to influence him when he had finally gained the title deeds to France. But Macmillan's Algiers success had been the product of very special circumstances. After 1958 Macmillan was no longer marshalling the General along the way the latter wished to go. Moreover de Gaulle had changed more since 1943 than Macmillan appreciated. 'You and I,' Macmillan wrote to Eisenhower seventeen years later, 'know from old experience how difficult he can be in one mood, and yet how accommodating in another.'[8] But by now the General was less emotional and less erratic than he had been under the pressures of wartime; the accommodating moments no longer recurred.

Perhaps most serious of all from Macmillan's point of view, the wartime friendship which both men were so keen to evoke proved more advantageous to de Gaulle than to himself. Rather than give him any handle over the General, it served to reinforce the trait of excessive optimism. Here the Prime Minister's activism created its own dangers. 'If you're in a great enterprise you buoy yourself up and hope,' he said during one of the television interviews he gave on the publications of his memoirs. But there was another remark in the same interview series, about Roosevelt's relationship with Stalin, which might also apply to the British Prime Minister. 'Like many statesmen he (Roosevelt) was apt to think that other statesmen will yield to his charms.'[9] Such vanity was always dangerous, not least when dealing with somebody thought of as an old friend. Algiers had helped make Macmillan vulnerable both to the equivocation which de Gaulle employed at Birch Grove and Château de Champs, and then to the ruthless *coup de grâce* delivered at Rambouillet. Thanks to such experiences as the bathing party at Tipasa, the Prime Minister could never quite bring himself to believe that he could become victim to the brutal methods which he knew de Gaulle to be capable of.

One final element in Macmillan's approach to the General should be noted – a certain fatalism which was always part of the Prime Minister's contradictory character. It obviously did not help that by 1962 Macmillan was becoming tired, or that EEC membership was never a 'cause' for him in the way the East-West Summit and the nuclear test ban treaty were. But the relative lack of fervency with which he pressed the British bid with de Gaulle compared with the way he had pressed the FTA in 1958 may also hint at a more fundamental problem. However much he hoped, Macmillan knew what a weak hand he held. He knew that de Gaulle did not respond to persuasion and argument, that there was little by way of pressure which he could bring to bear, and that his nuclear inducements were highly conditional. There was therefore simply no point in spending too much time and effort on the de Gaulle problem. He had done all he could, but in the final analysis the decision was out of his hands.

* * *

The consequences of the veto were severe. The General had inflicted one of the most dramatic and publicly humiliating reverses on British foreign policy of the post-war years, and one which could not be glossed over in the way in which Suez had been. Coming only a few weeks after Dean Acheson's much resented jibe on British decline, the veto served to dramatise the former American Secretary of State's merciless public diagnosis of Britain's predicament:

> ' The attempt to play a separate power role - that is, a role apart from Europe, a role based on a "special relationship" with the United States, a role based on being the head of a "commonwealth" which has no political structure, or unity, or strength, and enjoys a fragile and precarious economic relationship by means of the Sterling area and preferences in the British market - this role is about played out. Great Britain, attempting to work alone and to be a broker between the United States and Russia, has seemed to conduct policy as weak as its military power.'[10]

The panache of French foreign policy over the next few years, and the sense that France had found itself a post-colonial role, contrasts starkly with the defensive nature of British diplomacy of the 1960s. The realisation in Whitehall that there was no alternative to keep trying to get into an EEC to which the General was barring the door compounded the sense of drift and impotence which continued over the following decade. It was only after the 1982 Falklands war that Mrs. Thatcher could plausibly declare that 'we have ceased to be a nation in retreat'.[11]

How much de Gaulle gained from the veto is rather less clear. The General paid a price for an action which had been motivated by that love of commotion which Macmillan had once remarked on in Algiers, as well as by the fear of being 'ensnared' by the Brussels negotiations. He seriously strained relations with his EEC partners and, more important from his point of view, undermined the Franco-Germany treaty. Moreover, as the Soames affair would later demonstrate, the veto made it impossible for him to re-establish an effective political dialogue with Britain There would, as Couve de Murville and Wormser appreciated, have been subtler and less costly ways of blocking a British bid.

Subsequent events suggest that Paris had exaggerated the dangers posed by the British application. The General was certainly correct in believing that a large, if unavowed, part of Britain's objective in negotiating membership, was that of changing the character of the Community. Expansion inevitably ended the comfortable situation in which, in Macmillan's words, the EEC was 'a nice little club, not too big, not too small, under French hegemony'. Long-term it also reduced the hold of the French language in Brussels.[12] Yet it did not, at least in the short to medium term 'change everything' as de Gaulle had feared. Britain did not disrupt the critical Franco-German partnership once it eventually joined, and far from taking a lead as Macmillan had hoped, often seemed to be punching below its weight.

De Gaulle might perhaps claim at least some credit for this. Part of his objective in delaying British entry appears to have been to wait for France's rival to weaken further. 'Je la veux nue', 'I want her naked,' was his reported comment at the time. A less crude version has de Gaulle saying that Britain would only join Europe when the whole of its empire had finally gone. The ten year delay in British entry also contributed to the lack of enthusiasm which characterised British membership when it eventually did join.[13]

Yet if time helped work for the General, the explanation for the lack of challenge which Britain then offered the French position in Europe goes deeper. Paris had all along made too much of Anglo-French rivalry. Shrewd as the General was in diagnosing the 'insular' traditions of British policy, he underestimated how far these would handicap Britain's ability to maximise the advantages of EEC membership. He also seems to have missed the full implications of the British determination to continue the 'special relationship'. For whatever its very real downside from de Gaulle's point of view, London's determination to continue looking over its Atlantic shoulder to Washington had the advantage for Paris of serving to dull Britain's European ambitions. The need for France to share European leadership with Britain thus became less acute than the General (along with much of course of the French policy-making establishment) feared.

It is perhaps therefore at the personal rather than the political level that the impact of the veto was harshest. In a draft obituary of Macmillan written in

1962, Butler described the EEC decision as 'one of the most important economic and political decisions taken in peacetime since (the repeal of the Corn Laws in) 1846. The man was worthy of taking such a decision, and his reputation will live with it.'[14] Thanks to the General, the EEC bid proved at best an honourable failure, which reinforces the impression of an overambitious Prime Minister who found his foreign policy initiatives repeatedly thwarted. As with de Gaulle, the image of Don Quixote, repeatedly tilting against windmills, comes to mind.[15]

This, however, is scarcely a fair overall verdict on the Macmillan premiership. It was Macmillan's misfortune to have become Prime Minister at a time when Britain was undergoing what the US State Department described as 'adjustments of great complexity' concerned with the 'shift from major to lesser power status and its move towards the continent'. Complex adjustments, however skilfully managed, are not the stuff of which great reputations are made, and given the absence of any major domestic or foreign policy successes, Macmillan has inevitably been relegated to the second rank of post-war British Prime Ministers. If de Gaulle had helped to make Macmillan's political name in 1943, he had done more than his fair share to limit his eventual historical standing.[16]

The General's behaviour has been strongly criticised. Macmillan's official biographer, Alistair Horne, believes that he was 'treated monstrously by de Gaulle, from whom he personally deserved better things'. Paul Reynaud pointedly reminded French newspaper readers in 1963 that the *Entente* had saved France twice in thirty years, while Couve de Murville once privately described the veto as 'a kind of betrayal'.[17] Couve had of course a bad conscience over the affair. He had given misleading assurances to Heath just before the General's press conference, and must also have been aware of the fact that from the outset of the Brussels negotiations in autumn 1961, the French had been negotiating in the expectation that Britain would be unable or unwilling to pay the economic entry price they would demand.[18]

Betrayal, however, is a strong and emotive word. De Gaulle's career would certainly have taken a very different form without the help he had been given by Churchill and Macmillan. 'Washed up from a disastrous shipwreck upon the shores of England,' the General wrote of Churchill his in *War Memoirs*, 'what could I have done without his help?' On his return to power in 1958, de Gaulle immediately awarded the former British Prime Minister the Order of the Liberation.[19]

His *Memoirs of Hope* contain a reference to Macmillan which has already been partially quoted:

> 'We were, of course, old friends, ever since the period during the war when, as Churchill's minister, he was attached to me and my 'Committee' in Algiers. (sic) These memories, combined with the respect which I had for his character and the interest and enjoyment which I derived from his company, caused me to listen to him with

confidence and speak to him with sincerity. Besides, I admired England, still young in spite of her ancient trappings, thanks to her genius for adapting the modern to the traditional, and indomitable in the face of danger, as she had recently proved for her own salvation as well as that of Europe…Thus, Harold Macmillan found me disposed to reach agreement with him, *provided that it was possible for his country and mine to follow the same path*.'[20] (emphasis added)

For de Gaulle, friendship was strictly limited by national interest. The General believed that while men had friends, statesmen did not. He was no more willing to be constrained by old wartime ties than by the notions of community, partnership and shared values which other Western leaders saw as hallmarks of the alliances of the post-war world.[21] He would have thought it quite wrong to have done otherwise.

This was not Kennedy's view. Upbraided after Nassau for being soft on Macmillan, Kennedy replied, 'If you were in that kind of trouble you would want a friend.'[22] As leader of a superpower and senior member of the Anglo-American alliance, Kennedy could of course afford to be more generous. De Gaulle could not, but nor was he temperamentally disposed to such generosity. In the aftermath of the collapse of the negotiations for de Gaulle's plan for European political union in Spring 1962, an angry General accused Britain of having been an American satellite ever since Pearl Harbour, and the Low Countries and Scandinavian countries of being satellites of the British. 'The whole damn world dislikes us and detests our policy. It's natural therefore that we refuse to kneel before the Anglo-Saxons.' Had the General perhaps thought, wondered Peyrefitte who had witnessed the outburst, that.:

'without the English there would have been no Free France, no free Europe, no free world! Without them there would not have been de Gaulle!
But perhaps he knows the word of Lu Xun: "He who can take part courteously at a banquet to which he had been invited, but who can then politely and firmly tell his host 'leurs quatre verités' is a truly admirable man." '[23]

Peyrefitte recounts another, equally revealing, incident. Speaking after his 1963 press conference, de Gaulle predicted a Labour victory at the next British election. 'That Macmillan vanishes!' the General declared, and then sliced the air with the back of his hand, 'as pitiless as a Roman emperor turning down his thumb as though denying a reprieve to a defeated gladiator.'[24]

International politics are a rough business, and Macmillan had in no way been singled out by de Gaulle for specially ungrateful treatment. Churchill had at least as much reason to complain of ingratitude, as too had the Americans. Told in 1966 of the General's demand for the withdrawal of all American forces from France, Lyndon Johnson enquired with heavy irony whether the

Americans were also expected to remove their cemeteries. In the end Macmillan had been outwitted by one of the most formidable and ruthless operators on the international stage, who had no compunction about playing on the weakness of Macmillan's position, let alone Britain's. But he had also been outclassed.

Notes

ABBREVIATIONS

Catterall, *MD, 1950-57*	Peter Catterall, *The Macmillan Diaries, 1950-57*
De Gaulle, *CWM*	Charles de Gaulle, *The Complete War Memoirs, vols. i-iii*
De Gaulle, *Hope*	Charles de Gaulle, *Memoirs of Hope*
DBPO	*Documents on British Policy Overseas*
DDF	*Documents diplomatiques français*
FRUS	*Foreign Relations of the United States*
HMWD	Harold Macmillan, *War Diaries. The Mediterranean, 1943-45*
Horne, *Macmillan*	Alistair Horne, *Harold Macmillan, vol. i, 1894-1956; vol. ii 1957-86.*
Lacouture, *Rebel*	Jean Lacouture, *De Gaulle. The Rebel, 1890-1944*
Lacouture, *Ruler*	Jean Lacouture, *De Gaulle. The Ruler, 1945-70*
Macmillan, *Winds*	Harold Macmillan, *Winds of Change 1914-39*
Macmillan, *BW*	Harold Macmillan, *The Blast of War, 1939-45*
Macmillan, *Tides*	Harold Macmillan, *Tides of Fortune, 1945-55*
Macmillan, *Riding*	Harold Macmillan, *Riding the Storm, 1956-59*
Macmillan, *Pointing*	Harold Macmillan, *Pointing the Way, 1959-61*
Macmillan, *End*	Harold Macmillan, *At the End of the Day, 1961-63*
Peyrefitte, *C'était*	Alain Peyrefitte, *C'était de Gaulle, vols. i-iii*
Reilly, *Memoirs*	Sir Patrick Reilly, *Unpublished Memoirs*
Williams, *Frenchman*	Charles Williams, *The Last Great Frenchman. A Life of General de Gaulle*

INTRODUCTION. BATHING AT TIPASA

1   Macmillan, *BW*, p. 345. *HMWD*, p. 122. Reilly, *Memoirs*, Ms. Eng c.6919, p. 11.
2   *Keesings Contemporary Archives*, cols. 19198, 19-26. 1. 63.

3   John Grigg, *Lloyd George. War Leader, 1916-18* (Harmondsworth, 2003), pp. 295, 533. François Kersaudy, *Churchill and de Gaulle* (London,1990 ed.). Edward Heath, *The Course of My Life* (London, 1998), p. 369.
4   *Catterall, MD, 1950-57*, p. 361.
5   François Kersaudy, *De Gaulle et Roosevelt* (Paris, 2004), p. 302.
6   Alan Bennett et al., *Beyond the Fringe* (London, 1963), p. 48.
7   Robert Jackson, 'Non, merci', *Times Literary Supplement*, 3.6.05.
8   Timothy Garton Ash, *Free World* (London, 2004), p. 7.

CHAPTER 1. ANGLO-FRENCH CONTEMPORARIES
1   De Gaulle, *CWM, vol. i*, p. 3
2   Ibid.
3   Williams, *Frenchman*, p. 16.
4   de Gaulle, *CWM, vol. i*, p. 4
5   Ibid.
6   Lacouture, *Rebel*, p. 3.
7   Ibid., p.15. Stanley Hoffman, *Decline or Renewal?* (New York, 1974), p. 206.
8   Lacouture, *Rebel*, p. 18.
9   Ibid., pp. 18-20.
10 Willams, *Frenchman*, p. 59. Macmillan, *Pointing*, p. 185. FO371/153910. Personality notes.
11 Lacouture, *Rebel*, p. 108.
12 De Gaulle, *CWM, vol. i*, p. 6.
13 Lacouture, *Rebel*, p. 81.
14 Williams, *Frenchman*, p. 68.
15 Lacouture, *Rebel*, p. 146.
16 Ibid., pp. 144-5.
17 Ibid., p. 136. PREM11/4811. Despatch Paris, 19. 12. 62.
18 De Gaulle, *CWM, vol.* i., p. 16.
19 Williams, *Frenchman*, p. 81.
20 Lacouture, *Rebel*, p. 152.
21 PREM11/3783. Speech to American Newspaper Publishers Association Convention, 26. 4. 62.
22 Macmillan, *Winds*, pp. 34-5.
23 Ibid., pp. 47-8.
24 Ibid., p. 56.
25 Horne, *Macmillan, vol. i*, p. 8. Anthony Sampson, *Macmillan* (Harmondsworth, 1968), pp. 13-14.
26 Horne, *Macmillan, vol. i*, p.1.
27 Macmillan, *Winds*, pp. 55-7.
28 Ibid., pp. 36-7. Horne, *Macmillan, vol. i*, p. 12.
29 Ibid., p.11. Macmillan, *Winds*, p. 36.
30 Horne, *Macmillan, vol. i*, p. 14.
31 Macmillan, *Winds*, p. 45.
32 Robert Rhodes-James, *Anthony Eden and Harold Macmillan* (Conservative Political Centre, 1997), p. 5.
33 Macmillan, *Winds*, pp. 98-101.
34 Horne, *Macmillan, vol. i*, pp. 54-5, 57.
35 Ibid., pp. 84-90, 98. John Turner, *Macmillan* (London, 1994), p. 23.

36   Macmillan, *Winds,* pp. 174, 285.

37   Lord Blake, 'The Earl of Stockton', *Dictionary of National Biography, 1986-90* (Oxford, 1991), p. 278. Richard Davenport-Hines, *The Macmillans* (London, 1992), p.251.

38   Ibid., N. J. Crowson, 'Much Ado About Nothing: Macmillan and Appeasement' in Richard Aldous and Sabine Lee, *Harold Macmillan* (Basingstoke, 1999), p. 71.

39   Peter Hennessy, *The Prime Minister* (London, 2000), p. 254.

40   Crowson, 'Much Ado', p. 66.

41   Macmillan, *Winds,* pp. 572-3.

42   Sampson, *Macmillan,* p. 57.

43   Sir Gawain Bell, *An Imperial Twilight* (London, 1989), p. 101. Reginald Bevins, *The Greasy Pole* (London, 1965), p. 30.

44   L. Seidentop, 'Mr. Macmillan and the Edwardian Style' in Vernon Bogdanor and Robert Skidelsky (eds), *The Age of Affluence* (London, 1970), p. 26.

45   Horne, *Macmillan, vol. i,* p. 13. Horne, *Macmillan, vol. ii,* p. 160.

46   Eric Roussel, *Charles de Gaulle* (Paris, 2002), pp. 182-4.

47   F0371/182933. Valedictory despatch, Paris, 1. 2. 65.

48   Hoffmann, *Decline,* pp. 228-9. Julian Jackson, *Charles de Gaulle* (London, 1990), p.111.

49   Sampson, *Macmillan,* chapter one. Peter Clarke, *A Question of Leadership* (Harmondsworth, 1992), p. 231.

50   Reilly, *Memoirs,* Ms. Eng. c. 6923, p. 241.

51   John Barnes and David Nicolson (eds), *The Empire at Bay* (London, 1988), p. 841. Horne, *Macmillan, vol.* i, pp. 13-14, 42.

52   *Sunday Times,* 3. 4. 60. Andrew Shennan, *De Gaulle* (London, 1993), p. viii.

53   Hoffmann, *Decline,* p. 217.

54   Lord Egremont, *Wyndham and Children First* (London, 1968), p.194.

55   George Mallaby, *From My Level* (London, 1965), p. 62.

56   Seidentop, 'Mr Macmillan', p. 44. Lacouture, *Rebel,* p. 5.

57   Hennessy, *The Prime Minister,* p. 270. Sampson, *Macmillan,* p. 132.

58   Macmillan, *Winds,* pp. 100-1.

59   Williams, *Frenchman,* p. 106.

60   F0371/36013. Charles Peake, 3. 3. 43.

61   Hoffman, *Decline,* p. 223. Maurice Agulhon, *De Gaulle* (Paris, 2000), p. 13. Alex Danchev and Daniel Todman (eds), *Alanbrooke War Diaries,* (London, 2002 ed.), p. 101. F0660/49. 12. 6. 43.

62   De Gaulle, *CWM, vol. i,* p. 3.

63   Macmillan, *End,* p. 371.

CHAPTER 2. MESENTENTE CORDIALE

1   Williams, *Frenchman,* p. 424.

2   Eric Roussel, *Charles de Gaulle* (Paris, 2002), p. 951.

3   Peyrefitte, *C'était, vol. i,* pp. 153-4. Lacouture, *Ruler,* p. 351. F0371/153912. Special Political Brief for the Queen. PREM11/3002. Despatch Paris, 11.12.59.

4   F0146/4630. 'Britain through French Eyes. '

5   François Kersaudy, *Churchill and de Gaulle* (London, 1990 ed.), p. 33.

6   Philip Bell, *France and Britain, 1900-1940* (London, 1996), p. 20.

7   Robert Gibson, *Best of Enemies* (London, 1995), pp. 38-9.

8   PREM3/162/6. Despatch Algiers, 3. 1. 44.

9   Gibson, *Best*, p. 264.
10 Ibid., pp. 195-7.
11 Andrew Roberts, *Salisbury* (London, 1999), chapter 41.
12 James Morris, *Farewell the Trumpets* (Harmondsworth, 1969 ed.), p. 56.
13 Bell, *France and Britain*, p. 10. Kersaudy, *Churchill and de Gaulle*, pp. 33-4.
14 De Gaulle, *CWM, vol.* i, p. 4. Williams, *Frenchman*, p. 16.
15 *The Speeches of General de Gaulle* (London, 1943), p.103.
16 Kersaudy, *Churchill and de Gaulle*, p. 34.
17 Bell, *France and Britain*, p. 159.
18 Alan Sharp, 'Anglo-French Relations from Versailles to Locarno' in Alan Sharp and Glyn Stone (eds), *Anglo-French Relations in the Twentieth Century* (London, 2000), p.134.
19 Williams, *Frenchman*, p. 70. Bernard Ledwidge, *De Gaulle* (London, 1982), p.36.
20 De Gaulle, *CWM, vol. i.*, pp. 5-6.
21 Ibid., *vol. iii*, p. 719. Peyrefitte, *C'était, vol. i*, p. 154. Kersaudy, *Churchill and de Gaulle*, pp. 34-5. Lacouture, *Ruler*, p 220.
22 Bell, *France and Britain*, pp. 226-7.
23 Macmillan, *BW*, p. xvi.
24 Mark Pottle (ed.), *Champion Redoubtable* (London, 1999 ed.), p. 211. Horne, *Macmillan, vol. i*, pp. 125, 140.
25 Lacouture, *Rebel*, p. 186.
26 John Lukacs, *Five Days in London* (New Haven, 1999), pp. 182-3. Kersaudy, *Churchill and de Gaulle*, p. 77.
27 David Reynolds, '1940; Fulcrum of the Twentieth Century?', *International Affairs*, April 1990, p. 332.
28 De Gaulle, *CWM, vol. i*, p. 54. Kersaudy, *Churchill and de Gaulle*, p. 50.
29 Roussel, *De Gaulle*, pp. 56, 989. Lacouture, *Rebel*, p. 220. Philippe de Gaulle, *De Gaulle mon père*, (Paris, 2003), p. 161. Kersaudy, *Churchill and de Gaulle*, pp. 34-5. Gladwyn papers, 1/3/34, draft *Sunday Times* obituary.
30 De Gaulle, *CWM, vol i*, pp. 56-7. Philippe de Gaulle, *De Gaulle*, p. 163.
31 Ibid., p. 59.
32 Kersaudy, *Churchill and de Gaulle*, p. 63. Williams, *Frenchman*, p. 100.
33 De Gaulle, *CWM, vol. i*, p. 57.
34 Macmillan, *BW*, pp. 100-1.
35 Bell, *France and Britain*, p. 247.
36 De Gaulle, *CWM, vol. i*, p. 75.
37 Bell, *France and Britain*, pp. 247-8. Lacouture, *Rebel*, p. 204.
38 Julian Jackson, *France* (Oxford, 2001), p.185.
39 Robert Murphy, *Diplomat among Warriors* (London, 1964), p. 69. Jean-Louis Crémieux-Brilhac, 'The Background to the June 18 Broadcast' in Anne Corbett and Douglas Johnson (eds), *A Day in June,* (London, 2000), p. Peyrefitte, *C'était, vol. i*, pp. 62-3. *Speeches of Charles de Gaulle*, p. 6.
40 FC033/1007, 'The Death of General de Gaulle. ' Despatch Paris, 4. 12.70.
41 Raoul Aglion, *Roosevelt and De Gaulle* (London, 1988), p. 57.
42 Kersaudy, *Churchill and de Gaulle*, pp. 83-4, 87-8.
43 Piers Dixon, *Double Diploma* (London, 1968), p. 313.
44 Kersaudy, *Churchill and de Gaulle*, p. 211. *HMWD*, p. 335.
45 F0371/36301, 13. 7. 43. Simon Berthon, *Allies at War* (London, 2001), p. 161.
46 F0371/31948. Strang to Cadogan, 24. 1. 42. F0371/36013. Eden to Churchill, 2. 3. 43.

47   Williams, *Frenchman*, pp. 180-1. François Kersaudy, *De Gaulle et Roosevelt* (Paris, 2004), p. 286. Charles de Gaulle, *The Edge of the Sword* (London, 1960), pp. 60-1.
48   De Gaulle, *CWM, vol. i,* p. 58.
49   Max Egremont, *Under Two Flags* (London, 1997), p. 227.

CHAPTER 3. THE ANGLO-SAXON ALLIANCE

1   *FRUS, 1961-63, vol. xiii,* p. 674.
2   Williams, *Frenchman*, p. 112,
3   Macmillan, *BW,* p. 154.
4   François Kersaudy, *Churchill and de Gaulle* (London, 1990), p. 172. Simon Berthon, *Allies at War* (London, 2001), p. 147.
5   De Gaulle, *CWM, vol. ii,* p. 557. PREM11/4230. Macmillan-de Gaulle, 15-16. 12. 62. Alain Peyrefitte, *C'était, vol. ii,* pp. 84-5. Douglas Johnson, 'De Gaulle and France's Role in the World' in Hugh Gough and John Home (eds), *De Gaulle and the Twentieth Century* (London, 1994), p. 84.
6   De Gaulle, *CWM, vol. iii,* pp. 725-8.
7   Robert Murphy, *Diplomat among Warriors* (London, 1964), pp. 211-2. Arthur Funk, *Charles de Gaulle* (Oklahoma, 1959), pp. 85-6.
8   Berthon, *Allies,* p. 249. Lacouture, *Rebel,* p. 419. Warren Kimball (ed.), *Churchill and Roosevelt - the Complete Correspondence, vol. ii,* (Princeton, N. J., 1984), p. 104.
9   Murphy, *Diplomat,* p. 214.
10   Berthon, *Allies,* pp. 186-7.
11   Julian Jackson, *France* (Oxford, 2001), p. 447.
12   Sir Llewellyn Woodward, *British Foreign Policy in the Second World War, vol. ii* (London, 1971), p. 369. Stephen Ambrose, *The Supreme Commander* (London, 1969), p. 130.
13   F0954/l6. Minute Strang, 16. 12. 42. John Harvey (ed.), *The War Diaries of Oliver Harvey* (London, 1978), pp. 194-5. *FRUS, 1943, vol. ii,* p. 35. G. E. Maguire, *Anglo-American Policy towards the Free French* (Basingstoke, 1995), pp. 75-7.
14   Anthony Eden, *The Reckoning* (London, 1965), p. 355. Woodward, *British Foreign Policy,* pp. 376-7. PREM3/442/20A. Morton to Churchill, 3. 12. 42.
15   David Dilks (ed.), *The Diaries of Sir Alexander Cadogan* (London, 1971), p. 493. Michael Howard, *Grand Strategy, vol. iv* (London, 1972), p. 178. Harvey, *Diaries,* pp. 188-9.
16   Kimball, *Correspondence,* p. 22.
17   Macmillan, *BW,* pp. 236-7. Murphy, *Diplomat,* p. 117. Berthon, *Allies,* pp. 57-8. Kenneth Pendar, *Adventure in Diplomacy* (London, 1966 ed.), pp. 19-20.
18   Harvey, *Diaries,* p. 203. F0371/36118. Minute Eden, 7. 2. 43. F0371/36119. Mack personality note, 5. 2. 43.
19   Kimball, *Correspondence,* pp. 71, 90.
20   Macmillan, *BW,* pp. 216-7.
21   Lord Egremont, *Wyndham and Children First* (London, 1968), p. 193.
22   F0954/16. First Sea Lord to Admiral Cunningham, 30. 12. 42. M. R. D. Foot, 'Eisenhower and the British' in Guenther Bischof and Stephen Ambrose, *Eisenhower. A Centenary Reassessment* (Baton Rouge, 1995), pp. 44-5. David Stafford, *Roosevelt and Churchill* (London, 1999), pp. 194-6.
23   FO371/36113. Memo Strang, 25. 12. 43. Macmillan, *BW,* p. 218.
24   Funk, *De Gaulle,* p. 50. Kimball, *Correspondence,* p. 89.
25   Ibid., p. 90.
26   FO660/11. FO to Algiers 30. 12. 42. British Chiefs of Staff to Eisenhower, 31. 12. 42.

27 F0371/36167. Memorandum Comité Nationale Française. 6. 1. 43. Eden minute, 9. 1. 43.
28 *HMWD,* p. 4.
29 FO371/35167. Eisenhower to CCS, 31. 12. 42. D. K. R. Crosswell, *The Chief of Staff* (Greenwood, 1991), pp. 137, 144. Macmillan, *BW,* pp. 220-2. *FRUS, 1942, vol. ii,* pp. 495-6.
30 *HMWD,* p. 59.
31 Anthony Sampson, *Macmillan* (Harmondsworth, 1967), pp. 65-6. Murphy, *Diplomat,* p. 201.
32 FO371/36115, 13. 1. 43. Macmillan, *BW,* p. 290.
33 F0660/50. Macmillan to FO, 16. 6. 43. FO371/36119. Minute Strang, 20. 2. 43.
34 Lacouture, *Rebel,* p. 434. Général Giraud, *Le Seul but – la victoire* (Paris, 1949), p. 161. Général Catroux, *Dans la bataille de Mediterranêe* (Paris, 1949), p. 350. Ambrose, *Supreme Commander,* p. 192.
35 De Gaulle, *CWM, vol. ii,* p. 382. Murphy, *Diplomat,* pp. 214-5.
36 Ibid., p. 215. F0660/86. Dixon memo, 26. 1. 43. WO106/5233. FO to Washington, 2. 1. 43.
37 Egremont, *Wyndham,* p. 80. Macmillan, *BW,* p. 243.
38 Ibid.
39 Kersaudy, *Churchill and de Gaulle,* p. 238.
40 Eric Roussel, *Charles de Gaulle* (Paris, 2002), p. 343. Kersaudy, *Churchill and de Gaulle,* (Paris, 2004) p. 238.
41 Ibid., pp. 241-2, 245-6. De Gaulle, *CWM, vol. ii,* p. 387. *CWM, vol .i, Docs.,* pp. 126-8. Harvey, *Diaries,* p. 211. Williams, *Frenchman,* p. 211.
42 Elliott Roosevelt, *As He Saw It* (New York, 1946), p. 92. Macmillan, *BW,* p. 348.
43 De Gaulle, *CWM, vol. ii,* pp. 389-90.
44 Macmillan, *BW,* p. 175. Harvey, *Diaries,* pp. 137-8.
45 De Gaulle, *CWM, vol. ii,* p. 390.
46 Ibid, pp. 390-1, 393-4.
47 Ibid, pp. 396-7.
48 FO660/88. Dixon memo. Macmillan, *BW,* p. 249. Horne, *Macmillan, vol. i,* p. 170.
49 FO660/85. Anfa chronology. F0660/88. Dixon memo. Macmillan, *BW,* p. 252.
50 De Gaulle, *CWM, vol. ii,* p. 397.
51 Ibid., p. 399. F0371/36117. Mack minute, 28. 1. 43. Philippe de Gaulle, *De Gaulle mon père* (Paris, 2003), p. 285.
52 Ibid. *HMWD,* p. 10. Macmillan, *BW,* pp. 253-4.
53 F0660/85. Anfa chronology. FO954/8. Minute 2. 2. 43.
54 FO660/86. Eden to Macmillan, 4. 2. 43.
55 Funk, *De Gaulle,* p. 91. Macmillan, *BW,* pp. 256-60. Horne, *Macmillan, vol. i,* pp, 172-3.

CHAPTER 4. THE RESIDENT MINISTER

1 F0371/36117. Memo Mack, 28. 1. 43. Kenneth Pendar, *Adventure in Diplomacy* (London, 1966 ed.), p. 148. Eric Roussel, *Charles de Gaulle* (Paris, 2002), p. 350.
2 F0660/88. Macmillan to FO, 28. 1. 43. *HMWD,* p. 10. François Kersaudy, *De Gaulle et Roosevelt* (Paris, 2004), p. 256.
3 FO954/16. Macmillan to Eden, 21. 2. 43.
4 PREM3/442/6. Macmillan despatch, 'The Situation in North Africa. '
5 *FRUS, 1943, vol. ii,* pp. 55-6.
6 F0660/18. Macmillan to Makins, 27. 2. 43.

7   François Duchêne, *Jean Monnet* (New York, 1994), p. 111. WO106/5233. Washington to Macmillan, 24. 2. 43.

8   Jean Monnet, *Memoirs* (London, 1978), p. 186. Henri Giraud, *Le Seul but - la victoire* (Paris, 1949), p. 121. *FRUS, 1943, vol. ii,* p. 74. F0371/36123. Macmillan despatch, 'The North African New Deal. ' *HMWD,* p. 43. Duchêne, *Monnet,* p. 110. De Gaulle, *CWM, vol. ii,* pp. 407-8.

9   *HMWD,* p. 44. PREM3/182/6. Macmillan final despatch, Algiers, 3. 1. 44. WO106/5233. Tel. Macmillan, 14. 3. 43.

10 Guy de Charbonnières, *Le Duel Giraud-de Gaulle* (Paris, 1984), pp. 71-5. De Gaulle, *CWM, vol. ii,* p. 409.

11 Charles de Gaulle, *Lettres, notes et carnets, vol. v,* 1943-45 (Paris, 1983), 19. 3. 43.

12 *HMWD,* pp. 53,73.

13 Ibid., p. 55.

14 De Charbonnières, *Duel,* pp. 105-6. Arthur Funk, *Charles de Gaulle* (Oklahoma, 1959), p. 115.

15 Macmillan, *BW,* pp. 312-3. *HMWD,* pp. 57-8. PREM3/442/6. Macmillan despatch, 'The Weeks Between. '

16 *HMWD,* pp. 59-60.

17 Ibid., p. 72.

18 WO106/5233. Macmillan memorandum, 12. 4. 43. *HMWD,* pp. 68-72.

19 Ibid., p. 72. François Kersaudy, *Churchill and de Gaulle* (London, 1990), p. 270.

20 FO371/36173. Macmillan to Churchill, 29. 4. 43.

21 FO660/48. Macmillan to FO, 30. 4. 43.

22 De Gaulle, *CWM, vol. ii, Docs.,* pp. 157-9. De Charbonnières, *Duel,* pp. 146, 150.

23 *HMWD,* pp. 78-9.

24 Roussel, *De Gaulle,* pp. 355-6. De Charbonnières, *Duel,* pp. 148-50. FO371/361175. Tel. London, 6. 5. 43.

25 FO660/48. Letter Macmillan, 5. 4. 43. *HMWD,* p. 80.

26 Ibid., p. 81.

27 F0660/48. Macmillan to FO, 6. 5. 43.

28 *HMWD,* p. 82.

29 FO660/48. Macmillan to Makins, 13. 5. 43. Roussel, *De Gaulle,* p. 357. Duchêne, *Monnet,* p. 119.

30 *HMWD,* p. 84, Monnet, *Memoirs,* p. 196. Andre Kaspi, *La Mission de Jean Monnet à Alger* (Paris, 1971), p. 179.

31 *HMWD,* pp. 84-7. Macmillan, *BW,* pp. 318-9.

32 Ibid., p. 326. F0660/48. Letter Algiers, 17. 5. 43.

33 *FRUS, 1943, vol. ii,* pp. 109-10.

34 Ibid., pp. 111-2.

35 Roussel, *De Gaulle,* p. 358.

36 F0371/36047. Churchill to Attlee, 21. 5. 43. Attlee to Churchill, 23. 5. 43. Macmillan, *BW,* p. 327. Horne, *Macmillan, vol. i,* p. 185.

37 F0371/36047. Churchill to Attlee and Eden, 24. 5. 43.

38 FO660/49. Macmillan to Makins, 26. 5. 43.

39 De Gaulle, *CWM, vol. ii,* p. 418.

CHAPTER 5. JUNE CRISES

1   Lord Egremont, *Wyndham and Children First* (London, 1968), p. 89. François Kersaudy, *Churchill and de Gaulle* (London, 1990), p. 283.

2   Général Catroux, *Dans la bataille de Mediterranée* (Paris, 1949), p. 364. Horne, *Macmillan, vol. i*, p. 186. De Gaulle, *CWM, vol. ii*, p. 419. Philippe de Gaulle, *De Gaulle mon père* (Paris, 2003), pp. 287-8. F0660/24. Macmillan memo., 30. 3. 43. PREM3/442/6. Macmillan despatch, 'A Marriage Has Been Arranged. '
3   Kersaudy, *Churchill and de Gaulle*, p. 281. Williams, *Frenchman,* p. 225. Winston Churchill, *The Second World War, vol. iv* (London, 1951), p. 729. Warren Kimball, *Churchill and Roosevelt, vol. ii*, (Princeton, NJ, 1984), p. 228.
4   Ibid. John Harvey (ed.), *The War Diaries of Oliver Harvey* (London, 1998), p. 264.
5   Macmillan, *BW,* p. 328. *FRUS, 1943, vol. ii,* p. 121. Hervé Alphand, *L'Étonnement d'être* (Paris, 1977) p. 163.
6   PREM3/442/6. Macmillan despatch, 'A Marriage has been Arranged. ' FO660/49. Macmillan to FO, 1. 6. 42.
7   De Gaulle, *CWM, vol. ii*, pp. 421-2. Macmillan, *BW,* p. 330. *HMWD*, pp. 97-8.
8   Ibid., p. 98. F0660/49. Macmillan memo, 1. 6. 43.
9   FO660/49. Macmillan-Giraud, 1. 6. 43.
10 FO660/49. Macmillan-de Gaulle, 1. 6. 43. Macmillan, *BW,* pp. 330-2.
11 *HMWD*, pp. 99-101. De Gaulle, *CWM, vol. ii, Docs.*, p. 157. *FRUS, 1943, vol. ii,* pp. 129-30.
12 Williams, *Frenchman,* pp. 226-7.
13 De Gaulle, *CWM, vol. ii, Docs.* no. 203.
14 Charles de Gaulle, *Lettres, notes et carnets, vol. v, 1944-45* (Paris, 1983), p. 17. De Gaulle, *CWM, vol. ii*, pp. 423-4. Williams, *Frenchman,* p. 226. Macmillan, *BW,* p. 333.
15 Ibid., p. 338. FO660/49. Macmillan-Giraud, 2. 6. 43. Macmillan-de Gaulle, 2. 6. 43. Ben Pimlott (ed.), *The Second World War Diary of Hugh Dalton, 1940-45* (London, 1988), p. 122.
16 PREM3/442/6. Macmillan despatch, 'A Marriage Has Been Arranged. '
17 De Gaulle, *CWM, vol. ii, Docs.,* p. 181. *CWM, vol. ii,* p. 425. Jean Monnet, *Memoirs* (London, 1978), p. 200.
18 Robert Murphy, *Diplomat among Warriors* (London, 1984), p. 226.
19 *HMWD*, pp. 109-10. De Gaulle, *CWM, vol. ii,* p. 427.
20 F0660/49. Macmillan to de Gaulle, 4. 6. 43.
21 FO660/49. De Gaulle to Macmillan, 5. 6. 43.
22 PREM3/442/19. Macmillan to Churchill, 29. 5. 43. *HMWD*, pp. 125,7.
23 F0660/50. Macmillan to Churchill, 9. 6. 43.
24 Guy de Charbonnières, *Le Duel Giraud-de Gaulle* (Paris, 1984), p. 229.
25 Arthur Funk, *Charles de Gaulle* (Oklahoma, 1959), p. 130. François Kersaudy, *Roosevelt et de Gaulle* (Paris, 2004), p. 312. Williams, *Frenchman,* pp. 228-9. De Gaulle, *CWM, vol. ii, Docs.*, 184-5.
26 *HMWD*, pp. 113-7.
27 FO660/50. Macmillan to FO, 11. 6. 43. *FRUS, 1943, vol. ii,* p. 149.
28 Simon Berthon, *Allies at War* (London, 2001), pp. 274-5.
29 *HMWD*, p. 118. *FRUS, 1943, vol. ii,* p. 145. F0660/50. Roosevelt to Eisenhower, 10. 6. 43.
30 F0660/50. Churchill to Macmillan, 11. 6. 43. F0954/8. Churchill to Macmillan, 13. 6. 43.
31 Kersaudy, *Churchill and de Gaulle*, p. 287. Berthon, *Allies*, pp. 277-8.
32 Ibid., p. 278.
33 Macmillan, *BW,* p. 345.

34 F0660/50. Macmillan memo, 13. 6. 43. *HMWD*, p. 122. Bernard Ledwidge, *De Gaulle* (London, 1982), p. 154.

35 Egremont, *Wyndham*, pp. 87-8. *HMWD*, p. 77.

36 Ibid, p. 136. Macmillan, *BW*, p. 345.

37 FO660/50, Macmillan. memo., 14. 6. 43.

38 Ibid.

39 F0371/36305. Macmillan despatch, 'The Road to Recognition. '

40 *HMWD*, p. 124. F0660/50. Macmillan to FO, 16. 6. 43.

41 F037l/37176. Mack minute, 8. 6. 43. F0371/36127. Tel. Algiers, 19. 7. 43. *FRUS, 1943, vol. ii*, pp. 152-3. Funk, *De Gaulle*, p. 134.

42 Kimball, *Correspondence*, p. 255.

43 Ibid., p. 262. Kersaudy, *Churchill and de Gaulle*, p. 293. Harvey, *Diaries*, pp. 267-8. Anthony Eden, *The Reckoning* (London, 1965), p. 395.

44 F0660/50. Churchill to Macmillan, 17. 6. 43.

45 *HMWD*, pp. 125-6. Macmillan, *BW*, pp. 346-7. Berthon, *Allies*, p. 282. F0954/8. Macmillan to FO, 19. 6. 43.

46 *HMWD*, pp. 127-8.

47 Ibid., pp. 126-7. Macmillan, *BW*, pp. 348-9. De Gaulle, *CWM, vol. ii*, p. 432.

48 lbid., pp. 433-5.

49 *HMWD*, pp. 127-8. Harry Butcher, *Three Years with Eisenhower* (London, 1946), p. 283. De Gaulle, *Lettres, notes et carnets, 1943-45,* (Paris, 1983), p. 31.

50 Macmillan, *BW*, pp. 350-1.

51 Ibid., p. 351. *HMWD*, p. 131. De Gaulle, *CWM, vol. ii*, pp. 437-8. *CWM, vol. ii, Docs*, no. 225.

52 Ambrose, *Supreme Commander*, p. 202. *FRUS, 1943, vol. ii*, pp. 164-5. F0660 /51. Macmillan to Churchill, 22. 6. 43. Ledwidge, *De Gaulle*, p. 157. Berthon, *Allies*, pp. 283-4.

53 *The Papers of Dwight David Eisenhower, vol. ii* (Baltimore, 1970), p. 1212.

54 PREM3/121/1. Macmillan to Churchill, 22. 6. 43. Churchill to Mamillan, 23. 6. 43.

55 FO371/37168. *New Statesman*, 26. 6. 43.

56 FO954/8. Macmillan to FO 24. 6. 43. Williams, *Frenchman*, pp. 231-2.

57 Macmillan, *BW*, pp. 354-5. FO660/51. Macmillan-de Gaulle, 9. 7. 43.

58 Macmillan, *BW*, pp. 343-4. F0371/36299. Churchill to Eden, 12. 6. 43.

59 F0371/36299. Macmillan to FO, 17. 6. 43.

60 F0371/36299. Churchill to Eden, 20. 6. 43.

61 *HMWD*, p. 150.

62 FO371/36301. 'US Policy towards France. ' Undated draft memo for Cabinet.

63 Macmillan, *BW,* p. 355. FO660/45. Macmillan to FO, 14. 7. 43.

64 *HMWD*, pp. 167-8, 171. FO954/8. Churchill to Macmillan, 23. 7. 43. Macmillan to Churchill, 6. 7. 43.

65 Kimball, *Correspondence*, pp. 334-5.

66 Ibid., pp. 339-40.

67 F0371/36302. Churchill to Macmillan, 25. 8. 43. F0954/16. Eden to Macmillan, 25. 8. 43. Macmillan, *BW*, p. 360.

68 Ibid., p. 361.

CHAPTER 6. ALGIERS VALEDICTORY

1 *HMWD*, pp. 124-5.

2 Ibid., p. 145. FO660/106. Macmillan to Eden, 3. 8. 43.

3   De Gaulle, *CWM, vol. ii*, p. 54. Macmillan, *BW*, p. 409.
4   FO954/8. Churchill to Macmillan, 29. 9. 43. *HMWD*, p. 230.
5   Ibid., p. 230. Macmillan ministerial papers, c. 284. Macmillan to Churchill, 26. 9. 43. *HMWD*, p. 244.
6   Ibid., pp. 261-2.
7   Macmillan, *BW*, pp. 417-8. FO660/50. Macmillan-de Gaulle, 5. 11. 43.
8   Charles Williams, *Pétain* (London, 2005), pp. 447-53.
9   Macmillan, *BW*, pp. 417-20. FO660/150. Macmillan-de Gaulle, 18. 11. 43.
10 De Gaulle, *CWM, vol. ii*, p. 524. Reilly, *Memoirs*, Ms. Eng. c.6919, p. 17. PREM3/182/6. Final Algiers despatch, 3. 1. 44.
11 F0954/8. Churchill to Roosevelt, 13. 11. 43.
12 De Gaulle, *CWM, vol. ii*, pp. 524, 528. See also Macmillan *BW*, p. 425. Macmillan ministerial papers, c. 284, 1. 12. 43.
13 *HMWD*, pp. 298-300. Macmillan, *BW*, pp. 426-7. A. B. Gaunson *The Anglo French Clash in Lebanon and Syria* (Basingstoke, 1987), pp. 137-8.
14 *HMWD*, pp. 299-300.
15 Ibid, p. 312.
16 Ibid., pp. 331-5. Macmillan, *BW*, pp. 438-42. Macmillan ministerial papers, c. 284, 23. 12. 43.
17 FO371/36136. Churchill to Eden, 25. 12. 43. Macmillan, *BW*, pp. 442-3.
18 *HMWD*, p. 339.
19 Ibid, p. 348.
20 John Barnes and David Nicholson (eds), *The Empire at Bay* (London, 1988), p. 1021.
21 Nigel Nicolson (ed.), *Harold Nicolson Diaries and Letters, 1939-45,* (London, 1967), p. 367.
22 *HMWD*, pp. 113, 122.
23 PREM3/182/6. Macmillan, Final Algiers despatch, 3. 1. 44.
24 Ibid.
25 Arthur Funk, *Charles de Gaulle* (Oklahoma, 1959) p. 74. Williams, *Frenchman,* pp. 236-7.
26 Henri Giraud, *Le Seul but - la victoire* (Paris, 1949), p. 131.
27 PREM3/182/6. Macmillan, Final Algiers despatch, 3. 1. 44.
28 John Harvey (ed.), *The War Diaries of Oliver Harvey* (London, 1978), p. 226.
29 *HMWD*, p. 357.
30 Lord Egremont, *Wyndham and Children First* (London, 1968), p. 194. Anthony Sampson, *Macmillan* (Harmondsworth, 1967), pp. 65-6. Harvey, *Diaries*, p. 269. Horne, *Macmillan, vol. i*, p. 215.
31 Sampson, *Macmillan*, p. 70.
32 Miles Jebb (ed.), *The Diaries of Cynthia Gladwyn,* (London, 1996), p. 230.
33 John Charmley, 'Harold Macmillan and the Making of the French Committee of Liberation', *International History Review,* November 1982, p. 556. John Charmley, *British Policy towards General de Gaulle* (Unpublished D. Phil. thesis, Oxford, 1982), pp. 73-4. *HMWD*, p. 135.
34 Reilly, *Memoirs,* Ms. Eng. c.6919, p. 45. Horne, *Macmillan, vol. i*, p. 190. FO954/8. Catroux-Eden, 13. 4. 43.
35 Macmillan, *BW*, p. 237. *HMWD*, pp. 143, 293, 295.
36 PREM3/182/6. Macmillan, Final Algiers despatch, 3. 1. 44.
37 Horne, *Macmillan, vol. i*, pp. 160-1.
38 PREM3/182/6. Macmillan, Final Algiers despatch, 3. 1. 44.

39 René Massigli, *Une Comédie des Erreurs* (Paris, 1978), p. 22. David Dimbleby and David Reynolds, *An Ocean Apart* (London, 1988), p. 222. L. Seidentop, 'Mr Macmillan and the Edwardian Style' in Vernon Bogdanor and Robert Skidelsky, *The Age of Affluence* (London, 1970), p. 21. Cf. Gloria Maguire, *Anglo-American Policy towards the Free French* (Basingstoke, 1995), pp. 82-3.

40 Reilly M*emoirs*, Ms. Eng. c. 6919, p. 9. *Oxford Dictionary of National Biography, vol. 46* (Oxford, 2004), p. 427. Macmillan ministerial papers, c. 327, 27. 12. 59.

41 F0371/36167. Macmillan to Bridges, 13. 2. 43.

42 Macmillan ministerial papers, c. 283. Letter, 19. 4. 43. c. 327. Letter, 27. 12. 59.

43 Massigli, *Comédie*, pp. 22-3. Général Catroux, *Dans la bataille de Mediterranée* (Paris, 1949), p. 361.

44 Macmillan, *Fortune*, p. 209.

45 PREM11/2338. Macmillan minute, 22. 1. 57. Macmillan, *Pointing*, p. 410.

46 De Gaulle, *CWM, vol. ii*, p. 541.

47 Ibid., pp. 230-1, 541.

48 Anthony Eden, *The Reckoning* (London, 1965), p. 250.

CHAPTER 7. SUEZ, MESSINA AND ALGERIA

1 Lord Egremont, *Wyndham and Children First* (London, 1968), p. 194. Horne, *Macmillan, vol. i*, p. 223.

2 Ibid., pp. 295-6.

3 Catterall, *MD, 1950-7*, pp. 461, 490. Macmillan diary, 8. 6. 55. W. Scott Lucas, *Divided We Stand* (London, 1991), p. 80. Cf. Anthony Sampson, *Macmillan* (Harmondsworth, 1967), p. 110.

4 Hervé Alphand, *L'Étonnement d'être* (Paris, 1977), 17. 10. 43.

5 *The Listener*, 25. 9. 69. Ann Tusa, *The Last Division* (London, 1996), pp. 105-6. Macmillan papers, c. 333. Letter to Peggy Macmillan, 9. 8. 62. Hugo Young, *This Blessed Plot* (Macmillan, 1998), p. 2. Mark Deavin, *Harold Macmillan and the Origins of the 1961 British Application to Join the EEC* (Unpublished Ph. D. thesis, London, 1996), pp. 64-5.

6 Macmillan, *Tides*, p. 168.

7 Ibid, p. 194. Horne, *Macmillan, vol. i*, p. 321. *DBPO, Series ii, vol. i*, (London, 1986), pp. 813-5, 830-2, 844-6.

8 Ibid., p. 814. CAB129, c. c. (53) 108, 19. 3. 53.

9 Paul-Henri Spaak, *The Continuing Battle* (London, 1971), p. 230.

10 CAB128/29 CM (55) 19th. Concl., 30. 6. 55.

11 Catterall, *MD, 1950-7*, p. 443. F0371/116042. Meeting in Secretary of State's room, 29. 6. 55. James Ellison, *Threatening Europe* (Basingstoke, 2000), p. 18. John Young, '"The Parting of Ways"? Britain, the Messina Conference and the Spaak Committee, June-December 1955' in Michael Dockrill and John Young, *British Foreign Policy, 1945-56* (Basingstoke, 1989), p. 199.

12 Karl Kaiser, *Using Europe, Abusing the Europeans,* (Basingstoke, 1996), pp. 42-7. Alan Milward, *The Rise and Fall of National Strategy* (London, 2002), p. 229. Simon Burgess and Geoffrey Edwards, 'The Six Plus One. British Policy-making and the Question of European Economic Integration', *International Affairs,* Summer 1988, p. 406. Richard Lamb, *The Macmillan Years,* (London, 1995), pp. 106-7.

13 T234/106. Macmillan to Bridges, 1. 2. 56.

14 PREM11/1352. Eden-Mollet, 27. 9. 56. P. M. H. Bell, *Britain and France, 1940-94* (Harlow, 1997), pp. 136-7, 155-6.

15 Sampson, *Macmillan*, p. 121.
16 Jonathan Pearson, *Sir Anthony Eden and the Suez Crisis*. (Basingstoke, 2003), p. 29.
17 *FRUS, 1955-57, vol. xvi*, p. 329. Peter Mangold, *Success and Failure in British Foreign Policy* (Basingstoke, 2001), p. 104.
18 Catterall, *MD, 1950-7*, pp. 590-1, 607. Sampson, *Macmillan*, pp. 119-20. Lewis Johnman, 'Defending the Pound; the Economics of the Suez Crisis' in Anthony Gorst, Lewis Johnman and W. Scott Lucas, *Post War Britain, 1945-64* (London, 1989), pp. 170-1. Horne, *Macmillan, vol. i*, p. 413.
19 Lucas, *Divided*, p. 80.
20 *FRUS, 1955-57, vol. xvi*, p. 61.
21 Horne, *Macmillan, vol. i*, pp. 423-5. William Roger Louis, 'Harold Macmillan and the Middle East Crisis of 1958', *Proceedings of the British Academy*, no. 94, 1997, p. 213.
22 Horne, *Macmillan, vol. i*, pp. 444-5. Louis, *Divided*, p. 212.
23 Robert Rhodes-James, *Anthony Eden* (London, 1986), pp. 586-7.
24 Edward Heath, *The Course of My Life* (London, 1998), p. 179. Macmillan, *Riding*, p. 184.
25 Pearson, *Eden*, p. 168.
26 Horne, *Macmillan, vol. ii*, p. 18. George Hutchinson, *The Last Edwardian at No. 10* (London, 1980), pp. 42, 47.
27 Robert Marjolin, *Memoirs* (London, 1986), p. 297.
28 Lord Gladwyn, *Memoirs* (London, 1972), p. 285.
29 Peter Hennessey, *The Prime Minister* (London, 2000), p. 247.
30 Macmillan, *Riding*, chapter four.
31 Ibid., p. 240. *FRUS, 1955-7, vol. xxvii*, pp. 693-4.
32 Macmillan, *Riding*, p. 253.
33 *FRUS, 1955-7, vol. xxvii*, p. 719.
34 Macmillan, *Riding*, p. 253.
35 Ibid p. 320. *FRUS, 1955-7, vol. xxvii*, p. 785.
36 Michael Kandiah and Gillian Staerck 'Reliable Allies' in Wolfram Kaiser and Gillian Staerck (eds), *British Foreign Policy, 1955-64* (Basingstoke, 2000), pp. 150-1. Michael Dockrill, 'Restoring the Special Relationship - the Bermuda and Washington Conferences, 1957' in Dick Richardson and Glyn Stone (eds), *Decisions and Diplomacy* (London, 1995), pp. 218-9. Matthew Jones, 'Anglo-American Relations after Suez: the Rise and Decline of the Working Group Experiment and the French Challenge to NATO, 1957-9', *Diplomacy and Statecraft*, March 2003.
37 Macmillan, *Riding*, p. 323.
38 Horne, *Macmillan, vol. ii*, p. 58.
39 Macmillan, *Riding*, pp. 757-8.
40 Bruce Geelhoed and Anthony Edmonds, *Eisenhower, Macmillan and Allied Unity, 1957-60* (Basingstoke, 2003), p. 30.
41 *FRUS,1955-7, vol. xxvii*, p. 766. F0371/12933. Brief Bermuda. Tel. Bermuda 25. 3. 57. Jan Melissen, 'The Restoration of the Nuclear Alliance: Great Britain and Atlantic Relations with the US', *Contemporary Record*, Summer 1992, p. 78.
42 *FRUS, 1955-57, vol. xxvii*, p. 794. PREM11/1830B. Macmillan-Gaillard, November 1957. Macmillan, *Riding*, p. 331.
43 PREM11/2329. Gladwyn despatch, 14. 1. 58. Ellison, *Threatening*, p. 168.
44 'The Effects of Anglo-American Interdependence on the Long-term Interests of the United Kingdom', CAB 129 c. c. (58) 77.

45 Mathilde von Buelow, 'Paradoxes of Perception' (Unpublished M. Phil, thesis, Cambridge, 2001), p. 14.
46 Cf. Andrew Shennan, *De Gaulle* (London, 1993), p. 51.
47 Catterall, *MD, 1950-7,* p. 401.
48 De Gaulle, *CWM, vol. iii,* p. 997.
49 Shennan, *De Gaulle,* p. 77. Maurice Vaisse, 'Post-Suez France' in William Roger Louis and Roger Owen, *Suez, 1956* (Oxford, 1989), p. 339.
50 Macmillan diary, 16. 5. 58. Williams, *Frenchman,* p. 372.
51 Ibid., pp. 372-3
52 Ibid., p. 376.
53 Macmillan diary, 31. 6. 58. Lacouture, *Ruler,* p. 176.
54 De Gaulle, *Hope,* p. 19.

CHAPTER 8. THE OLD COMPANIONS

1   Williams, *Frenchman,* p. 363.
2   PREM11/2326. Macmillan-de Gaulle, 29-30. 6. 58. Macmillan, *Riding,* p.448.
3   Ibid.
4   Lord Gore-Booth, *With Great Truth and Respect* (London, 1974), p. 353.
5   Mathilde von Buelow, 'Paradoxes of Perception' (Unpublished M. Phil. thesis, Cambridge, 2001), p. 86.
6   PREM11/4152. Letter Rumbold, 14. 8. 63.
7   Macmillan, *Pointing,* p. 410.
8   De Gaulle, *Hope,* pp. 216-7.
9   Macmillan, *Riding,* p. 445. PREM11/2326. Macmillan-Chauvel, 2. 6. 58.
10 Macmillan, *Riding,* p. 445. Macmillan, *Pointing,* p. 112.
11 Ibid., p. 180.
12 Jean Chauvel, *Commentaire, vol. iii* (Paris, 1973), p. 347. Pierre Maillard, *De Gaulle et le problème allemand* (Paris, 2001 ed.), p. 128.
13 De Gaulle, *Hope,* pp. 210-11.
14 FO371/189233. Dixon Valedictory despatch, 1. 2. 65.
15 Horne, *Macmillan, vol. ii,* p. 25. Michael Kandiah and Gillian Staerck, 'Reliable Allies; Anglo-American Relations' in Wolfram Kaiser and Gillian Staerck (eds), *British Foreign Policy, 1955-64* (Basingstoke, 2000), p. 156. Arthur Schlesinger, *A Thousand Days* (London, 1965) p. 341. Harold Evans, *Downing Street Diary* (London, 1981), p. 144.
16 Macmillan, *End,* p. 473.
17 Macmillan, *Riding,* p. 445.
18 Macmillan papers, c. 349, 19. 6. 59. Macmillan to Sir F. Hoyer Millar, PREM11/2990. Macmillan-Chauvel, 4. 11. 59. *DDF, 1960, i,* p. 264.
19 De Gaulle, *Hope,* p. 216. Chauvel, *Commentaire,* pp. 273, 296.
20 PREM11/2998. Letter to the Queen, 14. 3. 60. PREM11/3325. Memorandum by the Prime Minister, 29. 12. 60-3. 1. 61.
21 FO371/153916. Home to PUS.
22 De Gaulle, *Hope,* pp. 166, 178-9. .
23 Edouard Jouve, *Le Général de Gaulle et la construction de l'Europe, vol. ii,* (Paris, 1967), p. 259. *FRUS, 1958-60, vol. vii,* p. 65.
24 Constantine Pagedas, *Anglo-American Relations and the French Problem* (London, 2000), p. 42.

25 Alex Danchev, *On Specialness* (Basingstoke, 1998), p. 4. T. G. Otte (ed.), *The Makers of British Foreign Policy* (Basingstoke, 2002), p. 238.

26 Nikita Khrushchev, *Khrushchev Remembers* (London, 1971), pp. 464-5.

27 John Ramsden, *Winds of Change* (London, 1996), pp. 147-8.

28 Maurice Vaisse, 'Politique Étrangère et la politique de défense dans la pensée et l'action du Général de Gaulle', *Espoir,* September 1993, p. 16. Williams, *Frenchman,* p. 394.

29 De Gaulle, *Hope,* p. 87.

30 Macmillan, *Pointing,* p. 156.

31 Chauvel, *Commentaire,* p. 317.

32 Lacouture, *Ruler,* pp. 351-2. De Gaulle, *Hope,* p. 217. De Gaulle, *CWM, vol. i,* pp. 102-3. PREM11/2338. Jebb interview de Gaulle, 20. 3. 58.

33 Ibid. Macmillan, *Pointing,* p. 180. C. L. Sulzberger, *The Last of the Giants* (London, 1970), p. 953.

34 Horne, *Macmillan, vol. ii,* p. 319. Cf. Lacouture, *Rebel,* p. 32.

35 Chauvel, *Commentaire,* pp. 253, 296. Lord Gladwyn, *Memoirs* (London, 1982), pp. 318-9.

36 FO371/153906. Killick memo, 27. 1. 60.

37 Gladwyn Papers, 1/3/34.

38 Macmillan, *Pointing,* p. 181.

39 Macmillan diary, 14. 2. 60.

40 Peyrefitte, *C'était, vol. i,* pp. 294-5. De Gaulle, *Hope,* p. 165.

41 Chauvel, *Commentaire,* p. 329.

42 PREM11/1352. Treasury memo, 22. 9. 56.

43 Colette Barber, 'The French Decision to Develop a Military Nuclear Programme in the 1950s', *Diplomacy and Statecraft,* March 1993, p. 103. FO371/161096. Briefs Rambouillet meeting, March 1961. PREM11/4230. Notes for the Prime Minister's Meeting with General de Gaulle.

44 De Gaulle, *Hope,* p. 149. Maurice Vaisse, *La Grandeur* (Paris, 1998), pp. 42-4.

45 Edward Fursdon, *The European Defence Community* (London, 1980), pp. 321-2.

46 Simon Burgess and Geoffrey Edwards, 'The Six Plus One', *International Affairs,* Summer 1988, pp. 401-2.

47 PREM11/3553. Tel. Paris, 16. 2. 61. FO371/153916. Tel. Paris, 19. 9. 60. FO371/145616. Macmillan visit Paris, 9-10. 3. 59. *DDF, 1959, i,* pp. 329-30. Macmillan papers, c. 343. Letter de Gaulle, 21. 10. 60. Chauvel, *Commentaire,* pp. 303, 328-9.

48 Saki Dockrill, *Britain's Retreat from East of Suez* (Basingstoke, 2002), p. 65.

49 Horne, *Macmillan, vol. ii,* p. 304.

50 CAB159/35 (61) 4th. meeting, 19. 1. 61.

51 Peyrefitte, *C'était, vol. ii,* p. 55. Henry Kissinger, *Diplomacy* (London, 1995), p. 598.

52 Robert Marjolin, *Memoirs* (London, 1989), p. 262. Lacouture, *Ruler,* pp. 455, 364.

53 FO146/4619. Dixon notes for use at meetings of ambassadors. Michael Foot, *Hansard,* 5th. Series, vol. 671, cols. 1021-2, 11. 2. 63. De Gaulle, *CWM, vol. i,* p. 230.

54 Paul Kennedy, *The Rise and Fall of the Great Powers* (London, 1989 ed.) p. 495.

55 FO371/161098. Briefs for Rambouillet. FO371/160462. Letter Paris, 7. 3. 61. Frank Costigliola, 'Kennedy, de Gaulle and the Challenge of Constitutionalism' in Robert Paxman and Nicholas Wahl (eds), *De Gaulle and the United States* (Oxford and Providence, 1994), p. 182.

56 Dockrill, *Retreat,* p. x.

57 Archives de la présidence de la République. 5AG1, Rambouillet, 13. 3. 60.

58 PREM11/4811. Despatch Paris, 19. 2. 62.

59 Charles Bohlen, *Witness to History* (London, 1973), p. 511. Michael Harrison, 'French Anti-Americanism under the Fourth Republic and the Gaullist Solution'' in Denis Lacorne *et al.*, *The Rise and Fall of French Anti-Americanism* (Basingstoke, 1990), pp. 176-7.

60 *FRUS, 1961-3, vol. xii*, p. 649. Peyrefitte, *C'était, vol. i*, pp. 367-8. Archives de la présidence de la République. 5 AG /5/171. De Gaulle-George Brown, 16. 12. 66.

61 *DDF, 1962, ii*, p. 543.

62 Institut Charles de Gaulle, *De Gaulle en son siècle, vol. v* (Paris, 1992), p. 447. Lacouture, *Ruler*, p. 420. Stanley Hoffman, *Decline or Renewal?* (New York, 1984), p. 284. De Gaulle, *Hope*, p. 255. Julian Jackson, *The Fall of France* (Oxford, 2003), p. 241.

63 PREM11/3712. De Zulueta note, 27. 6. 62. Scott to de Zulueta, 4. 12. 62.

64 Cyril Buffet, 'De Gaulle, the Bomb and Berlin' in John Gearson and Kari Schake (eds), *The Berlin Wall Crisis* (Basingstoke, 2002), p. 74. Peyrefitte, *C'était, vol. ii*, p. 32.

CHAPTER 9. IN SEARCH OF LOST FRIENDSHIP

1 Macmillan ministerial papers, c. 323. Macmillan to Lady Pam Berry, 28. 6. 58. Macmillan, *Riding*, p. 446. PREM11/2324. Brief Washington visit. PREM11/2339. Macmillan to Selwyn Lloyd, 6. 6. 58.

2 PREM11/2339. Tel. Washington, 3. 6. 58. *FRUS, 1958-60, vol. vii*, p. 19. De Gaulle, *CWM, vol. iii*, pp. 736-57.

3 Macmillan, *Riding*, p. 444.

4 PREM11/2326. Selwyn Lloyd to Jebb, 24. 6. 58.

5 PREM11/2339. Minute Rumbold, 2. 6. 58. F0371/137259. Minute Rumbold, 9. 6. 58.

6 Macmillan, *Riding*, p. 446.

7 PREM11/2330. Brook to Macmillan, 16. 6. 58

8 Macmillan, *Riding*, p. 447.

9 PREM11/2326. De Gaulle-Macmillan, 29-30. 6. 58.

10 *DDF, 1958, i*, p. 868. Jean Chauvel, *Commentaire, vol. iii* (Paris, 1973), pp. 253-4.

11 James Ellison, *Threatening Europe* (Basingstoke, 2000), pp. 150, 183, 195.

12 Miriam Camps, *Britain and the European Community, 1955-63* (London, 1964), p. 131. Robert Marjolin, *Memoirs* (London, 1989), pp. 319-20. Richard Lamb, *The Macmillan Years* (London, 1995), p. 112.

13 Lacouture, *Ruler*, p. 415.

14 Ibid, p. 420. Wilfrid Kohl, *French Nuclear Diplomacy* (Princeton, N. J., 1971), p. 15. McGeorge Bundy, *Danger and Survival* (New York, 1988), p. 481. Constantine Pagedas, *Anglo-American Strategic Relations and the French Problem,* (London, 2000), p. 1.

15 PREM11/2326. Paris brief.

16 PREM11/2326. Macmillan-Chauvel, 2. 6. 58.

17 FO371/137277. Macmillan-de Gaulle, 30. 6. 58. Macmillan-de Gaulle, 29-30. 6. 58. *DDF, 1958, i*, pp. 865-6, 883.

18 Chauvel, *Commentaire*, p. 254.

19 F0371/134505. FO Brief.

20 PREM11/2315. Macmillan to Selwyn Lloyd, 24. 6. 58.

21 Hugo Young, *This Blessed Plot* (London, 1998), p. 116.

22 PREM11/3334. Macmillan to Bligh, 16. 9. 60. George Ball, *The Past has Another Pattern* (New York, 1982), p. 209.
23 PREM11/2532. Selwyn Lloyd draft reply Macmillan, 26. 10. 58.
24 FO371/134505. Rumbold, 19. 7. 58. PREM11/2531. Tel. Paris, 11. 7. 58.
25 PREM11/2326. Macmillan-de Gaulle, 29-30. 6. 58.
26 Ibid.
27 *DDF, 1958, i,* p. 870.
28 Peyrefitte, *C'était, vol. i,* p. 300. De Gaulle, *Hope,* p. 186. Alan Milward, *The Rise and Fall of National Strategy* (London, 2002), p. 288.
29 *DDF, 1958, i,* pp. 870- 871. PREM11/2326. Macmillan-de Gaulle, 29-30. 6. 58. De Gaulle, *Hope,* p. 188.
30 Macmillan diary, 29-30. 6. 58.
31 Ibid., 4. 7. 58.
32 CAB128/32. c. c. (58) 51st. concl., 1. 7. 58. Macmillan, *Riding,* pp. 450-2.
33 Ibid., p. 631.
34 PREM11/2326. Macmillan-de Gaulle, 29-30. 6. 58.
35 PREM11/2326. Tel. Paris, 25. 6. 58.
36 Lamb, *Macmillan Years,* p. 35.
37 Frédéric Bozo, *Two Strategies for Europe* (Lanham, 2001), p. 14.
38 Ibid., pp. 14-15. Charles de Gaulle, *Lettres, notes et carnets, 1958-60* (Paris, 1985), p. 47.
39 PREM11/2387. Tel. Paris, 18. 7. 58.
40 PREM11/2335. Tel. NATO, 1. 1. 58. PREM11/2387. Tel. NATO, 18. 7. 58.
41 PREM11/2335. Macmillan to de Gaulle, 5. 8. 58. De Gaulle to Macmillan, 9. 8. 58. Tel. Paris, 2, 8. 8. 58. Letter Paris, 9. 8. 58.
42 *DDF, 1958, ii,* pp. 243, 244.
43 PREM11/2323. Macmillan to Selwyn Lloyd, 20. 7. 58.
44 PREM11/2323. Tel. Paris, 21. 7. 58. *DDF, 1958, ii,* p. 165.
45 Nigel Nicolson, *Portrait of a Marriage* (London, 1974 ed.), p. 219. Edward Heath, *The Course of My Life* (London, 1998), p. 215.
46 PREM11/2323. Tel. Paris, 29. 7. 58.
47 Macmillan, *Riding,* p. 527.
48 Horne, *Macmillan, vol. ii,* pp. 108-9. Macmillan diary, 3. 8. 58.
49 Macmillan papers, c. 324. Macmillan to de Gaulle, 2. 8. 58.
50 Macmillan, *Riding,* p.560.
51 Macmillan diary, 19,20. 8. 58. Horne, *Macmillan, vol. ii,* p.109.

CHAPTER 10. THE GENERAL STRIKES OUT

1 John Newhouse, *De Gaulle and the Anglo-Saxons* (New York, 1970), pp. 37-8. Reilly, Memoirs, Ms. Eng. c. 6925, p. 73.
2 Klaus-Juergen Mueller, *Adenauer and de Gaulle* (St. Antony's College, Konrad Adenauer Stiftung, 1992), pp. 7-8. Hans-Peter Schwarz, *Konrad Adenauer* (Oxford, 1995), pp. 360-3. Maurice Vaisse, *La Grandeur* (Paris, 1998), p. 226.
3 Mueller, *Adenauer,* p. 11.
4 De Gaulle, *Hope,* p. 174.
5 Newhouse, *De Gaulle,* p. 68.
6 Konrad Adenauer, *Erinnerungen,1955-9,* (Stuttgart, 1967), p. 434. Williams, *Frenchman,* pp. 396-7.
7 PREM11/3236. Macmillan-de Gaulle, 29. 5. 58. Edmond Jouve, *Le Général de Gaulle*

et la construction de l'Europe (Paris, 1967), p. 253. Jean-Marie Boegner, '1958: Le Général de Gaulle et l'acceptance de Traité de Rome', *Espoir,* June 1992, p. 28. Alain Peyrefitte, 'Un Singulier Paradox', *Espoir,* Octobre 1998, p. 51. Pierre Maillard, *De Gaulle et le problème allemand* (Paris, 2001 ed.), p. 160.

8   MAE, Cabinet de Ministre, No. 365. Echange de Message et notes. Colombey record.

9   Ibid.

10 *DDF, 1958, ii,* p. 344. Eric Roussel, *Charles de Gaulle,* (Paris, 2002), p. 617.

11 MAE, Cabinet de Ministre. Colombey record. *Paris Jour,* 5. 4. 60.

12 Maillard, *De Gaulle,* pp145-6. F0371/134509. Macmillan-Adenauer, 8. 10. 58.

13 PREM11/2326. Macmillan-de Gaulle, 29-30. 6. 58.

14 F0371/137277. Brief.

15 De Gaulle, *Hope,* p. 200.

16 Frédéric Bozo, *Two Strategies for Europe* (Lanham, 2001), p. 9. Constantine Pagedas, *Anglo-American Relations and the French Problem* (London, 2000), p. 140.

17 De Gaulle, *Discours et messages, 1958-62* (Paris, 1970), pp. 126-7. PREM 11/3775. Macmillan-de Gaulle, 2,3. 6. 62.

18 De Gaulle, *Hope,* pp. 202-3. *DDF, 1958, i,* p. 377. *DDF, 1958, ii,* p. 855. PREM11/2326. Macmillan-de Gaulle, 29-30. 6. 58. Bozo, *Two Strategies,* pp. 18-19.

19 Maillard, *De Gaulle,* p. 145.

20 F0371/137820. Tel. NATO, 8. 10. 58.

21 F0371/137820. Tel. NATO, 1. 10. 58. Macmillan, *Riding,* p. 453. Schwarz, *Adenauer,* pp. 370-1.

22 De Gaulle, *Hope,* pp. 202-3. Peyrefitte, *C'était, vol.* i, p. 352.

23 FO371/137825. Tel. FO, 7. 11. 58. Tel. NATO, 12. 11. 58. De Gaulle to Diefenbaker. George-Henri Soutou, *L' Alliance incertain* (Paris, 1996), p. 131.

24 FO371/137826. Tel. Washington, 5. 12. 58.

25 Maillard, *De Gaulle,* pp. 144-5.

26 FO371/137822. Tel. FO 22. 10. 58.

27 PREM11/2531. Tel. Paris, 11. 7. 58.

28 PREM11/2531. Macmillan to Maudling, 5. 8. 58. F0371/134505. Chauvel-Hoyer Millar, 8. 7. 58. F0371/134507. Chauvel-Hoyer Millar, 14. 8. 58.

29 MAE, Wormser papers, no. 40. Tel. Paris, 29. 7. 58. Note 30. 7. 58.

30 MAE, Cabinet de Ministre, no. 365. Echange de Messages et Notes, Colombey record. PREM11/2532. Maudling to Macmillan, 30. 9. 58.

31 PREM11/2532. Macmillan to Selwyn Lloyd, 15. 10. 58.

32 Macmillan, *Riding,* p. 455. CAB 129/95. Note by the Prime Minister, 3. 11. 58.

33 *DDF, 1958, ii,* p. 609. MAE, Wormser papers, draft note, Kojeve 13. 10. 58. Note, 20. 10. 58, 6. 11. 58. Frances Lynch, 'De Gaulle's First Veto', *Contemporary European History,* March 2000, pp. 127-8.

34 F0371/134510. Tel. Paris, 6. 11. 58.

35 F0371/134513. Selwyn Lloyd-Couve de Murville, 6. 11. 58. PREM11/2532. Macmillan-Couve de Murville, 6. 11. 58.

36 MAE, Wormser papers, no. 40. Note, 6. 11. 58.

37 Macmillan diary, 6. 11. 58.

38 Ibid. PREM11/3002 Macmillan to Diefenbaker, 6. 11. 58.

39 FO371/134510. Heathcoat-Amory to Macmillan, 7. 11. 58.

40 Macmillan, *Riding,* pp. 456-7.

41 Ibid., p. 457. Paul Gore-Booth, *With Great Truth and Respect* (London, 1974), p. 250.

42 Peyrefitte, *C'était, vol. i,* pp. 300, 37. Peyrefite, *Espoir,* Octobre, 1998, p. 51. De Gaulle, *Hope,* pp. 179-80. Lynch, *Veto,* pp. 127-8. *DDF, 1958, ii,* p. 898.

43 C. L. Sulzberger, *The Last of the Giants* (London, 1970), p. 40. Roussel, *De Gaulle,* pp. 619-20. Richard Lamb, *The Macmillan Years* (London, 1995), p. 110. MAE, Wormser papers, no. 40. Note 20. 10. 58.

44 De Gaulle, *Hope,* p. 188.

45 Lynch, *Veto,* p. 29.

46 *DDF, 1958, ii,* p. 704. Lynch, *Veto,* p. 131.

47 Ibid, p. 130. *DDF, 1958, ii,* pp. 754-6. FO371/134510. Discussion von Scherpenberg, 27. 10. 58.

48 Peyrefitte, *C'était, vol. i,* p. 353. Martin Schaad, *Bullying Bonn* (Basingstoke, 2000), pp. 104, 112-3. PREM11/2532. Memo. C. M. MacLehose.

49 FO371/134514, Gore-Booth to Caccia, 18. 11. 58. F0371/134520 Lord Perth to Selwyn Lloyd.

50 MAE, Wormser papers, no. 40. Note 13. 10. 58. *The Times,* 18. 11. 58. Miriam Camps, *Britain and the European Community* (London, 1964), p. 174.

51 Lamb, *The Macmillan Years,* pp. 122-3. Michael Charlton, *The Price of Victory* (London, 1983), pp. 225-6.

52 PREM11/2531. Maudling to Macmillan, 5. 8. 58.

53 Ibid. PREM11/2532. David Eccles, 8. 12. 58.

54 *DDF, 1958, ii,* pp. 673, 755.

55 MAE, Secrétariat Général, Entretiens et Messages, 1956-60, 17. 12. 58. PREM 11/2826. Selwyn Lloyd-de Gaulle, 17. 12. 58. F0371/134520. Couve-Jebb, 19. 12. 58.

56 MAE, Secrétariat-Général, Entretiens et Messages, 1956-60, De Gaulle-Fanfani, 18. 11. 58. Lynch, Veto p.121 .

57 Lord Gladwyn, *Memoirs* (London, 1972), p. 316.

58 Macmillan, *Pointing,* pp. 410-11.

CHAPTER 11. FORCING THE WAY

1   PREM11/2983. Macmillan to Bishop, 31. 7. 60.

2   Catterall, *MD, 1950-7,* pp. 452, 456.

3   Peter Mangold, *From Tirpitz to Gorbachev* (Basingstoke, 1998), p. 94.

4   Ibid., pp. 93-4. Sergei Khrushchev, *Nikita Khrushchev* (Pennsylvania, 2000), pp. 211-2.

5   William Taubman, *Khrushchev* (New York, 2003), p. 407.

6   Vladislav Zubok and Constantine Pleshakov, *Inside the Kremlin's Cold War* (Cambridge, Mass., 1996), pp. 195,8. Sergei Khrushchev, *Khrushchev,* p. 305.

7   Taubman, *Khrushchev,* pp. 396-7.

8   Ann Tusa, *The Last Division* (London, 1996), pp. 129-30. *FRUS, 1958-60, vol. viii,* pp. 86-7, 101.

9   Bernard Ledwidge, 'La Crise de Berlin; stratégie et tactique du Général de Gaulle' in Institut Charles de Gaulle, *De Gaulle en son siècle, vol. iv* (Paris, 1992), pp. 369, 373. Michel Debré, *Gouverner,* (Paris, 1988), pp. 412-3. Williams, *Frenchman,* pp. 313-4. Jean-Pierre Guichard, *De Gaulle face aux crises* (Paris, 2000), pp. 262, 264-5. PREM11/2685. De Gaulle to Macmillan, 25. 4. 59. *FRUS, 1958-60, vol. xviii,* p. 575.

10 CAB133/240. Macmillan-Eisenhower, 20. 3. 59. F0371/145616. Macmillan/de Gaulle, Debré, 9,10. 3. 59.

11 Macmillan, *Riding,* pp. 573, 8. John Gearson, *Harold Macmillan and the Berlin Wall*

Crisis (Basingstoke, 1998), pp. 62-3. Tusa, *Last Division,* pp. 136-8. Ledwidge, 'La Crise', pp. 370,376.

12 PREM11/2998. Macmillan-de Gaulle, 21. 12. 59.

13 John Gearson, 'British Policy and the Berlin Wall Crisis, *Contemporary Record,* Summer 1992, p. 130. Henry Kissinger, *Diplomacy* (London, 1995), p. 577. Macmillan, *Pointing,* p. 73. Horne, *Macmillan, vol. ii,* pp. 135-6.

14 Erin Mahan, *Kennedy, de Gaulle and Western Europe* (Basingstoke, 2002), p. 54. Macmillan, *Riding,* p. 257.

15 Mark Pottle (ed.), *Champion Redoubtable* (London, 1998), p. 392. *FRUS, 1958-60. vol. vii, pt. ii,* p. 846.

16 Macmillan, *Pointing,* pp. 74-5. Macmillan, *Riding,* pp. 597, 588.

17 Ibid., p. 57. Sergei Khrushchev, *Khrushchev,* pp. 305, 310-11.

18 Catterall, *MD, 1950-7,* p. 420.

19 PREM11/2716. Undated brief. PREM11/2990. Macmillan-Chauvel, 4. 11. 59. *The Listener,* 22. 6. 72. Anthony Sampson, *Macmillan* (Harmondsworth, 1967), p. 14. Stephen White, *Britain, Détente and Changing East-West Relations* (London, 1992), p.62. Arthur Schlesinger, *A Thousand Days* (London, 1965), pp. 340-1.

20 Macmillan diary, 6. 1. 59.

21 Sampson, *Macmillan,* p. 145.

22 Macmillan diary, 3. 5. 59.

23 CAB128/32 c. c. (58) 8th. Concl., 22. 1. 58. Kathleen Newman, *Britain and the Soviet Union* (Unpublished Ph. D. thesis, London, 1999), p. 93. Tusa, *Last Division,* pp. 128-30. Selwyn Lloyd papers, 4/22, 'Reflections on the FO. '

24 Macmillan, *Riding,* p. 559.

25 Ibid., p. 589.

26 Ibid., p. 583. Horne, *Macmillan, vol. ii,* pp.120-1. PREM11/2686. De Zulueta to Macmillan, 27. 7. 59.

27 Macmillan diary, 5. 2. 59. Gearson, *Harold Macmillan and the Berlin Wall Crisis,* p. 64. *DDF, 1959, i,* pp. 275, 277.

28 Newman, *Britain,* p. 106. Horne, *Macmillan, vol ii,* p. 120.

29 *FRUS, 1958-60, vol. viii,* p. 363. Richard Aldous, *Harold Macmillan and the Search for a Summit with the USSR, 1958-60* (Unpublished Ph. D thesis, Cambridge, 1993), p. 47.

30 Sir Curtis Keeble, 'Macmillan and the Soviet Union' in Richard Aldous and Sabine Lee, *Harold Macmillan* (Basingstoke, 1999), p. 211.

31 Sergei Khrushchev, *Khrushchev,* p. 308.

32 PREM11/2690. Macmillan-Khrushchev, 23,25,26. 2. 59.

33 PREM11/2716. Selwyn Lloyd to Caccia, 5. 3. 59. Gearson, *Harold Macmillan,* p. 77.

34 PREM11/2690. Reilly despatch, 16. 3. 59. Cf Sergei Khrushchev, *Khrushchev,* pp. 321, 327, 340.

35 Ibid, p. 308. Gearson, *Harold Macmillan,* p. 76. Gearson, *Contemporary Record,* p. 137. Keeble, 'Macmillan', p. 211.

36 CAB128/33 c. c. (59), l4th Concl., 4. 3. 59.

37 *DDF, 1959, i,* pp. 292-4.

38 F0371/145616. Macmillan-Debré/de Gaulle, 9-10. 3. 59.

39 PREM11/2716. Tel. Paris, 12. 3. 59.

40 F0371/145616. Macmillan-Debré/de Gaulle, 9-10. 3. 59.

41 Ibid. Macmillan diary, 9. 3. 59.

42 PREM 11/2716. Macmillan-Adenauer, 13. 3. 59. PREM11/2717. Letter Bonn, 31. 3. 59. *FRUS, 1958-60, vol. viii*, p. 1021. Macmillan, *Riding*, p. 640. Newman, *Britain*, p. 155.

43 *FRUS, 1958-60, vol. viii*, pp. 520, *vol. viv*, p. 842. Tusa, *Last Division*, pp. 160-2.

44 Macmillan, *Riding*, pp. 645-6. Macmillan diary, 21. 3. 59. *DDF, 1959, i*, p. 422.

45 PREM11/2717. Macmillan to Selwyn Lloyd, 2. 4. 59.

46 Charles de Gaulle, *Discours et messages, 1958-60*, (Paris, 1970), p. 86.

47 PREM11/2717. Selwyn Lloyd to Macmillan, 21. 5. 59. Macmillan, *Pointing*, pp. 63-4. *DDF, 1959, i*, p. 671. *FRUS, 1958-60, vol. viii*, pp. 860-1.

48 PREM11/2717. Tel. Geneva, 1. 6. 59. Macmillan, *Pointing*, p. 62. Zubok and Pleshakov, *Kremlin's Cold War*, p. 200. *DDF, 1959, i*, p. 239.

49 Archives de la présidence de la République, 5AG1. Macmillan to de Gaulle, 5. 6. 59.

50 *DDF, 1959, i.* pp. 790-1.

51 Macmillan, *Pointing*, p. 66.

52 PREM11/2685. Macmillan to Selwyn Lloyd, 10. 6. 59.

53 Macmillan, *Pointing*, pp. 66-67.

54 Ibid, p. 67. *FRUS,1958-60, vol.* viii, pp. 892-3.

55 PREM11/2685. Meeting No. 10 Downing Street, 14. 6. 59.

56 PREM11/2685. Macmillan to Jebb, 16. 6. 59. Tel. Paris, 16. 6. 59.

57 PREM11/2685. Tel. Washington, 17. 6. 59. Macmillan, *Pointing*, p. 71.

58 PREM11/2686. Macmillan to Eisenhower, 23 , 29. 6. 59. Macmillan diary, 27. 6. 59.

59 Newman, *Britain*, p. 212. Taubman, *Khrushchev*, p. 415.

60 Macmillan, *Pointing*, p. 70.

61 Ibid., p. 76. *FRUS, 1958-60, vol. viii*, pp. 972-3, 976-7. PREM11/2686. Herter to Selwyn Lloyd, 13. 7. 59. Selwyn Lloyd to Macmillan, 14. 7. 59.

62 Ibid., p. 78. PREM11/2686. Macmillan to Selwyn Lloyd, 22. 7. 59.

63 Macmillan diary, 23. 7. 59.

64 *FRUS, 1958-60, vol. viii*, pp. 1051-2.

65 Macmillan, *Pointing*, pp. 79-80.

66 Horne, *Macmillan, vol. ii*, p. 147. PREM11/2686. Macmillan to Selwyn Lloyd 27, 29. 7. 59.

67 *FRUS, 1958-60, vol. viii*, p. 1075.

68 Ibid., p. 1076.

69 Ibid., p. 1078.

70 Ibid., p. 1110.

CHAPTER 12. 'THE MOST TRAGIC DAY OF MY LIFE '

1 Macmillan, *Pointing*, pp. 80-2.

2 Curtis Keeble, 'Macmillan and the Soviet Union' in Richard Aldous and Sabine Lee, *Harold Macmillan* (Basingstoke, 1999), p. 215.

3 Macmillan, *Pointing*, p. 80. PREM11/2686. Selwyn Lloyd to Macmillan, 29. 7. 59.

4 PREM11/2290. Macmillan to Selwyn Lloyd, 4. 8. 59.

5 Macmillan diary, 30. 8. 59.

6 *DDF, 1959, ii*, p. 284.

7 Hervé Alphand, *L'Étonnement d'être* (Paris, 1977), p. 307.

8 PREM11/2990. Tel. F. O., 21. 10. 59.

9 PREM11/2990. Tel. Paris, 20. 10. 59. Selwyn Lloyd-Chauvel, 21. 10. 59. *DDF, 1959, ii*, p. 488. Alphand, *L'Étonnement*, p. 310.

10 PREM11/2990. Tel. Caccia to Macmillan, 10. 10. 59. Macmillan to Caccia, 12. 10. 59. Macmillan to de Gaulle, 17. 10. 59.

11 PREM11/2990. Macmillan-Chauvel, 4.11. 59. Macmillan, *Pointing*, p. 95.

12 Kathleen Newman, *Britain and the Soviet Union,* (Unpublished Ph. D. thesis, University of London, 1999), p. 256.

13 PREM11/2990. Selwyn Lloyd to Macmillan, 14. 11. 59.

14 *DDF, 1959, ii,* p. 664.

15 Macmillan, *Pointing,* p. 108. Horne, *Macmillan, vol. ii,* p. 218. PREM11/3480 Macmillan to the Queen, 23. 12. 59.

16 Macmillan, *Pointing,* pp. 101, 106-7, 8.

17 Ibid., p. 103.

18 Ibid., pp. 103, 195. Horne, *Macmillan, vol. ii,* p. 218. *DDF, 1959, ii,* p. 794.

19 *DDF, 1959, ii,* p. 664. PREM11/2991. Macmillan-de Gaulle, 20. 12. 59. De Gaulle, *Hope,* pp. 223-4. Macmillan, *Pointing,* p. 111.

20 Ibid., p. 110.

21 PREM11/3480. Macmillan to the Queen, 23. 12. 59.

22 PREM11/2991. Macmillan-de Gaulle, 21. 12. 59. *DDF, 1959, i,* p. 782.

23 Macmillan, *Pointing,* pp. 114-5.

24 Macmillan diary, 13. 3. 60. PREM11/2998. Macmillan-de Gaulle, 12-13. 3. 60. *DDF, 1960, i,* p. 265.

25 Jean-Pierre Guichard, *De Gaulle face aux crises* (Paris, 2000), p. 280.

26 Sergei Khrushchev, *Nikita Khrushchev* (Pennsylvania, 2000), p. 353.

27 William Taubman, *Khrushchev* (London, 2003), p. 452.

28 Michel Debré, *Gouverner* (Paris, 1988), p. 401.

29 De Gaulle, *Hope,* p. 232. Sergei Khrushchev, *Khrushchev,* p. 347.

30 Maurice Couve de Murville, *Une Politique étrangère,* (Paris, 1971), pp. 175-6.

31 *DDF 1960, i,* pp. 360-1. Strobe Talbott (ed.), *Khrushchev Remember. The Last Testament,* (London, 1974), p. 440.

32 René Bouscat, *De Gaulle-Giraud* (Paris, 1967), p. 94

33 *DDF 1960, i,* pp. 356-9, 367.

34 De Gaulle, *Hope,* p. 234. Talbott, *Khrushchev,* p. 442.

35 *DDF, 1960, i,* pp. 413, 500. Couve de Murville, *Politique,* p. 177. De Gaulle, *Hope,* p. 243.

36 Macmillan, *Pointing,* p. 187. PREM11/2992. Macmillan to Bishop, 21. 4. 60.

37 PREM11/2992. De Zulueta brief, 6. 5. 60.

38 Newman, *Britain,* pp. 275, 277. Stephen Ambrose, *Eisenhower* (New York, 1990), p. 515. Talbott, *Khrushchev,* p. 443. Fedor Burlatsky, *Khrushchev and the First Russian Spring* (London, 1991), pp. 155-6.

39 Michael Beschloss, *Mayday* (New York, 1986), pp. 241-2. Horne, *Macmillan, vol. ii,* pp. 224, 6. Sergei Khrushchev, *Khruschev,* pp. 368-73.

40 Ibid., p. 380.

41 Macmillan, *Pointing,* p. 201. Horne, *Macmillan, vol. ii,* p. 226.

42 PREM11/2992. Macmillan-Khrushchev, 15. 5. 60.

43 Talbott, *Khruhschev,* pp. 449, 451. Taubman, *Khrushchev,* pp. 455, 458-60. *DDF, 1960, i,* pp. 556-7.

44 Sergei Khrushchev, *Khrushchev,* p. 389. Macmillan, *Pointing,* pp. 202-3.

45 *FRUS, 1958-60, vol. ix,* p. 433. PREM11/2992. Paris records, 15. 5. 59. *DDF, 1960, i,* p. 659.

46 Macmillan, *Pointing,* p. 204.

47 Ibid.

48 De Gaulle, *Hope,* pp. 250-1.

49 Macmillan, *Pointing,* pp. 205-6. Sergei Khrushchev, *Khrushchev,* p. 390.

50 Dwight Eisenhower, *The White House Years* (London 1966), p. 556.

51 Couve de Murville, *Politique,* p. 180. De Gaulle, *Hope,* p. 248.

52 Macmillan, *Pointing,* pp. 207-8. *Listener,* 22. 6. 72. Richard Aldous, *Harold Macmillan and the Search for a Summit with the USSR, 1958-60* (Unpublished Ph. D. thesis, Cambridge, 1993), pp. 247-8. PREM11/2992. Macmillan-Khrushchev, 16. 5. 60.

53 Macmillan, *Pointing,* p. 209. Charles Bohlen, *Witness to History* (London, 1973), p. 469. PREM11/2992. Paris record, 17. 5. 60. *FRUS, 1958-60, vol. ix,* p. 475.

54 *DDF, 1960, i,* pp. 678-9.

55 Talbott, *Khrushchev,* p. 460.

56 PREM11/2992. Macmillan-Khrushchev, 18. 5. 59. Horne, *Macmillan, vol. ii,* p. 231. D. R. Thorpe, *Selwyn Lloyd* (London, 1989), pp. 302-3.

57 Aldous, *Macmillan,* p. 262.

58 De Gaulle, *Hope,* p. 253. Beschloss, *Mayday,* p. 310.

59 C. L. Sulzberger, *The Last of the Giants,* (London, 1970), p. 669. Selwyn Lloyd papers, Selo 4/22, 4/33. Alphand, *L'Étonnement,* p. 333. Richard Aldous, ' "A Family Affair" - Macmillan and the Art of Personal Diplomacy' in Richard Aldous and Sabine Lee, *Harold Macmillan and Britain's World Role* (Basingstoke, 1996), pp. 25-6. *FRUS, 1958-60, vol. xiv,* p. 515.

60 Macmillan ministerial papers, c. 343, 19. 5. 60.

61 Kendrick Oliver, *Kennedy, Macmillan and the Nuclear Test Ban Debate,* (Basingstoke, 1998), pp. 62, 72. David Nunnerley, *President Kennedy and Britain* (London, 1972), pp. 52-3. Henry Kissinger, *Diplomacy* (London, 1995), p. 586.

62 Jean Chauvel, *Commentaire, vol. iii* (Paris, 1973), p. 307. Thorpe, *Selwyn Lloyd.,* p. 301.

63 Sergei Khrushchev, *Khrushchev,* p. 305.

64 Macmillan diary, 10. 5. 59.

65 PREM11/3480. Macmillan to the Queen, 23. 12. 59.

CHAPTER 13. GRAND DESIGNS

1 Eric Roussel, *Charles de Gaulle* (Paris, 2002), p. 663. MAE, Europe, 1956-60, no. 169, Note. 16. 8. 60.

2 William Cohen, 'De Gaulle et l'Europe avant 1958' in *De Gaulle en son siècle vol. v,* (Paris, 1992), pp. 56-7. *DBPO Series ii, vol. i,* p. 814.

3 Jacques Bariety, 'Les Entretiens de Gaulle-Adenauer de Juillet 1960 en Rambouillet', *Revue d'Allemagne,* Avril-Juin 1997, pp. 168-9. Maurice Couve de Murville, *Une Politique étrangère* (Paris, 1971), p. 44.

4 Charles de Gaulle, *Discours et messages, 1958-62* (Paris, 1970), p. 244.

5 Couve de Murville, *Politique,* p. 244. MAE, Europe, 1956-60, no. 169, 16. 8. 60. Pierre Maillard, *De Gaulle et le problème allemand* (Paris, 2002 ed.), p. 165.

6 George-Henri Soutou, *L'Alliance incertain,* (Paris, 1996), p. 131.

7 Joseph Frankel, *British Foreign Policy, 1945-68* (London, 1975), p. 157.

8 *DDF, 1958, ii,* pp. 361-2. *DDF, 1960, ii,* p. 260. Lacouture, *Ruler,* p. 345. Soutou, *L'Alliance,* p. 124. Stanley Hoffman, *Decline or Renewal* (New York, 1974), p. 318. Peyrefitte, *C'était, vol. i,* pp. 366-7, 381.

9 Edmound Jouve, *Le Général de Gaulle et la construction de l'Europe* (Paris, 1967), pp. 244, 48. Peyrefitte, *C'était, vol. i,* pp. 158-9. Lacouture, *Ruler,* p. 345. Macmillan, *Pointing,* p. 427.

10 John Newhouse, 'De Gaulle and the Anglo-Saxons' in Douglas Brinkley and Richard Griffiths, *John F. Kennedy and Europe,* (Baton Rouge, 1999) p. 45. Ernst Weisenfeld, 'L'Europe de l'Atlantique a l'Oural; une formule, une vision, une politique' in Institut Charles de Gaulle, *De Gaulle en son siècle, vol. v,* p. 442.

11 Roussel, *De Gaulle,* p. 717. *DDF, 1960, ii,* p. 365.

12 MAE, Europe, 1956-60, no. 169. Note, 10. 8. 60. Europe, 1961-70, no. 211.

13. Macmillan, *Pointing,* p. 312.

14 Ibid., p. 312. Macmillan diary, 2. 11. 60.

15 PREM11/3325. Memo by the Prime Minister, 29. 12. 60-3. 1. 61. 'The Grand Design'.

16 PREM 11/3311. 'Short Version of the Grand Design. '

17 Macmillan, *Pointing,* p. 112. Constantine Pagedas, *Anglo-American Strategic Relations and the French Problem,* (London, 2000), p. 113. PREM11/3325. 'Grand Design. '

18 PREM11/3001. Talking points for State visit, April 1960.

19 PREM11/3334. Macmillan to Bligh. PREM11/2983. PREM11/2679. Briefing paper, Chequers weekend, 29. 11. 59. PREM11/3325. 'Grand Design.' Macmillan papers, c. 329. Letter to Maudling, 1. 8. 60. Macmillan diary, 27. 3. 60. Macmillan, *Pointing,* pp. 54-5, 113-4. James Ellison, *Threatening Europe* (Basingstoke, 2000), pp. 203-4.

20 F0371/153916. Jebb to Heath, 9. 9. 60. PREM11/2679. Chequers weekend discussion, 29. 11. 59.

21 Macmillan, *Pointing,* pp. 112-14.

22 PREM11/3480. Macmillan to the Queen.

23 FO371/152095. Hoyer Millar to Selwyn Lloyd, 23. 12. 59. F0371/152096. Hoyer Millar to Selwyn Lloyd, 26. 2. 60.

24 PREM11/3225. Norman Brook, 21. 1. 61.

25 PREM11/2679. Chequers weekend discussion, 29. 11. 59.

26 Pagedas, *Anglo-American,* pp. 46-7, 112-3. PREM11/2983. 'Joanna Southcott's Box'. Macmillan to Bishop, 31. 7. 60.

27 Soutou, *L'Alliance,* p. 134.

28 PREM11/2998. De Gaulle-Macmillan, 12-13. 3. 60. Macmillan diary, 13. 3. 60. *DDF, 1960, i,* pp. 264-6, 304, 318-9. Couve de Murville, *Politique,* p. 65.

29 MAE, Secrétariat Général, Entretiens et Messages, 1956-61, vol. 13. Note, Messmer, 18. 4. 60.

30 PREM11/3325. 'Grand Design. '

31 Pagedas, *Anglo-American,* pp. 119-22. PREM11/3325. Brook, 21. 1. 61. FO371/159668. Shuckburgh memo.

32 F0371/161097. Macmillan to Home, 25. 1. 61. FO371/159671. Home to Dixon, 24. 1. 61.

33 Macmillan, *Pointing,* p. 326.

34 *DDF, 1961, i,* p. 106. FO371/161097. Macmillan-de Gaulle, 28-9. 1. 61

35 Ibid. PREM11/4219. Letter Paris, 13. 6. 62.

36 FO371/161097. Macmillan-de Gaulle, 28-9. 1. 61.

37 *DDF 1961, i,* pp. 176-7. Macmillan, *Pointing,* p. 327. CAB128/35 Pt. 1 c. c. 3 (61) 31. 1. 61.

38 CAB128/35. Macmillan to Kennedy, 5. 4. 61. Macmillan to Canadian Cabinet, 11. 4. 61.

39 Ibid. George Ball, *The Past has Another Pattern* (New York, 1982), p. 214.

CHAPTER 14. THE $64,000 QUESTION

1   PREM11/3133. Minute Bishop, 22. 4. 60.
2   Sir Anthony Eden, *Full Circle* (London, 1960), p. 168.
3   Sabine Lee, 'Staying in the Game? Coming into the Game? Macmillan and European Integration' in Richard Aldous and Sabine Lee (eds), *Harold Macmillan and Britain's World Role* (Basingstoke, 1996), p. 140.
4   Jacqueline Tratt, *The Macmillan Government and Europe* (Basingstoke, 1996), pp. 122-3.
5   PREM11/4437. Macmillan to the Queen, 7. 8. 62. CAB134/1821. EQ (61) 4th, 17. 5. 61.
6   Tratt, *Macmillan Government*, pp. 180 184-5. CAB128/35. c. c. (61) 24th Concl., 26. 4. 61. CAB134/1821. EQ (61) 3rd, 9. 5. 61. EQ (61) 4th, 17. 5. 61.
7   FO371/153914. Macmillan-de Gaulle, 5. 4. 60.
8   FO371/154576. Minute Dean, 23. 6. 60. FO371/153916. Tel. Paris 18. 9. 60.
9   Peter Conradi, *Iris Murdoch* (London, 2002 ed.), p. 205. Sir Eric Roll, *Crowded Hours* (London, 1985), pp. 69, 108. FO371/158172. Letter, 25. 1. 61.
10 FO371/158172. Lee-Wormser, 28. 1. 61.
11 Richard Aldrich, *The Hidden Hand* (London, 2001), p. 616.
12 PREM11/3553. Chauvel-Heath, 14. 2. 61. Tel. Paris, 14. 2. 61.
13 FO371/158175. Lee-Wormser, 4. 4. 61. Memo, 5. 5. 61. Tel. Paris, 7. 5. 61. Cf. PREM11/3554. Tel. UKdel. EFTA, 29. 4. 61. Konrad Adenauer, *Erinnerungen, 1959-63* (Stuttgart, 1968), p. 110.
14 FO371/158176. Letter, 14. 5. 61.
15 Paul-Marie de la Gorce, 'De Gaulle et l'Angleterre', *Espoir*, Juin 2004, p. 12.
16 Peyrefitte, *C'était, vol. i*, pp. 363, 372. De Gaulle, *CWM, vol. i*, p. 230. Lacouture, *Ruler*, p. 131.
17 Peyrefitte, *C'était, vol. i*, p. 374. Pascaline Winand, *Eisenhower, Kennedy and the United States of Europe* (Basingstoke, 1993), p. 259. PREM11/3553. Tel. Paris, 16. 2. 61.
18 MAE. DE-CE, 1961-66, Préliminaires GB, no. 1410. Meeting Council of European Affairs, 31. 7. 62.
19 MAE, Europe, 1961-70, no. 211, Rélations avec la CEE. Note, 28. 8. 61.
20 Peyrefitte, *C'était, vol. i*, pp. 152, 366.
21 De Gaulle, *Hope*, p.188. Bernard Ledwidge, *De Gaulle* (London, 1982), p. 274. Hervé Alphand, *L'Étonnement d'être* (Paris, 1977), 17. 10. 43.
22 Peyrefitte, *C'était, vol. i*, pp. 109, 332. MAE, Secrétariat Général, Entretiens et Messages. De Gaulle to Krone, no. 14, 16. 6. 61. *DDF, 1960, ii*, p. 170.
23 *DDF, 1961, i*, p. 622. Adenauer, *Erinnerungen*, pp. 109-10.
24 *FRUS, 1961-3, vol. xiii*, pp. 424-5.
25 PREM11/3554. Undated Memo, Glaves-Smith.
26 *FRUS, 1961-3, vol. xiii*, p. 12.
27 MAE, DE-CE, 1961-66, no. 2071. Tel. 1. 6. 61. No. 2069. Note 13. 5. 61. FO371/158177. Letter UKdel. OEEC, 6. 6. 61. Letter Paris, 1. 6. 61. PREM11/3557. Maudling memos, 15. 6. 61. Richard Lamb, *The Macmillan Years* (London, 1995), pp. 149-50.
28 CAB128/35. c. c. (61) 24th. Concl., 26. 4. 61.
29 PREM11/3311. Macmillan to Kennedy, 23. 4. 61.
30 CAB133/297. Macmillan-Kennedy, 5. 4. 61. PREM11/3311. Kennedy to Macmillan, 8. 5. 61. Alphand, *L'Étonnement*, p. 342.
31 Macmillan diary, 11. 6. 61. CAB128/35 c. c. (51) 30th. Concl., 6. 6. 61.

32 Macmillan diary, 25. 6. 61.
33 Macmillan, *End,* pp. 16-17. PREM11/3558. Tel. Paris, 14. 7. 61.
34 PREM11/3559. Macmillan to Heath, 29. 7. 61.
35 Roll, *Crowded,* p. 108.
36 Macmillan, *End,* p. 7.
37 Piers Ludlow, *Dealing with Britain* (Cambridge, 1997), p. 93.
38 *FRUS, 1961-63, vol. xiii,* p. 85. Macmillan diary, 7. 2. 62, 21. 8. 62.
39 Macmillan papers, c. 344. Macmillan to de Gaulle, 22. 4. 61. De Gaulle to Macmillan, 2. 5. 61.
40 PREM11/3558. Dixon letter, 13. 7. 61.
41 Tratt, *Macmillan Government,* p. 154. Williams, *Frenchman,* pp. 404-5. PREM11/3339. Minute 19. 5. 61. Macmillan diary, 20. 5. 61.
42 PREM11/3757. Macmillan to Menzies, 3. 7. 61. Cf Macmillan papers, c. 331, 30. 9. 61, Article *Conservative Forum.*
43 PREM11/3556. Memo, Norman Brook, 7. 6. 61.
44 PREM11/3556. Heath to Macmillan, 14. 6. 61. PREM11/3557. Unsigned memo, 18. 6. 61. FO371/158178. Memos, Shuckburgh and Dixon, 7. 6. 61.
45 PREM11/3557. De Zulueta Memo, 16. 6. 61. PREM11/3780. 18. 6. 61. PREM11/3559. 'Timetable for the Week July 24-9. ' Archives de la présidence de la République, AG5/173. Tel. Chauvel. 28. 7. 61.

CHAPTER 15. NOT PERSUADING THE GENERAL

1 MAE, Rélations avec la CEE, Jan-Dec. 1961, no. 211. Tels. 31. 7. 61, 1. 8. 61. *Hansard,* 5th series, vol. 645, col. 930, 31. 7. 61.
2 Ibid., cols. 1507, 1545, 2. 8. 61.
3 PREM11/3559. Tels. Rome, Luxembourg and Hague, 28. 7. 61.
4 George Ball, *The Past has Another Pattern* (New York, 1982), p. 210.
5 Pascaline Winand, *Eisenhower, Kennedy and the United States of Europe* (Basingstoke, 1993), pp. 273-4. PREM11/3554. Note by the Prime Minister, 6. 4. 61.
6 PREM11/3559. Tel. Paris, 28. 7. 61.
7 De Gaulle, *Hope,* p. 188. Bernard Ledwidge, *De Gaulle,* (London, 1982), p. 278. Michel Debré, *Gouverner* (Paris, 1988), p. 440. Hervé Alphand, *L'Étonnement d'être* (Paris, 1977), p. 386.
8 *DDF, 1962, i,* pp. 138-9. Cf Horne, *Macmillan, vol. ii,* p. 432.
9 Piers Ludlow, 'A Mismanaged Application: Britain and the EEC, 1961-63', in Anne Deighton and Alan Milward, *Widening, Deepening and Accelerating* (Baden Baden, 1999), pp. 274-5.
10 Macmillan, *End,* p. 30.
11 Piers Ludlow, *Dealing with Britain* (Cambridge, 1997), p. 93. Piers Dixon, *Double Diploma* (London, 1968), p. 288.
12 Macmillan diary, 24. 11. 61.
13 Ludlow, *Dealing with Britain,* p. 240. FO371/164835. 'General de Gaulle's Attitude towards Britain's Entry into the Common Market', 16. 5. 62.
14 MAE, DE-CE, 1961-66, no. 2075. Note, Wormser, 20. 11. 61.
15 Sir Donald Maitland, *The Running Tide* (Bath, 2000), p. 53. FO371/177367. Commentary on Narrative Report, 8. 3. 63.
16 MAE, DE-CE, 1961-66, no. 1411, 15. 9. 62. FO371/164839. Couve de Murville to *Times* correspondent, 10. 9. 62.
17 Paul-Henri Spaak, *The Continuing Battle* (London, 1971), p. 473.

18 Macmillan diary, 6. 9. 61. Macmillan, *End*, p. 118. Sir Eric Roll, *Crowded Hours* (London, 1985), p. 112. Reilly, *Memoirs*, Ms. Eng. c. 5224, p. 105.
19 Macmillan, *Pointing*, pp. 412-5.
20 Ibid., pp. 415-7. Harold Evans, *Downing Street Diary* (London, 1981), p. 172.
21 Ibid. Macmillan, *Pointing*, p. 418. Edward Heath, *The Course of My Life* (London, 1998), p. 225.
22 PREM11/3561. Macmillan-de Gaulle, 24-25. 11. 61. *DDF, 1961, ii*, pp. 639-44, 646-49, 653-6. Peyrefitte, *C'était, vol. ii*, p. 19.
23 Macmillan, *Pointing*, p. 426. Evans, *Downing Street*, p. 174. Jean Chauvel, *Commentaire, vol. iii* (Paris, 1973), p. 348.
24 FO371/161246. Birch Grove brief.
25 MAE, DE-CE, Préliminaire, GB, no. 2075. Note, Négociations entre le marche commun et la Grande Bretagne, 20. 11. 61. Heath, *Course*, p. 225. Maurice Vaïsse, 'De Gaulle and the British Application to Join the Common Market' in George Wilkes, *Britain's Failure to Enter the Common Market* (London, 1997) p. 55.
26 PREM11/3561. Macmillan-de Gaulle, 24-5. 11. 61.
27 Ibid.
28 Ibid.
29 MAE, Europe-Grande Bretagne, 1961-70. Tel. London, 27. 11. 61.
30 Macmillan papers, c. 344. Letter to Commonwealth Prime Ministers, 2. 12. 61.
31 Macmillan diary, 29. 11. 61.
32 PREM11/3338. Letter Paris, 28. 11. 61. Letter de Gaulle, 20. 12. 61.
33 *DDF, 1961, ii*, p. 706.
34 Charles de Gaulle, *Lettres, notes et carnets, 1961-3* (Paris, 1986), p. 172.
32 Maurice Vaïsse, *La Grandeur* (Paris, 1998), p. 199.

CHAPTER 16. CHÂTEAU DE CHAMPS

1 Edward Heath, *The Course of My Life* (London, 1998), p. 220.
2 FO371/163832. Letter Paris, 10. 2. 62.
3 PREM11/3778. Macmillan to Home, 15. 4. 62. Macmillan, *End*, p. 65.
4 Étienne Burin des Roziers, *Retour aux sources* (Paris, 1986), pp. 51, 61-2. Pierre Gerbet, 'The Fouchet Negotiations for Political Union and the British Application' in George Wilkes, *Britain's Failure to Enter the European Community, 1960-63* (London, 1997), p. 139. Georges-Henri Soutou, 'Le Général de Gaulle, le plan Fouchet et l'Europe', *Commentaire*, Hiver 1990-1, pp. 763-4. FO371/171449. Paris despatch, 18. 2. 63. Paul-Marie de la Gorce, 'De Gaulle et l'Angleterre', *Espoir*, Juin 2004, p. 14.
5 *Keesings Contemporary Archives*, cols. 18827-8, 16-23. 6. 62. MAE. DE-CE, Préliminaires, 1961-66, no. 1409. Tel. London, 10. 5. 62. PREM11/3792. Macmillan-Chauvel, 19. 4. 62.
6 PREM11/3792. Tel. London, 16. 5. 62.
7 FO371/164835. 'General de Gaulle's attitude towards Britain's entry into the Common Market', 6. 5. 62.
8 Macmillan, *End*, p.118. Heath, *Course*, p. 226. PREM11/4019. De Zulueta to Macmillan, 18. 5. 62.
9 Horne, *Macmillan, vol. ii*, p. 326.
10 PREM11/3775. Tel. Paris, 23. 5. 62.
11 PREM11/3775. Memo Roll, 18. 5. 62.
12 Macmillan, *End*, p. 69.

13 Maurice Couve de Murville, *Une Politique étrangère* (Paris, 1971), p. 403. Macmillan, *End*, p. 120.

14 PREM11/3775. Macmillan to Home, 16. 5. 62.

15 Macmillan diary, 19. 5. 62. PREM11/3792. Macmillan-Chauvel, 19. 4. 62. PREM11/3775. Macmillan-de Courcel, 9. 5. 62. Constantine Pagedas, *Anglo-American Strategic Relations and the French Problem* (London, 2000), p. 204. Chauvel, *Commentaire, vol. iii* (Paris, 1973), p. 351.

16 MAE, DE-CE, Préliminaires, no. 1409. Tel. 10. 5. 62.

17 *FRUS, 1961-63, vol. xiii*, p. 1069.

18 PREM11/3783. Macmillan-Kennedy, 28. 4. 62. Macmillan-McNamara, 29. 4. 62.

19 PREM11/3712. Macmillan to Ormsby-Gore, 29. 5. 62. Pascaline Winand, *Eisenhower, Kennedy and the United States of Europe* (Basingstoke, 1993), p. 312. Pagedas, *Anglo-American*, p. 206.

20 Chauvel, *Commentaire*, p. 352. FO371/164835. Tel. Paris, 22. 5. 62.

21 PREM11/3775. Tel. Paris, 23. 5. 62. FO brief, 26. 5. 62.

22 Horne, *Macmillan, vol. ii*, p. 328. Michael Charlton, *The Price of Victory* (London, 1983), p. 285. PREM11/4151. Thorneycroft to Macmillan, 18. 7. 63.

23 De la Gorce, 'De Gaulle', p. 14. PREM11/3775. Macmillan-de Gaulle, 2-3. 6. 62.

24 Ibid. *DDF, 1962, i*, p. 567. PREM11/3712. Messmer-Watkinson, 7. 6. 62.

25 Erin Mahan, *Kennedy, de Gaulle and Western Europe* (Basingstoke, 2002), pp. 93, 105. Peyrefitte, *C'était, vol. i*, pp. 301-2.

26 Ibid. PREM11/3775. Macmillan-de Gaulle, 2-3. 6. 62. Stuart Ward, *Australia and the British Embrace* (Melbourne, 2001), p. 163.

27 *DDF, 1962, i*, pp. 547-8.

28 PREM11/3775. Macmillan-de Gaulle, 2-3. 6. 62.

29 Ibid.

30 Macmillan, *End*, p. 121. PREM11/3780. Letter Kennedy, 5. 6. 61. PREM11/3775. Letter to the Queen, 5. 6. 62.

31 Hervé Alphand, *L'Étonnement d'être* (Paris, 1977), p. 385. Peyrefitte, *C'était, vol. i*, pp. 300-2. Couve de Murville, *Politique étrangère*, p. 404. Des Roziers, *Retour*, p. 164. Nora Beloff, *The General Says No* (London, 1963), p. 151. FO371/166978. Discussion Wapler. Cf Bernard Lefort, *Souvenirs et secrètes des années Gaulliennes*, (Paris, 1999), 24. 6. 62.

32 PREM11/3775. Macmillan-de Gaulle, 2-3. 6. 62. Frédéric Bozo, *Two Strategies for Europe* (Lanham, 2001), p. 89. Piers Ludlow ' "Ne pleurez-pas, Milord", Macmillan and France from Algiers to Rambouillet' in Richard Aldous and Sabine Lee, *Harold Macmillan* (Basingstoke, 1999), p. 107. Archives de la présidence de la République. 5AG2. Note, 22. 5. 62.

33 *DDF, 1962, ii*, pp. 13-14, 37-8.

34 C. L. Sulzberger, *The Last of the Giants* (London, 1970), pp. 898, 902-3.

35 MAE, DE-CE, Préliminaires, no. 1410, Comtpe-rendu du Conseil sur les Affaires Européennes, 31. 7. 62. Piers Ludlow, *Dealing with Britain* (Cambridge, 1997), pp. 157-9.

36 Macmillan diary, 4,5. 8. 62.

37 PREM11/4437. Macmillan to the Queen, 7. 8. 62.

38 Piers Dixon, *Double Diploma* (London, 1968), p. 288.

39 Peyrefitte, *C'était, vol. i*, pp. 303-4.

CHAPTER 17. AUTUMN GALES

1   See Étienne Burin des Rozieres, *Retour aux sources,* (Paris, 1986.)

2   Ronald Hyam and Roger Louis (eds), *The Conservative Party and the End of Empire, 1957-64, Pt.2,* (London, 2000), p. 663. Macmillan, *End,* p. 114.

3   Hans-Peter Schwarz, *Konrad Adenauer* (Providence and Oxford, 1997), p. 609.

4   Peyrefitte, *C'était, vol. i,* pp. 153, 54. Charles Williams, *Frenchman,* pp. 421-2. Pierre Maillard, *De Gaulle et le problème allemande* (Paris, 2002 ed.), pp. 154-6.

5   *DDF, 1962, ii,* p. 40.

6   Ibid., p. 15. Konrad Adenauer, *Erinnerungen, 1959-63* (Stuttgart, 1968), p. 165. Olivier Bange, *The EEC Crisis of 1963* (Basingstoke, 2000), pp. 65-7. Maurice Vaisse, 'De Gaulle and the British "Application" to Join the Common Market' in George Wilkes (ed.), *Britain's Failure to Enter the European Community* (London, 1997), p. 58.

7   PREM11/4522. Adenauer television interview.

8   Schwarz, *Adenauer,* p. 619. Paul Legoll, *Charles de Gaulle et Konrad Adenauer* (Paris, 2004), p. 275.

9   PREM11/4219. Tel. Bonn, 7. 9. 62.

10 *DDF, 1962, ii,* p. 174.

11 Macmillan, *End,* p. 337.

12 Williams, *Frenchman,* p. 423. PREM11/4237. Tel. Paris, 27. 11. 62.

13 Macmillan, *End,* p. 338.

14 *FRUS, 1961-3, vol. xiii,* p. 1068.

15 Horne, *Macmillan, vol. ii,* p. 348. Macmillan diary, 6. 12. 62.

16 FO371/171449. Dixon despatch, 18. 2. 63.

17 John Ramsden, *The Winds of Change* (London, 1996), p. 146. Anthony Sampson, *Anatomy of Britain* (London, 1962), pp. 91, 620-1. Stuart Ward, ' "No Nation could be Broker," the Satire Boom and the Demise of Britain's World Role' in Stuart Ward, (ed.), *British Culture and the End of Empire* (Manchester, 2001). *Hansard* 5th series, vol 671, col. 1003, 11. 2. 63.

18 John Newhouse, *De Gaulle and the Anglo-Saxons* (New York, 1970), pp. 170-1. Frank Costigliola, 'The Failed Design', *Diplomatic History,* Summer 1984, p. 235.

19 Macmillan, *End,* p. 335. Macmillan diary, 3. 10. 62. Nigel Ashton, *Kennedy, Macmillan and the Cold War* (Basingstoke, 2002), pp. 161-5.

20 L. V. Scott, *Macmillan, Kennedy and the Cuban Missile Crisis* (Basingstoke, 1999), pp. 38, 189. PREM11/4437. Macmillan to the Queen, 20. 10. 62.

21 D. R. Thorpe, *Alec Douglas-Home* (London, 1996), p. 245.

22 Ernest May and Philip Zelikow, *The Kennedy Tapes* (Cambridge, Mass., 1997), p. 66. John Dickie, *"Special" No More* (London, 1994), pp. 106-7. Frank Costigliola, 'Kennedy, the European Allies and the Failure to Consult', *Political Science Quarterly,* Spring 1995, p. 107.

23 Maurice Vaisse, *La Grandeur* (Paris, 1998), pp. 153-4. Horne, *Macmillan, vol. ii,* pp. 383-4.

24 Ibid., pp. 375-6, 384. Macmillan, *End,* pp. 205, 209. CAB128/36 pt. 2 c. c. (62) 25. 10. 62.

25 PREM11/3689. Macmillan to de Gaulle, 22. 10. 62. Tel. Paris, 23. 10. 62. PREM11/3690. De Gaulle to Macmillan, 26. 10. 62.

26 PREM11/3689. Tel. Washington, 23. 10. 62. Scott, *Macmillan, Kennedy,* p. 184. Zelikow and May, *Tapes,* p. 625. Costigliola, *Political Science Quarterly,* p. 109.

27 CAB103/696. Macmillan to Trend, 22. 3. 73.

28 Thorpe, *Douglas Home*, pp. 239-40. David Dimbleby and David Reynolds, *An Ocean Apart* (London, 1988), pp. 234-5. Henry Brandon, *Special Relationship* (London, 1988), p. 160. Horne, *Macmillan, vol. ii*, pp. 382-3. May and Zelikow, *Tapes*, p. 692.

29 Horne, *Macmillan, vol. ii*, p. 371. Cf. Macmillan to Cabinet, CAB128/36 Pt. 2, c. c. (62) 63rd. Concl., 29. 10. 62.

30 Sorenson, BBC Radio 4, 16. 10. 02. May and Zelikow, *Tapes*, p. 692.

31 Horne, *Macmillan, vol. ii*, p. 382.

32 Macmillan papers, c. 334. Macmillan to Brook, 5. 11. 62.

33 Jean-Pierre Guichard, *De Gaulle face aux crises* (Paris, 2000), p. 310.

34 Peyrefitte, *C'était, vol. ii*, p. 23. Charles de Gaulle, *Lettres, notes et carnets, 1961-63* (Paris, 1986), 6. 11. 62.

35 PREM11/3691. Tel. Washington, 29. 10. 62. Frédéric Bozo, *Two Strategies for Europe* (Lanham, 2001), p. 87. Kendrick Oliver, *Kennedy, Macmillan and the Nuclear Test Ban Debate* (Basingstoke, 1998), p. 148.

36 Dimbleby and Reynolds, *Ocean*, p. 235. May and Zelikow, *Tapes*, pp. 625-6.

37 PREM11/4437. Macmillan to the Queen, 22. 11. 62. Macmillan, *End*, p. 337.

38 PREM11/4522. Minute de Zulueta, 12. 9. 62. FO371/164839. Tels. Paris, 1. 10. 62, 16. 10. 62. Macmillan diary, 3. 10. 62. Paul-Marie de la Gorce, 'De Gaulle et l'Angleterre', *Espoir*, Juin 2004, p. 15.

39 PREM11/4230. Letter Paris, 28. 11. 62.

40 PREM11/4230. Letter to FO, 6. 12. 62.

41 Macmillan diary, 1. 12. 62.

42 Macmillan, *End*, pp. 340-1. PREM11/4230. Notes for the Prime Minister's Meeting with General de Gaulle.

43 MAE, DE-CE, 1961-66, Préliminaires: GB, no. 1412. Note, 12. 12. 62.

44 Maurice Couve de Murville, *Une Politique étrangère* (Paris, 1971), p. 410.

45 *DDF, 1962, ii*, p. 535. Macmillan, *End*, pp. 345-6.

46 Richard Neustadt, *Report to JFK* (Ithaca, 1999), p. 85. Macmillan, *End*, p. 350.

47 Ibid., pp. 350-1. PREM11/4230. Macmillan-de Gaulle, 15-16. 12. 62. *DDF, 1962, ii*, p. 546.

48 Macmillan, *End*, p. 352.

49 PREM11/4230. Macmillan-de Gaulle, 15-16. 12. 62.

50 Ibid.

51 PREM11/4230. Tel. Paris, 16. 12. 62. De Gaulle, *Lettres, notes et carnets, 1961-63*, 21. 12. 62.

52 Richard Lamb, *The Macmillan Years* (London, 1995), p. 192. Neustadt, *Report*, p. 86.

53 Macmillan, *End*, pp. 354-5.

54 FO371/171447. Pisani to Soames, 9. 1. 63. FO371/171449. Dixon despatch, 18. 2. 63. Alan Milward, *The Rise and Fall of National Strategy*, (London, 2002), p. 480.

55 FO371/171443. Tel. Paris, 21. 12. 62. Peyrefitte, *C'était, vol. i*, p. 333. P. M. H. Bell, *France and Britain, 1940-94* (Harlow, 1997), pp. 196-7.

56 Edgard Pisani, *Le Général indivis* (Paris, 1974), pp. 108-9.

57 Ibid.

CHAPTER 18. TROUBLE WITH MISSILES

1 DEFE13/617. Watkinson to CDS, 9. 1. 62.

2 *FRUS, 1961-3, vol. xiii*, p. 1099.

3 Macmillan diary, 12. 6. 60. *FRUS, 1958-60, vol. vii, pt. ii*, p. 863.

4 AIR19/998. Draft memo, Watkinson, February 1960. Andrew Pierre, *Nuclear Politics*

(London, 1972), pp. 198-9. Constantine Pagedas, *Anglo-American Strategic Relations and the French Problem* (London, 2000), p. 276.

5   PREM11/3261. Heathcoat-Amory to Watkinson, 22. 4. 60.

6   Macmillan diary, 12. 6. 60. Ian Clark, *Nuclear Diplomacy and the Special Relationship* (Oxford, 1994), p. 189.

7   Ibid., p. 378. Donette Murray, 'Macmillan and Nuclear Weapons; the Skybolt Affair' in Richard Aldous and Sabine Lee, *Harold Macmillan. Aspects of a Political Life* (Basingstoke, 1999), pp. 220-25. Sir Solly Zuckerman, *Monkeys, Men and Missiles* (London, 1988), pp.240-1. Pierre, *Nuclear*, pp. 228-9. Horne, *Macmillan, vol. ii*, p. 435.

8   Richard Neustadt, *Report to JFK* (Ithaca, 1999), p. 77.

9   PREM11/4147. Macmillan to Ormsby-Gore, 14. 12. 62.

10 PREM11/3716. Note for Record, 14. 12. 62.

11 PREM11/4147. Draft Macmillan brief.

12 PREM11/3712. 'Rambouillet and Anglo-French Relations in the Nuclear Field', 6. 12. 62. PREM11/4147. FO to Dixon, 2. 1. 63 and draft Nassau brief. Lord Home, *The Way the Wind Blows* (London, 1976), p. 150. Peter Hennessy, *Muddling Through* (London, 1997 ed.), p. 112.

13 Macmillan, *End*, p. 344.

14 PREM11/4230. Macmillan-de Gaulle, 15-16. 12. 62.

15 Archives de la présidence de la République, 5AG2. Rambouillet briefs. *DDF, 1963, i*, p. 109. Maurice Vaisse, 'De Gaulle and the British "Application" to Join the Common Market' in George Wilkes (ed.), *Britain's Failure to Enter the European Community* (London, 1997), p. 68. PREM11/4230. *DDF, 1962, ii*, p. 539.

16 Clark, *Nuclear Politics*, p. 297.

17 *FRUS, 1961-3, vol. xiii*, pp. 289, 1073-5, 1078.

18 David Dimbleby and David Reynolds, *An Ocean Apart* (London, 1988), p. 239. Frank Costigliola, 'The Failed Design', *Diplomatic History*, Summer 1984, pp. 235-6. *DDF, 1962, ii*, p. 577.

19 Horne, *Macmillan, vol. ii*, p. 437.

20 PREM11/4147. Nassau, 19. 12. 62. Frank Costigliola, *Diplomatic History*, pp. 230-1, 237. Pascaline Winand, *Eisenhower, Kennedy and the United States of Europe* (Basingstoke, 1993), p. 316. Neustadt, *Report*, p. 43.

21 PREM11/4230. Macmillan-de Gaulle, 15-16. 12. 62.

22 PREM11/4147. Nassau, 19. 12. 62. *FRUS, 1961-63, vol. xiii*, pp. 1111-2.

23 Ibid., p. 1103. PREM11/4147. Nassau, 20. 12. 62.

24 *FRUS, 1961-63, vol. xiii*, p. 1105.

25 Horne, *Macmillan, vol. ii*, p. 439. Theodore Sorenson, *Kennedy* (London, 1965), pp. 558-9.

26 Neustadt, *Report*, pp. 60, 92. McGeorge Bundy, *Danger and Survival* (New York, 1988), p. 492. PREM11/4147. Macmillan to Butler, 20. 12. 62. *FRUS, 1961-63, vol. xiii*, p. 1079.

27 Neustadt, *Report*, p. 77. Nigel Ashton, *Kennedy, Macmillan and the Cold War* (Basingstoke, 2002), p. 24.

28 PREM11/4147. Nassau, 20. 12. 62.

29 Macmillan, *End*, p. 555.

30 Alan Bennet (et al.), *Beyond the Fringe* (London, 1963), pp. 48-9.

31 Sir Oliver Wright, 'Macmillan. A View from the Foreign Office' in Aldous and Lee, *Macmillan*, p. 9. Christopher Bellamy, 'The Decision that Dares Not Speak Its Name', *World Today*, May 2005, p. 10. Ashton, *Kennedy, Macmillan*, p. 191.

32 Ibid., p. 184. Clark, *Nuclear Politics*, p. 418.
33 PREM11/4147. Thorneycroft note, 30. 12. 62. Macmillan to Ormsby-Gore, 30. 12. 62.
34 Dimbleby and Reynolds, *Ocean*, p. 242. *FRUS, 1961-3, vol. xiii*, p. 1093.
35 Ibid., *vol. xi*, pp. 135-6, 148.
36 Ibid., *vol. xiii*, p. 743. *DDF, 1963, i*, 2. 1. 63. Mark Trachtenberg, *A Constructed Peace* (Princeton, NJ, 1999), pp. 365-6. Neustadt, *Report*, pp. 97, 101.
37 Ibid., p. 97.
38 Peyrefitte, *C'était, vol. i*, pp. 282, 341, 361.
39 Ibid., p. 346. FO371/171455. Tel. Paris, 18. 1. 63.
40 *Akten zur Auswaertigen Politik des Bundesrepublik Deutschland, 1963, i* (Munich, 1994), p. 116.
41 Peyrefitte, *C'était, vol. i*, pp. 346, 374. Bernard Ledwidge, *De Gaulle* (London, 1982), p. 283.
42 PREM11/4147. Tels. Paris, 21, 22. 12. 62.
43 FO371/171443. Letter Paris, 22. 12. 62.
44 Macmillan diary, 31. 12. 62.
45 Neustadt, *Report*, pp. 86-7.
46 PREM11/4147. Ministerial meeting, 31. 12. 62.
47 John Newhouse, 'De Gaulle and the Anglo-Saxons' in Douglas Brinkley and Richard Griffiths, *John F. Kennedy and Europe* (Baton Rouge, 1999), p. 45.
48 PREM11/4147. Macmillan to Ormsby-Gore, 31. 12. 62.
49 Pagedas, *Anglo-American*, p. 259.
50 *DDF, 1963, i*, no. 27. PREM11/4147. Ormsby-Gore to Macmillan, 2. 1. 63.
51 PREM11/4147. Tel. Paris, 2. 1. 63. Paul-Marie de la Gorce, 'De Gaulle et l'Angleterre', *Espoir*, Juin 2004, p. 15.
52 PREM11/4147. Tel. Paris, 2. 1. 63. *DDF, 1963, i*, pp. 3-5.
53 PREM11/4147. Tel. Paris, 2. 1. 63.
54 PREM11/4147. Tels. Paris, 3,4. 1. 63.
55 PREM11/4147. Tel. Paris, 4. 1. 63. PREM11/4148. Macmillan to Dixon, 10. 1. 63.
56 Charles de Gaulle, *Lettres, notes et carnets, 1961-63* (Paris, 1986), 4. 1. 63.
57 *FRUS, 1961-63, vol. xiii*, p. 1117.
58 Peyrefitte, *C'était, vol. i*, pp. 347-8.
59 PREM11/4151. Tel. Paris, 8. 1. 63. Oliver Bange, *The EEC Crisis of 1963* (Basingstoke, 2000), p. 100.
60 FO371/171455. Heath-Couve de Murville, 11. 1. 63.
61 Edward Heath, *The Course of My Life* (London, 1988) pp. 228-9. Macmillan, *End*, p. 365. Harold Evans, *Downing Street Diary*, (London, 1981), p. 245. Norah Beloff, *The General Says No* (Harmondsworth, 1963), p. 155.

CHAPTER 19. JUPITERISM AND AFTER

1 Peyrefitte, *C'était, vol. i*, p. 351.
2 *Keesings Contemporary Archives*, cols. 19107-9, 19-26. 1. 63.
3 FO371/171488. Tel. Paris, 7. 2. 63. Pierre Maillard, *De Gaulle et le problème allemand* (Paris, 2001 ed.), p. 195. Horne, *Macmillan, vol ii*, p. 446. Williams, *Frenchman*, p. 424. P. M. H. Bell, *Britain and France 1940-94* (Harlow, 1997), p. 200.
4 Edgard Pisani, *Le Général indivis* (Paris, 1974), p. 109. Peyrefitte, *C'était, vol. i*, p. 351.
5 PREM11/4523. Tel. Washington, 15. 1. 63. Paul-Henri Spaak, *The Continuing Battle* (London, 1971), p. 477. Piers Ludlow, *Dealing with Britain* (Cambridge, 1997), p. 215. Edward Heath, *The Course of My Life* (London, 1998), p. 230.

6   FO146/4630. 'Britain through French Eyes. '

7   PREM11/4523. Macmillan to Kennedy, 19. 1. 63. FO371/171444. Macmillan to Home, 15. 1. 63. *Daily Telegraph*, 15. 1. 63. CAB128/37. c. c. (63) 4th. Concl., 17. 1. 63

8   Heath, *Course*, pp. 231, 235. Pisani, *Le Général*, pp. 105-8.

9   Ludlow, *Dealing*, p. 216.

10   FO371/171446. Tel. Paris, 19. 1. 63.

11   FO371/171447. Tel. Paris, 25. 1. 63.

12   FO371/171444. FO to Bonn, 19. 1. 63. Oliver Bange, *The EEC Crisis of 1963* (Basingstoke, 2000), pp. 143-6, 149-50.

13   Ibid., p. 156.

14   Horst Osterheld, *Ich Gehe Nicht leichten Herzen*s (Mainz, 1986), pp. 182-4.

15   PREM11/4523. Tel. Paris, 23. 1. 63. Tel. Washington, 24. 1. 63. *DDF, 1963, i*, pp. 94-5, 108-9, 112 *Akten zur Auswaertigen Politik der Bundesrepublik Deutschland, 1963, i,* (Munich, 1994), pp. 129-30, 144-7.

16   PREM11/4523. Tel. Paris, 20. 1. 63. PREM11/4524. Tel. Bonn, 3. 2. 63. Erin Mahan, *Kennedy, de Gaulle and Western Europe* (Basingstoke, 2002), p. 152.

17   PREM11/4523. Note Macmillan to Cabinet, 22. 1. 63.

18   PREM11/4523. Tel. Brussels, 23. 1. 63.

19   PREM11/4523. Tel. Paris, 24. 1. 63.

20   PREM11/4523. Tel. Paris, 24. 1. 63.

21   George Ball, *The Past has Another Pattern* (New York, 1982), p. 271. *FRUS, 1961-63, vol. xiii*, pp. 157-8. Bange, *EEC Crisis*, pp. 188-92. Mahan, *Kennedy, de Gaulle*, p. 146. Vincent Jauvert, *L'Amérique contre de Gaulle* (Paris, 2000), pp. 107-11, 115-6.

22   FO371/169175. Tels. Moscow, 27. 1. 63, 6. 2. 63.

23   Peyrefitte, *C'était, vol. i*, pp. 369-70.

24   FO371/171447. Tel. Paris, 26. 1. 63.

25   PREM11/4523. Tel. Macmillan to Butler, 26. 1. 63.

26   Macmillan papers, c. 334. Letter to Lady Ava Waverley, 28. 1. 63. Macmillan diary, 28. 1. 63.

27   *Daily Mail*, 30. 1. 63. *Daily Herald*, 30. 1. 63. MAE, Europe. Grande-Bretagne, 1961-70, no. 261. Tel. London, 28. 1. 63.

28   Heath, *Course*, p. 235.

29   Ibid., p. 234. Bange, *EEC Crisis*, p. 220. Macmillan diary, 4. 2. 63.

30   MAE, Europe. Grande-Bretagne, 1961-70, no. 261. Tel. London, 30. 1. 63.

31   Ibid., 31. 1. 63. Macmillan, *End*, pp. 368-9.

32   MAE. Europe. Grande-Bretagne. Tel. London, 30. 1. 63. Richard Neustadt, *Report to JFK* (Ithaca, 1999), p. 107.

33   PREM11/452. Dixon to Heath and Home, 23. 1. 63. PREM11/4524. Heath to Macmillan, 29. 1. 63. Macmillan and Home to Heath, 29. 1. 63.

34   *Hansard*, 5th series, vol. 671, col. 962, 11. 2. 63.

35   *FRUS, 1961-63, vol. xiii*, p. 1128. Peyrefitte, *C'était, vol. i*, p. 356.

36   Anthony Sampson, *Macmillan* (Harmondsworth, 1968), p. 218. Hugo Young, *This Blessed Plot* (London, 1998), p. 144. Sir Oliver Wright, 'Macmillan. A View from the Foreign Office' in Richard Aldous and Sabine Lee (eds), *Harold Macmillan* (Basingstoke, 1999), p. 15.

37   Macmillan diary, 4. 2. 63.

38   FO371/171447. Tel. Brussels, 25. 1. 63. Macmillan, *End*, p. 373.

39   *Akten zur Auswaertigen Politik des Bundesrepublik Deutschland, 1963, i*, p. 72. Bange, *EEC Crisis*, p. 112. Horst Osterheld, 'Adenauer et de Gaulle: portraits comparées',

Espoir, Mars 1992, p. 6. Maillard, *De Gaulle*, pp. 190-4. Ludlow, *Dealing*, pp. 228, 230. PREM11/4524. Tel. Bonn, 29. 1. 63.

40 FO146/4618. Note 10. 4. 63. PREM11/4237. Letter Dixon, 5. 3. 63.

41 PREM11/4237. Macmillan to Home, 10. 3. 63. PREM11/4151. Thorneycroft to Macmillan, 26. 3. 63. Macmillan to Thorneycroft, 17. 4. 63.

42 PREM11/4151. Macmillan to Thorneycroft, 17. 7. 63. Macmillan to Home, 13. 7. 63. Home to Macmillan, 16. 7. 63.

43 PREM11/4151. Thorneycroft to Macmillan, 18,19. 7. 63.

44 MAE, Secrétariat Général, Entretiens and Messages, no. 19. 18. 7. 63. Macmillan diary, 17. 7. 63.

45 Sir Solly Zuckerman, *Monkeys, Men and Missiles*, (London, 1988), p. 307. Horne, *Macmillan, vol. ii*, p. 522.

46 Kendrick Oliver, *Kennedy, Macmillan and the Nuclear Test Ban Treaty*, (Basingstoke, 1998), p. 206. Horne, *Macmillan, vol. ii*, p. 524.

47 Maurice Vaisse, *La Grandeur* (Paris, 1998), p. 377.

48 Macmillan, *End*, p. 476.

49 Ibid., pp. 477-9.

50 PREM11/4151. Macmillan to Thorneycroft, 23. 7. 63.

51 PREM11/4151. Tel. Paris, 23. 7. 63.

52 Horne, *Macmillan, vol. ii*, p. 521.

53 PREM11/4152. Tel. Paris, 7. 8. 63.

54 PREM11/4152. Letter Dixon, 9. 9. 63. PREM11/4152. Letter Rumbold, 14. 8. 63.

55 Ibid.

56 PREM11/4152. Macmillan to Kennedy, 6 8. 63.

57 PREM11/4152. Letter Dixon, 9. 9. 63.

58 PREM11/4152. 'France and Nuclear Weapons', 12. 9. 63.

59 Macmillan diary, 20. 9. 63.

60 Ibid., 29. 8. 63.

61 Ibid., 17. 9. 63.

62 Charles de Gaulle, *Lettres, notes et carnets, 1961-3* (Paris, 1986), pp. 377-8. PREM11/4811. Letters Dixon, 16. 10. 63.

63 De Gaulle, *Lettres, notes et carnets, 1964-6* (Paris, 1987), p. 302. *1966-9*, (Paris, 1987), pp. 145-6.

64 Horne, *Macmillan, vol. ii*, p. 450.

65 *Dictionary of National Biography, 1961-70* (Oxford, 1981), p. 299. FO371/182933. Despatch Paris, 4. 2. 65.

66 CAB129/118 ii, CP(64) 102.

67 FCO30/414. Tel. Paris, 5. 2. 69. FCO30/418. Tel. Paris, 24. 3. 69.

68 FCO30/414. Stewart to Wilson, 11. 2. 69. Tel. Paris, 22. 4. 69.

69 Maillard, *De Gaulle*, p. 237.

CHAPTER 20. 'AT THE END OF THE DAY'

1 Étienne Burin des Roziers, *Retour aux sources* (Paris, 1986), p. 165.

2 FO371/151097. Macmillan-de Gaulle, 28-9. 1. 61.

3 DEFE7/2135. Brief, 5. 10. 62.

4 C. L. Sulzberger, *The Last of the Giants* (London, 1970), p. 956. PREM11/4152. De Zulueta-de Courcel, 24. 8. 63. Tel. Paris, 7. 8. 63.

5 FO146/4626. Discussion Admirality House, 31. 12. 62.

6 FO371/153912. Special Political Brief for the Queen.

7   PREM11/4524. Kennedy to Macmillan, 31. 1. 63.

8   FO371/152302. Macmillan to Eisenhower, 13. 8. 60.

9   *The Listener*, 21. 9. 67, 11. 10. 73.

10 Douglas Brinkley, 'Dean Acheson and John Kennedy - Combating Strains in the Atlantic Alliance' in Douglas Brinkley and Robert Griffiths, *John F. Kennedy and Europe* (Baton Rouge, 1999), p. 290.

11 Margaret Thatcher, *The Downing Street Years* (New York, 1995 ed.), p. 235.

12 CAB129/118 ii CP (64) 162. Despatch O'Neill, 25. 7. 64. Macmillan, *End*, p. 120.

13 FO371/169124. Letter Dixon, 16. 5. 63. Peyrefitte, *C'était, vol. i*, pp. 356, 377. Sir Michael Palliser, 'Cent ans d'Entente Cordiale', *Espoir*, Juin 2004, p. 26.

14 Nigel Ashton, *Kennedy, Macmillan and the Cold War* (Basingstoke, 2002), p. 140. Anthony Sampson, *Anatomy of Britain* (London, 1962), p. 339. Horne, *Macmillan, vol. ii*, p. 451.

15 Malcolm Muggeridge, 'England, Whose England?' in Arthur Koestler, *Suicide of a Nation* (London, 1963), p. 30.

16. *FRUS, 1961-3, vol. xiii*, p. 1064. Peter Hennessy, *The Prime Minister* (London, 2000), p. 352.

17 Horne, *Macmillan, vol. ii*, p. 451. Lacouture, *Ruler*, p. 359. Edward Heath, *The Course of My Life* (London, 1998), p. 235.

18 MAE, DE-CE,1961-66, Préliminaires: GB, no. 1412. Note, 12. 12. 62.

19 François Kersaudy, *Churchill and de Gaulle* (London, 1990 ed.), p. 76.

20 De Gaulle, *Hope*, p. 217.

21 Julian Jackson, *Charles de Gaulle* (London, 1990), p. 67.

22 Theodore Sorenson, *Kennedy* (London, 1965), p. 559.

23 Peyrifitte, *C'était, vol. i*, p. 299.

24 Ibid., p. 356.

Bibliography

OFFICIAL ARCHIVES

National Archives, Kew.
CAB65,128,129,133,159
FO146,371,660,954
PREM3,11

Archives Nationales, Paris
Archives de la présidence de la République, 5 AG.

Ministère des Affaires Étrangères, Paris (MAE.)
Europe, 1956-60, 1961-70.
Secrétariat Général, Entretiens et Messages.
DE-CE, 1961-66, Préliminaires, Grande-Bretagne.

UNPUBLISHED PAPERS

Sir Pierson Dixon, (private.)
Lord Gladwyn Papers, (Churchill College, Cambridge.)
Selwyn Lloyd Papers, (Churchill College, Cambridge.)
Harold Macmillan Diaries, (Bodleian Library, Oxford.) Ministerial Papers, (Bodleian Library, Oxford.)
Sir Patrick Reilly, Unpublished Memoirs and Papers (Bodleian Library, Oxford.)
Olivier Wormser Papers, (Quai d'Orsay, Paris.)

PUBLISHED DOCUMENTS

Akten zur Auswaertigen Politik des Bundesrepublic Deutschland, 1963,i, (R.Oldenbourg Verlag, Munich, 1994.)
Documents Diplomatiques Français, 1958-63 (Imprimerie Nationale, Paris, 1992-2000.)

Documents on British Policy Overseas, 1986 Series 2, vol.i (HMSO, London, 1986.)

Foreign Relations of the United States. Conferences at Washington, 1941-2 and Casablanca, 1943 (USGPO, Washington, 1968)

1942, vol.iii, Europe (1961.)

1943, vol.ii, Europe (1964.)

1955-57, vol.xxvii, Western Europe and Canada (1992)

1958-60, vol.vii, Western Europe, (1993.)

1958-60, vol.viii and vol.ix, The Berlin Crisis (1993.)

1961-3, vol.xiii, West Europe and Canada (1994)

vol.xi, Cuban Missile Crisis and Aftermath (1996.)

AUTOBIOGRAPHIES, DIARIES, LETTERS AND MEMOIRS

Konrad Adenauer, *Erinnerungen, 1955-59* (Deutsche Verlag Anstalt, Stuttgart, 1967.) *1959-63* (Deutsche Verlag Anstalt, Stuttgart, 1968.) *Teegespraeche, 1961-63* (Siedler Verlag, Berlin, 1992.)

Raoul Aglion, *Roosevelt and de Gaulle: Allies in Conflict. A Personal Memoir* (Free Press, New York, 1988.)

Hervé Alphand, *L'Étonnement d'être. Journal, 1939-73* (Fayard, Paris, 1977.)

George Ball, *The Past has Another Pattern. Memoirs* (W.W.Norton, New York, 1982.)

John Barnes and David Nicolson (eds), *The Empire at Bay. The Leo Amery Diaries, 1929-45* (Hutchinson, London, 1988.)

Charles Bohlen, *Witness to History, 1929-69* (Weidenfeld and Nicolson, London, 1973.)

General René Bouscat, *De Gaulle-Giraud. Dossier d'une mission* (Flammarion, Paris, 1967.)

Étienne Burin des Roziers, *Retour aux sources. 1962 L'année décisive* (Plon, Paris, 1986.)

Général Georges Catroux, *Dans la bataille de Méditerranée. Égypte, Levant, Afrique du Nord, 1940-44* (Juillard, Paris, 1949.)

Guy de Charbonnières, *Le Duel Giraud-de Gaulle* (Plon, Paris, 1984.)

Jean Chauvel, *Commentaire, vol.iii, 1952-62* (Fayard, Paris, 1973.)

Winston Churchill, *The Second World War, vol.iv. The Hinge of Fate* (Cassell, London, 1951.)

Maurice Couve de Murville, *Une Politique étrangère* (Plon, Paris, 1971.)

Michel Debré, *Gouverner. Mémoires, 1958-62* (Albin Michel, Paris, 1988.)

David Dilks (ed.), *The Diaries of Sir Alexander Cadogan, 1938-45* (Cassell, London, 1971.)

Lord Egremont, *Wyndham and Children First* (Macmillan, London, 1968.)

Dwight Eisenhower, *The White House Years. Waging Peace, 1956-61* (Heinemann, London, 1966.)

Harold Evans, *Downing Street Diary. The Macmillan Years, 1957-63* (Hodder and Stoughton, London, 1981.)

Charles de Gaulle, *The Complete War Memoirs* (Simon and Shuster, New York, 1972.) *Discours et messages, 1958-62* (Plon, Paris, 1970.) *The Edge of the Sword* (Faber, London, 1960.) *Lettres, notes et carnets, 1941-43* (Plon, Paris, 1982.) *1943-45* (Plon, Paris, 1983.) *1958-60* (Plon, Paris, 1985.) 1961-63 (Plon, Paris, 1986.) *Memoirs of Hope* (Weidenfeld and Nicolson, London, 1971.)

Général Henri Giraud, *Le Seul but - la victoire. Alger, 1942-44* (Juillard, Paris, 1949.)

Lord Gladwyn, *The Memoirs of Lord Gladwyn* (Weidenfeld and Nicolson, London, 1972.)

Lord Gore-Booth, *With Great Truth and Respect* (Constable, London, 1974.)

Andrei Gromyko, *Memoirs* (Hutchinson, London, 1989.)

John Harvey (ed.), *The War Diaries of Oliver Harvey* (Collins, London, 1978.)

Edward Heath, *The Course of My Life. My Autobiography*, (Hodder and Stoughton, London, 1998.)

Lord Home, *The Way the Wind Blows. An Autobiography* (Collins, London, 1976.)

Miles Jebb (ed.), *The Diaries of Cynthia Gladwyn* (Constable, London, 1996.)

Warren Kimball, *Churchill and Roosevelt. The Complete Correspondence, vol. ii Alliance Forged, November 1942-February 1944* (Princeton University Press, Princeton, N.J., 1984.)

Harold Macmillan, *War Diaries. The Mediterranean, 1943-5* (Macmillan, London, 1984.) *The Macmillan Diaries. The Cabinet Years*, 1950-57 (ed. Peter Caterall, Macmillan, London, 2003.) *Winds of Change, 1914-39* (Macmillan, London, 1966.) *The Blast of War, 1939-45* (Macmillan, London, 1967.) *Tides of Fortune, 1945-55* (Macmillan, London, 1969.) *Riding the Storm, 1956-9* (Macmillan, London, 1971.) *Pointing the Way, 1959-61* (Macmillan, London, 1972.) *At the End of the Day, 1961-3* (Macmillan, London, 1973.)

Donald Maitland, *The Running Tide. A View of International and other Public Affairs over Four Decades* (University of Bath Press, Bath, 2000.)

Robert Marjolin, *Architect of European Unity. Memoirs, 1911-86* (Weidenfeld and Nicolson, London, 1989.)

René Massigli, *Une Comédie des erreurs, 1943-56. Souvenirs et réflexions sur une étape de la construction européene* (Plon, Paris, 1978.)

Pierre Messmer, *Après tant de batailles. Mémoires* (Albin Michel, Paris, 1992.)

Jean Monnet, *Memoirs* (Collins, London, 1978.)

Alfred Mueller-Amack, *Auf dem Weg nach Europa. Errinerungen und Ausblicke* (Reiner Wunderlich, Tuebingen, and C.E.Poeschel, Stuttgart, 1971.)

Robert Murphy, *Diplomat among Warriors* (Collins, London, 1964.)

Nigel Nicolson (ed.), *Harold Nicolson. Diaries and Letters, 1939-45* (Collins, London, 1967.) *1945-62* (Collins, London, 1968.)

Horst Osterheld, *'Ich Gehe nicht leichten Herzens...' Adenauer's letzter Kanzler Jahre - eine dokumentarischer Bericht* (Gruenewald Verlag, Mainz, 1986.)

Kenneth Pendar, *Adventures in Diplomacy. The Emergence of General de Gaulle in North Africa* (Cassell, London, 1966.)

Alain Peyrefitte, *C'était de Gaulle, vol. i 'La France redevient la France'* (Fayard, Paris, 1994.) *vol.ii 'La France reprend sa position dans le monde'* (Fayard, Paris, 1997.) *vol iii 'Tout le monde a besoin d'une France qui marche'* (Fayard, Paris, 2000.)

Ben Pimlott (ed.), *The Second World War Diary of Hugh Dalton, 1940-45* (Cape, London, 1986.)

Edgard Pisani, *Le Général indivis* (Albin Michel, Paris, 1974.)

Mark Pottle (ed.), *Champion Redoubtable. The Diaries and Letters of Violet Bonham-Carter* (Phoenix, London, 1999 ed.)

Sir Eric Roll, *Crowded Hours* (Faber, London, 1985.)

Dean Rusk, *As I Saw It. A Secretary of State's Memoirs* (I.B.Tauris, London, 1991.)

Arthurs Schlesinger, *A Thousand Days. John F. Kennedy in the White House* (Deutsch, London, 1965.)

François Seydoux, *Mémoires d'outre-Rhin* (Bernard Grosset, Paris, 1975.)

Theodore Sorenson, *Kennedy* (Hodder and Stoughton, London, 1965.)

Paul-Henri Spaak, *The Continuing Battle. Memoirs of a European, 1936-66* (Weidenfeld and Nicolson, London, 1971.)

C.L.Sulzberger, *The Last of the Giants* (Weidenfeld and Nicolson, London, 1970.)

Strobe Talbott (ed.), *Khrushchev Remembers.* (Deutsch, London, 1971.) *Khrushchev. The Last Testament* (Deutsch, London, 1974.)

Harold Watkinson, *Turning Points. A Record of our Times* (Michael Russel, London,1986.)

SECONDARY WORKS

Richard Aldous and Sabine Lee (eds), *Harold Macmillan - Aspects of a Political Life* (Macmillan, Basingstoke, 1999.) *Macmillan and Britain's World Role* (Macmillan, Basingstoke, 1996.)

Stephen Ambrose, *The Supreme Commander. The War Years of General Dwight D. Eisenhower* (Cassell, London, 1969.)

Nigel Ashton, *Kennedy, Macmillan and the Cold War. The Irony of Interdependence* (Palgrave, Basingstoke, 2002.)

Simon Ball, *The Guardsmen. Harold Macmillan, Three Friends, and the World They Made* (HarperCollins, London, 2004.)

Oliver Bange, *The EEC Crisis of 1963. Kennedy, Macmillan, de Gaulle and Adenauer in Conflict* (Macmillan, Basingstoke, 2000.)

John Baylis, *Ambiguity and Deterrence. British Nuclear Strategy, 1945-64.* (Oxford University Press, Oxford, 1995.)

P.M.H.Bell, *Britain and France, 1900-1940. Entente and Estrangement* (Longman, Harlow, 1996.) *1940-94. The Long Separation* (Longman, Harlow, 1997.)

Norah Beloff, *The General Says No. Britain's Exclusion from Europe* (Penguin, Harmondsworth, 1963.)

Simon Berthon, *Allies at War* (HarperCollins, London, 2001.)

Michael Beschloss, *Mayday. Eisenhower, Khrushchev and the U2 Affair* (Harper Row, New York, 1986.)

Frédéric Bozo, *Two Strategies for France. De Gaulle, the United States and the Atlantic Alliance* (Rowman and Littlefield, Lanham, 2001.)

Douglas Brinkley and Richard Griffiths (eds), *John F.Kennedy and Europe* (Louisana State University Press, Baton Rouge, 1999.)

McGeorge Bundy, *Danger and Survival. Choices about the Bomb in the first Fifty Years* (Random House, New York, 1988.)

Philip Cerny, *The Politics of Grandeur. Ideological Aspects of de Gaulle's Foreign Policy* (Cambridge University Press, Cambridge, 1980.)

Michael Charlton, *The Price of Victory* (BBC, London, 1983.)

Philippe Chassaigne and Michael Dockrill (eds), *Anglo-French Relations. From Fashoda to Jospin,* (Palgrave, Basingstoke, 2002.)

Ian Clark, *Nuclear Diplomacy and the Special Relationship. Britain's Deterrent and America, 1957-62* (Oxford University Press, Oxford, 1994.)

Peter Clark, *A Question of Leadership. From Gladstone to Thatcher* (Penguin, Harmondsworth, 1992.)

Don Cook, *Charles de Gaulle. A Biography* (Secker and Warburg, London, 1984.)

D.K.R.Crosswell, *The Chief of Staff. The Military Career of General Walter Bedell-Smith* (Greenwood, 1991.)

Richard Davenport-Hines, *The Macmillans* (Heinemann, London, 1992.)

Anne Deighton and Alan Milward, *Widening, Deepening and Accelerating. The EEC, 1957-63* (Nomos Verlag, Baden Baden, 1999.)

David Dimbleby and David Reynolds, *An Ocean Apart. The Relationship between Britain and America in the Twentieth Century* (BBC/Hodder and Stoughton, London, 1988.)

Piers Dixon, *Double Diploma. The Life of Sir Pierson Dixon, Don and Diplomat* (Hutchinson, London, 1968.)

François Duchêne, *Jean Monnet. The First Statesman of Interdependence* (W.W.Norton, New York, 1994.)

Marcel Duval and Yves le Baut, *L'Arme nucléaire française. Pourquoi et comment?* (S.P.M., Paris, 1992.)

James Ellison, *Threatening Europe. Britain and the Creation of the European Community, 1955-58* (Macmillan, Basingstoke, 2000.)

Arthur Funk, *Charles de Gaulle. The Crucial Years* (University of Oklahoma Press, Norman, 1959.)

A.B.Gaunson, *The Anglo-French Clash in Lebanon and Syria* (Macmillan, Basingstoke, 1987.)

John Gearson, *Harold Macmillan and the Berlin Wall Crisis, 1958-62. The Limits of Interests and Force* (Macmillan, Basingstoke, 1998.)

Bruce Geelhoed and Anthony Edmonds, *Eisenhower, Macmillan and Allied Unity, 1957-61* (Palgrave, Basingstoke, 2003.)

Robert Gibson, *Best of Enemies. Anglo-French Relations since the Norman Conquest* (Sinclair Stevenson, London, 1995.)

Jean-Pierre Guichard, *De Gaulle face aux crises, 1940-68* (Cherche Midi, Paris, 2000.)

Michael Harrison, *The Reluctant Ally. France and the Atlantic Alliance* (Johns Hopkins University Press, Baltimore, 1981.)

Peter Hennessy, *The Prime Minister. The Office and its Holders since 1945* (Allen Lane, London, 2000.)

Stanley Hoffman, *Decline or Renewal? France since the 1930s* (Viking, New York, 1974.)

Alistair Horne, *Macmillan, vol.i, 1894-1956* (Macmillan, London 1988.) *vol.ii, 1957-86* (Macmillan, London, 1989.)

Michael Howard, *Grand Strategy, vol.iv, August 1942-September 1943* (HMSO, London, 1972.)

George Hutchinson, *The Last Edwardian at No.10. An Impression of Harold Macmillan* (Quartet, London, 1980.)

Institut Charles de Gaulle, *De Gaulle en son siècle, vol.iv, La Sécurité et l'indépendance de la France. vol.v, L'Europe* (Plon, Paris, 1972.)

Julian Jackson, *Charles de Gaulle* (Cardinal, London, 1990.) *France.The Dark Years, 1940-44.* (Oxford University Press, Oxford, 2001.)

Vincent Jauvert, *L'Amérique contre de Gaulle. Histoire secrète 1961-4* (Edition du Seuil, Paris, 2000.)

Edouard Jouve, *Le Général de Gaulle et la construction de l'Europe, 1940-66, vol. ii* (R.Pichon et R.Durand-Auzias, Paris, 1967.)

Wolfram Kaiser, *Using Europe, Abusing the Europeans. Britain and European Integration, 1945-63* (Macmillan, Basingstoke, 1996.)

Wolfram Kaiser and Gillian Staerck (eds), *British Foreign Policy, 1955-64. Contracting Options* (Macmillan, Basingstoke, 2000.)

Andre Kaspi, *La Mission de Jean Monnet à Alger, Mars-Octobre 1943* (Edition Richelieu, Paris, 1971.)

J.F.V.Keiger, *France and the World since 1870* (Arnold, London, 2001.)

François Kersaudy, *Churchill and de Gaulle* (Fontana, London, 1990 ed.) *De Gaulle et Roosevelt. Le Duel au sommet* (Perrin, Paris, 2004.)

Sergei Khrushchev, *Nikita Khrushchev and the Creation of a Superpower* (Pennsylvania State University Press, University Park, PA., 2000.)

Henry Kissinger, *Diplomacy* (Simon and Schuster, London, 1995.)

Wilfrid Kohl, *French Nuclear Diplomacy* (Princeton University Press, Princeton, NJ., 1971.)

Keith Kyle, *Suez* (Weidenfeld and Nicolson, London, 1991.)

Jean Lacouture, *De Gaulle, vol.i, The Rebel* (Harvill, London, 1990.) *vol.ii, The Ruler* (Harvill, London, 1991.)

Richard Lamb, *The Macmillan Years, 1957-63. The Emerging Truth* (John Murray, London, 1995.)

Bernard Ledwidge, *De Gaulle* (Weidenfeld and Nicolson, London, 1982.)

Sabine Lee, *An Uneasy Partnership. British-German Relations, 1955-61* (Universitaetsverlag, Dr.N.Brockmeyer, Bochum, 1996.)

Paul Legoll, *Charles de Gaulle et Konrad Adenauer. La cordiale entente* (L'Harmattan, Paris, 2004.)

William Roger Louis and Roger Owen (eds), *Suez, 1956. The Crisis and its Consequences* (Clarendon Press, Oxford, 1989.)

Piers Ludlow, *Dealing with Britain. The Six and the First UK Application to the EEC* (Cambridge University Press, Cambridge, 1997.)

Gloria Maguire, *Anglo-American Policy towards the Free French* (Macmillan, Basingstoke, 1995.)

Erin Mahan, *Kennedy, de Gaulle and Western Europe* (Palgrave, Basingstoke, 2002.)

Pierre Maillard, *De Gaulle et l'Europe. Entre la nation et Maastricht* (Tallandier, Paris, 1995.) *De Gaulle et le problème Allemand. Les leçons d'un grand dessein* (de Guibert, Paris, 2001 ed.)

Peter Mangold, *Success and Failure in British Foreign Policy. Evaluating the Record, 1900-2000* (Palgrave, Basingstoke, 2001.)

Alex May (ed.), *Britain, the Commonwealth and Europe. The Commonwealth and Britain's Application to Join the European Communities* (Palgrave, Basingstoke, 2001.)

Jan Melissen, *The Struggle for Nuclear Partnership. Britain and the United States and the Making of an Ambiguous Alliance, 1952-59* (Styx Publications, Groningen, 1993.)

Lois Pattison de Ménil, *Who Speaks for Europe? The Vision of Charles de Gaulle* (Weidenfeld and Nicolson, London, 1977.)

Alan Milward, *The Rise and Fall of National Strategy, 1945-63. The UK and the European Common Market* (Cass, London, 2002.)

Klaus-Jurge Mueller, *Adenauer and de Gaulle. De Gaulle and Germany: A Special Relationship* (St.Antony's College, Oxford/Konrad Adenauer Stiftung, 1992.)

Donette Murray, *Kennedy, Macmillan and Nuclear Weapons* (Macmillan, Basingstoke, 2000.)

Richard Neustadt, *Report to JFK. The Skybolt Crisis in Perspective* (Cornell University Press, Ithaca, 1999.)

John Newhouse, *De Gaulle and the Anglo-Saxons* (Viking, New York, 1970.)

David Nunnerley, *President Kennedy and Britain* (Bodley Head, London, 1972.)

Kendrick Oliver, *Kennedy, Macmillan and the Nuclear Test Ban Debate, 1961-63* (Macmillan, Basingstoke, 1998.)

Constantine Pagedas, *Anglo-American Strategic Relations and the French Problem, 1960-63. A Troubled Partnership* (Cass, London, 2000.)

Robert Paxton and Nicholas Wahl (eds), *De Gaulle and the United States. A Centennial Reappraisal* (Berg, Oxford, 1994.)

John Ramsden, *The Winds of Change. Macmillan to Heath, 1957-75* (Longman, London, 1996.)

Robert Rhodes-James, *Anthony Eden and Harold Macmillan* (Conservative Political Centre, London, 1997.)

Eric Roussel, *Charles de Gaulle* (Gallimard, Paris, 2002.)

Anthony Sampson, *Anatomy of Britain* (Hodder and Stoughton, London, 1962.) *Macmillan. A Study in Ambiguity* (Penguin, Harmondsworth, 1967.)

Martin Schaad, *Bullying Bonn. Anglo-German Diplomacy on European Integration, 1955-61* (Macmillan, Basingstoke, 2000.)

L.V.Scott, *Macmillan, Kennedy and the Cuban Missile Crisis. Political, Military and Intelligence Aspects* (Macmillan, Basingstoke, 1999.)

W.Scott-Lucas, *Divided We Stand. Britain, the United States and the Suez Crisis* (Hodder and Stoughton, Sevenoaks, 1991.)

Simon Serfaty, *France, de Gaulle and Europe. The Policy of the Fourth and Fifth Republics toward the Continent* (Johns Hopkins, Baltimore, 1968.)

Andrew Shennan, *De Gaulle* (Longman, London, 1993.)

George-Henri Soutou, *L'Alliance incertain. Les Rapports politiques et stratégiques franco-alle-mandes, 1954-96* (Fayard, Paris, 1996.)

Sir Edward Spears, *Two Men who Saved France. Pétain and de Gaulle* (Eyre and Spottiswoode, London, 1966.)

Hans-Peter Schwarz, *Konrad Adenauer. A German Politician and Statesman in a Period of War, Revolution and Restoration, vol.ii* (Berghahn, Providence and Oxford, 1997.)

Alan Sharp and Glyn Stone (eds), *Anglo-French Relations in the Twentieth Century. Rivalry and Cooperation* (Routledge, London, 2000.)

William Taubman, *Khrushchev. The Man and his Era* (Free Press, New York, 2003.)

D.R.Thorpe, *Alec Douglas-Home* (Sinclair Stevenson, London, 1996.) *Selwyn Lloyd* (Cape, London, 1989.)

Jacqueline Tratt, *The Macmillan Government and Europe. A Study in the Process of Policy Development* (Macmillan, Basingstoke, 1996.)

John Turner, *Macmillan* (Longman, London, 1994.)

Ann Tusa, *The Last Division. Berlin and the Wall* (Hodder and Stoughton, London, 1996.)

Maurice Vaisse, *La Grandeur. Politique étrangère du Général de Gaulle, 1958-69* (Fayard, Paris, 1998.)

Neville Waites, *Troubled Neighbours. British-French Relations in the Twentieth Century* (Weidenfeld and Nicolson, London, 1981.)

Stuart Ward, *Australia and the British Embrace. The Demise of the Imperial Ideal.* (Melbourne University Press, Melbourne, 2001.)

George Wilkes (ed.), *Britain's Failure to Enter the European Community, 1961-63. The Enlargement Negotiations and Crises in European, Atlantic and Commonwealth Relations* (Cass, London, 1997.)

Charles Williams, *The Last Great Frenchman. A Life of Charles de Gaulle* (Abacus, London, 1995 ed.)

Pascaline Winand, *Eisenhower, Kennedy and the United States of Europe* (Macmillan, Basingstoke, 1993.)

Sir Llewellyn Woodward, *British Foreign Policy in the Second World War, vol.ii* (HMSO, London, 1971.)

Hugo Young, *This Blessed Plot. Britain and Europe from Churchill to Blair* (Macmillan, London, 1998.)

Vladislav Zubok and Constantine Pleshakov, *Inside the Kremlin's Cold War* (Harvard University Press, Cambridge, Mass., 1996.)

ARTICLES AND PAMPHLETS

Nigel Ashton '"A Rear Guard Action." Harold Macmillan and the Making of British Foreign Policy' in T.G.Otte (ed.), *The Makers of British Foreign Policy. From Pitt to Thatcher* (Palgrave, Basingstoke, 2002.)

Colette Barbier, 'The French Decision to develop a Military Nuclear Programme in the 1950s', *Security Studies*, Autumn 1995.

Jacques Bariéty, 'Les Entretiens de Gaulle-Adenauer de Juillet 1960 en Rambouillet. Prélude au plan Fouchet et au Traité d'Elysée', *Revue d'Allemagne*, Avril-Juin 1997.

Lord Blake, 'The Earl of Stockton ' in *Dictionary of National Biography, 1986-90* (Oxford, 1991.)

Jean-Paul Bled, 'Des Conceptions européens du Général de Gaulle à la veille de son retour au pouvoir', *Revue d'Allemagne*, Avril-Juin 1997.

Jean-Marc Boegner, '1958: Le Général de Gaulle et l'acceptation de Traité de Rome', *Espoir*, Juin 1992.

Peter Boyle, 'The British Government's View of the Cuban Missile Crisis', *Contemporary History*, Autumn 1996.

Cyril Buffet, 'De Gaulle, the Bomb and Berlin. How to use a Political Weapon' in John Gearson and Kori Schake (eds), *The Berlin Wall Crisis. Perspectives on Cold War Alliances* (Palgrave, Basingstoke, 2002.)

Simon Burgess and Geoffrey Edwards, 'The Six Plus One. British Policy-Making and the Question of European Integration, 1955', *International Affairs*, Summer 1988.

John Charmley, 'Harold Macmillan and the Making of the French Committee of Liberation', *International History Review*, November 1982.

Frank Costigliola, 'The Failed Design. Kennedy, de Gaulle and the Struggle for Europe', *Diplomatic History*, Summer 1994. 'Kennedy, the European Allies and the Failure to Consult', *Political Science Quarterly*, Spring 1995.

Maurice Couve de Murville, 'Principles d'une politique étrangère', *Espoir*, Decembre 1987.

Richard Davies, 'Why did the General do it? De Gaulle, Polaris and the French Veto of Britain's Application to Join the Common Market', *European History*, July 1998.

Paul-Marie de la Gorce, 'De Gaulle et l'Angleterre', *Espoir,* Juin 2004.

David Dilks, *De Gaulle and the British* (University of Hull Press, Hull, 1994.) *Rights, Wrongs and Rivalries. Britain and France in 1945* (University of Hull Press, 1995.)

Michael Dockrill, 'Restoring the "Special relationship". The Bermuda and Washington Conferences, 1957' in Dick Richardson and Glyn Stone (eds), *Decisions and Diplomacy. Essays in Twentieth Century International History* (Routledge, London, 1995.)

David Dutton, 'Anticipating Maastricht. The Conservative Party and Britain's First Application to the Join the European Community', *Contemporary Record*, Winter 1993.

Espoir, Juin 1983 ed. 'De Gaulle et Grande Bretagne.'

Arthur Funk, 'The "Anfa" Memorandum. An Incident at the Casablanca Conference', *Journal of Modern History*, September 1954.

John Gearson, 'British Policy and the Berlin Wall Crisis, 1958-61', *Contemporary Record*, Summer 1992.

Philip Gordon, 'Charles de Gaulle and the Nuclear Revolution', *Security Studies*, Autumn 1995.

Georges Jessula, '1943: De Gaulle à Alger. Les "Carnets" d'Harold Macmillan', *Revue d'histoire diplomatique*, 1991, nos.3-4.

Douglas Johnson, 'De Gaulle and France's Foreign Policy' in Hugh Gough and John Horne (eds), *De Gaulle and the Twentieth Century* (Arnold, London, 1994.)

Lewis Johnman, 'Defending the Pound. The Economics of the Suez Crisis, 1956' in Anthony Gorst, Lewis Johnman and W.Scott-Lucas, *Post-War Britain, 1945-64. Themes and Perspectives* (Pinter/ICBH, London, 1989.)

Matthew Jones, 'Anglo-American Relations after Suez. The Rise and Decline of the

Working Group Experiment', *Diplomacy and Statecraft*, March 2003. 'Macmillan, Eden, the War in the Mediterranean and Anglo-American Relations', *Twentieth Century British History*, vol.viii, no.i.

Wolfram Kaiser, 'The Bomb and Europe. Britain, France and the EEC Entry Negotiations, 1961-63', *Journal of European Integration History*, vol.i, no.i, 1995. *The Listener*, Macmillan interviews, 8.9.66, 21.9.67, 25.9.69, 13.5.71, 22.6.72, 11.10.73.

William Roger Louis, 'Harold Macmillan and the Middle East Crisis of 1958' *Proceedings of the British Academy*, 1994.

N.Piers Ludlow, ' "A Conditional Application." British Management of the First Attempt to seek Membership of the EEC, 1961-63', in Anne Deighton (ed.), *Building Post-war Europe. National Decision-Makers and European Institutions* (Macmillan, Basingstoke, 1995.) 'Le Paradox Anglais. Britain and Political Union', *Revue d'Allemagne*, Avril-Juin 1997.

Frances Lynch, 'De Gaulle's First Veto. France, the Rueff Plan and the Free Trade Area', *Contemporary European History*, March 2000.

Jan Melissen, 'The Restoration of the Nuclear Alliance. Great Britain and Atomic Negotiations with the United States, 1957-58', *Contemporary Record*, Summer 1992.

Yves-Henri Nouailhat, 'De Gaulle, la Grande Bretagne et la construction européene, 1958-69', *Espoir*, Juin 1992.

Horst Osterheld, 'Adenauer et de Gaulle. Portraits comparées', *Espoir*, Mars 1992.

Constantine Pagedas, 'The Limits of Personal Influence.' 'Harold Macmillan and Anglo-French Relations, 1961-63' in T.G.Otte and Constantine Pagedas (eds), *Personalities, War and Diplomacy. Essays in International History* (Cass, London, 1997.)

Sir Michael Palliser, 'Cent Ans d'Entente Cordiale', *Espoir*, Juin 2004.

Alain Peyrefitte, 'Une Singulier paradoxe', *Espoir*, Octobre 1998.

Gary Rawnsley, 'How Special is Special? The Anglo-American Alliance during the Cuban Missile Crisis', *Journal of Contemporary History*, Winter 1995.

Martin Schaad, 'Plan G. "A Counterblast"? Britain's Policy towards the Messina Countries', *Contemporary European History*, March 1998.

Larry Seidentop, 'Mr. Macmillan and the Edwardian Style' in Vernon Bogdanor and Robert Skidelsky (eds), *The Age of Affluence* (Macmillan, London, 1970.)

George-Henri Soutou, 'France and the Cold War, 1944-63', *Diplomacy and Statecraft*, December 2001. 'French Policy towards European Integration' in Michael Dockrill (ed.), *Europe within the Global System, 1938-60. Great Britain, France, Italy and Germany. From Great Powers to Regional Powers* (Universitaetsverlag, Dr.N. Brechmeyer, Bochum, 1995.) 'Le Général de Gaulle, le plan Fouchet et l'Europe', *Commentaire*, Hiver, 1990-91.

Kristian Steinnes, 'The European Challenge. Britain's EEC Applicaiton in 1961', *Contemporary European History*, March 1998.

Simon Toschi, 'Washington-London-Paris. An Untenable Triangle, 1960-63', *Journal of European Integration History, vol.i, no.ii*, 1995.

Maurice Vaisse, 'Le Traité de Moscou', *Revue d'Histoire Diplomatique*, 1993, i.. 'Politique étrangère et politique de défense dans la pensée et l'action du Général de Gaulle', *Espoir*, Septembre 1993.

Jeffrey Vanke, 'An Impossible Union. Dutch Objections to the Fouchet Plan, 1959-62', *Cold War History*, October 2001.

Geoffrey Warner, 'Why the General said No', *International Affairs*, October 2002.

Sydney Zebel, 'Harold Macmillan's Appointment as Minister at Algiers, 1942. The Military, Political and Diplomatic Background', *Journal of the Rutgers University Library*, December 1979.

UNPUBLISHED THESES

Richard Aldous, *Harold Macmillan and the Search for a Summit with the USSR, 1958-60* (Ph.D., Cambridge, 1993.)

John Charmley, *British Policy towards General de Gaulle, 1942-44* (D.Phil., Oxford, 1982.)

Mark Deavin, *Harold Macmillan and the Origins of the 1961 British Application to Join the EEC* (Ph.D., London, 1996.)

Kathleen Paul Newman, *Britain and the Soviet Union. The Search for an Interim Agreement on West Berlin, November 1958-May 1960* (Ph.D., London, 1999.)

Christopher van Houten, *British and United States Policy towards France*, (Ph.D., Cambridge, 1996.)

Mathilde von Buelow, *Paradoxes of Perception. The JIC and France, 1956-63* (M.Phil., Cambridge, 2001.)

Index